M000206932

The Life of John Newton
by Richard Cecil

edited by Marylynn Rouse

for
Chris and Howard Wilson

The Life of John Newton

Richard Cecil

edited by
Marylynn Rouse

Christian Focus

Published in 2000
by
Christian Focus Publications,
Geanies House, Fearn, Ross-shire,
IV20 1TW, Great Britain.

Cover design by Owen Daily

"My history is briefly expressed in Deuteronomy 32:10,

He found him in a desert land, and in the waste howling wilderness; he led him about, he instructed him, he kept him as the apple of his eye.

He found me in a howling wilderness indeed! He has led me about into a variety of situations, and in them all He watched over me, and kept me as the apple of His eye."

John Newton

CONTENTS

The following hymn (*Olney Hymns*, 1779, Book 2, Hymn 26) by John Newton seems an authentic outline of the chapters of his life, 'being,' as he says of all his hymns, 'the fruit and expression of my experience'.

What contradictions meet
In ministers' employ!
It is a bitter sweet,
A sorrow full of joy:
No other post affords a place
For equal honour, or disgrace!

Who can describe the pain
Which faithful preachers feel;
Constrained to speak, in vain,
To hearts as hard as steel?
Or who can tell the pleasures felt,
When stubborn hearts begin to melt?

They pray and strive, their rest departs,
Till Christ be formed in sinners hearts,
Too oft they find their hopes deceived,
Then, how their inmost souls are grieved!
No harvest-joy can equal theirs,
To find the fruit of all their cares.

On what has now been sown
Thy blessing, Lord, bestow;
The power is thine alone,
To make it spring and grow:
Do thou the gracious harvest raise,
And thou, alone, shalt have the praise.

John Roque's Map of Wapping, 1746

*Used by kind permission of Guildhall Library, Corporation of London,
whose first Librarian was taken under the wing of "one John Newton"
when his father died.*

David Jenning's
Independent Meeting House
in Old Gravel Lane,
where Newton was baptised

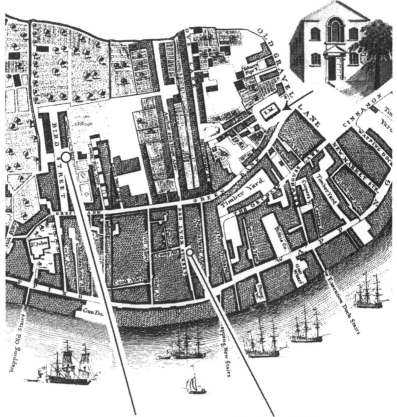

Alexander Clunie was living in
Bird Street when he met Newton
at St Kitts

John Newton lived in
Red Lyon Street as a child

TOWER OF LONDON

CHIEF DATES IN JOHN NEWTON'S LIFE

(dates up to 1752 are in Old Style)

24 July 1725	born to John and Elizabeth Newton, Wapping, London
26 July 1725	baptised at Old Gravel Lane Independent Meeting, Wapping
11 July 1732	John's mother died; his father remarried shortly after (to Thomasina)
1733-35	sent to a private boarding school in Stratford, Essex
1735-1743	mostly on Mediterranean voyages
25 Feb 1743	press-ganged to HMS *Harwich*
9 May 1745	transferred to the Guinea trader, *Pegasus*
1745-47	slave on Guinea Coast, West Africa
Feb 1747	fetched home in the *Greyhound*
10 March 1748	subjected to a storm at sea which began his conversion
Aug 1748 – Dec 1749	First Mate in the *Brownlow*
1 Feb 1750	married Mary Catlett at St Margaret's, Rochester
Aug 1750 – Oct 1751	Master of the *Duke of Argyle* slave trader
28 June 1750	his father drowned swimming in Hudson Bay, Canada
June 1752 – Aug 1753	Master of the *African* slave trader: first voyage
Oct 1753 – Aug 1754	Master of the *African* slave trader: second voyage
May 1754	at St Kitts, West Indies, met Captain Alexander Clunie, who established him in his faith
Nov 1754	a fit ended his sea career
Aug 1755	began employment as Surveyor of Tides in Liverpool
4 Aug 1758	committed himself in prayer to entering the ministry
29 April 1764	ordained deacon of St Peter's and St Paul's, Olney, by the Bishop of Lincoln
17 June 1764	ordained priest
Aug 1764	published his *Narrative*
1779	published *Olney Hymns*
8 Dec 1779	instituted as rector of St Mary Woolnoth, London
15 Dec 1790	his wife died
23 Dec 1790	preached at Polly's funeral from Habukkuk 3:17,18
May 1800	preached a Funeral Sermon for William Cowper from Exodus 3:2,3
Oct 1806	the last time he was in the pulpit at St Mary Woolnoth, preaching on the first anniversary of the Battle of Trafalgar
21 Dec 1807	Newton died, about 8.15 pm
31 Dec 1807	Newton was buried at St Mary, Woolnoth; Henry Foster read the Service (with 30 ministers present)
3 Jan 1808	Richard Cecil preached Newton's Funeral Sermon in St Mary Woolnoth
25 Jan 1893	The remains of John and Mary Newton were re-interred at Olney (removal from St Mary Woolnoth required for the construction of the London Underground)

FOREWORD

The author of *Amazing Grace* and many other famous hymns was one of the best loved and most influential of the early evangelicals.

His story was extraordinary. A sailor who was flogged for desertion, afterwards a slave in West Africa in all but name and then, when rescued, a slave trader. He was converted in a great storm at sea. Although his path to assurance and service was slow, the ex-slaver, ex-lecher, ex-atheist became a true minister of the gospel and a doughty ally of William Wilberforce in the abolition of the slave trade.

Richard Cecil was his first biographer. Cecil had known "Mr N.", as he calls him, in his later years and the book became a classic. It has long been out of print. Marylynn Rouse has done a good service in editing a new edition but she has done far more. She has found out a great deal about Newton which Cecil did not know so that he becomes a fully rounded figure, and just as lovable. Wisely, Marylynn does not splatter Cecil's pages with footnotes or insertions, so the reader gets the full flavour of Cecil's prose, quaint as it occasionally reads.

Instead, she adds an appendix to each chapter, writing much new material from her very thorough researches. Newton's friends and opponents come alive. Passages in poems of Wordsworth, Coleridge and of course Cowper which Newton inspired are brought to hand. Cecil drew upon Newton's autobiography, *An Authentic Narrative* and on his *Letters to a Wife*, but in the Olney museum is a leather bound set of the two volumes of *Letters*, specially interleaved by Newton himself. I remember the thrill of first reading his own notes and additions in his rather difficult handwriting. Much of these are now easily available here. Marylynn has also discovered unpublished letters and other treasures and she adds a most useful Who's Who.

The 'old African blasphemer' never forgot that amazing grace had 'saved a wretch like me'. He always sought to exalt Christ by his ministry and his life. This new edition is a very useful addition to the general reader's knowledge of the man and his period but above all, like Newton, it shows how sweet the name of Jesus sounds in a believer's ear.

John Pollock

EDITORIAL COMMENT

Richard Cecil's *Life of Newton* was originally published in just three sections: the main "Memoirs", followed by "Remarks made by Mr Newton in Familiar Conversation" and by Cecil's own "General Observations". When the biography was first printed, many of its readers would have known or heard of Newton and his contempories. To make it easier to add some background information, I have divided the first section into nine chapters, roughly co-inciding with specific periods in Newton's life. Where Cecil used footnotes they appear at the bottom of the appropriate page, but the references and chapter appendices are additional material.

A *Who's Who* is included after Cecil's work, to help keep track of Newton's many acquaintances. Rather than being a collection of brief biographies, it highlights their connections with Newton.

The *Appendices* commencing on page 343 contain previously unpublished or little known writings of Newton's.

Marylynn Rouse

PREFACE

The *Memoirs* of the Hon. and Rev. William Bromley Cadogan,[1] and those of John Bacon, Esq.[2] were written at the particular request of their relations: but in publishing these of the late Rev. John Newton, I profess myself a volunteer: and my motives were the following: When I perceived my venerable friend bending under a weight of years, and considered how soon, from the very course of nature, the world must lose so valuable an instructor and example, when I reflected how common it is for hasty and inaccurate accounts of extraordinary characters to be obtruded on the public by venal writers, whenever more authentic documents are wanting; above all, when I considered how striking a display such a life affords of the nature of true religion, of the power of divine grace, of the mysterious but all-wise course of Divine Providence, and of the encouragement afforded for our dependence upon that providence in the most trying circumstances, I say, on these accounts, I felt that the leading features of such a character should not be neglected, whilst it was easy to authenticate them correctly.

Besides which, I have observed a want of books of a certain class for young people; and have often been enquired of by Christian parents for publications that might amuse their families, and yet tend to promote their best interests. The number, however, of this kind which I have seen, and that appeared unexceptionable, is but small. For, as the characters and sentiments of some men become *moral blights* in society, men, whose mouths seldom open but, like that of sepulchres, they discover the putridity they contain, and infect more or less whoever ventures within their baneful influence; so the reformed subject of these *Memoirs* was happily a remarkable instance of the reverse: the change that took place in his heart, after such a course of profligacy, affords a convincing demonstration of the truth and force of Christianity. Instead of proceeding as a *blight* in society, he became a blessing: his future course was a striking example of the beneficial effects of the Gospel; and that not only from the pulpit, and by his pen, but also by his conversation in the large circle of his acquaintance, of which there is yet living a multitude of witnesses.

Impressed, therefore, with the advantages which I conceived would result from the publication of these *Memoirs*, I communicated my design some years ago to Mr. N. Whatever tended to promote that cause in which his heart had long been engaged, I was sure would not fail to obtain his concurrence. He accordingly promised to afford whatever materials might be necessary, beyond those which his printed *Narrative*[3] contained. He promised also to read over and revise whatever was added from my own observation; and he soon after brought me an account in writing, containing every thing memorial which he recollected before the commencement of his *Narrative*. I shall, therefore, detain the reader no longer than to assure him that the whole of the following *Memoirs*, (except what relates to Mr. N.'s character), was submitted to him in MS while he was capable of correcting it, and that it received his sanction.

April, 1808

R.C.

Appendix to Preface

The Narrative

Newton's *Narrative* was originally written as a series of autobiographical letters to his Baptist friend John Fawcett. A friend of Fawcett's asked Newton if he would expand on these letters and arranged for sponsorship to have them printed.

The *Narrative* was published in 1764 while Newton was curate-in-charge at Olney. It created a bit of a stir in the town to have such extraordinary details of their Church of England clergyman's background made known. He wrote to a friend, "The people stare at me since reading them, and well they may. I am indeed a wonder to many."[4] Concerned that the letters should be of spiritual value, he added, "but let me beg you likewise to help them with your prayers, that they may be not only sold, but read, not only read, but accompanied with the blessing and unction of the Holy Spirit, that they may be a means to awaken the careless, confirm the wavering, and comfort the wounded."

Although Cecil quotes copiously from the *Narrative* I have taken the liberty of extending some of his extracts in a few places [in square brackets] where it seemed of special interest, as the information was, in Cecil's time, more widely known than now.

MEMOIRS
OF THE

REV. JOHN NEWTON,

LATE RECTOR OF ST. MARY WOOLNOTH,
AND ST. MARY
WOOLCHURCH HAW;

WITH
GENERAL REMARKS
ON HIS
LIFE, CONNECTIONS, AND CHARACTER.

BY THE
REV. RICHARD CECIL, M.A.

MINISTER OF ST. JOHN'S CHAPEL,
BEDFORD ROW,
LONDON.

CHAPTER 1

EARLY LIFE
1725-1741

These Memoirs seem naturally to commence with the *Account* mentioned in the Preface, and which I here transcribe:

"I was born in London the 24th of July, 1725, old style.[1] My parents, though not wealthy, were respectable. My father was many years master of a ship in the Mediterranean trade. In the year 1748 he went Governor of York Fort in Hudson's Bay, where he died in the year 1750.

"My mother was a dissenter, a pious woman, and a member of the late Dr. Jennings's church. She was of a weak, consumptive habit, loved retirement, and, as I was her only child, she made it the chief business and pleasure of her life to instruct me, and bring me up in the nurture and admonition of the Lord. I have been told, that, from my birth, she had, in her mind, devoted me to the ministry; and that, had she lived till I was of a proper age, I was to have been sent to St. Andrew's in Scotland to be educated. But the Lord had appointed otherwise. My mother died before I was seven years of age.

"I was rather of a sedentary turn, not active and playful, as boys commonly are, but seemed as willing to learn as my mother was to teach me. I had some capacity, and a retentive memory. When I was four years old, I could read, (hard names excepted), as well as I can now: and could likewise repeat the answers to the questions in the *Assembly's Shorter Catechism*,[2] with the proofs; and all Dr. Watts's smaller *Catechisms*,[3] and his *Children's Hymns*.[4]

"When my father returned from sea, after my mother's death, he married again. My new mother was the daughter of a substantial grazier at Aveley in Essex. She seemed willing to adopt and bring me up; but, after two or three years, she had a son of her own, who engrossed the old man's notice. My father was a very sensible, and a moral man, as the world rates morality; but neither he, nor my step-mother, was under the impressions of religion: I was, therefore, much left to myself, to mingle with idle and wicked boys; and soon learnt their ways.

"I was never at school but about two years; from my eighth to my tenth year. It was a boarding-school at Stratford, in Essex. Though my father left me much to run about the streets, yet, when under his eye, he kept me at a great distance. I am persuaded he loved me, but he seemed not willing that I should know it. I was with him in a state of fear and bondage. His sternness, together with the severity of my schoolmaster, broke and overawed my spirit, and almost made me a dolt; so that part of the two years I was at school, instead of making a progress, I nearly forgot all that my good mother had taught me.

"The day I was eleven years old, I went on board my father's ship in Longreach. I made five voyages with him to the Mediterranean. In the course of the last voyage, he left me some months at Alicant in Spain, with a merchant, a particular friend of his. With him I might have done well, if I had behaved well: but, by this time, my sinful propensities had gathered strength by habit: I was very wicked, and therefore very foolish; and, being my own enemy, I seemed determined that nobody should be my friend.

"My father left the sea in the year 1742. I made one voyage afterwards to Venice, before the mast; and, soon after my return, was impressed on board the *Harwich*. – Then began my awfully mad career, as recorded in the *Narrative*; to which, and to the *Letters to a Wife*,[5] I must refer you for any further dates and incidents.

                                        "I am truly yours,
                                        "JOHN NEWTON."
                                                        "Dec. 19, 1795."

A few articles may be added to this account from the *Narrative*, where we find that his pious mother stored his "memory with whole chapters, and smaller portions of Scripture, catechisms, hymns, and poems; and often commended him with many prayers and tears to God:" that, in his sixth year he began to learn Latin, though the intended plan of his education was soon broken – and that he lost this valuable parent, July 11th, 1732.

We also find that, after his father's second marriage, he was sent to the school above-mentioned: and, in the last of the two years he spent there, a new usher came, who observed and suited his temper. He prosecuted Latin, therefore, with great eagerness; and, before he was ten years old, he had reached and maintained the first post in the second class, which, in that school, read Tully and Virgil. But, by being pushed forward too fast, and not properly grounded (a method too common in inferior schools) he soon lost all he had learned.

In the next and most remarkable period of Mr. N.'s life, we must be conducted by the *Narrative* above mentioned. It has been observed, that, at eleven years of age, he was taken by his father to sea. His father was a man of remarkably good sense, and great knowledge of the world. He took much care of his son's morals, but could not supply a mother's part. The father had been educated at a Jesuits' College near Seville in Spain; and had an air of such distance and severity in his carriage, as discouraged his son, who always was in fear when before him, which deprived him of that influence he might otherwise have had.

From this time to the year 1742 Mr. N. made several voyages, but at considerable intervals. These intervals were chiefly spent in the country, excepting a few months in his fifteenth year, when he was placed, with a very advantageous prospect, at Alicant already mentioned.

About this period of his life, with a temper and conduct exceedingly various, he was often disturbed with religious convictions; and being from a child fond of reading, he met with Bennet's *Christian Oratory*,[6] and though he understood little of it, the course of life it recommended appeared very desirable. He therefore began to pray, to read the Scriptures, to keep a diary, and thought himself religious; but soon became weary of it, and gave it up. He then learnt to curse and to blaspheme; and was exceedingly wicked when out of view of his parents, though at so early a period.

Upon his being thrown from a horse near a dangerous hedge-row, newly cut, his conscience suggested to him the dreadful consequence of appearing in such a state before God. This put him, though but for a time, upon breaking off his profane practices; but the consequences of these struggles between sin and conscience, was, that on every relapse he sunk into still greater depths of wickedness. He was roused again, by the loss of a companion who had agreed to go with him one Sunday on board a man of war. Mr. N. providentially coming too late, the boat had gone without him, and was overset, by which his companion and several others were drowned. He was exceedingly affected at the funeral of this companion, to think that by the delay of a few minutes (which at the time occasioned much anger) his life had been preserved: but this also was soon forgotten. The perusal of the *Family Instructor* [7] produced another temporary reformation. In short, he took up and laid aside a religious profession three or four different times, before he was sixteen years of age.

"All this while," says he, "my heart was insincere. I often saw the necessity of religion, as a means of escaping hell; but I loved sin, and was unwilling to forsake it. – I was so strangely blind and stupid, that, sometimes, when I have been determined upon things which I knew were sinful, I could not go on quietly till I had first dispatched my ordinary task of prayer, in which I grudged every moment of the time: when this was finished, my conscience was in some measure pacified, and I could rush into folly with little remorse."

But his last reform was the most remarkable. "Of this period," says he, "at least of some part of it, I may say, in the Apostle's words, *After the strictest sect of our religion, I lived a Pharisee.* [8] I did everything that might be expected from a person entirely ignorant of God's righteousness, and desirous to establish his own. I spent the greatest part of every day in reading the Scriptures, and in meditation and prayer. I fasted often; I even abstained from all animal food for three months. I would hardly answer a question for fear of speaking an idle word: I seemed to bemoan my former miscarriages very earnestly, and sometimes with tears: in short, I became an Ascetic, and endeavoured, as far as my situation would permit, to renounce society, that I might avoid temptation."

This reformation, it seems, continued for more than two years. But he adds, "it was a poor religion: it left me in many respects under the power of sin: and, so far as it prevailed, only tended to make me gloomy, stupid, unsociable, and useless."

That it was a poor religion, and quite unlike that which he afterwards possessed, will appear from what immediately follows: for, had it been taken up upon more scriptural ground, and attended with that internal evidence and satisfaction which true religion only brings, he could not so soon have fallen a dupe to such a writer as Shaftesbury. It was at a petty shop at Middleburgh, in Holland, that he first met with a volume of the *Characteristicks*. [9] The declamation, called by his Lordship a "Rhapsody", suited the romantic turn of his mind. Unaware of its tendency, he imagined he had found a valuable guide. This book was always in his hand, till he could nearly repeat the "Rhapsody." Though it produced no immediate effect, it operated like a slow poison, and prepared the way for all that followed.

Appendix to Chapter 1

Newton's birthplace
John Newton was born in Wapping, not far from the Tower of London. Wapping was a nautical hamlet, home in Newton's lifetime to men such as Captain James Cook, the navigator, and Captain William Bligh, who endured mutiny on the *Bounty*.

Since the fifteenth century the stretch along the Thames between the Tower and Wapping had been "the usual Place of Execution for hanging of Pirates and Sea-Rovers, at the low Water Mark, there to remain till three Tides had overflowed them", but when the Gallows were moved, it became "a Continual Street, or rather a filthy straight Passage, with Lanes and Alleys of small Tenements or Cottages, inhabited by Saylors and Victuallers, along by the River of *Thames*, almost to *Radcliff*, a good Mile from the Tower."[10] Little more than thirty years before Newton's birth the infamous Judge Jeffreys, the Hanging Judge, was captured in Wapping while trying to escape disguised as a sailor, just a few yards from the house where the Newtons were to live.

The evangelist George Whitefield, friend of John and Charles Wesley, used to preach on weekdays at Wapping Chapel (later called St. John's) around 1737, but it was not until 1755 that Newton first met him.

His Parents and David Jennings
John's parents were Captain John Newton and Elizabeth. The distance between father and son in those early years had lessened by the time Newton heard, at sea, that his father had died. He wrote to his wife, "Had not the news of my dear father's death been accompanied by these confirmations of your health and your affection to me, I should have felt it more heavily, for I loved and revered him. But enough of this. My tears drop upon the paper." [11]

His mother attended the Independent Meeting in Old Gravel Lane, Wapping New Stairs.[12] It appears from Land Tax records[13] that the Newtons and Elizabeth's pastor, Dr. David Jennings, lived next door but one to each other in Red Lyon Street, Wapping, in 1730.

David Jennings was a close friend of Isaac Watts, composer of *When I survey the wondrous Cross*. Newton particularly enjoyed Watts's hymns as a child and later used them as the basis for composing the lyrics of his own. Jennings also had strong links with Philip Doddridge, the dissenting pastor who wrote many valuable works including *The Family Expositor* (a paraphrase of New Testament themes for family worship) and hymns such as *Hark the glad sound, the Saviour comes*; *O happy day that fixed my choice on Thee, my Saviour and my God*; *O God of Bethel, by whose hand Thy people still are fed.*

As Newton attributes so much to his mother's early teaching and prayers, it is particularly interesting to note a section of one of David Jennings's *Sermons to Young People*,[14] preached while Elizabeth Newton was still alive and John would have been about five or younger. Jennings challenged the parents from 1 Chronicles 29:19, *And give unto Solomon my son a perfect heart.* "Did you ever pray this prayer for your children in good earnest? Lord, give them a perfect heart. What pains have you taken to instruct and teach them the good ways of holiness? ...O! be earnest and importunate with God, be daily intercessors with him for the souls of your dear children. Beg it of him, who is the God of grace, that he would give your children a perfect heart." Such was the faithfulness of both pastor and mother for the child who was later to write, "'Twas grace that taught my heart to fear, and grace my fears relieved."

In another of these sermons, Jennings preached from Philemon 10, 11, "We have likewise, in this epistle, a memorable instance of richness and freeness of the grace of God, for the encouragement of the meanest and vilest sinners to fly to him for mercy." *Amazing grace, how sweet the sound that saved a wretch like me* ... the prayers of a mother were answered in such a remarkable way, more than she could have asked or imagined, many years after her death, and that despite the depths to which her son had sunk. Chapter 5 reveals another interesting link with his mother's prayers.

After his conversion Newton sought out spiritual advice from David Jennings and corresponded with him for several years until Jennings's death in 1762. Newton began the New Year of 1753 by writing to him, "I think it has been a prevalent custom in most ages and countries for clients to begin the new year with address to their respective patrons: considering myself in the former capacity, it immediately occurred to me, that Dr. Jennings was on all accounts the most proper and most worthy person I could regard in the latter."[15]

Old Gravel Lane continued as an Independent Chapel until 1885, when it was "unable, from circumstances of neighbourhood, to maintain a separate pastor". It was temporarily closed for repair and re-opened in 1887 as a Mission Hall under the London Congregational Union. The last mention of it in the *Congregational Year Book* is in 1913, when it had no members but ministered to 98 children.

His Step-Mother
The son born to John's father and his step-mother, Thomasina, was William, who was baptised in Aveley parish church on 8 September 1736.[16] Newton had another brother, Harry, who was a Lieutenant in the Royal Navy in Boston, America, and a sister, Thomasina, who married a Christian, Benjamin Nind.[17] Following Captain Newton's death, Thomasina remarried, but John was not much impressed by this union. In his biography of Newton, *Amazing Grace*, John Pollock mentions the interesting connection he himself has with Aveley. His father-in-law, the late Sir Richard Barrett-Lennard, Bt., O.B.E., was the great-great-great-grandson of the owner of the Belhus Estate, where Thomasina's father was a grazier on the tenant farm "Moor Hall".

His first voyage to sea
Writing to Walter Taylor in 1784, Newton confided, "I have likewise another reason for wishing to see Southampton. I was there so long ago as the year '36, in the shape of a little sailor boy. My father was master of a ship, and took in a lading of corn for Spain. It was my first voyage to sea. I love to revisit the spots where I spent a part of my early life; it revives the ideas of things and events long passed, and I hope the contrast between my situation then, and what it is now, will strike me, when I return to the same place, with some profitable impressions; for, alas! at the best I am too faintly affected with a review of the wonderful way by which the Lord has led me this far through the wilderness."[18]

The Family Instructor
One of the books which had an early effect on Newton, *The Family Instructor*, was published anonymously but later attributed to Daniel Defoe, author of *Robinson Crusoe* and several hundred other publications. It consists of imaginary conversations between fathers and their children, masters and servants and husbands and wives.

Each chapter is followed by notes evaluating spiritual attitudes with suggestions on how improvements could have been made. The author's aim is described in his introduction to the first section:

"The Father represented here, appears knowing enough, but seems to be one of those professing Christians who acknowledge God in their Mouths, *yet take no effectual Care* to honour him with their Practice; that live in a round of Religion, as a thing of course; have not the Power of Godliness, nor much of the Form; a kind of Negative Christian, a God-I-thank thee Pharisee, Sound in Knowledge, but negligent in Conversation, Orthodox in Opinion, but Hetrodox in Practice; and that I have found out such a Person, is to signify that let him be *where* he will, and *who* he will, this work is calculated to reprove and admonish him."

CHAPTER 2

AT SEA
1742–1745

About the year 1742, his father, having lately come from a voyage, and not intending to return to sea, was contriving for Mr. N.'s settlement in the world. But, to settle a youth who had no spirit for business, who knew but little of men or things, who was of a romantic turn, a medley, as he expressed it, of religion, philosophy, and indolence, and quite averse to order, must prove a great difficulty. At length a merchant in Liverpool [Joseph Manesty], an intimate friend of the father, and afterwards a singular friend to the son, offered to send him for some years to Jamaica, and undertook the charge of his future welfare. This was consented to, and preparation made for the voyage, which was to be prosecuted the following week. In the mean time, he was sent by his father on some business to a place, a few miles beyond Maidstone in Kent. But the journey, which was designed to last but three or four days, gave such a turn to his mind, as roused him from his habitual indolence, and produced a series of important and interesting occurrences.

A few days before this intended journey, he received an invitation to visit some distant relations in Kent. They were particular friends of his mother, who died at their house, but a coolness having taken place upon his father's second marriage, all intercourse between them had ceased. As his road lay within half a mile of the house, and he had obtained his father's leave to call on them, he went thither, and met with the kindest reception from these friends. They had two daughters. It seems the eldest had been intended, by both the mothers, for his future wife. Almost at the first sight of this girl, then under fourteen years of age, he was impressed with such an affection for her, as appears to have equalled all that the writers of romance have imagined.

"I soon lost," says he, "all sense of religion, and became deaf to the remonstrances of conscience and prudence: but my regard for her was always the same; and I may perhaps venture to say, that none of the scenes of misery and wickedness I afterwards experienced

ever banished her a single hour together from my waking thoughts
for the seven following years."

His heart being now riveted to a particular object, every thing
with which he was concerned appeared in a new light. He could not
now bear the thought of living at such a distance as Jamaica, for four
or five years, and therefore determined not to go thither. He dared
not communicate with his father on this point; but, instead of three
days, he stayed three weeks in Kent, till the ship had sailed, and then
he returned to London. His father, though highly displeased, became
reconciled; and, in a little time, he sailed with a friend of his father to
Venice.

In this voyage, being a common sailor, and exposed to the company
of his comrades, he began to relax from the sobriety which he had
preserved, in some degree, for more than two years. Sometimes,
pierced with convictions, he made a few faint efforts, as formerly, to
stop; and though not yet absolutely profligate, he was making large
strides towards a total apostasy from God. At length he received a
remarkable check by a dream, which made a very strong, though not
abiding, impression upon his mind.

I shall relate this dream in his own words, referring to the *Narrative*
those who wish to know his opinion of dreams, and his applications
of this one in particular to his own circumstances.

"The scene, presented to my imagination, was the harbour of
Venice, where we had lately been. I thought it was night, and my
watch upon the deck; and that, as I was walking to and fro by myself,
a person came to me (I do not remember from whence), and brought
me a ring, with an express charge to keep it carefully; assuring me,
that, while I preserved that ring, I should be happy and successful:
but if I lost or parted with it, I must expect nothing but trouble and
misery. I accepted the present and the terms willingly, not in the
least doubting my own care to preserve it, and highly satisfied to
have my happiness in my own keeping. I was engaged in these
thoughts, when a second person came to me, and, observing the ring
on my finger, took occasion to ask me some questions concerning it.
I readily told him its virtues, and his answer expressed a surprise at
my weakness in expecting such effects from a ring. I think he reasoned
with me some time, upon the impossibility of the thing; and at length
urged me, in direct terms, to throw it away. At first I was shocked at
the proposal, but his insinuations prevailed. I began to reason and

doubt, and at last plucked it off my finger, and dropped it over the ship's side into the water, which it had no sooner touched, than I saw, at the same instant, a terrible fire burst out from a range of mountains (a part of the Alps), which appeared at some distance behind the city of Venice. I saw the hills as distinct as if awake, and that they were all in flames. I perceived, too late, my folly; and my tempter, with an air of insult, informed me, that all the mercy God had in reserve for me was comprised in that ring, which I had wilfully thrown away. I understood that I must now go with him to the burning mountains, and that all the flames I saw were kindled on my account. I trembled, and was in a great agony; so that it was surprising I did not then awake: but my dream continued; and, when I thought myself upon the point of a constrained departure, and stood self-condemned, without plea or hope, suddenly, either a third person, or the same who brought the ring at first (I am not certain which) came to me, and demanded the cause of my grief. I told him the plain case, confessing that I had ruined myself wilfully, and deserved no pity. He blamed my rashness, and asked if I should be wiser, supposing I had my ring again. I could hardly answer to this, for I thought it was gone beyond recall. I believe, indeed, I had not time to answer, before I saw this unexpected friend go down under the water, just in the spot where I had dropped it, and he soon returned, bringing the ring with him: the moment he came on board, the flames in the mountains were extinguished, and my seducer left me. Then was *the prey taken from the hand of the mighty, and the lawful captive delivered.*[1] My fears were at an end, and with joy and gratitude I approached my kind deliverer to receive the ring again; but he refused to return it and spoke to this effect: 'If you should be entrusted with this ring again, you would very soon bring yourself into the same distress: you are not able to keep it, but I will preserve it for you, and, whenever it is needful, will produce it on your behalf.' Upon this I awoke, in a state of mind not to be described: I could hardly eat, or sleep, or transact my necessary business, for two or three days: but the impression soon wore off, and in a little time I totally forgot it; and I think it hardly occurred to my mind again till several years afterwards."

[*Narrative:*

"Those who acknowledge Scripture will allow that there have been monitory and supernatural dreams, evident communications from Heaven, either directing or foretelling future events: and those who are acquainted with the history and experience of the people of God, are well assured, that such intimations have not been totally withheld in any period down to the present times. Reason, far from contradicting this supposition, strongly pleads for it, where the process of reasoning is rightly understood and carefully pursued. So that a late eminent writer [Andrew Baxter on the *vis inertiæ*[2]], who I presume is not generally charged with enthusiasm, undertakes to prove, that the phenomenon of dreaming is inexplicable at least, if not absolutely impossible, without taking in the agency and intervention of spiritual beings, to us invisible. I would refer the incredulous to him. For my own part, I can say, without scruple, *The dream is certain, and the interpretation thereof sure.*[3] I am sure I dreamed to the following effect; and I cannot doubt, from what I have seen since, that it had a direct and easy application to my own circumstances, to the dangers in which I was about to plunge myself, and to the unmerited deliverance and mercy which God would be pleased to afford me in the time of distress.

"It will appear in the course of these papers, that a time came, when I found myself in circumstances very nearly resembling those suggested by this extraordinary dream, when I stood helpless and hopeless upon the brink of an awful eternity; and I doubt not that, had the eyes of my mind been then opened, I should have seen my grand enemy, who had seduced me wilfully to renounce and cast away my religious professions, and to involve myself in the most complicated crimes; I say, I should probably have seen him pleased with my agonies, and waiting for a permission to seize and bear away my soul to his place of torment. I should perhaps have seen likewise, that Jesus, whom I had persecuted and defied, rebuking the adversary, challenging me for his own, as a brand plucked out of the fire, and saying, 'Deliver him from going down to the pit: I have found a ransom.'[4] However, though I saw not these things, I found the benefit; I obtained mercy. The Lord answered for me in the day of my distress; and blessed be his name, he who restored the ring, (or what was signified by it,) vouchsafes to keep it. O what an unspeakable comfort is this, that I am not in my own keeping! 'The Lord is my shepherd.'[5]

I have been enabled to trust my all in his hands; and I know in whom I have believed. Satan still desires to have me, that he might sift me as wheat; but my Saviour has prayed for me, that my faith may not fail. Here is my security and power; a bulwark against which the gates of hell cannot prevail. But for this, many a time and often (if possible) I should have ruined myself since my first deliverance: nay, I should fall, and stumble, and perish still, after all that the Lord has done for me, if his faithfulness were not engaged in my behalf, to be my sun and shield even unto death. *Bless the Lord, O my soul.*[6]]

Nothing remarkable took place in the following part of that voyage. Mr. N. returned home in December 1743; and, repeating his visit to Kent, protracted his stay in the same imprudent manner he had done before. This so disappointed his father's designs for his interest, as almost to induce him to disown his son. Before any thing suitable offered again, this thoughtless son, unmindful of the consequences of appearing in a *checked shirt*, was marked by a lieutenant [Thomas Ruffin] of the *Harwich* man of war, who immediately impressed and carried him on board a tender. This was at a critical juncture, as the French fleets were hovering upon our coast; so that his father was incapable of procuring his release. A few days after, he was sent on board the *Harwich*, at the Nore. Here a new scene of life was presented; and, for about a month much hardship endured. As a war was daily expected, his father was willing he should remain in the navy, and procured him a recommendation to the captain [Philip Carteret], who sent him upon the quarter-deck as a midshipman. He might now have had ease and respect, had it not been for his unsettled mind and indifferent behaviour. The companions he met with here completed the ruin of his principles: though he affected to talk of virtue, and preserved some decency, yet his delight and habitual practice was wickedness.

His principal companion [James Mitchell] was a person of talents and observation, an expert and plausible infidel, whose zeal was equal to his address. "I have been told," says Mr. N., "that afterwards he was overtaken in a voyage from Lisbon in a violent storm: the vessel and people escaped, but a great sea broke on board, and swept him into eternity." Being fond of this man's company, Mr. N. aimed to display what smattering of reading he had: his companion, perceiving that Mr. N. had not lost all the restraints of conscience, at first spoke in favour of religion; and, having gained Mr. N.'s confidence, and perceiving his attachment to the *Characteristicks*, he soon convinced his pupil that he had never understood that book. By objections and arguments Mr. N.'s depraved heart was soon gained. He plunged into infidelity with all his spirit; and, like an unwary sailor who quits his post just before a rising storm, the hopes and comforts of the gospel were renounced at the very time when every other comfort was about to fail.

In December, 1744, the *Harwich* was in the Downs, bound to the East Indies. The captain gave Mr. N. leave to go on shore for a day; but, with his usual inconsideration, and following the dictates of a restless passion, he went to take a last leave of the object with which he was so infatuated. Little satisfaction attended the interview in such circumstances, and on new year's day he returned to the ship. The captain was so highly displeased at this rash step, that it occasioned ever after the loss of his favour.

At length they sailed from Spithead, with a very large fleet. They put in to Torbay, with a change of wind; but sailed the next day, on its becoming fair. Several of the fleet were lost at leaving the place; but the following night the whole fleet was greatly endangered upon the coast of Cornwall, by a storm from the southward. The ship on which Mr. N. was abroad escaped unhurt, though several times in danger of being run down by other vessels; but many suffered much: this occasioned their putting back to Plymouth.

While they lay at Plymouth, Mr. N. heard that his father, who had an interest in some of the ships lately lost, was come down to Torbay. He thought that if he could see his father, he might easily be introduced into a service which would be better than pursuing a long and uncertain voyage to the East Indies. It was his habit in those days *never to deliberate*. As soon as the thought occurred, he resolved to leave the ship at all events: he did so, and in the worst manner possible. He was sent one day in the boat to prevent others from desertion, but betrayed his trust, and deserted himself. Not knowing which road to take, and fearing to enquire lest he should be suspected, yet having some general idea of the country, he found, after he had travelled some miles, that he was on the road to Dartmouth. That day and part of the next every thing seemed to go on smoothly. He walked fast, and thought to have seen his father in about two hours, when he was met by a small party of soldiers, whom he could not avoid or deceive; they brought him back to Plymouth, through the streets of which he proceeded guarded like a felon. Full of indignation, shame, and fear, he was confined two days in the guardhouse; then sent on ship-board, and kept a while in irons: next he was publicly stripped and whipped, degraded from his office, and all his former companions forbidden to show him the least favour, or even to speak to him. As midshipman he had been entitled to command, in which (being sufficiently haughty and vain) he had not been temperate: but was now in his turn brought down to a level with the lowest, and exposed to the insults of all.

The state of his mind at this time can only be properly expressed in his own words:

"As my present situation was uncomfortable, my future prospects were still worse: the evils I suffered were likely to grow heavier every day. While my catastrophe was recent, the officers and my quondam brethren were something disposed to screen me from ill usage; but during the little time I remained with them afterwards, I found them cool very fast in their endeavours to protect me. Indeed they could not avoid such conduct without running a great risk of sharing with me; for the captain, though in general a humane man, who behaved very well to the ship's company, was almost implacable in his resentment, and took several occasions to show it, and the voyage was expected to be (as it proved) for five years. Yet nothing I either felt or feared distressed me so much as to see myself thus forcibly torn away from the object of my affections, under a great improbability of seeing her again, and a much greater of returning in such a manner as would give me hope of seeing her mine.

"Thus I was as miserable on all hands as could well be imagined. My breast was filled with the most excruciating passions; eager desire, bitter rage and black despair. Every hour exposed me to some new insult and hardship, with no hope of relief or mitigation; no friend to take my part, nor to listen to my complaint. Whether I looked inward or outward, I could perceive nothing but darkness and misery. I think no case, except that of a conscience wounded by the wrath of God, could be more dreadful than mine. I cannot express with what wishfulness and regret I cast my last looks upon the English shore: I kept my eyes fixed upon it, till, the ship's distance increasing, it insensibly disappeared; and, when I could see it no longer, I was tempted to throw myself into the sea, which (according to the wicked system I had adopted) would put a period to all my sorrows at once. But the secret hand of God restrained me."

During his passage to Madeira, Mr. N. describes himself as a prey to the most gloomy thoughts. Though he had deserved all, and more than all he had met with from the captain, yet pride suggested that he had been grossly injured; "and this so far," says he, "wrought upon my wicked heart, that I actually formed designs against his life, and that was one reason which made me willing to prolong my own. I was sometimes divided between the two, not thinking it practicable to affect both. The Lord had now to appearance given me up to judicial hardness; I was capable of any thing. I had not the least fear of God before my eyes, nor (so far as I remember) the least sensibility of conscience. I was possessed with so strong a spirit of delusion, that I believed my own lie, and was firmly persuaded that after death I should cease to be. Yet the Lord preserved me! Some intervals of sober reflection would at times take place: when I have chosen death rather than life, a ray of hope would come in (though there was little probability for such a hope) that I should yet see better days, that I might return to England, and have my wishes crowned, if I did not wilfully throw myself away. In a word, my love to Mrs. N. was now the only restraint I had left; though I neither feared God nor regarded man, I could not bear that *she* should think meanly of me when I was dead."

Mr. N. had now been at Madeira some time. The business of the fleet being completed, they were to sail the following day: on that memorable morning he happened to be late in bed, and would have continued to sleep, but that an old companion, a midshipman, came down, between jest and earnest, and bid him rise. As he did not immediately comply, the midshipman cut down the hammock in which he lay; this obliged him to dress himself; and though very angry, he durst not resent it, but was little aware this person without design, was a special instrument of God's providence. Mr. N. said little, but went upon deck, where he saw a man putting his own clothes into a boat, and informed Mr. N. he was going to leave the ship. Upon enquiry, he found that two men from a Guinea ship [the *Pegasus*], which lay near them, had entered on board the *Harwich*, and that the commodore, (the late Sir George Pocock) had ordered the captain to send two others in their room. Inflamed with this information, Mr. N. requested that the boat might be detained a few minutes: he then entreated the lieutenants to intercede with the captain that he might be dismissed upon this occasion: though he had formerly behaved ill to these officers, they were moved with pity, and were disposed to serve him. The captain, who had refused to exchange him at Plymouth, though requested by Admiral Medley, was easily prevailed with now. In little more than half an hour from his being asleep in bed, he found himself discharged, and safe on board another ship: the events depending upon this change, will show it to have been the most critical and important.

Appendix to Chapter 2

Relations
Newton's relations in Kent were the Catletts. George Catlett was Customs Officer in Chatham. His wife, Elizabeth, was said to be a distant cousin of Elizabeth Newton's. Their children were Mary (Polly), Elizabeth, John Churchill (Jack) and George. There were also two other daughters, Sarah and Susanna, born before George, who appear to have died prematurely. Newton fell in love with Mary.

Mary's sister Elizabeth married James Cunningham at St. Mary's, Chatham, in March, 1764. They lived in Rochester before moving to Fifeshire. Both parents and two of their children had died by 1783, leaving only their daughter Elizabeth (Eliza) who was taken into the Newtons' home.

Mary's brother Jack was a solicitor. Newton constantly tried to direct his thoughts to faith in Christ, appealing to the lawyer's mind to observe "that I have one evident advantage over you in judging, namely, that I have experienced the good and evil on *both* sides, and you only on *one*."[7] Jack died the year after he received this letter. Newton felt there was reason to believe he had changed his ways before his death.

Mary's brother George married Sarah Kite at St Mary's, Dover, on 3 February 1767. Their daughter Elizabeth (Betsy) was born at noon on Thursday 22 June 1769. Her mother died in childbirth. Betsy was orphaned and adopted by the Newtons in 1774. It was she who looked after Newton in his old age.

In Newton's *Narrative* he replied to a request from Thomas Haweis for more details of his relationship with Mary:

"Amongst other things, you desired a more explicit account of the state and progress of my courtship, as it is usually phrased. This was the point in which I thought it especially became me to be very brief; but I submit to you; and this seems a proper place to resume it, by telling you how it stood at the time of my leaving England. When my inclinations first discovered themselves, both parties were so young, that no-one but myself considered it in a serious view. It served for tea-table talk amongst our friends; and nothing further was expected from it. But afterwards, when my passion seemed to have abiding effects, so that in an interval of two years it was not at all abated, and especially as it occasioned me to act without any regard to prudence or interest, or my father's designs; and as there was a coolness between him and the family, her parents began to consider it as a matter of consequence; and when I took my last leave of them, her mother, at the same time that she expressed the most tender affection for me, as if I had been her own child, told me, that though she had no objections to make, upon a supposition, that at a maturer age there should be a probability of our engaging upon a prudent prospect, yet as things then stood, she thought herself obliged to interfere; and therefore desired I would no more think of returning to their house, unless her daughter was from home, till such time as I could either prevail with myself entirely to give up my pretensions, or could assure her that I had my father's express consent to go on. "

He adds that Mary had penetration to see her absolute power over him, "and prudence to make a proper use of it; she would neither understand my hints, nor give me room to come to a direct explanation."

He wrote to her as the *Harwich* was waiting to depart in January 1745:

"My uncle's officiousness (which I am determined never to forgive) has made the length of this voyage, much more acceptable than it would otherwise have been; since if I were to stay in England I must be obliged to submit to live from you; and on that hard condition all countries are nearly alike to me. There is I know not what within me, that bears me up, and assures me I shall certainly come home again; but whether it will be to any purpose; whether I shall be happy in you, or no, is what I long to know, yet should dread to be resolved in: I will not mortify myself to think I shall return to find you in another's possession, before I have had an opportunity of showing what I would do to deserve you; for if I were not firmly assured, no person living can so tenderly regard you as myself, I could be almost content to resign you for your own sake.

"You are not ignorant that your Mother has strictly forbad me troubling you with my letters, and you will suppose no doubt that I shall be glad if you receive this without her intercepting it, and consequently that it would give me a great pleasure to hear that you had done so."[8]

Polly's aunt, Mrs. Eversfield, helped in forwarding their letters.

The dream

In a letter to John Ryland, many years later,[9] Newton recalls a custom in Venice, where a vessel called the Bucentaur, goes out to sea with the Doge and certain nobles to perform an ancient ritual where a gold ring is thrown overboard.

"The Bucintoro returning to the Molo [Quayside]", Canaletto's famous painting, from the Royal Collection, depicts this ceremony of thanksgiving for the bounty the sea brought to Venice. Perhaps this ritual served as the framework for Newton's dream.

CHAPTER 3

A SERVANT OF SLAVES
1745–1747

The ship he now entered was bound to Sierra Leone, and the adjacent parts of what is called the Windward Coast of Africa. The Commander [Captain Guy James Penrose] knew his father, received him kindly, and made professions of assistance; and probably would have been his friend, if, instead of profiting by his former errors, he had not pursued a course, if possible, more worse. He was under some restraint on board the *Harwich*; but, being now among strangers, he could sin without disguise. "I well remember," says he, "that while I was passing from one ship to the other, I rejoiced in the exchange with this reflection, that I might now be as abandoned as I pleased, without any control; and from this time, I was exceedingly vile indeed, little, if any thing, short of that animated description of an almost irrecoverable state, which we have in 2 Peter 2:14. I not only sinned with a high hand myself, but made it my study to tempt and seduce others, upon every occasion: nay, I eagerly sought occasion, sometimes to my own hazard and hurt." By this conduct he soon forfeited the favour of his captain; for, besides being careless and disobedient, upon some imagined affront, he employed his mischievous wit in making a song to ridicule the captain as to his ship, his designs, and his person; and he taught it to the whole ship's company.

He thus proceeded for about six months, at which time the ship was preparing to leave the coast; but, a few days before she sailed the captain died. Mr. N. was not upon much better terms with his mate [Josiah Blunt], who succeeded to the command, and upon some occasion had treated him ill. He felt certain that if he went in the ship to the West Indies, the mate would have him put on board a man of war, a consequence more dreadful to him than death itself; to avoid this, he determined to remain in Africa, and pleased himself with imagining it would be an opportunity of improving his fortune.

Upon that part of the coast there were a few white men settled, whose business it was to purchase slaves, etc. and sell them to the ships at an advanced price. One of these, who had first landed in circumstances similar to Mr. N.'s, had acquired considerable wealth. This man [Amos Clow] had been in England, and was returning in the same vessel with Mr. N. of which he owned a quarter part. His example impressed Mr. N. with hopes of the same success, and he obtained his discharge upon condition of entering into the trader's service, to whose generosity he trusted without precaution of terms. He received, however, no compensation for his time on board the ship, but a bill upon the owners in England; which, in consequence of their failure, was never paid: the day, therefore, on which the vessel sailed, he landed upon the island of Benanoes, like one ship-wrecked, with little more than the clothes upon his back.

"The two following years," says he, "of which I am now to give some account, will seem as an absolute blank in my life: but, I have seen frequent cause since to admire the mercy of God in banishing me to those distant parts, and almost excluding me from all society, at a time when I was big with mischief, and, like one infected with a pestilence, was capable of spreading a taint wherever I went. But the Lord wisely placed me where I could do little harm. The few I had to converse with were too much like myself; and I was soon brought into such abject circumstances, that I was too low to have any influence. I was rather shunned and despised than imitated; there being few even of the negroes themselves, during the first year of my residence, but thought themselves too good to speak to me. I was as yet an outcast, ready to perish; but the Lord beheld me with mercy, he even now bid me *live*; and I can only ascribe it to his secret upholding power, that what I suffered in a part in this interval did not bereave me either of my life or senses."

The reader will have a better idea of the station Mr. N. was now in, by his brief sketch of it.

"From Cape de Verd, the most western point of Africa, to Cape Mount, the whole coast is full of rivers: the principal are the Gambia, Rio Grande, Sierra Leone, and Sherbro. Of the former, as it is well known, and as I was never there, I need say nothing. The Rio Grande (like the Nile) divides into many branches near the sea. On the most northerly, called Cacheo, the Portuguese have a settlement. The most southern branch, known by the name of Rio Nuna, is, or was, the usual boundary of the white men's trade northward. Sierra Leone is a mountainous peninsula, uninhabited, and I believe inaccessible, upon account of the thick woods, excepting those parts which lie

near the water. The river is large and navigable. From hence, about
twelve leagues to the south-east, are three contiguous islands, called
the Benanoes, twenty miles in circuit: this was about the centre of
the white men's residence. Seven leagues further, the same way, lie
the Plantanes, three small islands, two miles distant from the continent,
at the point which forms one side of the Sherbro. The river is more
properly a *sound*, running within a long island, and receiving the
confluence of several large rivers: "rivers unknown to song," but far
more deeply engraven in my remembrance than the Po or Tiber. The
southernmost of these has a very peculiar course almost parallel to
the coast; so that in tracing it a great many leagues upwards, it will
seldom lead one above three miles, and sometimes not more than
half a mile from the sea shore."

Mr. N.'s new master had resided near Cape Mount, but at this
time had settled at the Plantanes, on the largest of the three islands. It
is low and sandy, about two miles in circumference, and almost
covered with palm-trees. They immediately began to build a house.
Mr. N. had some desire to retrieve his time and character, and might
have lived tolerably well with his master, if this man had not been
much under the direction of a black woman ["P.I."], who lived with
him as a wife, and influenced him against his new servant. She was a
person of some consequence in her own country, and he owed his
first rise to her interest. This woman, for reasons not known, was
strangely prejudiced against Mr. N. from the first. He also had
unhappily a severe fit of illness, which attacked him before he had
opportunity to show what he could or would do in the service of his
master. Mr. N. was sick when his master sailed in a shalop to Rio
Nuna, and was left in the hands of this woman. He was taken some
care of at first; but, not soon recovering, her attention was wearied,
and she entirely neglected him. Sometimes it was with difficulty he
could procure a draught of cold water, when burning with a fever!
His bed was a mat, spread upon a board or chest, with a log for his
pillow. Upon his appetite returning, after the fever left him, he would
gladly have eaten, but *no one gave unto him*.[1] She lived in plenty, but
scarcely allowed him sufficient to sustain life, except now and then,
when in the highest of good humour, she would send him victuals in
her own plate after she had dined. And this (so greatly was he
humbled) he received with thanks and eagerness, as the most needy
beggar does an alms. "Once," says he, "I well remember, I was called

to receive this bounty from her own hand: but, being exceedingly weak and feeble, I dropped the plate. Those who live in plenty can hardly conceive how this loss touched me: but she had the cruelty to laugh at my disappointment; and, though the table was covered with dishes (for she lived much in the European manner), she refused to give me any more. My distress has been at times so great, as to compel me to go by night, and pull up roots in the plantain (though at risk of being punished as a thief) which I have eaten raw upon the spot, for fear of discovery. The roots I speak of are very wholesome food, when boiled or roasted, but as unfit to be eaten raw in any quantity as a potato. The consequence of this diet, which, after the first experiment, I always expected and seldom missed, was the same as if I had taken tartar emetic; so that I have often returned as empty as I went: yet necessity urged me to repeat the trial several times. I have sometimes been relieved by strangers; yea even by the slaves in the chain, who have secretly brought me victuals (for they durst not be seen to do it) from their own slender pittance. Next to pressing want, nothing sits harder upon the mind than *scorn* and *contempt*, and of this likewise I had an abundant measure."

When slowly recovering, the same woman would sometimes pay Mr. N. a visit; not to pity or relieve, but to insult him. She would call him worthless and indolent, and compel him to walk; which when he could scarcely do, she would set her attendants to mimic his motions, to clap their hands, laugh, throw limes at him, and sometimes they would even throw stones. But though her attendants were forced to join in this treatment, Mr. N. was rather pitied than scorned, by the meanest of her slaves, on her departure.

When his master returned from the voyage, Mr. N. complained of ill usage, but was not credited; and, as he did it in her hearing, he fared worse for it. He accompanied his master in his second voyage, and they agreed pretty well, till his master was persuaded by a brother trader that Mr. N. was dishonest. This seems to be the only vice with which he could not be charged; as his honesty seemed to be the last remains of a good education which he could now boast of: and though his great distress might have been a strong temptation to fraud, it seems he never once thought of defrauding his master in the smallest matter. The charge, however, was believed, and he was condemned without evidence. From that time he was used very hardly: whenever his master left the vessel, he was locked upon deck with a pint of rice for his day's allowance, nor had he any relief till his master return. "Indeed," says he, "I believe I should have been nearly starved, but for an opportunity of catching fish sometimes. When fowls were killed for my master's own use, I seldom was allowed any part but the entrails, to bait my hooks with; and, at what we call *slack-water*, that is, about the changing of the tides, when the current was still, I used generally to fish, (at other times it was not practicable) and I very often succeeded. If I saw a fish upon my hook, my joy was little less than any other person would have found in the accomplishment of the scheme he had most at heart. Such a fish, hastily broiled, or rather half burnt, without salt, sauce, or bread, has afforded me a delicious meal. If I caught none, I might, if I could, sleep away my hunger till the next return of *slack-water*, and then try again.

"Nor did I suffer less from the inclemency of the weather, and the want of clothes. The rainy season was now advancing; my whole suit was a shirt, a pair of trousers, a cotton handkerchief instead of a cap, and a cotton cloth about two yards long, to supply the want of upper garments: and, thus accoutred, I have been exposed for twenty, thirty, perhaps near forty hours together, in incessant rains, accompanied with strong gales of wind, without the least shelter, when my master was on shore. I feel to this day some faint returns of the violent pains I then contracted. The excessive cold and wet I endured in that voyage, and so soon after I had recovered from a long sickness, quite broke my constitution and my spirits: the latter were soon restored, but the effects of the former still remain with me, as a needful memento of the service and wages of sin."

In about two months they returned, and the rest of the time which Mr. N. spent with his master was chiefly at the Plantanes, and under the same regimen as has been mentioned. His heart was now bowed down, but not at all to a wholesome repentance. While his spirits sunk, the language of the prodigal was far from him; destitute of resolution, and almost of all reflection, he had lost the fierceness which fired him when on board the *Harwich*, and rendered him capable of the most desperate attempts; but he was no further changed than a tiger tamed by hunger.

However strange it may appear, he attests it as a truth, that, though destitute both of food and clothing, and depressed beyond common wretchedness, he could sometimes collect his mind to mathematical studies. Having bought Barrow's *Euclid*[2] at Plymouth, and it being the only volume he brought ashore, he used to take it to remote corners of the island, and draw his diagrams with a long stick upon the sand. "Thus," says he, "I often beguiled my sorrows, and almost forgot my feelings, and thus without any other assistance I made myself in a good measure master of the first six books of Euclid."

With my staff I passed this Jordan, and now I have become two bands.[3] These words of Jacob might well affect Mr. N. – when remembering the days in which he was busied in planting some lime or lemon trees. The plants he put into the ground were no higher than a young gooseberry bush. His master and mistress, in passing the place, stopped a while to look at him; at length his master said, "Who knows but by the time these trees grow up and bear, you may go home to England, obtain the command of a ship, and return to reap the fruits of your labours? We see strange things sometimes happen."

"This," says Mr. Newton, "as he intended it, was a cutting sarcasm. I believe he thought it full as probable that I should live to be King of Poland: yet it proved a prediction; and they (one of them at least) lived to see me return from England, in the capacity he had mentioned, and pluck some of the first limes from these very trees. How can I proceed in my relation, till I raise a monument to the divine goodness, by comparing the circumstances in which the Lord has since placed me, with what I was in at that time? Had you seen me, sir, then go so pensive and solitary in the dead of night to wash my one shirt upon the rocks, and afterwards put it on wet, that it might dry upon my back while I slept; had you seen me so poor a figure, that when a ship's boat came to the island, shame often constrained me to hide myself in the woods, from the sight of strangers; especially had you known that my conduct, principles, and heart, were still darker than my outward condition – how little would you have imagined, that one, who so fully answered to the στυγητοι μισουντες* of the Apostle, was reserved to be so peculiar an instance of the providential care, and exuberant goodness of God! – There was, at that time, but one earnest desire of my heart, which was not contrary and shocking both to religion and reason: that *one* desire, though my vile licentious life rendered me peculiarly unworthy of success, and though a thousand difficulties seemed to render it impossible, the Lord was pleased to gratify."

---

*Hateful and hating [Titus 3:3]

Things continued thus nearly twelve months. In this interval Mr. N. wrote two or three times to his father, describing his condition, and desiring his assistance; at the same time signifying, that he had resolved not to return to England, unless his parent were pleased to send for him. His father applied to his friend at Liverpool, who gave orders accordingly, to a captain of his who was then fitting out for Gambia and Sierra Leone.

Some time within the year, Mr. N. obtained his master's consent to live with another trader [Mr. Williams] who dwelt upon the same island. This change was much to his advantage, as he was soon decently clothed, lived in plenty, was treated as a companion, and trusted with his effects to the amount of some thousand pounds. This man had several factories, and white servants in different places; particularly one in Kittam, the river already described as running so near along the sea coast. Mr. N. was soon appointed there, and had a share in the management of business, jointly with another servant [McCraig]. They lived as they pleased; business flourished; and their employer was satisfied.

"Here," says he, "I began to be wretch enough to think myself *happy*. There is a significant phrase frequently used in those parts, that such a white man is growing *black*. It does not intend an alteration of complexion, but disposition. I have known several, who settling in Africa after the age of thirty or forty, have, at that time of life, been gradually assimilated to the tempers, customs, and ceremonies of the natives, so far as to prefer that country to England: they have even become dupes to all the pretended charms, necromancies, amulets, and divinations of the blinded negroes, and put more trust in such things than the wiser sort among the natives. A part of this spirit of infatuation was growing upon me (in time, perhaps, I might have yielded to the whole): I entered into closer engagements with the inhabitants, and should have lived and died a wretch among them, if the Lord had not watched over me for good. Not that I had lost those ideas which chiefly engaged my heart to England, but a despair of seeing them accomplished made me willing to remain where I was. I thought I could more easily bear the disappointment in this situation than nearer home. But, as soon as I had fixed my connections and plans with these views, the Lord providentially interposed to break them in pieces, and save me from ruin, in spite of myself."

Appendix to Chapter 3

In slavery

The woman with whom Mr. Clow lived was described some years later by Newton in a letter to his wife as having a name which sounded like "P.I. (those two letters pronounced distinctly, and not in one syllable, as Pi, exactly sound her name)".[4]

William Wordsworth was intrigued by reading, in the *Narrative*, of Newton's self-taught lessons in Euclid on the shores of his captive island. He asked his sister, Dorothy, to copy out the passage for him and used the idea in *The Prelude*, quoting Newton verbatim at times:

> And as I have read of one by shipwreck thrown
> With fellow sufferers whom the waves had spared
> Upon a region uninhabited,
> An island of the deep, who having brought
> To land a single volume and no more –
> A treatise of geometry – was used,
> Although of food and clothing destitute,
> And beyond common wretchedness depressed,
> To part from company and take this book,
> Then first a self-taught pupil in those truths,
> To spots remote and corners of the isle
> By the seaside, and draw his diagrams
> With a long stick upon the sand, and thus
> Did often beguile his sorrow, and almost
> Forget his feeling... [5]

Some thirty years after this event, Newton was to write to a young man training for the ministry, whose curriculum included mathematical studies, warning him of the dangers of pride in his research: "I believe I had naturally a turn for the mathematics myself, and dabbled in them a little way; and though I did not go far, my head, sleeping and waking, was stuffed with diagrams and calculations. Everything I looked at that exhibited either a right line or a curve, set my wits a wool-gathering. What then must have been the case had I proceeded to the interior *arcana* of speculative geometry? I bought my namesake's *Principia*;[6] but I have reason to be thankful that I left it as I found it, a sealed book, and that the bent of my mind was drawn to something of more real importance before I understood it."[7]

The Lime trees

A CMS missionary visiting the Plantanes in 1820 recorded in his Journal,[8] "After breakfast we went in search of the lime-trees which were planted by the late Rev. John Newton, when he was wandering like a lost sheep over this island." They found the trees cut down, with new shoots sprouting – a picture perhaps of the spiritual change in the old Newton, for he also found in the library of the chief, George Caulker, a hymn-book with translations, "and as several of the hymns in that book were composed by the late Rev. John Newton, it is probable that some of his hymns are now sung in the Sherbro tongue, on the very spot were he in ignorance wandered, and planted lime-trees for his amusement!"

Rivers unknown to song

Newton's description of the Sherbro river (page 36) is a very appropriate quote from James Thomson's *Hymn*, which was added to his collected *Seasons* in 1730:

> Should fate command me to the farthest verge
> Of the green earth, to distant barbarous climes,
> *Rivers unknown to song*; where first the sun
> Gilds Indian mountains, or his setting beam
> Flames on th' Atlantic isles; 'tis nought to me,
> Since God is ever present, ever felt,
> In the void waste as in the city full;
> And where He vital breathes there must be joy.

Thomson [1700-1748] was a friend of Riccaltoun, whom Newton greatly admired, and was tutor to the son of Charles Talbot, Lord Chancellor, the uncle of William Talbot, vicar of Kineton. The Shakespearean actor, David Garrick, performed Thomson's work at Drury Lane. But Thomson's best known piece is still heard annually by an audience of millions – *Rule Brittania.*

CHAPTER 4

THE BEGINNINGS OF A NEW LIFE
1747–1748

In the mean time, the ship, that had orders to bring Mr. N. home, arrived at Sierra Leone. The captain made enquiry for Mr. N. there, and at the Bonanas: but finding he was at a great distance, thought no more about him. A special providence seems to have placed him at Kittam just at this time; for the ship coming no nearer than the Bonanas, and staying but a few days, if he had been at the Plantanes he would not probably have heard of her till she had sailed: the same must have certainly been the event had he been sent to any other factory, of which his new master had several. But though the place he went to was a long way up the river, much more than a hundred miles distant from the Plantanes, yet by its peculiar situation, already noticed, he was still within a mile of the sea coast. The interposition was also more remarkable, as at that very juncture he was going in quest of trade directly from sea; and would have set out a day or two before, but that they waited for a few articles from the next ship that came, in order to complete the assortment of goods he was to take with him.

They used sometimes to walk to the beach, in hopes of seeing a vessel pass by; but this was very precarious, as at that time the place was not resorted to by ships of trade: many passed in the night, others kept a considerable distance from the shore, nor does he remember that any one had stopped while he was there.

In Feb. 1747, his fellow-servant walking down to the beach in the forenoon, saw a vessel [the *Greyhound*] sailing by, and made a smoke in token of trade. She was already beyond the place, and the wind being fair, the captain demurred about stopping: had Mr. N.'s companion been half an hour later, the vessel would have been beyond recall: when he saw her come to an anchor, he went on board in a canoe, and this proved the very ship already spoken of, which brought an order for Mr. N.'s return. One of the first questions the captain put was concerning Mr. N., and understanding he was so near, the captain came on shore to deliver his message.

"Had," says he, "an invitation from home reached me when I was sick and starving at the Plantanes, I should have received it as life from the dead; but now, for the reasons already given, I heard it at first with indifference." The captain [Captain Swanwick], however, unwilling to lose him, framed a story, and gave him a very plausible account of his having missed a large packet of letters and papers, which he should have brought with him, but said he had it from his father's own mouth, as well as from his employer, that a person lately dead had left Mr. N. £400 per annum, and added, that if embarrassed in his circumstances, he had express orders to redeem Mr. N., though it should cost one half of his cargo. Every particular of this was false, nor could Mr. N. believe what was said about the estate; except, that, as he had some expectations from an aged relation [Great-Aunt Henrietta], he thought a part of it might be true.

But though his father's care and desire to see him, was treated so lightly, and would have been insufficient alone to draw him from his retreat, yet the remembrance of Mrs. N., the hopes of seeing her, and the possibility that his accepting this offer might once more put him in the way of gaining her hand, prevailed over all other considerations.

The captain further promised (and in this he kept his word) that Mr. N. should lodge in his cabin, dine at his table, and be his companion, without being liable to service. Thus suddenly was he freed from a captivity of about fifteen months. He had neither a thought nor a desire of this change one hour before it took place; but, embarking with the captain, he in a few hours lost sight of Kittam.

[*Narrative:*

"How much is their blindness to be pitied, who can see nothing but chance in events of this sort! so blind and stupid was I at that time: I made no reflection, I sought no direction in what had happened: like a wave of the sea driven by the wind, and tossed, I was governed by present appearances, and looked no farther. But he who is eyes to the blind, was leading me in a way that I knew not.

"Now I am in some measure enlightened, I can easily perceive, that it is in the adjustment and concurrence of these seemingly fortuitous circumstances, that the ruling power and wisdom of God are most evidently displayed in human affairs. How many such casual events may we remark in the history of Joseph, which had each a necessary influence on his ensuing promotion! If he had not dreamed, or if he had not told his dream; if the Midianites had passed by a day sooner, or a day later; if they had sold him to any person but Potiphar; if his mistress had been a better woman; if Pharaoh's officers had not displeased their lord; or if any, or all of these things had fallen out in any other manner or time than they did, all that followed had been prevented; the promises and purposes of God concerning Israel, their bondage, deliverance, polity, and settlement, must have failed: and as all these things tended to, and centred in, Christ, the promised Saviour, the desire of all nations would not have appeared. Mankind had been still in their sins, without hope, and the counsels of God's eternal love in favour of sinners defeated. Thus we may see a connection between Joseph's first dream and the death of our Lord Jesus Christ, with all its consequences. So strong, so secret, is the concatenation [series of links] between the *greatest* and the *smallest* events. What a comfortable thought is this to a believer, to know, that amidst all the various interfering designs of men, the Lord has one constant design, which he cannot, will not, miss, namely, his own glory in the complete salvation of his people; and that he is wise, and strong, and faithful, to make even those things which seem contrary to this design, subservient to promote it."]

The ship in which he embarked as a passenger was on a trading voyage for gold, ivory, dyer's wood, and bees' wax. Such a cargo requires more time to collect than one of slaves. The captain began his trade at Gambia, had been already four or five months in Africa; and during the course of a year after Mr. N. had been with him, they ranged the whole coast as far as Cape Lopez, which lies about a degree south of the equinoctial [equator], and more than a thousand miles further from England than the place from whence he embarked.

"I have," says he, "little to offer worthy of notice in the course of this tedious voyage. I had no business to employ my thoughts, but sometimes amused myself with mathematics: excepting this, my whole life, when awake, was a course of most horrid impiety and profaneness. I know not that I have ever since met so daring a blasphemer. Not content with common oaths and imprecations, I daily invented new ones: so that I was often seriously reproved by the captain, who was himself a very passionate man, and not at all circumspect in his expressions. From the relation I at times made him of my past adventures, and what he saw of my conduct, and especially towards the close of the voyage, when we met with many disasters, he would often tell me, that to his grief, he had a Jonah on board; that a curse attended me wherever I went; and that all the troubles he met with in the voyage were owing to his having taken me into his vessel."

Although Mr. N. lived long in the excess of almost every other extravagance, he was never, it seems, fond of drinking: his father was often heard to say that while his son avoided drunkenness, some hopes might be entertained of his recovery. Sometimes, however, in a frolic, he would promote a drinking bout; not through love of liquor, but disposition to mischief: the last proposal he made of this kind, and at his own expense, was in the river Gabon whilst the ship was trading on the coast.

Four or five of them sat down one evening to try who could hold out longest in drinking Geneva and rum alternately: a large sea-shell supplied the place of a glass. Mr. N. was very unfit for such a challenge, as his head was always incapable of bearing much liquor: he began, however, and proposed as a toast, some imprecation against the person who should start first: this proved to be himself. Fired in his brain, he arose and danced on the deck like a madman, and while he was thus diverting his companions, his hat went overboard. Seeing the ship's boat by moonlight, he endeavoured eagerly to throw himself over the side into the boat, that he might recover his hat. His sight however deceived him, for the boat was not (as he supposed) within his reach, but perhaps twenty feet from the ship's side. He was, however, half overboard, and would in the space of a moment have plunged into the water, when somebody caught hold of his clothes, and pulled him back. This was an amazing escape, as he could not swim, had he been sober: the tide ran very strong: his companions were too much intoxicated to save him, and the rest of the ship's company were asleep.

Another time at Cape Lopez, before the ship left the coast, he went with some others into the woods, and shot a buffalo, or wild cow; they brought part of it on board, and carefully marked the place (as he thought) where the rest was left. In the evening they returned to fetch it, but set out too late. Mr. N. undertook to be their guide; but, night coming on before they could reach the place, they lost their way. Sometimes they were in swamps, and up to the middle in water; and when they recovered dry land, they could not tell whether they were proceeding towards the ship, or the contrary way. Every step increased their uncertainty, the night grew darker, and they were entangled in thick woods, which perhaps the foot of man had never trodden, and which abound with wild beasts: besides which, they had neither light, food, nor arms, while expecting a tiger to rush from behind every tree. The stars were clouded, and they had no compass whereby to form a judgement which way they were going. But it pleased God to secure them from the beasts; and, after some hours' perplexity, the moon arose, and pointed out the eastern quarter. It appeared then, that, instead of proceeding towards the sea, they had been penetrating the country; at length, by the guidance of the moon, they recovered the ship.

These, and many other deliverances, produced at that time no salutary effect. The admonition of conscience, which from successive repulses had grown weaker and weaker, at length entirely ceased; and, for the space of many months, if not for some years, he had not a single check of that sort. At times he was visited with sickness, and believed himself to be near death, but had not the least concern about the consequences. "In a word," says he, "I seemed to have every mark of final impenitence and rejection: neither judgments nor mercies made the least impression on me."

At length, their business being finished, they left Cape Lopez; and, after a few days' stay at the island of Annabona, in order to lay in provisions, they sailed homeward about the beginning of January 1748. From Annabona to England is perhaps more than seven thousand miles, if the circuits are included, which it is necessary to make on account of the trade-winds. They sailed first westward, till near the coast of Brazil, then northward, to the banks of Newfoundland, without meeting any thing extraordinary. On these banks they stopped half a day to fish for cod: this was then chiefly for diversion, as they had provision enough, and little expected that those fish (as it afterwards proved) would be all they would have to subsist on. They left the banks, March 1st, with a hard gale of wind westerly, which pushed them fast homewards. By the length of this voyage in a hot climate, the vessel was greatly out of repair, and very unfit to endure stormy weather. The sails and cordage were likewise very much worn; and many such circumstances concurred to render what followed imminently dangerous.

Among the few books they had on board was Stanhope's Thomas-a-Kempis:[1] Mr. N. carelessly took it up, as he had often done before,

to pass away the time, but which he read with the same indifference
as if it were a romance. But, in reading it this time, a thought occurred
– *What if these things should be true!* He could not bear the force of
the inference, and therefore shut the book, concluding, that, true or
false, he must abide the consequences of his own choice; and put an
end to these reflections by joining in the vain conversation which
came in his way.

"But now," says he, "*the Lord's time was come*, and the conviction
I was so unwilling to receive was deeply impressed upon me by an
awful dispensation."

He went to bed that night in his usual carnal security; but was
awakened from a sound sleep by the force of a violent sea which
broke upon board: so much of it came down as filled the cabin in
which he lay with water. This alarm was followed by a cry from the
deck that the ship was sinking. He essayed to go upon the deck but
was met upon the ladder by the captain, who desired him to bring a
knife. On his return for the knife, another person went up in his place,
who was instantly washed overboard. They had no leisure to lament
him, nor did they expect to survive him long, for the ship was filling
with water very fast. The sea had torn away the upper timbers on one
side, and made it a mere wreck in a few minutes; so that it seems
almost miraculous that any survived to relate the story. They had
immediate recourse to the pumps, but the water increased against
their efforts: some of them were set to bailing, though they had but
eleven or twelve people to sustain this service. But, notwithstanding
all they could do, the vessel was nearly full, and with a common
cargo must have sunk; but having a great quantity of bees' wax and
wood on board, which were specifically lighter than water, and
providentially receiving this shock in the very crisis of the gale,
towards morning they were enabled to employ some means for safety,
which succeeded beyond hope. In about an hour's time, day began to
break, and the wind abated: they expended most of their clothes and
bedding to stop the leaks: over these they nailed pieces of boards;
and, at last, perceived the water to subside.

At the beginning of this scene Mr. N. was little affected: he pumped
hard, and endeavoured to animate himself and his companions. He
told one of them, that in a few days this distress would serve for a
subject over a glass of wine; but the man, being less hardened than
himself, replied with tears, "No, it is too late now." About nine

o'clock, being almost spent with cold and labour, Mr. N. went to speak with the captain, and, as he was returning, said, almost without meaning, "If this will not do, the Lord have mercy upon us:" thus expressing, though with little reflection, his desire of mercy for the first time within the space of many years. Struck with his own words, it directly occurred to him, *What mercy can there be for me!* He was, however, obliged to return to the pump, and there continued till noon, almost every passing wave breaking over his head, being, like the rest, secured by ropes, that they might not be washed away. He expected, indeed, that every time the vessel descended in the sea she would rise no more: and though he dreaded death Now, and his heart foreboded the worst, if the Scriptures, which he had long opposed, were true; yet he was but half convinced, and remained for a time in a sullen frame, a mixture of despair and impatience. He thought, if the Christian Religion were true, he could not be forgiven: and was therefore expecting, and almost at times wishing, to know the worst of it.

The following part of his *Narrative* will, I think, be best expressed in his own words: "The 10th, that is, in the present style, the 21st of March, is a day much to be remembered by me, and I have never suffered it to pass wholly unnoticed since the year 1748. On that day the Lord sent from on high, and delivered me out of deep waters. – I continued at the pump from *three* in the morning till near *noon*, and then I could do no more. I went and lay down upon my bed, uncertain, and almost indifferent whether I should rise again. In an hour's time I was called; and, not being able to pump, I went to the helm, and steered the ship till midnight, excepting a small interval for refreshment. I had here leisure and convenient opportunity for reflection. I began to think of my former religious professions, – the extraordinary turns of my life, – the calls, warnings, and deliverances I had met with, – the licentious course of my conversation, – particularly my unparalleled effrontery in making the gospel history (which I could not be sure was false, though I was not yet assured it was true) the constant subject of profane ridicule. I thought, allowing the Scripture promises, there never was or could be such a sinner as myself; and then, comparing the advantages I had broken through, I concluded at first, that my sins were too great to be forgiven. The Scripture likewise seemed to say the same: for I had formerly been well acquainted with the Bible, and many passages, upon this occasion, returned upon my memory; particularly those awful passages, Proverbs 1:24-31, Hebrews 6:4, 5, 6 and 2 Peter 2:20, which seemed so exactly to suit my case and character, as to bring with them a presumptive proof of a divine original.

"Thus, as I have said, I waited with fear and impatience to receive my inevitable doom. Yet, though I had thoughts of this kind, they were exceeding faint and disproportionate: it was not till after (perhaps) several years that I had gained some clear views of the infinite righteousness and grace of Christ Jesus my Lord, that I had a deep and strong apprehension of my state by nature and practice: and, perhaps, till then, I could not have borne the sight. So wonderfully does the Lord proportion the discoveries of sin and grace: for he knows our frame, and that if he were to put forth the greatness of his power, a poor sinner would be instantly overwhelmed, and crushed as a moth.

"But, to return. When I saw, beyond all probability, that there was still hope of respite, and heard about six in the evening that the ship was freed from water, there arose a gleam of hope. I thought I saw the hand of God displayed in our favour. I began to pray; I could not utter the prayer of faith: I could not draw near to a reconciled God, and call him *Father*: my prayer was like the cry of the ravens, which yet the Lord does not disdain to hear. I now began to think of that Jesus whom I had so often derided: I recollected the particulars of his life, and of his death; a death for sins not his *own*, but as I remembered, for the sake of those, who in their distress should put their trust in him. And now I chiefly wanted evidence. The comfortless principles of infidelity were deeply riveted; and I rather *wished* than believed these things were real facts. You will please to observe, that I collect the strain of the reasonings and exercises of my mind in one view; but I do not say that all this passed at one time. The great question now was how to obtain *faith*. I speak not of an appropriating faith (of which I then knew neither the nature nor necessity,) but how I should gain an assurance that the Scriptures were of divine inspiration, and a sufficient warrant for the exercise of trust and hope in God.

"One of the first helps I received (in consequence of a determination to examine the New Testament more carefully) was from Luke 11:13. I had been sensible, that, to profess faith in Jesus Christ, when in reality, I did not believe his history, was no better than a mockery of the heart-searching God; but there I found a SPIRIT spoken of, which was to be communicated to those who ask it. Upon this I reasoned thus: If this book be true, the promise in this passage must be true likewise. I have need of that very Spirit by which the whole was written, in order to understand it aright. He has engaged here to give that Spirit to those who ask: I must therefore pray for it; and, if it be of God, he will make good his own word. My purposes were strengthened by John 7:17. I concluded from thence, that, though I could not say from my heart that I believed the Gospel, yet I would, for the present, take it for granted: and that, by studying it in this light, I should be more and more confirmed in it.

"If what I am writing could be perused by our modern infidels, they would say, (for I too well know their manner) that I was very desirous to persuade myself into this opinion. I confess I was; and so would they be, if the Lord should show them, as he was pleased to show me at that time, the absolute necessity of some expedient to interpose between a righteous God and a sinful soul: upon the Gospel scheme, I saw, at least a peradventure of hope; but, on every other side, I was surrounded with black, unfathomable despair."

The wind now being moderate, and the ship drawing near to its port, the ship's company began to recover from their consternation, though greatly alarmed by their circumstances. They found that the water having floated their moveables in the hold, all the casks of provision had been beaten to pieces by the violent motion of the ship. On the other hand, their livestock had been washed overboard in the storm. In short, all the provisions they saved, except the fish lately caught on the banks for amusement, and a little of the pulse kind, which used to be given to the hogs, would have supported them but a week, and that at a scanty allowance. The sails, too, were mostly blown away; so that they advanced but slowly, even while the wind was fair. They imagined they were about a hundred leagues from land, but were in reality much further. Mr. N's leisure was chiefly employed in reading, meditation on the Scriptures, and prayer for mercy and instruction.

Things continued thus for about four or five days, till they were awakened one morning by the joyful shouts of the watch upon deck, proclaiming the sight of land, with which they were all soon raised. The dawning was uncommonly beautiful; and the light, just sufficient to discover distant objects, presented what seemed a mountainous coast, about twenty miles off, with two or three small islands: the whole appeared to be the north-west extremity of Ireland, for which they were steering. They sincerely congratulated one another, having no doubt that if the wind continued, they should be in safety and plenty the next day. Their brandy, which was reduced to a little more than a pint, was, by the captain's orders, distributed among them; who added, "We shall soon have brandy enough." They likewise ate up the residue of their bread, and were in the condition of men suddenly reprieved from death.

But, while their hopes were thus excited, the mate [Hardy] sunk their spirits, by saying, in a graver tone, that he wished "it might prove land at last." If one of the common sailors had first said so, the rest would probably have beaten him. The expression, however, brought on warm debates, whether it was land or not: but the case was soon decided; for one of their fancied islands began to grow red from the approach of the sun. In a word, their land was nothing but clouds: and, in half an hour more, the whole appearance was dissipated.

Still, however, they cherished hope from the wind continuing fair; but of this hope they were soon deprived. That very day, their fair wind subsided into a calm; and, the next morning, the gale sprung up from the south-east, directly against them, and continued so for more than a fortnight afterwards. At this time the ship was so wrecked, that they were obliged to keep the wind always on the broken side, except when the weather was quite moderate; and were thus driven still further from their port in the north of Ireland, as far as Lewis, among the western isles of Scotland. Their station now was such, as deprived them of any hope of relief from other vessels. "It may indeed be questioned," says Mr. N., "whether our ship was not the very first that had been in that part of the ocean at the same time of the year."

Provisions now began to fall short. The half of a salted cod was a day's subsistence for twelve people: they had no stronger liquor than water, no bread, hardly any clothes, and very cold weather. They had also incessant labour at the pumps, to keep the ship above water. Much labour and little food wasted them fast, and one man died under the hardship. Yet their sufferings were light compared with their fears. Their bare allowance could continue but little longer; and a dreadful prospect appeared of their being either starved to death, or reduced to feed upon one another.

At this time Mr. N. had a further trouble, peculiar to himself. The captain, whose temper was quite soured by distress, was hourly reproaching him as the sole cause of the calamity, and was confident that his being thrown overboard would be the only means of preserving them. The captain, indeed, did not intend to make the experiment; but "the continued repetition of this in my ears," says Mr. N., "gave me much uneasiness; especially as my conscience seconded his words: I thought it very probable, that all that had befallen us was on my account, that I was at last found out by the powerful hand of God, and condemned in my own breast."

While, however, they were thus proceeding, at a time when they were ready to give up all for lost, and despair appeared in every countenance, they began to conceive hope from the wind's shifting to the desired point, so as best to suit that broken part of the ship, which must be kept out of the water, and so gently to blow, as their few remaining sails could bear. And thus it continued at an unsettled time of the year, till they were once more called up to see land, and which was really such. They saw the island of Tory, and the next day anchored in Lough Swilly, in Ireland, on the 8th of April, just four weeks after the damage they had sustained from the sea. When they came into this port, their very last victuals were boiling in the pot, and before they had been there two hours, the wind, which seemed to have been providentially restrained till they were in a place of safety, began to blow with great violence; so that if they had continued at sea that night, they must, in all human estimation, have gone to the bottom! "About this time," says Mr. N., "I began to know that there is a God, who hears and answers prayer."

Mr. N.'s history is now brought down to the time of his arrival in Ireland, in the year 1748; and the progress he had hitherto made in religion will be best related in his own words. I shall, therefore, make a longer extract than usual, because it is important to trace the operation of real religion in the heart. Speaking of the ship in which he lately sailed, he says, "There were no persons on board to whom I could open myself with freedom concerning the state of my soul: none from whom I could ask advice. As to books, I had a New Testament, Stanhope, already mentioned, and a volume of Bishop Beveridge's Sermons,[2] one of which, upon our Lord's Passion, affected me much. In perusing the New Testament, I was struck with several passages, particularly that of the fig-tree, Luke 13, the case of St. Paul, 1 Timothy, but particularly that of the Prodigal, Luke 15. I thought *that* had never been so nearly exemplified as by myself. And then the goodness of the Father in receiving, nay, in running to meet such a son, and this intended only to illustrate the Lord's goodness to returning sinners. Such reflections gaining upon me, I continued much in prayer: I saw that the Lord had interposed *so far* to save me, and I hoped he would do more. Outward circumstances helped in this place to make me more serious and earnest in crying to him who alone could relieve me; and sometimes I thought I could be content to die even for want of food, so I might but die a believer.

"Thus far was I answered, that before we arrived in Ireland, I had a satisfactory evidence in my own mind of the truth of the Gospel, as considered in itself, and of its exact suitableness to answer all my needs. I saw, that, by the way they were pointed out, God might declare not his mercy only, but his justice also, in the pardon of sin, on account of the obedience and sufferings of Jesus Christ. My judgement, at that time, embraced the sublime doctrine of God *manifest in the flesh, reconciling the world unto himself.*[3] I had no idea of those systems, which allow the Saviour no higher honour than that of an *upper servant*, or at the most of a *demi-god*. I stood in need of an Almighty Saviour, and such an one I found described in the New Testament. Thus far the Lord had wrought a marvellous thing: I was no longer an infidel: I heartily renounced my former profaneness, and had taken up some right notions; was seriously disposed, and sincerely touched with a sense of the undeserved mercy I had received, in being brought safe through so many dangers. I was sorry for my past misspent life, and purposed an immediate reformation. I was quite freed from the habit of swearing, which seemed to have been as deeply rooted in me as a second nature. Thus, to all appearance, I was a new man.

"But, though I cannot doubt that this change, so far as it prevailed, was wrought by the Spirit and power of God, yet still was I greatly deficient in many respects. I was in some degree affected with a sense of my enormous sins, but I was little aware of the innate evils of my heart. I had no apprehension of the spirituality and extent of the law of God; or of the hidden life of a Christian, as it consists in Communion with God by Jesus Christ: a continual dependence on him for hourly supplies of wisdom, strength and comfort, was a mystery of which I had as yet no knowledge. I acknowledged the

Lord's mercy in pardoning what was past, but depended chiefly upon my own resolution to do better for the time to come. I had no Christian friend or faithful minister to advise me that my strength was no more than my righteousness; and, though I soon began to enquire for serious books, yet not having spiritual discernment, I frequently made a wrong choice; and I was not brought in the way of evangelical preaching or conversation (except the few times when I heard, but understood not) for six years after this period. Those things the Lord was pleased to discover to me gradually. I learnt them here a little, and there a little, by my own painful experience, at a distance from the common means and ordinances, and in the midst of the same course of evil company and bad examples I had been conversant with for some time.

"From this period I could no more make a mock at sin, or jest with holy things: I no more questioned the truth of Scripture, or lost a sense of the rebukes of conscience. Therefore I consider this as the beginning of my return to God, or rather of *his* return to me; but I cannot consider myself to have been a believer (in the full sense of the word) till a considerable time afterwards."

While the ship was refitting at Lough Swilly, Mr. N. repaired to Londonderry, where he soon recruited his health and strength. He was now a serious professor, went twice a day to the prayers at Church, and determined to receive the sacrament the next opportunity. When the day came, he arose very early, was very earnest in his private devotions, and solemnly engaged himself to the Lord; not with a formal, but sincere surrender, and under a strong sense of the mercies which he lately received. Having, however, as yet but an imperfect knowledge of his own heart, and of the subtlety of Satan's temptations, he was afterwards seduced to forget the vows of God that were upon him. Yet he felt a peace and satisfaction in the ordinance of that day, to which he had hitherto been an utter stranger.

The next day he went on a shooting party with the mayor of the city, and some of the gentlemen. As he was climbing up a steep bank, and pulling his fowling-piece in a perpendicular direction after him, it went off so near his face as to destroy the corner of his hat. The remark he makes on this ought not to be omitted: "Thus, when we think ourselves in the greatest safety, we are no less exposed to danger than when all the elements seem conspiring to destroy us. The Divine Providence, which is sufficient to deliver us in our utmost extremity, is equally necessary to our preservation in the most peaceful situation."

During their stay in Ireland, Mr. N. wrote home. The vessel he was in had not been heard of for eighteen months, and was given up for lost. His father had no expectation of hearing that his son was alive; but received his letter a few days before he embarked from London to become governor of York Fort, in Hudson's Bay, where he died.

He had intended to take his son with him, had he returned to England in time. Mr. N. received two or three affectionate letters from his father; and hoped, that, in three years more, he should have had the opportunity of asking his forgiveness for the uneasiness his disobedience had occasioned; but the ship that was to have brought his father home came without him. It appears he was seized with the cramp, while bathing, and was drowned before the ship arrived in the bay. Before his father's departure from England, he had paid a visit in Kent, and given his consent to the union that had been so long talked of.

Mr. N. arrived at Liverpool the latter end of May 1748, about the same day that his father sailed from Nore. He found, however, another father in the gentleman whose ship had brought him home [Joseph Manesty]. This friend received him with great tenderness, and the strongest assurances of assistance; yet not stronger than he afterwards fulfilled, for to this instrument of God's goodness he felt he owed everything. "Yet," as Mr. N. justly observes, "it would not have been in the power even of this friend, to have served me effectually, if the Lord had not met me on my way home, as I have related. Till then I was like the man possessed with the *Legion*. No arguments, no persuasion, no views of interest, no remembrance of the past, nor regard to the future, could have restrained me within the bounds of common prudence; but now I was, in some measure, restored to my senses."

This friend immediately offered Mr. N. the command of a ship, which, upon mature consideration, he, for the present, declined. He prudently considered, that, hitherto, he had been unsettled and careless; and that he had better, therefore, make another voyage, and learn obedience, and acquire further experience in business, before he ventured to undertake such a charge. The mate of the vessel, in which he came home, was preferred to the command of a new ship [the *Brownlow*], and Mr. N. engaged to go in the station of mate with him [Captain Hardy].

There was something so peculiar in Mr. N.'s case after this extraordinary deliverance, and because others in like circumstances might be tempted to despair, that I think it proper to make another extract from his "Narrative"; as such accounts cannot be well conveyed but in his own words.

"We must not make the experience of others in all respects a rule to ourselves, nor our own a rule to others: yet these are common mistakes, and productive of many more. As to myself, every part of my case has been extraordinary. I have hardly met a single instance resembling it. Few, very few, have been recovered from such a dreadful state: and the few, that have been thus favoured, have generally passed through the most severe convictions; and, after the Lord has given them peace, their future lives have been usually more zealous, bright, and exemplary than common. Now as, on the one hand, my convictions were very moderate, and far below what might have been expected from the dreadful review I had to make: so on the other my first beginnings in a religious course were as faint as can be well imagined. I never knew that season alluded to, Jeremiah 2:2, Revelation 2:4, usually called the time of *first love*. Who would not expect to hear, that, after such a wonderful and unhoped-for deliverance as I had received, and after my eyes were in some measure enlightened to see things aright, I should immediately cleave to the Lord and his ways with full purpose of heart, and consult no more with flesh and blood? But, alas! it was far otherwise with me. I had learned to pray: I set some value upon the word of God; and was no longer a libertine: but *my soul* still *cleaved to the dust.*[4] Soon after my departure from Liverpool, I began to intermit and grow slack in waiting upon the Lord: I grew vain and trifling in my conversation; and, though my heart smote me often, yet my armour was gone, and I declined fast: and, by the time we arrived at Guinea, I seemed to have forgotten all the Lord's mercies and my own engagements: and was, profaneness excepted, almost as bad as before. The enemy prepared a train of temptations, and I became his easy prey: for about a month he lulled me asleep in a course of evil, of which, a few months before, I could not have supposed myself any longer capable. How much propriety is there in the Apostle's advice, *Take heed lest any of you be hardened through the deceitfulness of sin.*"[5]

[*Narrative*:
"O, who can be sufficiently upon their guard? Sin first deceives, and then it hardens. I was now fast bound in chains; I had little desire, and no power at all, to recover myself. I could not but at times reflect how it was with me: but if I attempted to struggle with it, it was in vain. I was just like Samson, when he said, 'I will go forth, and shake myself as at other times';[6] but the Lord was departed, and he found himself helpless in the hands of his enemies. By the remembrance of this interval, the Lord has often instructed me since, what a poor creature I am in myself, incapable of standing a single hour, without continual fresh supplies of strength and grace from the fountain head."]

Appendix to Chapter 4

The Rescue

Newton confided in Thornton almost 30 years later, "At the very time when the ship appeared so critically, and brought me off the coast, I had formed the horrid design of fighting a man who had affronted me (and who was too strong for me) with pistols, and in a few days should have put it in execution."[7]

The storm

At the age of seventy-seven Newton reflected again on these events:

"My Gracious Lord, Thou hast preserved me to see another anniversary of that great, awful, and merciful day, when I was upon the point of sinking with all my sins and blasphemies upon my head into the pit which has no bottom, and must have sunk, had not Thine eye pitied me, and preserved me in a manner which appears to me little less miraculous, than all the wonders Thou didst perform for Israel in Egypt and at the Red Sea.

"O I have now cause to praise Thee for that terrible storm, which first shook my infidelity, and made me apprehensive that death was not, as my corrupt heart had persuaded me, an eternal sleep.

"I thank Thee, likewise, for the subsequent month, when we expected to be starved, or reduced to feed upon one another and had it not been for this protected season of distress, my first serious impressions might have worn off, but Thou fixed and increased them, so that by the time we arrived in Ireland, I was no longer an *infidel*.

Not one of my fellow sufferers was affected as I was. Well may I say with wonder and gratitude, Why me, O Lord, Why me?"[8]

Lessons from Jonah

Newton must have recalled the captain's threats to throw him overboard when, years later, he began to preach from the book of Jonah at St. Mary Woolnoth. "It bears a resemblance to my own history, and I need not go far, nor consult many books, to explain the workings of the heart of man, from Jonah's case. The recollection of many parts of my past life, and many feelings of my own heart to this day, will furnish me with something to say upon it. When the path of duty led me to the East, I have foolishly and obstinately set my face to the West. I have suffered by storms, which my own sins have raised, and if I never was in the belly of a fish, I have been in my own apprehensions, in the mouth of Hell! I have had my gourds likewise, and while I have been admiring them a worm has been sent to the root. Some of them have faded, and some of them are still spared. The crowning wonder and mercy of all is, that I am still spared myself!"[9]

CHAPTER 5

ON BOARD
1748–1754

In this voyage Mr. N.'s business, while upon the coast, was to sail in the long-boat from place to place, in order to purchase slaves. The ship, at this time, was at Sierra Leone, and he at the Plantanes, the scene of his former captivity, and where everything he saw tended to remind him of his present ingratitude. He was now in easy circumstances, and courted by those who had once despised him. The *lime trees* he had formerly planted were growing tall, and promised fruit upon his return with a ship of his own. Unaffected, however, with these things, he needed another providential interposition to rouse him; and, accordingly, he was visited with a violent fever, which broke the fatal chain, and once more brought him to himself. Alarmed at the prospect before him, he thought himself now summoned away. The dangers and deliverances through which he had passed – his earnest prayers in time of trouble – his solemn vows before the Lord at his table – and his ungrateful returns for all his goodness, were present, at once, to his mind. He began then to wish that he had sunk in the ocean when he first cried for mercy. For in a short time, he concluded that the door of hope was quite shut. Weak and almost delirious, he arose from his bed, crept to a retired part of the island, and here found a renewed liberty in prayer: daring to make no more resolves, he cast himself upon the Lord, to do with him as he should please. – It does not appear that any thing new was presented to his mind, but that, in general, he was enabled to hope and believe in a Crucified Saviour.

After this the burden was removed from his conscience; and not only his peace, but his health, was gradually restored when he returned to the ship: and, though subject to the effects and conflicts of sin dwelling in him, yet he was ever after delivered from its power and dominion.

His leisure hours, in this voyage, were chiefly employed in acquiring Latin, which he had now almost forgotten. This desire took place from an imitation he had seen of one of Horace's Odes in a Magazine. In this attempt at one of the most difficult of the poets, he had no other help than an old English translation, with Castalio's Latin Bible. He had the edition *in usum Delphini*; and, by comparing the Odes with the interpretation, and tracing such words as he understood from place to place by the index, together with what assistance he could get from the Latin Bible, he thus, by dint of hard industry, made some progress. He not only understood the sense of many Odes, and some of the Epistles, but "I began," says he, "to relish the beauties of the composition: acquired a spice of what Mr. Law calls *classical enthusiasm*;[1] and, indeed, by this means, I had Horace more *ad unguem*,[2] than some who are masters of the Latin tongue: for my helps were so few, that I generally had the passage fixed in my memory before I could fully understand its meaning."

During the eight months they were employed upon the coast, Mr. N.'s business exposed him to innumerable dangers, from burning suns, chilling dews, winds, rains, and thunder-storms, in an open boat: and on the shore from long journeys through the woods; and from the natives, who in many places are cruel, treacherous, and watchful of opportunities of mischief. Several boats, during this time, were cut off: several white men were poisoned: and from his own boat, he buried six or seven people with fevers. When going on shore, or returning, he was more than once overset by the violence of the surf, and brought to land half dead, as he could not swim. Among a number of such escapes, which remained upon his memory, the following will mark the singular providence that was over him.

On finishing their trade, and being about to sail to the West Indies, the only service Mr. N. had to perform in the boat was to assist in bringing the wood and water from the shore. They were then at Rio Cestors. He used to go into the river, in the afternoon, with the sea breeze, to procure his loading in the evening, in order to return on board in the morning with the landwind. Several of these little voyages he had made; but the boat was grown old, and almost unfit for use. This service, likewise, was almost completed. One day, having dined on board, he was preparing to return to the river as formerly: he had taken leave of the captain, received his orders, was ready in the boat, and just going to put off. In that instant the captain came up from the cabin, and called him on board again. Mr. N. went expecting further orders, but the captain said he *had taken it into his head* (as he phrased it) that Mr. N. should remain that day in the ship, and accordingly ordered another man to go in his room. Mr. N. was surprised at this, as the boat had never been sent away without him before. He asked the captain the reason of his resolution, but none was assigned, except, as above, that so he would have it. The boat therefore, went without Mr. N. but returned no more: it sunk that night in the river; and the person who supplied Mr. N.'s place was drowned! Mr. N. was much struck, when news of the event was received the next morning. The captain himself, though quite a stranger to religion, even to the denying of a Particular Providence, could not help being affected: but declared that he had no other reason for countermanding Mr. N. at that time, but that it came suddenly into his mind to detain him.

A short time after he was thus surprisingly preserved, they sailed for Antigua; and from thence to Charlestown, in South Carolina. In that place there were many serious people: but, at this time, Mr. N. was little capable of availing himself of their society; supposing that all who attended public worship were good Christians, and that whatever came from the pulpit must be very good. He had two or three opportunities, indeed, of hearing a minister of eminent character and gifts [Josiah Smith], whom, though struck with his manner, he did not rightly understand. Almost every day, when business would permit, he used to retire into the woods and fields (being his favourite oratories) and began to taste the delight of communion with God, in the exercises of prayer and praise: and yet so much inconsistency prevailed, that he frequently spent the evening in vain and worthless company. His relish, indeed, for worldly diversions was much weakened: and he was rather a spectator than a sharer in these pleasures; but he did not as yet see the necessity of absolutely relinquishing such society. It appears that compliances of this sort, in his present circumstances, were owing rather to a want of light than to any obstinate attachment. As he was kept from what he *knew* to be sinful, he had, for the most part, peace of conscience; and his strongest desires were towards the things of God. He did not as yet apprehend the force of that precept, *abstain from all appearance of evil;*[3] but he very often ventured upon the brink of temptation. He did not break with the world at once, as might have been expected; but was gradually led to see the inconvenience and folly of first one thing, and then another; and, as such, to give them up.

[*Annotated Letters to a Wife*, 21 February 95
The religion I then possessed, my Lord, Thou knowest, scarcely deserved the name. My views of truth were very imperfect; my conduct, though not grossly criminal, was very defective and inconsistent. I have wondered that in those early times, I should aim at, attain, and in general preserve, such a measure of dependence upon Thy providential care. But I can remember many trying occasions when it afforded me strong support, though I hardly know upon what it was founded. The state of my mind, then, seems not to have warranted me to apply Thy promises to myself. For I knew little of Thee as a Saviour, and while I trusted Thee in temporals, I was not aware of my greatest wants and dangers. In my spiritual concerns, I chiefly depended upon myself. I knew I had been very bad, I had a desire to be better, and thought I should in time make myself so. Surely if I had any light, it was but as the first and faintest streak of dawn. Yet if this glimmering had not been from Thee, it could not have advanced. Thou who wilt not forsake the work of Thine own hands, nor break the bruised reed, nor quench the smoking flax, wast pleased to pardon, accept and bring me forward. May the remembrance of Thy patience and gentleness towards me, teach me forbearance and candour to others, in whom I observe the smallest indications of a desire to seek and serve Thee!]

They finished their voyage, and arrived in Liverpool. When the ship's affairs were settled, Mr. N. went to London, and from thence he soon repaired to Kent. More than seven years had now elapsed since his first visit. No views of the kind seemed more chimerical [fanciful] than his; or could subsist under greater discouragements: yet, while he seemed abandoned to his passions, he was still guided by a hand that he knew not, to the accomplishment of his wishes. Every obstacle was now removed – he had renounced his former follies – his interest was established – and friends on all sides consenting. The point was now entirely between the parties immediately concerned; and, after what had passed, was easily concluded: accordingly their hands were joined, February the 1st, 1750.

"But alas!" says he, "this mercy, which raised to me all I could ask or wish in a temporal view, and which ought to have been an animating motive to obedience and praise, had a contrary effect. I rested in the gift, and forgot the giver. My poor narrow heart was satisfied. A cold and careless frame, as to spiritual things, took place, and gained ground daily. Happy for me, the season was advancing; and, in June, I received orders to repair to Liverpool. This roused me from my dream; and I found the pains of absence and separation fully proportioned to my preceding pleasure.* Through all my following voyage, my irregular and excessive affections were as thorns in my eyes, and often made my other blessings tasteless and insipid. But He, who doeth all things well, over-ruled this likewise for good: it became an occasion of quickening me in prayer, both for her and myself: it increased my indifference for company and amusement: it habituated me to a kind of voluntary self-denial, which I was afterwards taught to improve to a better purpose."

[*Narrative*
While I remained in England, we corresponded every post; and all the while I used the sea afterwards, I constantly kept up the practice of writing, two or three times a week (if weather and business

---

* He wrote to Mrs. Newton from St. Alban's, and in his letter inserted a prayer for his own health and that of Mrs. N. [The prayer was: Gracious God! favour me and my dearest Mary with health, and a moderate share of the good things of this life! Grant that I may be always happy in her love, and always proving deserving of it! For the rest, the empty gewgaws and gilded trifles, which engage the thoughts of multitudes, I hope I shall be always able to look upon them with indifference.] From his interleaved copy of his *Letters to a Wife*, I extract the following remarks on this letter.

"This prayer includes all that I at that time knew how to ask for; and had not the Lord given me more than I then knew how to ask or think, I should now be completely miserable. The prospect of this separation was terrible to me as death: to avoid it, I repeatedly purchased a ticket in the lottery; thinking, 'Who knows but I may obtain a considerable prize, and be thereby saved from the necessity of going to sea?' Happy for me, the lot which I then considered as casual was at thy disposal. The money, which I could not with prudence have spared at the time, was lost: all my tickets proved blanks, though I attempted to bribe thee, by promising, if I succeeded, to give a considerable part to the poor. But these blanks were truly prizes. Thy mercy sent me to sea against my own will. To thy blessing, and to my solitary sea hours, I was indebted for all my temporal comforts and future hopes.

"Thou wert pleased likewise to disappoint me by thy providence of some money which I expected to receive on my marriage; so that, excepting our apparel, when I sailed from Liverpool on my first voyage, the sum total of my worldly inventory was – seventy pounds in debt."

permitted,) though no conveyance homeward offered for six or eight months together. My packets were usually heavy: and as not one of them at any time miscarried, I have to the amount of nearly 200 sheets of paper now lying in my bureau of that correspondence. I mention this little relief by which I contrived to soften the intervals of absence, because it had a good effect beyond my first intention. It habituated me to think and write upon a great variety of subjects; and I acquired, insensibly, a greater readiness of expressing myself than I should otherwise have attained. As I gained more ground in religious knowledge, my letters became more and more serious; and, at times, I still find an advantage in looking them over; especially as they remind me of many providential incidents, and the state of my mind at different periods in these voyages, which would otherwise have escaped my memory.]

Mr. N. sailed from Liverpool in August 1750, commander of a good ship [the *Duke of Argyle*]. He had now the control and care of thirty persons; and he endeavoured to treat them with humanity, and to set them a good example.* He likewise established public worship according to the Liturgy of the Church of England, officiating himself twice every Lord's Day. He did not proceed further than this, while he continued in that occupation.

Having now much leisure, he prosecuted the study of Latin with good success. He remembered to take a Dictionary this voyage; and added Juvenal to Horace; and, for prose authors, chose Livy, Caesar, and Sallust. He was not aware of the mistake of beginning with such difficult writers; but, having heard Livy highly commended, he was resolved to understand him: he began with the first page, and made it a rule not to proceed to a second till he understood the first. Often at a stand, but seldom discouraged, here and there he found a few lines quite obstinate, and was forced to give them up, especially as his edition had no notes. Before, however, the close of that voyage, he

---

* I have heard Mr. Newton observe, that, as the commander of a slave-ship, he had a number of women under his absolute authority: and, knowing the danger of his situation on that account, he resolved to abstain from flesh in his food, and to drink nothing stronger than water, during the voyage; that, by abstemiousness, he might subdue every improper emotion: and that, upon his setting sail, the sight of a certain point of land was the signal for his beginning a rule which he was enabled to keep.

informs us that he could, with a few exceptions, read Livy almost as readily as an English author.

Other prose authors, he says, cost him but little trouble; as, in surmounting the former difficulty, he had mastered all in one. In short, in the space of two or three voyages, he became quite tolerably acquainted with the best classics. He read Terence, Virgil, several pieces of Cicero; and the modern classics, Buchanan [*Narrative*: "I prefer Buchanan's Psalms[4] to a whole shelf of Elzivir's"], Erasmus, and Casimir: and made some essays towards writing elegant Latin.

"But, by this time," he observes, "the Lord was pleased to draw me nearer to himself, and to give me a fuller view of the pearl of great price – the inestimable treasure hid in the field of the Holy Scripture: and, for the sake of this, I was made willing to part with all my newly-acquired riches. I began to think that life was too short (especially my life) to admit of leisure for such elaborate trifling. Neither poet nor historian could tell me a word of Jesus: and I therefore applied myself to those who could. The classics were at first restrained to one morning in the week, and at length laid aside."

This, his First Voyage after his marriage, lasted the space of fourteen months, through various scenes of danger and difficulty; but nothing very remarkable occurred: and, after having seen many fall on his right hand and on his left, he was brought home in peace, November 2, 1751.

In the interval between his first and second voyage, he speaks of the use he found in keeping a sort of diary; of the unfavourable tendency of a life of ease, among his friends; and of the satisfaction of his wishes proving unfavourable to the progress of grace: upon the whole, however, he seems to have gained ground, and was led into further views of Christian Doctrine and Experience by Scougal's *Life of God in the Soul of Man*,[5] Hervey's *Meditations*,[6] and the *Life of Colonel Gardiner*.[7] He seems to have derived no advantages from the preaching he heard, or the Christian acquaintance he had made: and, though he could not live without prayer, he durst not propose it, even to his wife, till she first urged him to the social practice of it.

In a few months, the returning season called him abroad again;*

---

* Mr. N. had an unexpected call to London; and, on his return, when within a few miles of Liverpool, he mistook a marle-pit for a pond, and, in attempting to water his horse, both the horse and the rider plunged in it overhead. He

and he sailed from Liverpool in a new ship [The *African*], July 1752. "I never knew," says he, "sweeter or more frequent hours of divine communion, than in my two last voyages to Guinea, when I was almost secluded from society on shipboard, or when on shore among the natives. I have wandered through the woods, reflecting on the singular goodness of the Lord to me, in a place where, perhaps, there was not a person who knew me for some thousand miles round. Many a time, upon these occasions, I have restored the beautiful lines of Propertius to the right owner: lines, full of blasphemy and madness, when addressed to a creature; but full of comfort and propriety, in the mouth of a believer."

> *Sic ego desertis possim benè vivere sylvis*
> *Quò nulla humano sit via trita pede:*
> *Tu mihi curarum requies, in nocte vel atra*
> *Lumen, et in solis tu mihi turba locis.*

PARAPHRASED

> *In desert woods, with thee, my God,*
> *Where human footsteps never trod,*
> *How happy could I be!*
> *Thou my repose from care, my light*
> *Amidst the darkness of the night,*
> *In solitude my company.*

In the course of this voyage, Mr. N. was wonderfully preserved through many unforeseen dangers. At one time there was a conspiracy among his own people to become pirates, and take possession of the ship: when the plot was nearly ripe, they watched only for opportunity: two of them were taken ill in one day; and one of them died: this suspended the affair, and opened a way to its discovery. The slaves on board frequently plotted insurrections; and were sometimes upon the very brink of one when it was disclosed. When at a place called Mana, near Cape Mount, Mr. N. intended to go on shore the next morning to settle some business; but the surf of the sea ran so high, that he was afraid to attempt landing: he had often ventured at a worse time; but then feeling a backwardness which he could not account for, the high surf furnished a pretext for indulging it: he

was afterwards told, that, near that time, three persons had lost their lives by a mistake of the same kind.

therefore returned to the ship without doing any business. He afterwards found, that, on the day he intended to land, a scandalous and groundless charge had been laid against him, which greatly threatened his honour and interest, both in Africa and England; and would perhaps have affected his life, had he landed: the person most concerned in this affair [Thomas Bryan] owed him about a hundred pounds, which he sent in a huff; and otherwise, perhaps, would not have paid it at all: Mr. N. heard no more of this accusation till the next voyage; and then it was publicly acknowledged to have been a malicious calumny, without the least shadow of foundation.

But as these things did not occur every day, Mr. N. prosecuted his Latin, being very regular in the management of his time. He allotted about eight hours to sleep and meals, eight hours to exercise and devotion, and eight hours to his books; and thus, by diversifying his engagements, the whole day was agreeably filled up.

From the coast he went to St. Christopher's, where he met with a great disappointment: for the letters which he expected from Mrs. N. were, by mistake, forwarded to Antigua. Certain of her punctuality in writing, if alive, he concluded, by not hearing from her, that she was surely dead. This fear deprived him of his appetite and rest, and caused an incessant pain in his stomach; and, in the space of three weeks, he was near sinking under the weight of an imaginary stroke. "I felt," says he, "some severe symptoms of that mixture of pride and madness, commonly called a broken heart; and, indeed, I wonder that this case is not more common. How often do the potsherds of the earth presume to contend with their Maker! and what a wonder of mercy it is, that they are not all broken! This was a sharp lesson, but I hope it did me good; and, when I had thus suffered for some weeks, I thought of sending a small vessel to Antigua. I did so, and she brought me several packets, which restored my health and peace; and gave me a strong contrast of the Lord's goodness to me, and of my unbelief and ingratitude towards him."

In August, 1753, Mr. N. returned to Liverpool. After that voyage, he continued only six weeks at home; and, in that space, nothing very memorable occurred.

We now follow Mr. N. in his Third Voyage to Guinea. It seems to be the shortest of any that he had made; and is principally marked by an account of a young man who had formerly been a midshipman, and his intimate companion on board the *Harwich*. This youth [Job

Lewis], at the time Mr. N. first knew him, was sober; but was afterwards deeply affected with Mr. N.'s then libertine principles. They met at Liverpool, and renewed their former acquaintance. As their conversation frequently turned upon religion, Mr. N. was very desirous to recover his companion. He gave him a plain account of the manner and reasons of his own change, and used every argument to induce him to relinquish his infidelity. When pressed very close, his usual reply was, that Mr. N. was the first person who had given him an idea of his liberty; which naturally occasioned many mournful reflections in the mind of his present instructor. This person was going master to Guinea himself; but, meeting with disappointment, Mr. N. offered to take him as a companion, with a view of assisting him in gaining future employment; but, principally, that his arguments, example, and prayers, might be attended with good effect. But his companion was exceedingly profane; grew worse and worse; and presented a lively, but distressing picture, continually before Mr. N.'s eyes, of what he himself had once been. – Besides this, the man was not only deaf to remonstrance himself, but laboured to counteract Mr. N.'s influence upon others: his spirit and passions were likewise so exceedingly high, that it required all Mr. N.'s prudence and authority to hold him in any degree of restraint. At length Mr. N. had an opportunity of buying a small vessel [The *Racehorse*], which he supplied with a cargo from his own ship. He gave his companion the command of it, and sent him away to trade on the ship's account. When they parted, Mr. N. repeated and enforced his best advice: it seemed greatly to affect his companion at the time; but, when he found himself released from the restraint of his instructor, he gave a loose to every appetite; and his violent irregularities, joined to the heat of the climate, soon threw him into a malignant fever, which carried him off in a few days. He seems to have died convinced, but not changed: his rage and despair struck those who were about him with horror; and he pronounced his own fatal doom before he expired, without any sign that he either hoped or asked for mercy. – I hope the reader will deem the features of this awful case, though a digression from the principal subject, too instructive to be omitted.

Mr. N. left the coast in about four months, and sailed for St. Christopher's. Hitherto he had enjoyed a perfect and equal state of health in different climates for several years: but, in this passage, he was visited by a fever, which gave him a very near prospect of eternity.

He was, however, supported in a silent composure of spirit, by the faith of Jesus; and found great relief from those words, *He is able to save to the uttermost.*[8] He was for a while troubled, either by a temptation or by the fever disordering his faculties, that he should be lost or overlooked amidst the myriads that are continually entering the unseen world; but the recollection of that scripture – *The Lord knoweth them that are his*[9] – put an end to his doubts. After a few days, he began to amend; and, by the time they arrived in the West Indies, he was perfectly recovered.

In this way he was led, for about the space of six years. He had learnt something of the evils of his heart – had read the Bible over and over – had perused several religious books – and had a general view of Gospel Truth: but his conceptions still remained confused in many respects; not having, in all this time, met with one acquaintance qualified to assist in his enquiries.

On his arrival at St. Christopher's, he found a captain of a ship from London, a man of experience in the things of God [Captain Alexander Clunie]. For near a month, they spent every evening together on board each other's ships alternately; prolonging their visits till near day-break. While Mr. N. was an eager recipient, his companion's discourse not only informed his understanding, but inflamed his heart – encouraged him in attempting social prayer – taught him the advantage of Christian converse – put him upon an attempt to make his profession more public, and to venture to speak for God. His conceptions now became more clear and evangelical: he was delivered from a fear, which had long troubled him, of relapsing into his former apostasy; and taught to expect preservation, not from his own power and holiness, but from the power and promise of God. From this friend he likewise received a general view of the present state of religion, and of the prevailing errors and controversies of the times; and a direction where to enquire, in London, for further instruction. Mr. N.'s passage homewards gave him leisure to digest what he had received. He arrived safely at Liverpool, August, 1754.*

---

* In a MS note on a letter from sea, in the interleaved copy of his *Letters to a Wife*, before mentioned, Mr. Newton remarks:– "I now enter my 70th year. Still Thou art singularly bountiful to me: still I have reason to think myself favoured as to externals beyond the common lot of mortals. Thou didst bear me above the removal of her I most valued, to the admiration of all who knew me. The best part of my childhood and youth was vanity and

His stay at home, however, was intended to be but short; and, by the beginning of November, he was ready again for sea. But the Lord saw fit to over-rule his design. It seems, from the account he gives, that he had not had the least scruple as to the lawfulness of the Slave Trade: he considered it as the appointment of Providence: he viewed this employment as respectable and profitable: yet he could not help regarding himself as a sort of jailer; and was sometimes shocked with an employment so conversant with chains, bolts, and shackles. On this account he had often prayed that he might be fixed in a more humane profession; where he might enjoy more frequent communion with the people and ordinances of God, and be freed from those long domestic separations which he found it so hard to bear. His prayers were now answered, though in an unexpected way.

Mr. N. was within two days of sailing, and in apparent good health; but, as he was one afternoon drinking tea with Mrs. N. he was seized with a fit, which deprived him of sense and motion. When he had recovered from this fit, which lasted about an hour, it left a pain and dizziness in his head, which continued with such symptoms, as induced the physicians to judge it would not be safe for him to proceed on the voyage. By the advice of a friend, therefore, to whom the ship [the *Bee*] belonged, he resigned the command on the day before she sailed: and thus he was not only freed from that service, but from the future consequences of a voyage which proved extremely calamitous. The person, who went in his room, died; as did most of the officers, and many of the crew.

---

folly: but, before I attained the age of man, I became exceeding vile indeed; and was seated in the chair of the scorner, in early life. The troubles and miseries I for a time endured, were my own. I brought them upon myself, by forsaking Thy good and pleasant paths; and choosing the ways of the transgressors, which I found very hard: they led to slavery, contempt, famine and despair.

"But my recovery from that dreadful state was wholly of Thee. Thou didst prepare the means, unthought of and undesired by me. How nice were the turns upon which my delivery from Africa depended! Had the ship passed one quarter of an hour sooner, I had died there a wretch, as I had lived. But Thou didst pity and hear my first lispings in prayer, at the time the storm fell upon me. Thou didst preserve from sinking and starving. Thus I returned home; and Thou didst provide me friends, when I was destitute and a stranger."

Appendix to Chapter 5

On the Brownlow
During his voyage as mate on board the *Brownlow* Newton
corresponded with his father from the River Festers, perhaps recalling
also his own grim experience in the *Greyhound*:

"If you are a virtuoso it will not be impertinent to give you some
account of a monstrous fish I lately caught here which was 16 foot
broad and his liver only weighed near 200 pounds. I have heard some
people who would invalidate the story of Jonah, pretend that there is
no fish capable of swallowing a man, but I believe if this had met one
of them in the water, he would have convinced him to the contrary,
for he had a mouth 2 foot 3 inches wide, and a proportionable
swallow."[10]

Return to the Plantanes
The Revd. John Campbell, a friend of Newton's, relates these
incidents in his *Conversational Remarks of John Newton*:[11]

"Upon being asked whether he ever met again with the black
woman who had treated him so harshly when he was in Africa, Mr.
N. replied, 'Oh yes, when I went there as a captain of a ship, I sent
my longboat ashore for her. This soon brought her on board. I desired
the men to fire guns over her head in honour of her, because she had
formerly done me so much good, though she did not mean it. She
seemed to feel it like heaping coals of fire on her head. I made her
some presents, and sent her ashore. She was evidently most
comfortable when she had her back to my ship.

" 'I just recollect a circumstance that happened to me when I first
stepped ashore on the beach at that time. Two black females were
passing; the first who noticed me observed to her companion, that
'there was Newton, and, what do you think, he has got shoes!' 'Ay,'
said the other, 'and stockings too!' They had never seen me before
with either.' "

As Captain of the Duke of Argyle and the African
Some extracts from Newton's log book illustrate the trials he
encountered as a Captain during these years:[12]

On board the *Duke of Argyle* at the Bonanas 1750:

Wednesday 21st November
Fair weather, fresh land and sea breezes. In the afternoon Mr. Clow and PI being on board, one of their people who had assisted me in securing Will Lees [a disorderly crew member] at the Plantanes, coming inadvertently too near him as he sat upon the windlace, he unexpectedly struck at him with the carpenter's maul, and but just missed his head; the maul grazing on his breast. Had this been offered to any of the people of the Main Land or this Island it might have been of very dangerous consequence, but having PI with me, a laced hat made up the matter. Put Lees in handcuffs and stapled him down to the deck, at which proceeding 2 others, Tom Creed and Tom True, behaved with a good deal of insolence, these three having been in a close cabal since the fighting affair at Sierra Leone. I bore it as well as I could, being resolved to apply to the Man of War tomorrow.

Thursday 22nd November
At 9 am set out in the Punt with Will Lees in irons to deliver him to the *Surprize* Man of War at Sierra Leone. Had a strong SE tornado all the way to the cape with hard rain and a great sea, that I was several times afraid the Punt would have filled with us, but by the favour of good Providence got safe round the rock at 4 pm and on board the *Surprize* by 6. Waited on Capt. Baird and discharged my man.

Friday 23rd November
Fair weather, variable winds. In the morning waited upon Capt. Baird to beg he would make the Bonanas in his way down, to rid me of the rest of my mutineers, which he consented to, though he did not otherwise intend to call there. He desired I would stay on board the *Surprize* to show him where to anchor, he having nobody on board that was acquainted there.

On board the *African* at Mana 1752:

Wednesday 15th November
Little winds any way, a great deal of rain, thunder and lightning. The yaul returned at 9 am, Jemmy Cole having taken her quite to his town to land the goods which is almost half way to C. Mount. Her

long stay making me very uneasy gave occasion to the discovering a plot some of our people have been concerned in, which I can suppose to be no less than the seizing the ship. William Cunneigh, the informer, told me he had been solicited by Richard Swain to sign what he called a round robin, a term which I was before a stranger to. I cannot but acknowledge a visible interposition of Divine Providence in this affair for, though I cannot yet find the bottom of it, I have reason to think the sickness we have had on board within these 3 days has prevented a black design when it was almost ripe for execution and the unexpected stay of the boat brought it to light. I thought myself very secure from any danger of this kind, as everybody behaved very quiet the whole voyage, and I do not remember the least complaint or grievance. Richard Swain was then in the yaul; as soon as he came on board I put him in double irons. He seemed to be much surprised and pretends he knows nothing of the matter. The others [of] whom I have suspicion are at present too ill to bear examining.

Thursday 16th November
Very uncertain weather, rain, thunder and lightning as yesterday all the morning, and mostly calm: at 10 am the yaul went in to the beach with Mr. Tucker, but he could not get on shore – came back again at 4 pm. I hope the boatswain and one of our sick are in a fair way of recovery: for we are at present so weak that we can do nothing when the yaul is away, but be upon our guard against the slaves and the round robin gentlemen: and what makes it more difficult I am not yet able to find out who are or are not in the gang. In the evening looked at the anchor – found it clear.

Friday 17th November
Fair weather land & sea breeze, with a small leeward current. Sent the yaul inshore with Mr. Tucker and he landed safe... In the evening made some farther discovery concerning the round-robins: Joseph Forrester and Peter Mackdonald were, it seems, parties and were providentially both taken sick in one day; the latter is so ill that I hardly expect he can live [he died two days later], but the former I think recovered enough to be put in irons. My second witness is John Sadler, who says when he was in the boat at Shebar he heard Swain and Forrester talk to each other, but in a distant manner, that he could

not understand then what they intended. The one said somebody should pay for it and the other that he was sure all the ship's company would join him if he spoke the word. But at another time he heard Joseph Forrester in plain terms say that he would kill Mr. Welsh [the First Mate] and the doctor, or at least leave only just alive. He likewise says that when the yaul was on shore on Wednesday Swain endeavoured to persuade him and the rest to go off with her.

On board the *African* at Shebar 1752:

Monday 11th December
Fair weather mostly calm. By the favour of Divine Providence made a timely discovery to day that the slaves were forming a plot for an insurrection; surprized 2 of them attempting to get off their irons, and upon farther search in their rooms upon the information of 3 of the boys found some knives, stones, shot etc. and a cold chisel. Upon enquiry there appeared 8 principally concerned: 4 men in projecting the mischief and 4 boys in supplying them with the above instruments; put the boys in irons and slightly in the thumbscrews, to urge them to a full confession. We have already 36 men out of our small number...

The Slave Trade
As this chapter highlights the time Newton spent as the captain of a slave-trader, it is fitting to add here that some thirty years later he was to appear before the Prime Minister, William Pitt, and a committee of the Privy Council[13] to testify on a commerce he then regarded as "so iniquitous, so cruel, so oppressive, so destructive, as the African Slave Trade".[14] His *Thoughts upon the African Slave Trade* were published in 1788. In this he wrote, "I hope it will always be a subject of humiliating reflection to me, that I was once an active instrument in a business at which my heart now shudders."

He wrote to his friend William Bull in 1792, "When I was assured that Mr. Wilberforce would renew his motion in the House this session, I preached (as I did last year) about the slave-trade. I think myself bound in conscience to bear my testimony at least, and to wash my hands from the guilt which if persisted in, now things have been so thoroughly investigated and brought to light, will, I think, constitute a national sin of scarlet and crimson dye. A motion since made in the Common Council for a petition to parliament on the subject has been negatived. If the city want a motto, I would furnish them with *'Virtus post nummos.'*[15] If the business miscarries again, I shall fear not only for the poor slaves, but for ourselves."[16]

Correspondence with David Jennings while at sea

His letters to David Jennings show the growth of a pastoral concern both for his crew and on a wider scale. He was known for his humane treatment of the sailors (apart from the thumbscrews, I guess). But additionally his gifts as pastor and communicator, in speech and in writing, can be seen coming to the fore. Some extracts of his correspondence with Jennings particularly illustrate this:

"When I consider these things, the unhappy degeneracy of the generality of sailors, their number and the vast importance and concern they are (in this nation especially) to the welfare of the state, and what various accidents and evils have arisen from the sources I have pointed at, and when I remember at the same time, that notwithstanding all the just complaints of the spreading of vice, there perhaps was never any age or nation since the apostles' days blessed with greater degrees of Gospel light, or with better or more exemplary (I wish I could say more numerous of such) teachers of the ways of happiness, or of a brighter or more extensive charity; when I see so many excellent books coming out every day from persons of all persuasions, with directions, incentives and devotions adapted to almost every condition and circumstance: I say when I take all these things together, I cannot but wonder that the poor sailors, and they only should as it were by a general consent, be forgot, as though they were either not capable or not worthy of instruction. When it pleased God, first to permit me the command and charge of a ship's company, I determined with myself to imitate Joshua's resolution as far as it should be practicable, and nothing but an indispensable necessity has prevented me, from requiring from all on board a solemn observation of the sabbath day (we cannot in our voyages command more frequent public opportunities) and here I find myself at a great loss in what manner to regulate our Devotions. I could not judge myself equal to the task of conceived prayer before a number of people, especially of such as would be too apt to take offence at an indifferent performance, and no forms, that I have met with, have been suitable to the particular circumstances of our calling. I was at last forced to take up with the common prayer of the Church of England, which, though it contains many things that I think excellent, yet the breaks, the repetitions and indeed the expressions in some places, render it in my opinion, but an indifferent rule for such congregations as mine, who have but little knowledge of religion in general, and as little judgement or charity to make allowance for what may seem exceptionable; besides that in this likewise there seems to be no provision made for seamen as such; the few Collects designedly for the sea, being only applicable to particular cases which seldom happen. To remedy this I venture to compose a short prayer of my own, relating entirely to our own wants and views, which I write down and deliver amongst the rest always in the same words that the service may be of a piece. I likewise take the liberty of leaving out or changing, to make the whole to the best of my judgement as suitable as possible, and after all there are many things that I wish altered, yet it has pleased God so far to bless the sincerity of my intention, that there are few moments of my life afford me a more real pleasure, than when I am thus attempting the part of the Minister to about twenty-five people who have all one design to bespeak a blessing upon, and numberless mercies to acknowledge in common. After this long introduction I come to my proposal, which is that for the amending the depravity of morals and promoting the public service and worship of God Almighty which under these many hindrances is almost discontinued; a book of advices and devotions might be composed adapted entirely to the business and occasions of seamen. I have seen a little treatise called the *Seamen's Monitor*,[17] and another by Mr. Flavel entitled *Navigation Spiritualized*,[18] and they are both very good as far as they extend, and to my own knowledge have been blessed as means of reforming some: but they neither come up to what I would wish. I have likewise read a sermon preached at Liverpool to a Ship's Company by Mr. Basont, and our friend Mr. Breckel has published a sort of comment upon St. Paul's voyage, I suppose with the same view; but I judge them both far inferior to those I first mentioned, and the latter by placing his criticisms in the wrong part of the book, has I am afraid discouraged many from reading so far, as to where he writes to the purpose. I would not presume to engage your own pen in this affair because I know your time is already forestalled, otherwise, perhaps, no undertaking in equal compass, might contribute more to the good of mankind or the glory of God, but it will be sufficient if you devolve the business to some person who you shall judge fit; though I am persuaded let who will undertake it, it will come out with greater advantage both to itself and to the world, if attended with your inspection and recommendation. If you think this design deserves encouragement, I hope you will bear with my taking the liberty of giving a few hints with regard to the execution, as being a party concerned and so far a judge of what is most wanted. The Devotional part should be the largest as being hitherto in a manner untouched: it would be very convenient to have the prayers for Lord's day service so divided in three parts as to give opportunity for reading a chapter in the Old or New Testament between each, there being many poor creatures amongst us who perhaps never hear the word of God at any other time." [19]

Jennings suggested instead that Newton write such a book. Newton was disappointed and replied, "I have not a choice or fixedness of style to venture appearing in print in this nice [scrupulously] censorious age, least of all could I presume to compose prayers for others, who have so much need to borrow help from others, for I look upon this as the most difficult kind of writing, to perform it well, and otherwise it is better let alone; for in this case I think a good intention is not sufficient alone. I know indeed that when God pleases, the most unsuitable and weak means have often great effects. But the ordinary course of Providence, in raising up so many excellent pens to bless and improve this age, is argument enough to persuade me to desist." [20]

Newton's meeting with the captain from a London ship at St. Kitts (the British nickname for St. Christopher) was to mark a turning point in his life. He wrote to David Jennings: [21]

"I cannot omit mentioning what I look upon as a special mercy and favour which I lately received. Like Elijah I was ready to think I was in a manner serving my God alone, with respect to the generality of those of my own profession, and the inhabitants of this dry and barren land, where there are hardly any waters, any streams of gospel communion and experiences to be found, but I have met with a brother sailor, a Brother Captain too, whose acquaintance I esteem beyond any temporal advantage that could have fallen to me; as he is an acquaintance of yours, I shall only tell you his name is Alexander Clunie; it is quite needless I am sure to say anything of his character, but as I delight to impart to you what relates to myself, I must insert how great an instrument of good it has pleased the Almighty Giver of grace to make him unto me; in the one week (for it is no more we have been acquainted) I find my affections more lively, my grace more active and my evidences of assurance more clear than I ever yet attained to in my life.

"We spend the whole time we can command from our business together at the sacrifice of almost all our common acquaintance and sometimes having been together the most part of the day are hardly able to part at midnight. My life of late, compared with what it was, has seemed a heaven upon earth, and I trust I shall have lasting, I may say indeed, everlasting cause to bless God on his behalf.

St. Christopher 7 June 1754"

The previous year, as Newton headed for St. Kitts, he had prayed for help in using the opportunities for speaking and living as a Christian. Remembering how he had failed then, he again set aside a day for thanksgiving for a safe passage and to ask for grace and help, praying, "Lord, grant that it may be more effectual than then ... O Lord, I beseech thee let me no longer resolve and pray in vain; strengthen me by thy grace and direct me by thy wisdom that I may upon all occasions strive to promote thy honour and glory; and know how to speak a word in season." After having his prayers answered so fully in the fellowship he received from Captain Clunie, he added in his diary, "I now see that I had not that perfect dependence on Jesus my Saviour and him only for justification and acceptance as I thought I had.... May his example strengthen me to *go and do likewise*, to endeavour to teach others those comforts wherewith I myself have been comforted.... May it be my constant aim that thy kingdom may come and thy will be done in earth as it is in heaven."[22]

Captain Alexander Clunie

Alexander Clunie worshipped at the Stepney Meeting[23] under the ministry of Samuel Brewer. Reflecting again on Newton's mother's prayers, it is interesting to note that Samuel Brewer was a close friend of David Jennings, her pastor. Their churches were no more than a mile apart. In fact Jennings had been Brewer's tutor and was invited to preach at his ordination in Stepney. He had given the charge from 2 Timothy 4:5, *But watch thou in all things, endure afflictions, do the work of an evangelist, make full proof of thy ministry.* Clunie became a member of Brewer's church on 3rd January 1754, shortly before setting sail for St. Kitts. At that time he lived in Bird Street, Wapping, less than four hundred yards from Newton's childhood home in Red Lyon Street. Forty-four years after Elizabeth Newton's death, and although John was about forty-four thousand miles from home, it was a neighbour and friend of her pastor who met up with the son she had prayed for so earnestly, to lead him deeper into the things of God and to direct him to helpful teaching and fellowship at his birthplace on his return to London. Unknown to everyone at the time, this was to be Newton's last voyage and the beginning of his entrance into the ministry for which his mother had so longed and prayed.

Newton delighted to keep in touch with Clunie. His letters to him between 1761 and 1770 were published as *The Christian Correspondent*.[24] Throughout his Christian life he made a strong point of looking back thankfully on past experiences. Writing to Clunie in February 1761 he recalled his gratitude to him for the time he had spent instructing him and encouraging him at this crucial stage of his spiritual life, "Your conversation was much blessed to me at St. Kitts, and the little knowledge I have of men and things, took its first rise from thence."

Newton's marriage

John and Mary were married at St. Margaret's, Rochester. "My first regard for her was truly a *passion*," he wrote to a friend, Mrs. Coffin, "strong as ever writers of romance imagined. Neither absence, nor distance, nor the unhappy scenes of profligacy in which I was too long engaged, could extinguish it; and from the moment I had a prospect of gaining her, it sprung up with renewed force. At length the Lord gave her to me: we lived together more than forty years in harmony, and, if possible, with increasing affection."[25]

He described her as "the main hinge upon which all the principal events of my life had turned ... an excellent wife ... my faithful friend, my judicious counsellor; *we had but one heart between us*."

CHAPTER 6

SURVEYING THE TIDE
1755–1764

As Mr. N. was now disengaged from business, he left Liverpool, and spent most of the following year in London, or in Kent. Here he entered upon a new trial, in a disorder that was brought upon Mrs. N. from the shock she received in his late illness: as he grew better, she became worse, with a disorder which the physicians could not define, nor medicine remove. Mr. N. was therefore placed for about eleven months in what Dr. Young calls the

> -------- Dreadful post of observation,
> Darker every hour.[1]

The reader will recollect that Mr. N.'s friend at St. Christopher's had given him information for forming a religious acquaintance in London: in consequence of this, he became intimate with several persons eminent for that character: and profited by the spiritual advantages which a great city affords, with respect to the means of grace.

[*Narrative:*
"I first applied to Mr. Brewer, and chiefly attended upon his ministry when in town. From him I received many helps, both in public and private; for he was pleased to favour me with his friendship from the first. His kindness and the intimacy between us, has continued and increased to this day; and of all my many friends, I am most deeply indebted to him. The late Mr. Hayward was my second acquaintance, a man of choice spirit, and an abundant zeal for the Lord's service. I enjoyed his correspondence till near the time of his death. Soon after, upon Mr. Whitefield's return from America, my two good friends introduced me to him; and though I had little personal acquaintance with him until afterwards, his ministry was exceedingly useful to me. I had likewise access to some religious societies, and became known to many excellent Christians in private life. Thus, when at

London, I lived at the fountain-head, as it were, for spiritual advantages."]

When he was in Kent, his advantages were of a different kind: most of his time he passed in the fields and woods: "It has been my custom," says he, "for many years to perform my devotional exercises *sub dio*,[2] when I have opportunity; and I always find these scenes have some tendency to refresh and compose my spirits. A beautiful, diversified prospect gladdens my heart. When I am withdrawn from the noise and petty works of men, I consider myself as in the great temple which the Lord has built for his own honour."

During this time he had to weather two trials, the principal of which was Mrs. N.'s illness; she still grew worse, and he had daily more reason to fear that hour of separation which appeared to be at hand. He had likewise to provide some future settlement: the African trade was overdone that year, and his friends did not care to fit out another ship, till that which had been *his*, returned. Though a provision of food and raiment had seldom been with him a cause of great solicitude, yet he was some time in suspense on this account; but, in August following, he received a letter, informing him that he was nominated to a post which afforded him a competency, both unsought and unexpected. When he had gained this point, his distress respecting Mrs. N. was doubled: he was obliged to leave her in the greatest extremity of pain and illness, and when he had no hope that he should see her again alive: he was, however, enabled to resign her and himself to the divine disposal; and, soon after he was gone, she began to amend; and recovered so fast, that, in about two months, he had the pleasure to meet her at Stone, on her journey to Liverpool.

From October, 1755, he appears to have been comfortably settled at Liverpool, and mentions his having received, since the year 1757, much profit from his acquaintance in the West Riding of Yorkshire. "I have conversed," says he, "at large among all parties, without joining any: and, in my attempts to hit the *golden mean*, I have sometimes drawn too near the different extremes; yet the Lord has enabled me to profit by my mistakes." Being at length placed in a settled habitation, and finding his business would afford him much leisure, he considered in what manner he could improve it. Having determined, with the Apostle, to know *nothing but Jesus Christ, and him crucified*,[3] he devoted his life to the prosecution of spiritual knowledge, and resolved to peruse nothing but in subservience to this design. But as what follows will appear most natural, and be best expressed in his own words, I shall transcribe them from the conclusion of his *Narrative*.

"This resolution," says Mr. N., "divorced me (as I have already hinted) from the classics and mathematics. My first attempt was to learn so much Greek as would enable me to understand the New Testament and Septuagint: and, when I had made some progress this way, I entered upon the Hebrew the following year: and, two years afterwards, having surmised some advantages from the Syriac Version, I began with that language. You must not think that I have attained, or ever aimed at, a critical skill in any of these: I had no business with them, but as in reference to something else. I never read one classic author in the Greek: I thought it too late in life to take such a round in this language as I had done in the Latin: I only wanted the signification of scriptural words and phrases, and for this I thought I might avail myself of Scapula [Johannis Scapula's *Lexicon*], the Synopsis, and others, who had sustained the drudgery before me. In the Hebrew, I can read the Historical Books and Psalms with tolerable ease; but, in the Prophetical and difficult parts, I am frequently obliged to have recourse to Lexicons, &c. However, I know so much as to be able, with such helps as are at hand, to judge for myself the meaning of any passage I have occasion to consult.

"Together with these studies, I have kept up a course of reading the best writers in divinity that have come to my hand, in the Latin and English tongues, and some French (for I picked up the French at times, while I used the sea). But, within these two or three years, I have accustomed myself chiefly to writing, and have not found time to read many books besides the Scriptures.

"I am the more particular in this account, as my case has been something singular: for, in all my literary attempts, I have been obliged to strike out my own path by the light I could acquire from books; as I have not had a teacher or assistant since I was ten years of age.

"One word concerning my views to the ministry, and I have done. I have told you, that this was my dear mother's hope concerning me; but her death, and the scenes of life in which I afterwards engaged, seemed to cut off the probability. The first desires of this sort in my own mind arose many years ago, from reflection on Galatians 1:23,24. I could but wish for such a public opportunity to testify the riches of divine grace. I thought I was, above most living, a fit person to proclaim that faithful saying, that *Jesus Christ came into the world to save the chief of sinners*;[4] and, as my life had been full of remarkable turns, and I seemed selected to show what the Lord could do, I was in some hopes that perhaps, sooner or later, he might call me into his service.

"I believe it was a distant hope of this that determined me to study the Original Scriptures; but it remained an imperfect desire in my own breast, till it was recommended to me by some Christian friends. I started at the thought when first seriously proposed to me: but, afterwards, set apart some weeks to consider the case, to consult my friends, and to entreat the Lord's direction. The judgement of my friends, and many things that occurred, tended to engage me. My first thought was to join with the Dissenters, from a presumption that I could not honestly make the required subscriptions: but Mr. Crook, in a conversation upon these points, moderated my scruples; and, preferring the Established Church in some respects, I accepted a title from him, some months afterwards, and solicited ordination from the late Archbishop of York. I need not tell you I met with a refusal, nor what steps I took afterwards to succeed elsewhere. At present, I desist from any applications. My desire to serve the Lord is not weakened; but I am not so hasty to push myself forward as I was formerly. It is sufficient that he knows how to dispose of me, and that he both can and will do what is best. To him I commend myself: I trust that his will and my true interest are inseparable."

A variety of remarks occurred to me while abridging the *Narrative*, but I refrained from putting them down, lest, by interrupting its course, and breaking the thread of the history, I should rather disgust than profit the reader. I have heard Mr. N. relate a few additional particulars, but they were of too little interest to be inserted here: they went, however, like natural incidents, to a further authentication of the above account, had it needed any other confirmation than the solemn declaration of the pious Relator. Romantic relations, indeed, of unprincipled travellers, which appear to have no better basis than a disposition to amuse incredulity, to exhibit vanity, or to acquire gain, may naturally raise suspicion, and produce but a momentary effect at most on the mind of the reader: but facts, like the present, manifest such a display of the Power, Providence, and Grace of God;

and, at the same time, such a deep and humbling view of human depravity, when moved and brought forth by circumstances, as inexperience can scarcely credit, but which must arrest the eye of pious contemplation, and open a new world of wonders.

I must now attempt to conduct the reader, without the help of Mr. N.'s *Narrative*, finished Feb. 2, 1763; to which, as I have already observed, he referred me for the former and most singular part of his life. When I left the above account with him for revision, he expressed full satisfaction as to all the facts related; but said, he thought I had been too minute even in the abridgement, since the *Narrative* itself had been long before the public. I remarked, in reply, that the *Narrative* contained a great variety of facts; that these Memoirs might fall into the hands of persons who had not seen the *Narrative*; but that without some abridgement of it, no clear view could be formed of the peculiarity of his whole dispensation and character; and, therefore, that such an abridgement appeared to be absolutely necessary, and that he had recommended it at my first undertaking the work. With these reasons he was well satisfied. I now proceed to the remaining, though less remarkable part of his life.

Mr. Manesty, who had long been a faithful and generous friend of Mr. N. having procured him the place of tide-surveyor in the port of Liverpool, Mr. N. gives the following account of it. – "I entered upon business yesterday. I find my duty is to attend the tides one week, and visit the ships that arrive, and such as are in the river; and the other week to inspect the vessels in the docks; and thus, alternately, the year round. The latter is little more than a sinecure; but the former requires pretty constant attendance, both by day and night. I have a good office, with fire and candle, and fifty or sixty people under my direction; with a handsome six-oared boat and a coxswain, to row me about in form."*

We cannot wonder that Mr. N. latterly retained a strong impression of a Particular Providence, superintending and conducting the steps of man; since he was so often reminded of it in his own history. The following occurrence is one of many instances. Mr. N. after his reformation, was remarkable for his punctuality: I remember his often sitting with his watch in his hand, lest he should fail in keeping his next engagement. This exactness with respect to time, it seems, was

---

* *Letters to a Wife*, vol. 2 p.7

his habit while occupying his post at Liverpool. One day, however, some business had so detained him, that he came to his boat much later than usual, to the surprise of those who had observed his former punctuality. He went out in the boat, as heretofore, to inspect the ship; but the ship blew up just before he reached her. It appears, that, if he had left the shore a few minutes sooner, he must have perished with the rest on board.

This anecdote I had from a clergyman, upon whose word I can depend; who had been long in intimate habits with Mr. N. and who had it from Mr. N. himself: the reason of its not appearing in his letters from Liverpool to Mrs. N. I can only suppose to be, his fearing to alarm her with respect to the dangers of his station.

But another providential occurrence, which he mentions in those letters, I shall transcribe.

"When I think of my settlement here, and the manner of it, I see the appointment of Providence so good and gracious, and such a plain answer to my poor prayers, that I cannot but wonder and adore. I think I have not yet told you, that my immediate predecessor in office, Mr. C[roxton], had not the least intention of resigning his place on the occasion of his father's death; though such a report was spread about the town without his knowledge; or, rather, in defiance of all he could say to contradict it. Yet to this false report I owe my situation. For it put Mr. Manesty upon an application to Mr. Salusbury, the member for the town; and, the very day he received the promise in my favour, Mr. C. was found dead in his bed; though he had been in company, and in perfect health, the night before. If I mistake not, the same messenger, who brought the promise, carried back the news of the vacancy to Mr. S. at Chester. About an hour after, the Mayor applied for a nephew of his; but though it was only an hour or two, he was too late. Mr. S. had already written, and sent off the letter, and I was appointed accordingly. These circumstances appear to me extraordinary, though of a piece with many other parts of my singular history. And the more so, as, by another mistake, I missed the land-waiter's place, which was my first object, and which I now see, would not have suited us nearly so well. I thank God, I can now look through instruments and second causes, and see his wisdom and goodness immediately concerned in fixing my lot."

Mr. N. having expressed, near the end of his *Narrative*, the motives which induced him to aim at a regular appointment to the ministry in the Church of England, and of the disappointment he met with in his first making the attempt, the reader is further informed, that, on December 16, 1758, Mr. N. received a title to a curacy from the Rev. Mr. Crook and applied to the Archbishop of York, Dr. Gilbert, for ordination. The Bishop of Chester having countersigned his testimonials, directed him to Dr. [Thomas] Newton, the Archbishop's Chaplain. He was referred to the Secretary, and received the softest refusal imaginable. The Secretary informed him, that he had "represented the matter to the Archbishop; but his Grace was inflexible in supporting the Rules and Canons of the Church ," etc.

Travelling to Loughborough, Mr. N. stopped at Welwyn; and, sending a note to the celebrated Dr. Young, he received for answer, that the Doctor would be glad to see him. He found the Doctor's conversation agreeable, and answerable to his expectation respecting the author of the *Night Thoughts*. The Doctor likewise seemed pleased with Mr. N. He approved Mr. N.'s design of entering the ministry, and said many encouraging things upon the subject; and, when he dismissed Mr. N. desired him never to pass near Welwyn without calling upon him.

Mr. N., it seems, had made some small attempts at Liverpool, in a way of preaching or expounding. Many wished him to engage more at large in those ministerial appointments to which his own mind was inclined; and he thus expresses his motives in a letter to Mrs. N. in answer to the objections she had formed. "The late death of Mr. Jones, of St. Saviour's, has pressed this concern more closely upon my mind. I fear it must be wrong, after having so solemnly devoted myself to the Lord for his service, to wear away my time, and bury my talents in silence (because I had been refused orders in the Church) after all the great things he has done for me."*

In a note annexed, he observes that the influence of his judicious and affectionate counsellor moderated the zeal which dictated this letter, written in the year 1762 – that, had it not been for her, he should probably have been precluded from those important scenes of service, to which he was afterwards appointed: but, he adds, "The exercises of my mind upon this point, have not been peculiar to myself. I have known several persons, sensible, pious, of competent abilities, and cordially attached to the Established Church; who, being wearied out with repeated refusals of ordination, and perhaps not

---

* *Letters to a Wife*, vol. 2 p.79

having the advantage of such an adviser as I had, have at length struck into the itinerant path, or settled among the Dissenters. Some of these, yet living, are men of respectable characters, and useful in their ministry; but their influence, which would once have been serviceable to the true interests of the Church of England, now rather operates against it."

In the year 1764, Mr. N. had the curacy of Olney proposed to him, and was recommended by Lord Dartmouth to Dr. Green, Bishop of Lincoln; of whose candour and tenderness he speaks with much respect. The Bishop admitted him as a candidate for orders. "The examination," says he, "lasted about an hour, chiefly upon the principal heads of divinity. As I was resolved not to be charged hereafter with dissimulation, I was constrained to differ from his Lordship in some points; but he was not offended: he declared himself satisfied, and has promised to ordain me, either next Sunday, in town, or the Sunday following, at Buckden. – Let us praise the Lord!"*

Appendix to Chapter 6

Samuel Brewer
Samuel Brewer was the pastor of the Independent Meeting at Stepney from 1746 to 1796. He was a very significant person in the Newtons' lives. They often stayed with him when in London and he spent some time with them at Olney vicarage. Mary Newton always referred to him in her letters to John as "dear Mr. Brewer".

His parents named him Samuel, trusting that he would follow his Biblical namesake into the ministry. Samuel did not experience the same conviction and it was with difficulty that his father got him at least to agree to studying for a year at a dissenting academy in London. They set out together in spite of Samuel's "great disinclination". On the way through Stratford, Essex (where Newton had been at school a couple of years earlier), they paused at a church. "At that time there was a Latin inscription on the church porch, to which his father particularly directed his attention: 'My son,' says he, 'read this.' He did – *'Seek ye first the kingdom of God, and his righteousness.'* It affected him much. And, though it did not immediately produce a saving conversion, the impression was lasting; for he frequently remarked to his friends, that he seldom, if ever, repeated the passage

* *Letters*, etc. p89

without recollecting the circumstance."[5]

Brewer was converted during his first year under the preaching of Dr. Guyse. "His good father constantly invited half a dozen members of the church, famous in their day for faith in Christ and zeal for the doctrinal truths, to set apart a day in prayer for a blessing on his preparatory studies and on the labours of the important office for which he was designed." Samuel was called to be pastor of the Stepney Meeting in his early twenties. Some accounts state that there were only seven members of the church at the time. Brewer is quoted as saying that the individuals of the congregation were not so numerous as the pews. However, in addition to the seven male members, there were also twenty-five female members of the church – a force to be reckoned with. One of the deacons thought Brewer too young and felt he needed a longer trial, "upon which the sisters of the church withdrew, one and all, into the yard, and pleaded with tears until the deacon withdrew his objection." Brewer was amused to relate ever after that he had been "chosen pastor of the church by the sisters".

His preaching always aimed at the heart and the church was strengthened through his ministry. He was a friend of George Whitefield's. He held the weekday lectureship in several places, such as Pinner's Hall, where Christians from all denominations met in religious societies. By the end of his life his own congregation numbered two or three hundred. His successor, George Ford, took as his text for Brewer's funeral sermon Acts 11.24: *For he was a good man and full of the Holy Ghost and of Faith. And much people was added unto the Lord.* He summarised Brewer's life by saying, "He upheld the doctrine best calculated to give glory to God and to do good to the souls of men." [6]

Stepney Meeting House, dating back to 1674, was originally almost opposite St. Dunstan's in the East. The first minister to oversee this meeting, Henry Burton, had earlier been sentenced to life imprisonment for accusing the Archbishop of popery and had his ears cut off. Archbishop Laud, however, was later beheaded for treason and Burton was pardoned. He became an Independent. When Brewer began his ministry in Stepney there were still "secret" apartments between the roof and ceiling with access via a trap-door linked to an alarm bell. Part of one of the walls of the "new" chapel in 1863 remains on this site, currently a city farm, but the present

church is now lower down Stepney Way, near Jubilee Street. With
the amalgamation of Presbyterian and Congregational Churches into
the United Reformed Church in 1972, John Knox Chapel joined with
it, though the name of Stepney Meeting was retained.

George Whitefield

One of the first people Newton met in London, through Brewer's
introduction, was George Whitefield. In an undated letter to his wife
he described a service of his he attended:[7]

"Do my dearest Polly excuse my staying till Thursday; some new
engagements have offered for tomorrow, but I chiefly wait to hear
Mr. Whitefield once more, which it is said will be the last time of his
preaching till he returns from his Circuit. However you may be assured
that if he does oftener, neither he nor anybody else shall detain me
from you another day – hitherto I have been willing to strike while
the iron is hot as the saying is, and indeed as I came up with a good
design, so it has pleased God to bless it greatly to me: and without
his blessing it signifies little who we hear. But I am persuaded now I
have tried, that there is something extraordinary in this persecuted
despised man, beyond any common attainments, beyond any other
person perhaps, which the present or the former age has known. I
received the sacrament from him at the Tabernacle Sunday morning:
there were none present but communicants, and none of those, but
such as having either passed a suitable examination of strangers, or
bringing sufficient vouches from some Minister whom he knew and
could depend on, received a ticket of admission the day before; yet
notwithstanding this caution, I believe we were not less than twelve
hundred people met together with one heart and soul, though of
different forms and persuasions church folks, baptists, presbyterians
etc.; in short any that agreed in the grand fundamentals of our faith
and bore testimony of a suitable practice. He used the office of the
Church of England, interspersing at times exhortations and discourses
after the manner of the dissenters, and every ten minutes or oftener
we stopped and sung part of a hymn, I suppose 20 different times in
all or more. The number of persons, the beauty of singing, the decency
and regularity of the whole service joined to the noble and enlivening
views he led us into, by his powerful and evangelical discourses, all
being blessed by God to my benefit, was such a resemblance and
foretaste of heaven as it is not possible to describe. I believe there

were very few there who could not say as the disciples of our Lord, did not our hearts burn within us, while he talked to us. The service lasted 3 hours, though there was no sermon. I have heard him preach 5 times, always in a different manner, according as he had a different view, or a different audience; the last was this morning which exceeded all the rest, it was really beyond my imagination. I believe there were hardly 10 people in the congregation, which was pretty large, of any seriousness at all, who could not refrain from tears; mine I am sure were tears of joy: Mr. Brewer's eyes were full often and he was forced to hide his face. He and Mr. Heyward and many of the most owned and honoured preachers about town seize every opportunity of hearing him, though they come 2 or 3 miles, and they all say, they think themselves in a manner unfit and ashamed to go into a pulpit after him. I trust I shall as you say in yours be able to bring down something with me, that may be useful to us both, and that I may be like the scribe well instructed who brings out of his treasure things new and old: I am sure I have enjoyed the rich opportunities for this purpose, for besides Mr. Whitefield, I have heard Mr. Brewer twice, Mr. Rollins and another once each."

"Devotional Exercises"[8]

He spent much time in prayer, longing that he would be placed under those who "teach and understand the truth as it is in Jesus; who in their degree can say with their great master, *We speak that which we know and testify that which we have seen*." Meanwhile he was thankful that the Lord had "in some measure brought me to see the nothingness of my own abilities, and my natural propensity to error and falsehood."

His diary notes for a morning in April read, "Prayed over a part of 8th Romans in a way of paraphrase with some readiness. I greatly fail in the duty of meditation and am forced to use some artifice with myself to do it at all; thus sometimes I turn them into a prayer form, sometimes I suppose myself in imaginary conversation, sometimes that I am called upon to speak to a point. Without something of this sort I am not able to engage myself to attend with any fixedness of thought, and with it, alas! how seldom, I would remember to pray for grace and direction in this matter that my delight may be in the Law of God to meditate therein day and night."

Settling in Liverpool

Newton left for Liverpool to start his new employment as Surveyor of Tides in August 1755 while Polly remained in Kent, still very ill, "in extreme agony with the bilious cholic."⁹ He felt that the eyes of men and perhaps of angels were on him to see if his actions would be consistent with his profession of trust in God and submission to his will. "Such times as these," he wrote in his diary, "are the tests which will distinguish believers from worldlings – thus Abraham, Job and David were tried." He revealed the cost of his departure:

"I am going to leave her when I would most earnestly choose to be with her, to leave her at the uncertainty of ever seeing her again, to take possession of an office which without her will be a burden. This is the language of sense, but faith talks in a different strain, only my ears are deaf to hear, and my heart heavy to understand."

On the third anniversary of her death in 1793, he must have had this occasion in mind when he wrote a hymn in memory of her which began:

> Enough of the language of sense,
> Still harping on sorrow and death!
> I turn my attention from thence,
> To hear the glad tidings of faith.
> For faith has intuitive skill
> (Believers best know what I mean)
> To pierce through the veil at her will,
> And realise objects unseen.[10]

In Liverpool Newton first attended the ministry of pastor John Johnson, founder of the Johnsonian Baptists. The weekend he arrived, Johnson preached from Isaiah 40:31, *They shall run and not be weary*.[11] The 3 main points of his sermon were:

1) that the Christian's life is comparable to a race
2) that they who run, only run in the strength of the Lord and
3) that not withstanding all the trials and oppositions, they shall undoubtedly come off victorious

It was just the encouragement that he needed. That evening Johnson preached again from the same verse, this time of the prize they were running for. He first showed what it was not: it could not be meant of the love of God, of peace with God, of renewing grace, of pardon of sin, of justification, of salvation or everlasting glory, for all these sprang from the free mercy of the Sovereign God's decree.

Then he went on to say that there was, however, a prize which in some sense depended on our own endeavours and was well worth striving for, and this included assurance of hope, victory over our spiritual enemies and usefulness to the church of God. Though these were also the free gift of God, they would rise and fall in proportion to our watchfulness.

The following Sunday Johnson preached twice again from Isaiah 40:31, focussing on *They shall walk and not faint.* Newton went along to the midweek meeting on Wednesday to hear Johnson speaking from Psalm 48:12 on the Rock of Ages. Next time they met they were to share their thoughts on *consider his palaces*, based on the next verse.

To his great pleasure Whitefield came to Liverpool in September 1755 and Newton wrote enthusiastically to his wife:

"He came to town on Wednesday, preached on that evening, twice yesterday, and so will continue preaching twice a day while he stays.... I made myself known to him the first night; went to see him, and conversed with him the next morning, when he invited me to supper. I went home with him from the preaching, and stayed till ten o'clock. So we are now very great; and very thankful I would be for the privilege. May the Lord yet give him to see that his labour of love amongst us is not in vain! However he is, as he was formerly, very helpful to me. He warms my heart, makes me more indifferent to cares and crosses, and strengthens my faith."[12]

"Mr. Whitefield left us yesterday morning; I accompanied him on foot a little way out of town, till the chaise overtook us. I have had more of his company than would have come to my share at London in twelvemonth. I heard him preach nine times, supped with him three times, and dined with him once at Mr. Fisher's, and on Sunday he dined with me. I cannot say how much I esteem him, and hope, to my dying day, I shall have reason to bless God in his behalf. Having never been here before but one night, he was not known or regarded by the fashionable folks, though several of them went to hear him. But many of the poorer sort are enquiring after him with tears."[13]

Whitefield spoke on John 21:17 *Lovest thou Me?* (from *Olney Hymns*, it would appear Newton never forgot this sermon); Isaiah 25:4 *A Refuge from the storm* (he preached this at 5 am, on the storms of guilt, sin, affliction, temptation, death, God's eternal wrath); Hebrews 2:3 *How shall we escape, if we neglect so great a salvation?*

John 6:35 *I am the Bread of Life*; John 14:6 *I am the Way* (the way to pardon, to righteousness, to sanctification; the way as our Intercessor and example); Revelation 3:20 *Behold I stand at the door and knock*; Ephesians 5:14 *Awake thou that sleepest*. Newton added that "he divided his applications as usual so that everyone had something."[14]

Newton's whole-hearted involvement with Whitefield's visit to Liverpool earned him the title of "the young Whitefield" (and also resulted in the conversion of his landlady). At Whitefield's suggestion he became acquainted with another Liverpool Baptist Pastor, Mr. Oulton (Johnson's group was an off-shoot from this church). Newton's assessment of him was that, "He is not as lively a preacher as Mr. Johnson, nor perhaps so deep in delivering the doctrines, but I dare say he is a sound and experimental preacher and deals more in application than the other, which I have always found the most useful part of a sermon to me: indeed I should not have sought him out but that Mr. Whitefield recommended him as an excellent and humble man."[15]

Newton used his spare time in reading. The life of the Puritan Joseph Alleine, written by his wife, drew tears from his eyes. "O what a cumber-ground, what a Nicodemus am I, when compared with such," he cried out in prayer. "O for a portion of his zeal, his prudence, in my life. Bless me, even me also, O Lord, with some degree of usefulness, with some endeavours to show my gratitude for thy unmerited distinguishing goodness before I go hence and am no more seen. O my cowardice, my self-seeking, my shameless shame. Lord, forgive me and mend me for thy name's sake." [a reference to one of his favourite quotes: "Notwithstanding I am already converted, well may I say with good old Herbert, Lord, break, or rather, mend me."]

In October Polly was well enough to join him. In January 1756 the Newtons moved into a house in Edmund Street, off Oldhall Street, in Liverpool.

Friends in Yorkshire

Newton found a special quality of ministry in his visits from Liverpool into Yorkshire. He described the county to Clunie as being "like Eden, the garden of the Lord, watered on every side by the streams of the Gospel".[16]

He enjoyed fellowship with William Grimshaw of Haworth, Henry

Venn of Huddersfield, John Fawcett (Baptist) of Hebden Bridge, James Scott (Independent) of Heckmondwike, Harry Crook, John Edwards (Presbyterian) in Leeds and Benjamin Ingham of the Moravian settlement at Yeadon.

It was his friendship with John Fawcett which led to much of the material for Cecil's *Life of Newton* becoming available. Newton's *Narrative* was originally written as a series of autobiographical letters to Fawcett.

While on these visits to Yorkshire, Newton had opportunities for preaching. The first time that Edwards invited him to preach, Newton eventually agreed against his will and better judgment. "He met a party at Mr. E.'s house to tea, and seems to have enjoyed himself very much. After tea he was told there was a private room at his service prior to preaching. 'O,' said he, 'I am prepared!'" [17]

"At the appointed time the service commenced, and after prayer Mr. Newton read his text, which was, *'I have set the Lord always before me; because he is at my right hand I shall not be moved.'* He began fluently; but in a few minutes he lost all recollection of his plan; was confused, stopped, and desired Mr. Edwards to come up and finish the service. Mr. Edwards urged him to proceed; but Mr. Newton left the pulpit, which Mr. Edwards ascended, and concluded with an address to the audience on the importance of the Spirit's agency to help our infirmities. Such was the confusion occasioned by the young preacher's failure, that for some time after he could not see two or three persons standing together in the street without suspecting that he himself must be the subject of their conversation." [18]

Discussing the incident with Harry Crook a couple of days later, Newton realised he had been "too hasty in making that essay and too adventurous in refusing the aid of notes." [19]

The next time he preached he used notes, but still ended despondently. "The moment I began my eyes were riveted to the book, from a fear that if I looked off I should not readily find the line again. Thus with my head hanging down (for I was near-sighted), and fixed like a statue, I conned over my lesson like a boy learning to read, and did not stop till I came to the end. I am convinced that unless I can speak warmly from my heart, God helping me, it will be in vain." [20]

He also preached in the Baptist and Moravian chapels and societies of John Fawcett and Benjamin Ingham.

One of his most valued associates in Yorkshire was Henry Venn. Their friendship lasted many years. In old age Newton reminisced on these days: "Seen or unseen you will always be dear to me, as you ought. Particularly for the benefits the Lord made you an instrument of conveying to me, when I used to visit you at Huddersfield, from Liverpool. It was then a critical time with me, and I had good reason to look up to you as a father, and a guide of my youth."[21]

William Grimshaw of Haworth was a unique character. Newton wrote his *Memoirs*[22] and tells us that in addition to his immediate responsibilities Grimshaw established two circuits for visiting "which, with some occasional variations, he usually traced every week, alternately. One of these, he often pleasantly called his idle week, because he seldom preached more than 12 or 14 times. His sermons in his working or busy week, often exceeded the number of 24, and sometimes amounted to 30."

Grimshaw preached two-hour sermons in market language. Newton described the effect, "Frequently a sentence, which a delicate hearer might judge quaint or vulgar, conveyed an important truth to the ear and fixed it in the memory for years after the rest of the sermon and the general subject were forgotten. I may give my judgment upon this point, something in his own way, by quoting a plain and homely proverb, which says, That is the best cat which catches the most mice."

The last time they were together, standing on a hill near Haworth (perhaps the top of Penistone Hill, where there is a panoramic 360° view of the area), Grimshaw told Newton how his congregation had grown from almost nothing to between 300 and 500 communicants, depending on the weather, "of the greater part of whom, so far as man who cannot see the heart (and can therefore only determine by appearance, profession and conduct) may judge, I can give almost as particular account as I can of myself. I know the state of their progress in religion. By my frequent visits and converse with them, I am acquainted with their several tempers, trials and exercises, both personal and domestic, both spiritual and temporal, almost as intimately as if I had lived in their families."

Many of the nonconformist pastors in the area had sat at Grimshaw's feet for instruction before entering their ministries (and continued to afterwards). Newton was no exception in benefiting from his ministry:

"I number it amongst the many great mercies of my life, that I was favoured with his notice, edified (I hope) by his instruction and example, and encouraged and directed by his advice at the critical time when my own mind was much engaged with a desire of entering the ministry. I saw in him, much more clearly than I could have learnt from books or lectures, what it was to be a faithful and exemplary minister of the gospel; and the remembrance of him has often both humbled and animated me.

"Had it been the will of God, methought I could have renounced the world to have lived in these mountains with such a minister, and such a people, but from hence likewise I was constrained to move."

Considering entering the ministry
Newton also took every opportunity to hear John Wesley and talk with him whenever he visited Liverpool. He wrote to Wesley on 14 November 1760, after one of his visits to Yorkshire:

"I forgot to tell you in my last that I had the honour to appear as a Methodist preacher. I was at Haworth – Mr. Grimshaw was pressing and prevailed. I spoke in his house to about one hundred and fifty persons – a difficult auditory, in my circumstances, about half Methodists and half Baptists. I was afraid of displeasing both sides; but my text (John 1:29) led me to dwell upon a point in which we were all agreed, and before I had leisure to meddle with doctrines, as they are called, the hour was expired. In short, it was a comfortable opportunity.

"Methinks, here again, you are ready to say, Very well; why not go on in the same way? What more encouragement can you ask, than to be assisted and accepted? But, however it may do for a time or so, I have not the strength of body or mind sufficient for an itinerant preacher; my constitution has been broken for some years. To ride a horse in the rain, or more than above thirty miles in a day, usually discomposes and unfits me for anything; then you must allow me to pay some regard to flesh and blood, though I would not consult them. I have a maintenance now in my hands, the gist of a kind Providence, and I do not see that I have a call to involve myself, and a person who has entrusted all her concerns to me (and must share in whatever I feel), in want and difficulties. I have likewise an orphan sister, for whom it is my duty to provide; consequently it cannot be my duty to disable myself from fulfilling what I owe her. And still the weightiest difficulty remains; too many of the preachers are very different from

Mr. Grimshaw; and who would wish to live in the fire? So that, though I love the people called Methodists, and vindicate them from unjust aspersions on all occasions, and suffer the reproach of the world for being one myself, yet it seems not practicable for me to join them further than I do. For the present I must remain as I am, and endeavour to be as useful as I can in private life, till I can see further. I shall always be obliged to you for your free sentiments in my case."[23]

Newton received an invitation at the end of 1759 to become the pastor of Cow Lane Independent Chapel in Warwick. (It was later renamed Brooke Street and is currently used for commercial offices.) It was a new church which had just been formed a couple of years before, following a secession in the town.[24] The Vennor family, dissatisfied with moves to Arianism amongst the Presbyterians, had left them, taking some members with them. They spent some time under John Ryland at the Baptist church, then withdrew to form their own worship meeting in an upper room in the High Street. Their invitation to Newton came shortly after their chapel in Cow Lane was built. The long awaited opportunity to enter the ministry brought him mixed feelings. "Now a call seems to await me, flesh and blood are alarmed at the undertaking, and seem to say, keep back; but I cannot, I dare not... "[25]

Newton shared his dilemma with John Wesley. He had wanted to enter the Church of England rather than become a dissenting pastor, but just couldn't get past the bishops.

Wesley recorded in his *Journal*:[26]

Thursday 20 March 1760
"I had a good deal of conversation with Mr. Newton. His case is very peculiar: our Church requires that Clergymen should be men of learning, and to this end have a university education: but how many have a university education and yet no learning at all? Yet these men are ordained! Meantime one of eminent learning as well as unblameable behaviour, cannot be ordained, 'because he was not at the university!' What a mere farce is this? Who would believe that any Christian Bishop would stoop to so poor an evasion?"

Newton had time off from his tide-surveying duties in a slack period and went to Warwick in May 1760, after a day of fasting and prayer, where he ministered for the next three months. He just missed having the fellowship of John Ryland, who had been ministering at the Castle Hill Baptist Church in Warwick for thirteen years but had moved on to College Lane, Northampton, a few months earlier.

During his ministry in Warwick, Ryland had rented accommodation in St. Mary's Vicarage. When some complaints reached the incumbent, Dr. Tate, for having an Anabaptist living in the vicarage, he replied, "What would you have me do? I have brought the man as near to the church as I can, but I cannot force him to enter it."[27]

On his last Sunday in Warwick Newton wrote to Mary, who was staying at her family's home in Kent:

"I spoke in the afternoon from Judges 16:20,21; in the evening from John 1:29. The place was much crowded, and numbers much affected; indeed I wonder not at it, for the very text is a sermon, if attentively read, and I was greatly favoured in my meditations upon it. May he of whom it is spoken have all the glory. I cannot express the reluctance of the people to part with me, nor how exceeding anxious they are about my return, but I keep my promise to Mr. Brewer, & leave them in suspense."[28]

He had been able to extend his leave through the kind "piecing and ekeing" of the Collector, John Colquitt jnr., and was even able to obtain a further extension on his return to Liverpool in order to meet Mary on her journey home, "for I told him a sad story what a poor disconsolate thing I was without you."[29]

In November 1760 he received another pressing invitation from Warwick. "I cannot but think it amounts to a clear call." William Romaine advised him to accept it, but Samuel Brewer recommended caution. It was Brewer's advice which proved judicious, as a problem had developed with one of the church members. After a visit to Warwick many years later Newton reflected, "The people among whom my mouth was first opened, and where I found some sweet encouragement in my entrance on the ministry, will always be dear to me; they are at present but few, but those few are lively and steady."[30]

In a Funeral Sermon for Newton in 1808, Samuel Palmer referred to the following incident which occurred while Newton was at Warwick, feeling that it had influenced his decision: "Hearing that Mr. Beddome was to preach at the Baptists' meeting in that town, he desired that his own congregation would shut up their meeting house,

that he and they might go to hear him. Though most of them agreed
to the proposal, others were so much offended, as to throw out bitter
reflections both on him and them."[31]

Hindmarsh refers to another possible explanation given in John
Byrom's Journal, which notes that there were differences between
Newton and the congregation in maintenance, rather than in doctrine.[32]

In 1759 Newton had been invited to accept an Independent charge
when he was in Yorkshire at James Scott's. "Had this come some
months sooner, I would have willingly complied, but I am embarked
so far on the other side I shall not stop till I have tried the *dernier
ressort*.... I have only now to appeal to my Lord of Canterbury, and
to leave the situation with the Lord; for I think upon a refusal there,
which I am prepared to expect, that I will retract the pursuit, and take
up the conclusion Mr. Romaine has already made for me, that it is
not the will of the Lord I should appear on that side."[33]

Much affected by the death in 1762 of Mr. Jones of St. Saviour's,
Southwark, Newton felt an urgency to get into the ministry and wrote
to Rev. Caleb Warhurst, Independent minister at Manchester, "I
should be glad of an opportunity to see Mr. Scott ... to let him know
that I am disposed to accept a call within his connection .... If I should
not have an opportunity to meet Mr. Scott, will you tell him, so far as
I know my own heart, I have quite done with the established church,
so called, not out of anger or despair, but from a conviction that the
Lord has been wise and good in disappointing my views in that
quarter; and I believe if the admission I once so earnestly sought was
now freely offered, I could hardly, if at all, accept it."[34]

In February 1764 Newton received proposals from a Presbyterian
church in Yorkshire.

He had recently written a series of eight letters about his life to
his Baptist friend John Fawcett. Thomas Haweis, curate to Martin
Madan at the Lock Hospital in London, saw these and asked Newton
to expand on them. Newton replied with fourteen letters in three days.
Haweis passed them on to Lord Dartmouth, who had offered the
curacy of Olney to Haweis. Haweis suggested Newton be appointed
to Olney instead of him.

The result was that Newton had a rapid series of meetings in
London with Lord Dartmouth, Moses Browne (the incumbent) and
the Bishop of Lincoln, in whose diocese Olney lay.

During this time he wrote home to his wife:

Thursday 5 April 1764
"I hope I could retire to Olney and be happy, if the Lord made me the instrument of good to the people there, though neither they nor I should be spoke of beyond the bounds of the Parish.... The Lord has indeed led me in a way that I knew not, and it seems highly probable the acquaintance I have found among persons to whom I had so little reason to expect being known, is designed for some important purpose."[35]

The points on which he differed from the Bishop of Lincoln at his examination in London were "a few expressions in the Burial and Baptism offices and in the Catechism, which I cannot fully approve."[36]

After taking his first funeral in Olney, Newton recorded in his diary, "ventured to omit a clause in one of the prayers, as I propose to do in such cases hereafter."[37]

He later commented to a clergy friend, "Although a passable Churchman, I cannot undertake to vindicate every expression in our baptismal service." He felt the Reformers had been impeded by some in Edward VI's time who "would not accept the Scriptures alone as the sufficient rule of faith and practice, but prevailed to superadd the fathers of the first six centuries. Afterwards Elizabeth with her *semper eadem* forbade all further alterations. But the Gospel purity was soon corrupted, and some of the fathers were but mothers (old women) in divinity. However, their authority gave sanction to several expressions and sentiments which the Scripture does not warrant, particularly with regard to baptism. The Sacraments are of Divine institution, but I do not think either of them confers grace *ex opera operato*. The rubric tells us gravely that those who die in infancy may be saved if baptised; I believe they may be and are saved whether baptised or not; for I cannot think that the salvation of a soul depends upon a negligent or drunken minister, who cannot be found when wanted to baptise a dying infant. The fathers, or some of them, did indeed speak of baptism and regeneration or the new birth as synonymous; but while the Scripture, experience and observation contradict them, I pay little regard to their judgment."[38]

In his lectures on the church catechism in 1765, before explaining the Creed he cautioned his hearers that "it is not the repeating this Creed by rote like a parrot that will prove any to be a Christian, unless there is likewise the true knowledge and experience of the heart, of what is said with the lips."[39]

CHAPTER 7

CURATE IN CHARGE AT OLNEY
1764–1779

Mr. N. was ordained Deacon at Buckden, April 29, 1764; and Priest, in June, the same year.[1] In the parish of Olney he found many who not only had evangelical views of the truth, but had also long walked in the light and experience of it. The vicarage was in the gift of the Earl of Dartmouth, the nobleman to whom Mr. N. addressed the first twenty-six letters in his *Cardiphonia*.[2] The earl was a man of real piety, and most amiable disposition: he had formerly appointed the Rev. Moses Brown to the vicarage.

Mr. Brown was a faithful minister, and a good man; of course, he had afforded wholesome instruction to the parishioners of Olney: he had also been the instrument of a sound conversion in many of them. He was the author of a poetical piece, entitled *Sunday Thoughts*,[3] a translation of Professor Zimmerman's *Excellency of the Knowledge of Jesus Christ*, etc. But Mr. Brown had a numerous family, and met with considerable trials in it; he too much resembled Eli, in his indulgence of his children. He was also under the pressure of pecuniary difficulties, and had therefore accepted the Chaplaincy of Morden College, Blackheath, while Vicar of Olney.

Mr. N. in these circumstances, undertook the Curacy of Olney, in which he continued near sixteen years, previous to his removal to St. Mary Woolnoth, to which he was afterwards presented by the late John Thornton, Esq.

As Mr. N. was under the greatest obligations to Mr. Thornton's friendship while at Olney, and had been enabled to extend his own usefulness by the bounty of that extraordinary man, it may not be foreign to our subject, to give some general outline of Mr. Thornton's character in this place.

It is said of Solomon, that *the Lord gave him largeness of heart, even as the sand on the sea shore*:[4] such a peculiar disposition for whatever was good or benevolent was also bestowed on Mr. Thornton. He differed as much from rich men of ordinary bounty, as they do from others who are parsimonious. Nor was this bounty the result of occasional impulse, like a summer shower, violent and short: on the contrary, it proceeded like a river, pouring its waters through various countries, copious and inexhaustible. Nor could those obstructions of imposture and ingratitude, which have often been advanced as the cause of damming up other streams, prevent or retard the course of this. The generosity of Mr. Thornton, indeed, frequently met with such hindrances, and led him to increasing discrimination; but the stream of his bounty never ceased to hold its course. Deep, silent, and overwhelming, it still rolled on, nor ended even with his life.

But the fountain from whence this beneficence flowed, and by which its permanency and direction were maintained, must not be concealed. Mr. Thornton was a Christian. Let no one, however, so mistake me here, as to suppose that I mean nothing more by the term CHRISTIAN, than the state of one, who, convinced of the truth of Revelation, gives assent to its ordinances – and maintains, externally, a moral and religious deportment. Such a one may have *a name to live while he is dead*:[5] he may have *a form of godliness without the power*[6] of it – he may even be found denying and ridiculing that power – till, at length, he can only be convinced of his error at an infallible tribunal; where a *widow,* who gives but a mite, or a *publican,* who smites on his breast, shall be preferred before him.

Mr. Thornton was a Christian indeed; that is, he was alive to God by a spiritual regeneration. With this God he was daily and earnestly transacting that infinitely momentous affair, the salvation of the souls of others. Temperate in all things, though mean in nothing, he made provision for doing good with his opulence; and seemed to be most in his element when appropriating a considerable part of his large income to the necessities of others.

But Mr. Thornton possessed that discrimination in his attempts to serve his fellow creatures, which distinguishes an enlightened mind. He habitually contemplated man, as one who has not only a *body*, subject to want, affliction, and death; but a *spirit* also, which is immortal, and must be happy or miserable for ever. He felt, therefore, that the noblest exertions of charity are those which are directed to the relief of the noblest part of our frame. Accordingly he left no mode of exertion untried to relieve man under his natural ignorance and depravity. To this end, he purchased Advowsons and Presentations, with a view to place in parishes the most enlightened, active and useful ministers. He employed the extensive commerce in which he was engaged, as a powerful instrument for conveying immense quantities of Bibles, Prayer Books, and the most useful publications, to every place visited by our trade. He printed, at his sole expense, large editions of the latter for that purpose; and it may safely be affirmed, that there is scarcely a part of the known world, where such books could be introduced, which did not feel the salutary influence of this single individual.

Nor was Mr. Thornton limited in his views of promoting the interests of real religion, with what sect soever it was connected. He stood ready to assist a beneficial design in every party, but would be the creature of none. General good was his object: and, wherever or however it made its way, his maxim seemed constantly to be, *Valeat quantum valere potest.*[7]

But the nature and extent of his liberality will be greatly misconceived, if any one should suppose it *confined* to moral and religious objects, though the grandest and most comprehensive exertions of it. Mr. Thornton was a philanthropist, on the largest scale – the friend of man, under all his wants. His manner of relieving his fellow-men was princely. Instances might be mentioned of it, were it proper to particularise, which would surprise those who did not know Mr. Thornton. They were so much out of ordinary course and expectation, that I know some, who felt it their duty to enquire of him, whether the sum they had received was sent by his intention or by mistake. – To this may be added, that the manner of presenting his gifts was as delicate and concealed, as the measure was large.

Besides this constant course of private donations, there was scarcely a public charity, or occasion of relief to the ignorant or necessitous, which did not meet with his distinguished support. His only question was, "May the miseries of man in any measure be removed or alleviated?" Nor was he merely distinguished by stretching out a liberal hand: his benevolent heart was so intent on doing good, that he was ever inventing and promoting plans for its diffusion at home or abroad.

He who wisely desires any end, will as wisely regard the means. In this Mr. Thornton was perfectly consistent. In order to execute his beneficent designs, he observed frugality and exactness in his personal expenses. By such prospective methods, he was able to extend the influence of his fortune far beyond those, who, in still more elevated stations, are slaves to expensive habits. Such men meanly pace in the trammels of the tyrant Custom, till it leaves them scarcely enough to preserve their conscience, or even their credit; much less to employ their talents in Mr. Thornton's nobler pursuits. He, however, could *afford* to be generous; and, while he was generous, did not forget his duty in being *just*. He made ample provision for his children; and though, while they are living, it would be indelicate to say more, I am sure of speaking truth, when I say – they are so far from thinking themselves impoverished by the bounty of their father, that they contemplate with the highest satisfaction the fruit of those benefits to society which he planted – which it may be trusted will extend with time itself – and which, after his example, they still labour to extend.

But, with all the piety and liberality of this honoured character, no man had deeper views of his own unworthiness before his God. To the Redeemer's work alone, he looked for acceptance of his person and services: he felt that all he did, or could do, was infinitely short of that which had been done for him, and of the obligations that were thereby laid upon him. It was his abasedness of heart towards God, combined with the most singular largeness of heart towards his fellow-creatures, which distinguished JOHN THORNTON among men.

To this common patron of every useful and pious endeavour, Mr. N. sent the *Narrative* from which the former part of these Memoirs is extracted. Mr. Thornton replied in his usual manner, that is, by accompanying his letter with a valuable bank note; and, some months after, he paid Mr. N. a visit at Olney. A closer connection being now formed between friends who employed their distinct talents in promoting the same benevolent cause, Mr. Thornton left a sum of money with Mr. N. to be appropriated to the defraying of his necessary expenses, and the relief of the poor. "Be hospitable," said Mr. Thornton, "and keep open house for such as are worthy of entertainment. Help the poor and needy. I will statedly allow you £200 a year, and readily send whatever you have occasion to draw for more." – Mr. N. told me, that he thought he had received of Mr. Thornton upwards of £3,000 in this way, during the time he resided at Olney.

The case of most ministers is peculiar in this respect. Some among them may be looked up to, on account of their publicity and talents: they may have made great sacrifices of their personal interest, in order to enter on their ministry, and may be possessed of the warmest benevolence; but, from the narrowness of their pecuniary circumstances, and from the largeness of their families, they often perceive that an ordinary tradesman in their parishes can subscribe to a charitable or popular institution much more liberally than themselves. This would have been Mr. N.'s case, but for the above-mentioned singular patronage.

A minister, however, should not be so forgetful of his dispensation, as to repine at his want of power in this respect. He might as justly estimate his deficiency by the strength of the lion, or the flight of the eagle. The power communicated to *him* is of another kind: and power of every kind belongs to God, who gives gifts to every man severally as he will. The two mites of the widow were all the power of *that* kind, which was communicated to her; and her bestowment of her two mites was better accepted, than the large offerings of the rich man. The powers, therefore, of Mr. Thornton and of Mr. N., though of a different order, were both consecrated to God; and each might have said, *Of thine own have we given thee.*[8]

Providence seems to have appointed Mr. N.'s residence at Olney, among other reasons, for the relief of the depressed mind of the poet COWPER. There has gone forth an unfounded report, that the deplorable melancholy of Cowper was, in part, derived from his residence and connections in that place. The fact, however, is the reverse of this; and, as may be of importance to the interests of true religion to prevent such a misrepresentation from taking root, I will present the real state of the case, as I have found it attested by the most respectable living witnesses: and, more especially, as confirmed by a MS written by the poet himself, at the calmest period of his life, with the perusal of which I was favoured by Mr. N.[9]

It most evidently appears, that symptoms of Mr. Cowper's morbid state began to discover themselves in his earliest youth. He seems to have been at all times disordered, in a greater or less degree. He was sent to Westminster school at the age of nine years, and long endured the tyranny of an elder boy, of which he gives an affecting account in the paper above mentioned; and which "*produced*," as one of his biographers observes, who had long intimacy with him, "*an indelible effect upon his mind through life.*" – A person so naturally bashful and depressed as Cowper, must needs find the profession of a Barrister a further occasion of anxiety. The post obtained for him by his friends in the House of Lords overwhelmed him; and the remonstrances which those friends made against his relinquishing so honourable and lucrative an appointment (but which soon after actually took place) greatly increased the anguish of a mind already incapacitated for business. To all this were added events, which, of themselves, have been found sufficient to overset the strongest minds: namely, the decease of his particular friend and intimate, Sir William Russel, and his meeting with a disappointment in obtaining a lady [his cousin, Theodora Cowper], upon whom his affections were placed.

But the state of a person, torn and depressed (not by his *religious connections*, but) by adverse circumstances, and these meeting a naturally morbid sensibility, *long before he knew Olney, or had formed any connection* with its inhabitants, will best appear from some verses which he sent at this time to one of his female relations, and for the communication of which we are indebted to Mr. Hayley:[10]

> "Doom'd as I am, in solitude to waste
> The present moments, and regret the past;
> Depriv'd of every joy I valued most,
> My friend torn from me, and my mistress lost:
> Call this not gloom I wear, this anxious mien,
> The dull effect of humour or of spleen!
> Still, still I mourn, with each returning day,
> Him snatch'd by fate, in early youth, away;
> And her, through tedious years of doubt and pain,
> Fix'd in her choice, and faithful – but in vain.
> See me ere yet my destin'd course half done,
> Cast forth a wand'rer on a wild unknown!
> See me, neglected on the world's rude coast,
> Each dear companion of my voyage lost!
> Nor ask, why clouds of sorrow shade my brow,
> And ready tears wait only leave to flow:
> Why all that soothes a heart, from anguish free,
> All that delights the happy – palls with me!"

Under such pressures, the melancholy and susceptible mind of Cowper received, from evangelical truth, the first consolation which it ever tasted. It was under the care of Dr. Cotton, of St. Alban's, (a physician as capable of administering to the spiritual as to the natural maladies of his patients) that Mr. C. first obtained a clear view of those sublime and animating doctrines, which so distinguished and exalted his future strains as a poet. Here, also, he received that settled tranquillity and peace, which he enjoyed for several years afterwards. So far, therefore, was his constitutional malady from being produced or increased by his evangelical connexions, either at St. Albans or at Olney, that he seems never to have had any settled peace but from the truths he learned in these societies. It appears, that, among them alone, he found the only sunshine he ever enjoyed, through the cloudy day of his afflicted life.

It appears also, that, while at Dr. Cotton's, Mr. Cowper's distress was for a long time entirely removed, by marking that passage in Romans 3:25, *Him hath God set forth to be a propitiation, through faith in his blood, to declare his righteousness for the remission of sins that are past.* In this Scripture he saw the remedy which God provides for the relief of a guilty conscience, with such clearness, that for *several years* after, his heart was filled with love, and his life occupied with prayer, praise, and doing good to his needy fellow-creatures.

Mr. N. told me, that, from Mr. Cowper's first coming to Olney, it was observed he had studied his Bible with such advantage, and was so well acquainted with its design, that not only his troubles were removed, but that, to the end of his life, he never had clearer views of the Gospel, than when he first became an attendant upon them – that (short intervals excepted) Mr. Cowper enjoyed a course of peace for several successive years – that, during this period, the inseparable attendants of a lively faith appeared, by Mr. Cowper's exerting himself to the utmost of his power in every benevolent service he could render to his poor neighbours – and that Mr. N. used to consider him as a sort of Curate, from his constant attendance upon the sick and afflicted, in that large and necessitous parish.

But the malady, which seemed to be subdued by the strong consolations of the Gospel, was still latent; and only required some occasion of irritation, to break out again, and overwhelm the patient. Any object of constant attention that shall occupy a mind previously disordered, whether fear, or love, or science, or religion, will not be so much the CAUSE of the disease, as the accidental OCCASION of exciting it. Cowper's Letters show us how much his mind was occupied at one time by the truths of the Bible, and at another time by the fictions of Homer; but his melancholy was originally a constitutional disease – a physical disorder, which, indeed, could be *affected* either by the Bible or by Homer, but was utterly distinct in its nature from the mere matter of either. And, here, I cannot but mark this necessary distinction; having often been witness to cases where religion has been assigned as the proper *cause* of insanity, when it has been only an *accidental* occasion, in the case of one *already* affected.* Thus COWPER's malady, like a strong current, breaking down the banks which had hitherto sustained the pressure and obliquity of its course, prevailed against the supports he had received, and precipitated him again into his former distress.

I enquired of Mr. N. as to the manner in which Mr. Cowper's disorder returned, after an apparent recovery of nearly nine years' continuance: and was informed, that the first symptoms were discovered one morning, in his conversation, soon after he had undertaken a new engagement in composition.

As a general and full account of this extraordinary genius is already before the public, such particulars would not have occupied so much room in these Memoirs, but with a view of removing the false statements that have been made.

Of great importance also was the vicinity of Mr. N.'s residence to that of the Rev. Mr. Thomas Scott, then curate of Ravenstone and Weston Underwood, and now Rector of Aston Sandford; a man,

---

* I have been an eye-witness of several instances of this kind of misrepresentation; but will detain the reader with mentioning only one. I was called to visit a woman whose mind was disordered; and, on my observing that it was a case which required the assistance of a physician, rather than that of a clergyman, her husband replied, "Sir, we sent to you, because it is a religious case: her mind has been injured by constantly reading the Bible." "I have known many instances," said I, "of persons brought to their senses by reading the Bible; but it is possible, that too intense an application to that, as well as to any other subject, may have disordered your wife." – "There is every proof of it," said he, and was proceeding to multiply his proofs, till his brother interrupted him by thus addressing me:

"Sir, I have no longer patience to stand by, and see you imposed on. The truth of the matter is this: my brother has forsaken his wife, and been long connected with a loose woman. He had the best of wives in her, and one who was strongly attached to him: but she has seen his heart and property given to another; and in her solitude and distress, went to the Bible, as the only consolation left her. Her health and spirits, at length, sunk under her troubles; and there she lies distracted, not from reading her Bible, but from the infidelity and cruelty of her husband." – Does the reader wish to know what reply the husband made to this? He made no reply at all, but left the room with confusion of face!

whose ministry and writings have since been so useful to mankind. This Clergyman was nearly a Socinian; he was in the habit of ridiculing evangelical religion, and laboured to bring over Mr. N. to his own sentiments. Mr. Scott had married a lady from the family of a Mr. Wright, a gentleman in his parish, who had promised to provide for him. But Mr. Scott's objections to subscription arose so high, that he informed his patron it would be in vain to attempt providing for him in the Church of England; as he could not conscientiously accept a Living, on the condition of subscribing its Liturgy and Articles. "This," said Mr. N. "gave me hopes of Mr. Scott's being sincere, however wrong his principles."

But the benefit which Mr. Scott derived from his neighbour, will best appear in his own words.*

"I was," says he, "full of proud self-sufficiency, very positive, and very obstinate: and, being situated in the neighbourhood of some of those whom the world calls Methodists, I joined in the prevailing sentiment; held them in sovereign contempt; spoke of them with derision; declaimed against them from the pulpit, as persons full of bigotry, enthusiasm, and spiritual pride; laid heavy things to their charge; and endeavoured to prove the doctrines, which I supposed them to hold, (for I never read their books) to be dishonourable to God, and destructive of morality. And though, in some companies, I chose to conceal part of my sentiments: and, in all, affected to speak as a friend to universal toleration: yet, scarcely any person could be more proudly and violently prejudiced against both their persons and principles than I then was.

"In January, 1774, two of my parishioners, a man and his wife, lay at the point of death. I had heard of the circumstance; but, according to my general custom, not being sent for, I took no notice of it: till one evening, the woman being now dead, and the man dying, I heard that my neighbour Mr. N. had been several times to visit them. Immediately my conscience reproached me with being shamefully negligent in sitting at home within a few doors of dying persons, my general hearers, and never going to visit them. Directly it occurred to me, that, whatever contempt I might have for Mr. N.'s *doctrines*, I must acknowledge his *practice* to be more consistent with the ministerial character than my own. He must have more zeal and love for souls than I had, or he would not have walked so far to

*Scott's *Force of Truth*, [1779], p. 11, etc. 5th edtn.

visit, and supply my lack of care to those who, as far as I was concerned, might have been left to perish in their sins.

"This reflection affected me so much, that, without delay, and very earnestly, yea, with tears, I besought the Lord to forgive my past neglect; and I resolved thenceforth to be more attentive to this duty: which resolution, though at first formed in ignorant dependence on my own strength, I have by divine grace been enabled hitherto to keep. I went immediately to visit the survivor; and the affecting sight of one person already dead, and another expiring in the same chamber, served more deeply to impress my serious convictions.

"It was at this time that my correspondence with Mr. N. commenced. At a Visitation, May 1775, we exchanged a few words on a controverted subject, in the room among the Clergy, which I believe drew many eyes upon us. At that time he prudently declined the discourse; but, a day or two after, he sent me a short note, with a little book for my perusal [*Omicron*]. This was the very thing I wanted: and I gladly embraced the opportunity which, according to my wishes, seemed now to offer; God knoweth, with no inconsiderable expectations that my arguments would prove irresistibly convincing, and that I should have the honour of rescuing a well-meaning person from his enthusiastical delusions.

"I had, indeed, by this time conceived a very favourable opinion of him, and a sort of respect for him; being acquainted with the character he sustained even among some persons, who expressed a disapprobation of his doctrines. They were forward to commend him as a benevolent, disinterested, inoffensive person, and a laborious minister. But, on the other hand, I looked upon his religious sentiments as a rank fanaticism; and entertained a very contemptuous opinion of his abilities, natural and acquired. Once I had the curiosity to hear him preach; and not understanding his sermon, I made a very great jest of it; where I could do it without giving offence. I had also read one of his publications; but, for the same reason, I thought the greater part of it whimsical, paradoxical, and unintelligible.

"Concealing, therefore, the true motives of my conduct, under the offer of friendship and a professed desire to know the truth (which amidst all my self-sufficiency and prejudice, I trust the Lord had even then given me) with the greatest affectation of candour, and of a mind open to conviction, I wrote him a long letter; purposing to draw from him such an avowal and explanation of his sentiments, as might introduce a controversial discussion of our religious differences.

"The event by no means answered my expectation. He returned a very friendly and long answer to my letter; in which he carefully avoided the mention of those doctrines which he knew would offend me. He declared that he believed me to be one who feared God, and was under the teaching of his Holy Spirit: that he gladly accepted my offer of friendship, and was no ways inclined to dictate to me; but that, leaving me to the guidance of the Lord, he would be glad, as occasion served from time to time, to bear testimony to the truths of the Gospel; and to communicate his sentiments to me on any subject, with all the confidence of friendship.

"In this manner our correspondence began; and it was continued, in the interchange of nine or ten letters, till December in the same year. Throughout I held my purpose, and he his. I made use of every endeavour to draw him into controversy, and filled my letters with definitions, enquiries, arguments, objections, and consequences, requiring explicit answers. He, on the other hand, shunned every thing controversial as much as possible, and filled his letters with the most useful and least offensive instructions: except that, now and then, he dropped his hints concerning the necessity, the true nature, and the efficacy of faith, and the manner in which it was to be sought and obtained; and concerning some other matters, suited, as he judged, to help me forward in my enquiry after truth. But they much offended my prejudices, afforded me matter of disputation, and at that time were of little use to me.

"When I had made this little progress in seeking the truth, my acquaintance with Mr. N. was resumed. From the conclusion of our correspondence, in December, 1775, till April 1777, it had been wholly dropped. To speak plainly, I did not care for his company: I did not mean to make use of him as an instructor: and I was unwilling the world should think us in any way connected. But, under discouraging circumstances, I had occasion to call upon him; and his discourse so comforted and edified me, that my heart, being by his means relieved from its burden, became susceptible of affection for him. From that time I was inwardly pleased to have him for my friend; though not, as now, rejoiced to call him so. I had, however, even at that time, no thoughts of learning doctrinal truth from him, and was ashamed to be detected in his company; but I sometimes stole away to spend an hour with him. About the same period, I once heard him preach, but still it was foolishness to me; his sermon being principally upon the believer's experience, in some particulars, with which I was unacquainted. – So that, though I loved and valued him, I considered him as a person misled by enthusiastical notions; and strenuously insisted that we should never think alike till we met in heaven."

Mr. Scott, after going on to particularise his progress in the discovery of truth, and the character of Mr. N. as its minister, afterwards adds:

"The pride of reasoning, and the conceit of superior discernment, had all along accompanied me; and, though somewhat broken, had yet considerable influence. Hitherto, therefore, I had not thought of hearing any person preach; because I did not think any one in the circle of my acquaintance capable of giving me such information as I wanted. But, being at length convinced that Mr. N. had been right, and that I had been mistaken, in the several particulars in which we differed, it occurred to me, that having preached these doctrines so long, he must understand many things concerning them to which I was a stranger. Now, therefore, though not without much remaining prejudice, and not less in the character of a judge than of a scholar, I condescended to be his hearer, and occasionally to attend his preaching, and that of some other ministers. I soon perceived the benefit; for, from time to time the secrets of my heart were discovered to me, far beyond what I had hitherto noticed; and I seldom returned from hearing a sermon, without having conceived a meaner opinion of myself – without having attained to a further acquaintance of my deficiencies, weaknesses, corruptions, and wants – or without being supplied with fresh matter for prayer, and directed to greater watchfulness. I likewise learned the use of experience in preaching; and was convinced, that the readiest way to reach the hearts and consciences of others, was to speak from my own. In short, I gradually saw more and more my need of instruction, and was at length brought to consider myself as a very novice in religious matters. Thus I began experimentally to perceive our Lord's meaning, when he says, *Except ye receive the kingdom of heaven as a little child, ye shall in no wise enter therein.*"[11]

If I have seemed to digress in dwelling so long on these three characters, let the reader consider the importance of the facts, and their intimate connection with Mr. N.'s history: and let me inform him, that the author has a design much nearer his heart than that of *precision* in setting forth the history of an individual; namely, that of exhibiting the nature and importance of vital and experimental religion: he therefore gladly brings forward any fact found in his way, which may tend to illustrate it.

But to return to the more immediate subject of these Memoirs.

In the year 1776, Mr. N. was afflicted with a tumour, or wen, which had formed on his thigh; and, on account of its growing more large and troublesome, he resolved to undergo the experiment of extirpation. This obliged him to go to London for the operation, which was successfully performed, October 10th, by the late Mr. Warner, of Guy's Hospital. I remember hearing him speak several years afterwards of this trying occasion: but the trial did not seem to have affected him as a painful operation, so much as a critical opportunity in which he might fail in demonstrating the patience of a Christian under pain. "I felt," said he, "that being enabled to bear a very sharp operation with tolerable calmness and confidence, was a greater favour granted to me than the deliverance from my malady."*

While Mr. N. thus continued faithfully discharging the duties of his station, and watching for the temporal and eternal welfare of his flock, a dreadful fire broke out at Olney, Oct. 1777. Mr. N. took an active part in comforting and relieving the sufferers: he collected upwards of £200 for them; a considerable sum of money, when the poverty and late calamity of the place are considered. Such instances of benevolence towards the people, with the constant assistance he afforded the poor by the help of Mr. Thornton, naturally led him to expect that he should have so much influence as to restrain gross

---

* The following reflections on this occasion occur in Mr. N.'s diary. – "Thou didst support me, and make this operation very tolerable. The cure, by thy blessing, was happily expedited: so that on Sunday the 27th, I was enabled to go to church and hear Mr. F[oster], and the Sunday following to preach for him. The tenderness and attention of Dr. and Mrs. F[ord], with whom we were, I cannot sufficiently describe; nor, indeed, the kindness of many other friends. To them I would be thankful, my Lord, but especially to thee: for what are creatures, but instruments in thy hand, fulfilling thy pleasure? At home, all was preserved quiet; and I met with no incident to distress or disturb me while absent. The last fortnight I preached often, and was hurried about in seeing my friends: but though I had little leisure or opportunity for retirement, and my heart, alas! as usual, sadly reluctant and dull in secret; yet, in public, thou wert pleased to favour me with liberty."

licentiousness on particular occasions. But to use his own expression, he had "lived to bury the old crop, on which any dependence could be placed." He preached a Weekly Lecture, which occurred that year on the 5th of November; and, as he feared that the usual way of celebrating it at Olney might endanger his hearers in their attendance at the church, he exerted himself to preserve some degree of quiet on that evening. Instead, however, of hearkening to his entreaties, the looser sort exceeded their former extravagance, drunkenness, and rioting; and even obliged him to send out money, to preserve his house from violence ["*Tell it not in Gath*," wrote Newton to Thornton[12]]. This happened but a year before he finally left Olney. When he related this occurrence to me, he added, that he believed he should never have left the place while he lived, had not so incorrigible a spirit prevailed in a parish which he had long laboured to reform.

But I must remark here, that this is no solitary fact, nor at all unaccountable. The Gospel, we are informed, is not merely *a savour of life unto life*, but also *of death unto death*.[13] Those, whom it does not *soften*, it is often found to *harden*. Thus we find St. Paul *went into the synagogue and spake boldly for the space of three months, disputing and persuading the things concerning the kingdom of God. But, when divers were hardened, and believed not, but spake evil of that way before the multitude, he departed from them.*[14]

The strong man armed,[15] seeks to keep his *house and goods in peace*; and if a Minister is disposed to let this *sleep of death*[16] remain, that Minister's *own* house and goods may be permitted to remain in peace also. Such a Minister may be esteemed by his parish as a good kind of man – quiet, inoffensive, candid, &c. and if he discovers any zeal, it is directed to keep the parish in the state he found it; that is, in ignorance and unbelief, worldly-minded and hard-hearted – the very state of peace in which *the strong man armed* seeks to keep his palace or citadel, the human heart.

But, if a Minister, like the subject of these Memoirs, enters into the design of his commission – if he be alive to the interest of his own soul, and that of the souls committed to his charge: or, as the Apostle expresses it, *to save himself and those that hear him*,[17] he may depend upon meeting in his own experience the truth of that declaration, *Yea, all that will live godly in Christ Jesus, shall suffer persecution*,[18] in one form of it or another. One of the most melancholy sights we behold is, when any part of the Church, through prejudice, joins the World in throwing the stone. There is, however, such a determined enmity to godliness itself, in the breasts of a certain class of men existing in most parishes, that whatever learning and good sense are found in their Teacher – whatever consistency of character or blameless deportment he exhibits – whatever benevolence or bounty (like that which Mr. N. exercised at Olney) may constantly appear in his character – such men remain irreconcilable. They will resist every attempt made to appease their enmity. God alone, who changed the hearts of Paul and of Newton, can heal these bitter waters.

I recollect to have heard Mr. N. say on such an occasion, "When God is about to perform any great work, he generally permits some great opposition to it. Suppose Pharaoh had acquiesced in the departure of the children of Israel – or that they had met with no difficulties in the way – they would, indeed, have passed from Egypt to Canaan with ease: but they, as well as the Church in all future ages, would have been great losers. The wonder-working God would not have been seen in those extremities which make his arm so visible – A *smooth passage* here would have made but a *poor story*."

But under such disorders, Mr. N. in no one instance that I ever heard of, was tempted to depart from the line marked out by the precept and example of his Master. He continued to *bless them that persecuted him*;[19] knowing that *the servant of the Lord must not strive, but be gentle unto all men, apt to teach, patient.*[20] To the last day he spent among them, he went straight forward, *in meekness instructing those that opposed, if God peradventure might give them repentance to the acknowledging of the truth.*

But, before we take a final leave of Olney, the reader must be informed of another part of Mr. N.'s labours. He had published *A Volume of Sermons*[21] before he took Orders, dated Liverpool, Jan. 1, 1760. In 1774 [incorrectly printed as 1762 in Cecil], he published his *Omicron*; to which his letters, signed *Vigil*,[22] were afterwards annexed. In 1764, appeared his *Narrative*: in 1767, *a Volume of sermons, preached at Olney*:[23] in 1769, his *Review of Ecclesiastical History*:[24] and, in 1779, *a Volume of Hymns*;[25] of which some were composed by Mr. Cowper, and distinguished by a C. To these succeeded, in 1781, his valuable work, *Cardiphonia*. But more will be said of these in their place.

Appendix to Chapter 7

Ordination

Moses Browne, the existing incumbent of Olney, had also had a difficult path into the ministry, not having been to university. His poetry had gained the attention of Isaac Watts, who had been asked to judge the entries for a competition in the *Gentleman's Magazine*. His winning poem was entitled *The Consummate State of Man*. Watts took a kind and almost parental interest in him from then on. His cause was also taken on by James Hervey, George Whitefield and the Countess of Huntingdon. Whitefield referred to him as "Poor Mr. Browne", a description echoed by Newton writing to his wife from London:

"Browne ... Poor man he is worthy of much compassion. I was not willing to add to his difficulties by leaving him to think that I would use any influence with his friends to increase his difficulties. Let him keep the title; the name of vicar is a feather in the cap which I can easily spare, and if he desires to have a reserve of £18 or £20 p. ann. from the living, his embarrassments are so great that I know not how to object."[26]

Newton's letters to Haweis were being considered for publication at the same time. He had not anticipated this. They had also been instrumental in opening the way for his ordination. "And all that has or may happen seems eventually owing to the letters I wrote to Mr. Fawcett of which I at the time expected to hear nothing of further."[27]

He wrote to Polly from London on 19 April 1764, "If I can I will bring a copy of my historical letters [the *Narrative*] down with me, but am not sure. I believe not withstanding all my reluctance gainsaying my friends will prevail to have them in print soon after I am in Priest's orders, I have nobody that in any measure joins on my side to prevent their publication but Lady Dartmouth, and she seems to be giving ground and ready to yield the point. She has not yet read those I wrote to Mr. Haweis; when she has I expect she will be of the same mind as the rest. Mr. Brewer, though you know him to be cautious and prudent, is very warm for it. After all as you are the Heroine of the Tragedy it is but right you should have a share in the consultation."[28]

The prospect of finally entering the ministry moved him deeply. He told her the next week, "My heart is *something* though I dare not say *sufficiently* affected with the important prospect before me – to stand in a most public point of view, to take the charge of thousands, to answer the incessant demands of stated and occasional services – to *be* what I *preach*, and to *preach* what I *ought* – O what zeal, faith, patience, watchfulness, humility and courage will these things call for. My only hope is in the name and power of Jesus – may that precious name be as ointment poured forth to your soul and mine – may that power be triumphantly manifested in our weakness."[29]

On his return to Liverpool from being licensed at Buckden as a deacon, he was asked to preach for two of the clergymen who had signed his testimonials. His own comment on the sermon he preached in St. George's Church was:

"I hope I was enabled to speak the truth. Some were pleased, but many disgusted. I was thought too long, too loud, too much extempore. I conformed to their judgment, so far as I lawfully might, on the Sunday when I preached at the other church in the morning and at the Infirmary in the afternoon."[30]

On 21 May 1764 Newton left Liverpool and set up home in Olney, where he was to remain for the next sixteen years. The Bishop of Lincoln ordained him as priest on 17 June. On 21 June 1764 Newton wrote to Clunie saying, "On Thursday 28th, that is, this day sev'nnight, I propose to preach my first weekly lecture." [31] He began with John 4:38, *I sent you to reap that whereon ye bestowed no labour: other men laboured, and ye are entered into their labours.* A section of a later series of Olney lectures, on Romans 8:26-34, has recently been published as *The Searcher of Hearts*[32] by Christian Focus Publications, who will be publishing more of Newton's lectures, sermon notes and correspondence.

The Thorntons:

John Thornton was Governor of the Bank of England. His son, Henry, was a founder member of the British and Foreign Bible Society (formed in 1804), who met often with William Wilberforce (nephew of John's half-sister Hannah), James Stephen, Charles and Robert Grant, Henry Drummond and Zachary Macaulay at Lord Teignmouth's house on the corner of Clapham Common. Also included in their gatherings was John Venn, the vicar of Clapham and son of Newton's friend, Henry Venn of Huddersfield. A powerful group for moral reform and taking the initiative in Christian mission, they were later referred to as the Clapham Sect. From this group came the monthly journal, the *Christian Observer*, a Society for the Better Observance of Sunday, the Proclamation Society for Suppression of Vice, support for overseas missions and enormous efforts towards the abolition of slavery.

Henry Thornton's generosity matched his father's. Amongst others he helped was Patrick Brontë, father of the Brontë sisters Emily Jane, Anne and Charlotte. Brontë had left Ireland in 1802 with £7 to study at Cambridge University. During the course of these studies Henry Martyn, then the curate of Charles Simeon, wrote to Thornton about Brontë's needs. Thornton and Wilberforce agreed to sponsor him. Brontë was later appointed to the church in Haworth where William Grimshaw had worked so tirelessly, and had left his mark on the sounding board above the pulpit: *I determined not to know anything among you, save Jesus Christ, and him crucified* (1 Corinthians 2:2). *For me to live is Christ, and to die is gain* (Philippians 1:21). William Grimshaw A.B. Minister 1742."

William Cowper:
In Cowper's own account of his experience at Dr. Cotton's asylum, he describes picking up a Bible "for comfort and instruction" and reading Romans 3:25. "Immediately I received strength to believe it, and the full beams of the Sun of Righteousness shone upon me. I saw the sufficiency of the atonement he had made, my pardon sealed in his blood, and all the fullness and completeness of his justification. In a moment I believed, and received the gospel. Whatever my friend Madan had said to me, long before, revived in all its clearness, with demonstration of the Spirit and with power."[33]

He wrote his first hymn in response: *How blest thy creature is, O God.*[34] Verses 2 and 3 particularly describe his experience:

> Through all the storms that veil the skies,
> And frown on earthly things,
> The Sun of Righteousness he eyes,
> With healing on his wings.
>
> Struck by that light, the human heart,
> A barren soil no more,
> Sends the sweet smell of grace abroad,
> Where serpents lurk'd before.*

---

* Isaiah 35:7 [*Olney Hymns*]

When he left St. Albans, Cowper decided not to return to London. He looked for a quieter life in Huntingdon, where he took private lodgings in June 1765. He found a firm friend in William Unwin, son of the rector and a student at Cambridge. Cowper soon found himself very much at home with the Unwins, so much so in fact that he moved in with them and became "a sort of adopted son in this family".[35] Meanwhile a friend of Newton's, Dr. Conyers, was studying divinity at Cambridge and had learned from young William Unwin that his mother, Mary, was a devout Christian. He asked Newton to call in on her. A few days before Newton arrived, Mary's husband was thrown from his horse and died from a fractured skull. When Newton called he found the family in distress.

Mary Unwin and Cowper longed to leave Huntingdon. Cowper asked his aunt, Judith Madan, to pray for them to find a spiritual ministry somewhere, "that it may please the Good Shepherd to feed us in his own pasture".[36] He asked for his cousin Martin Madan's help in knowing where the gospel was preached. They were willing to go anywhere except London. Newton offered to help them find accommodation in Olney. When a house seemed to become available in Emberton, just outside Olney, Cowper cautiously wrote to his aunt in July 1767, reluctant to stop other enquiries in case this opportunity fell through, though confident that the Lord would provide something for them. He added, "Mr. Newton seems to have conceived a great desire to have us for neighbours, and I am sure we shall think ourselves highly favoured to be committed to the care of such a pastor. May we be enabled to hold him in double honour for his work's sake, according to the will of the great Shepherd of us all!"[37]

They were not able to obtain this house. Pressures were mounting for them in Huntingdon. Cowper wrote again to his aunt, "I am weary of this place.... I want to be with the Lord's people, having great need of the quickening intercourse and the communion of his saints.... The Lord seems to have filled the hearts of Mr. and Mrs. Newton with Christian tenderness and affection towards us, the number of the flock there is considerable, and they all dwell together as becomes brethren, in unity. So that the Lord seems to be drawing us out of this wilderness with one hand, and driving us out with the other."[38]

The next month, September 1767, he wrote to her from Olney, "It is fit I should acknowledge the goodness of the Lord in bringing me to this place, abounding with palm trees and wells of living water.

The Lord put it into my heart to desire to partake of his ordinances and to dwell with his people, and has graciously given me my heart's desire: nothing can exceed the kindness and hospitality with which we are received here by his dear servant Newton: and to be brought under the ministry of so wise and faithful a steward of His holy mysteries is a blessing for which I can never be sufficiently thankful. May our heavenly Father grant that our souls may thrive and flourish in some proportion to the abundant means of grace we enjoy: for the whole day is but one continued opportunity either of seeking Him, or conversing about the things of His kingdom."[39]

When Cowper first moved to Olney he stayed at the vicarage with the Newtons for almost five months before moving into his own accommodation at *Orchard Side*, now kept as the Cowper and Newton Museum, in the Market Square (many of Cowper's original possessions and some of Newton's can be seen there). Once when the annual fair outside proved too noisy for Cowper he sought refuge again in the vicarage, his overnight stay extending to fourteen months before he was willing to return home.

Newton's diary for 1767 has this entry for Thursday 3 December, the day of their evening lectures: "Acts 2:14, 18, Mr. Cooper's servant much affected."[40] Cowper wrote to tell his aunt that both of his servants had been brought to faith, adding that "the man servant, you may remember, is the same that attended me at St. Alban's. What various methods does the good Shepherd use, and how wonderful is he in many of those dispensations by which he brings his people within the sound of the gospel. We had no sooner taken possession of our own house, than I found myself called to lead the prayers of the family. A formidable undertaking you may imagine to a temper and spirit like mine. I trembled at the apprehension of it, and was so dreadfully harassed in the conflict I sustained upon this occasion in the first week, that my health was not a little affected by it. But there was no remedy, and I hope the Lord brought me to that point, to choose death rather than a retreat from duty. In my first attempt he was sensibly present with me, and has since favoured me with very perceptible assistance. My tears begin to wear off, I get rather more liberty of speech at last, if not of spirit, and have some hope that having opened my mouth he will never suffer it to be closed again, but rather give increase of utterance and zeal to serve him and never leave me till he has made the dumb to speak and the stammering tongue like the pen of a ready writer!"[41]

Cowper took an active part in the church life, participating in the prayer meetings and visiting the sick. He was a special encouragement to the lace makers who lived next door.

When his brother John was taken dangerously ill for the second time in six months, Cowper went again to be with him, hoping also to have the opportunity to share with him the faith which John had so long resisted. John was a minister but held very liberal views. William was delighted to find that John allowed him to pray with him. While he was there Newton wrote often to assure him of the whole church's support back in Olney, "Prayer is made both for him and for you among us publicly, and from house to house." He added what he said Mr. Philip Henry called "a word upon the wheels" for his encouragement: "Considering how much his best interest is laid upon your heart, the pleasure he expressed at your arrival, his willingness to hear your prayers for him, and the liberty you find to improve every moment of speaking, I am willing to hope, that you will be made a messenger of light and peace to his soul. The Lord's hand is not shortened that he cannot save. He can do great things in a small time, as you know from your own experience. In a moment, in the twinkling of an eye, he can command light to shine out of darkness. If he speaks, it is done.... One glimpse of the worth of the soul, the evil of sin, and the importance of eternity, will effect that which hath been in vain attempted by repeated arguments. I hope the Lord will be with your heart and mouth, and that he will afford you the *mollia tempora fandi!*[42] and direct your words to the heart. Perhaps now you may be heard when you touch upon your own most singular case, and declare the manner and the effects of the Lord's wonderful dealing with yourself, which, as it cannot be gainsayed, so neither can it be accounted for upon any other principles than those of the Scripture, respecting the power, grace and all-sufficiency of Jesus to save to the uttermost."[43]

Cowper himself wrestled in prayer for his brother.[44] He said to him, "You have many friends who love you, and are willing to do all they can to serve you; but it is not the lot of every sick man, how much soever he may be beloved, to have a friend that can pray for him." His brother replied, "That is true, and I hope God will have mercy on me." But that night, worn out with struggling for breath, he said, "Brother, I seem to be marked out for misery." Cowper writes,

"That moment I felt my heart enlarged, and such a persuasion of the love of God towards him was wrought in my soul, that I replied with confidence, and, as if I had the authority to say it, 'But that is not your case; you are marked out for mercy'."

In his next letter Newton spoke of the Great Physician, "to whom all cases are equally easy, and whose compassion is equal to his power. If he who does all things well sees it best, he can and he will restore him; if not, he is able to give *him* such a view of what is beyond the grave, as would make him desirous to depart, and to be with Christ; and make *you* perfectly willing to resign him. This is my prayer: – that he may find to live is Christ, and to die, gain; for this I commend him to Him who is the Way, the Truth, and the Life, who has overcome death, and him that has the power of death, and is exalted to save to the uttermost. That word Uttermost has an extensive meaning: it includes a conquest over all difficulties, and a supply of all that is necessary.... As to myself, my very heart sinks at the apprehension of sharp trials; the Lord has long dealt with a marvellous accommodation to my weakness in this respect; what supports me when I look forward to them is, a persuasion of his nearness, faithfulness, and all-sufficiency; but I know there is a great difference between viewing the battle at a distance, and being actively engaged in it."[45]

Cowper's sketch continues, "On Saturday the 10th of March, about three in the afternoon, he suddenly burst into tears, and said with a loud cry, 'Oh, forsake me not!' I went to his bed-side, when he grasped my hand, and presently, by his eyes and countenance, I found that he was in prayer." The nurse offered John hartshorn or lavender, "but he replied, 'None of these things will serve my purpose.' I said, 'But I know what would, my dear, don't I?' He answered, 'You do, brother.'

"Having continued some time silent, he said, 'Behold, I create new heavens and a new earth,' – then, after a pause, 'Ay, and he is able to do it too.'

"I left him for about an hour, fearing lest he should fatigue himself with talking, and because my surprise and joy were so great that I could hardly bear them. When I returned he threw his arms about my neck, and, leaning his head against mine, he said, 'Brother, if I live, you and I shall be more like one another than we have been. But whether I live or live not, all is well, and will be so; I know it will; I have felt that which I never felt before; and I am sure that God has visited me with this sickness to teach me what I was too proud to learn in health.... I have often studied these points, and studied them with great attention, but was blinded by prejudice; and, unless He, who alone is worthy to unloose the seals, had opened the book to me, I had been blinded still. Now they appear so plain, that though I am convinced no comment could ever have made me understand them, I wonder I did not see them before.'"

That evening John told his brother, "I have peace in myself... I have learned *that* in a moment, which I could not have learned by reading many books for many years... I should delight to see the people at Olney... I should rejoice in an hour's conversation with Mr. Newton, and, if I live, shall have much discourse with him upon these subjects."

Newton told Cowper that he would share the good news of his brother's conversion with the church at the next prayer meeting. "When we shall meet on Tuesday evening, I purpose to impart it to the people in a body, by reading your letter; my heart jumps at representing to myself, how they will look, how they will feel, how they will pray and give thanks, when they hear what God has wrought!"[46] His knowledge of both spiritual warfare and Cowper's disposition caused him to add a word of caution to him also, "You need not wonder if, upon this very affecting and important occasion, the enemy attempts his utmost to disturb you.... He knows how nearly you are concerned in these things, and therefore, so far as he is permitted, will cut you out trouble."

Cowper's brother died in the autumn of 1770. The loss took its emotional toll on him. He had been devastated by his mother's death in early life and every subsequent loss of a close friend or relative seemed to trigger off the same sense of despair and abandonment.

Newton's preface to the *Olney Hymns* explains how he sought to help his friend at this time: "A desire of promoting the faith and comfort of sincere Christians, though the principal, was not the only motive to this undertaking. It was likewise intended as a monument, to perpetuate the remembrance of an intimate and endeared friendship. With this pleasing view I entered upon my part, which would have been smaller than it is, and the book would have appeared much sooner, and in a very different form, if the wise, though mysterious, providence of GOD had not seen fit to cross my wishes. We had not proceeded far upon our proposed plan, before my dear friend was prevented, by a long and affecting indisposition, from affording me any farther assistance. My grief and disappointment were great; I hung my harp upon the willows, and for some time thought myself determined to proceed no farther without him."

Newton later continued writing a hymn a week alone, until there were well over three hundred. Some confusion arose in subsequent editions of the *Olney Hymns* as to how many Cowper had contributed, confirmed in a letter by him to Thomas Park, dated 3 January 1793,[47] "You asked me a long time since a question concerning the *Olney Hymns*, which I do not remember that I have ever answered. Those marked C. are mine, one excepted, which, though it bears that mark, was written by Mr. Newton. I have not the collection at present, and therefore cannot tell you which it is." T. S. Grimshawe,[48] consulting the original edition, put the number at sixty-seven, explaining that there had been a printer's error due to the Roman numeral 'C' having been misread as Cowper's initial. The reprint of the original attributes sixty-seven to Cowper.

A letter from Newton to his wife on 7 July 1772 comments on Cowper being "in the depths", but it was in the early hours of the morning of 2 January 1773 that Newton was called urgently to *Orchard Side* where Cowper was severely depressed, convinced he should take his life.

In his (incomplete) *Memoirs* of Cowper Newton states: "For nearly twelve years we were seldom separated for seven hours at a time, when we were awake, and at home: the first six I passed daily admiring and aiming to imitate him: during the second six, I walked pensively with him in the valley of the shadow of death."[49]

When Cowper continued to be seriously ill, Newton felt that he needed medication and corresponded with Cowper's aunt, Judith Madan. It was her son, Martin, who had given William spiritual help after his attempted suicide in 1763 before he was admitted to Dr. Cotton's asylum. She replied:

"I cannot conclude it *entirely* a spiritual cause, as I well know the state of the *blood*, or *weakness* of the *nerves*, will occasion gloom over the gayest and *brightest scenes* of life (and *such* I take *those* of religion to be; if anything can be taken that may correct the *blood* and *strengthen* the *nerves* I entirely agree Sir with you, (as I think I mentioned in my former letter) that the name of *Dr. C[otton]* and any application to him, should *be a secret.*"[50]

Newton's own feelings on possible causes of doubts and depression were already well established before he met Cowper. While he felt the lace makers' low spirits were due to being cooped up indoors all day without fresh air or exercise, he was perceptive of other possible causes. Writing to Hannah Wilberforce in 1764 of the possibility of overcharging oneself with guilt he said, "Some things which abate the comfort and alacrity of our Christian profession are rather impediments than properly sinful, and will not be imputed to us by him who knows our frame, and remembers that we are but dust. Thus, to have an infirm memory, to be subject to disordered, irregular, or low spirits, are faults of the constitution, in which the will has no share, though they are all burdensome and oppressive, and sometimes needlessly so by our charging ourselves with guilt on their account. The same may be observed of the unspeakable and fierce suggestions of Satan, with which some people are pestered, but which shall be laid to him from whom they proceed, and not to them who are troubled and terrified, because they are forced to feel them."[51]

Newton continued to spend time with Cowper every day that he was in Olney. Mary Newton and Cowper enjoyed each other's company. She was very concerned for him and he delighted in amusing her. At Olney she adopted the term of endearment "Sir" Cowper, in keeping with the villagers' respect for him. She wrote to John from Kent, "thank you and dear Mrs. Unwin for your prayers, dear Sir Cowper for his love. I love and thank him for all his prayers and kindness to me. I soon lost my headache."[52]

When the Newtons moved to London Cowper wrote to Mary, sometimes in verse. She sent him gifts of fish whenever she could. He understood her reluctance for letter writing and took some of the pressure off her:

"Dear Madam
When I write to Mr. Newton, he answers me by letter; when I write to you, you answer me in fish. I return you many thanks for the mackerel and lobster. They assured me in terms as intelligible as pen and ink could have spoken, that you still remember *Orchard Side*; and though they never spoke in their lives, and it was still less to be expected from them that they should speak, being dead, they gave us an assurance of your affection that corresponds exactly with that

which Mr. Newton expresses towards us in all his letters."[53]

But he felt their absence from Olney very deeply:

"The vicarage-house became a melancholy object as soon as Mr. Newton had left it; when you left it, it became more melancholy: now it is actually occupied by another family, even I cannot look at it without being shocked. As I walked in the garden this evening, I saw the smoke issue from the study chimney, and said to myself, That used to be a sign that Mr. Newton was there; but it is so no longer."[54]

Before leaving Olney Newton persuaded Cowper to receive a friend of his, William Bull, the Independent minister from the nearby village of Newport Pagnell. It proved a good move. Cowper enjoyed the company of Bull, who dined with him at least once a fortnight.

He described Bull to Mary Unwin's son William, "A Dissenter, but a liberal one; a man of letters and of genius; a master of a fine imagination, or rather not master of it – an imagination which, when he finds himself in the company he loves and can confide in, runs away with him into such fields of speculation as amuse and enliven every other imagination that has the happiness to be of the party. At other times he has a tender and delicate sort of melancholy in his disposition, not less agreeable in its way. No men are better qualified for companions in such a world as this than men of such a temperament. Every scene of life has two sides, – a dark and a bright one; and the mind that has an equal mixture of melancholy and vivacity is best of all qualified for the contemplation of either. He can be lively without levity, and pensive without dejection. Such a man is Mr. Bull. But he smokes tobacco! Nothing is perfect. *Nihil est ab omni parte beatum.*"[55]

When Bull absent-mindedly left his tobacco box at Cowper's one day, he received it back with the following verses in praise of the supposed nymph of the river where his Orinoco tobacco grew:

> So may thy votaries increase
> And fumigation never cease.
> May Newton with renew'd delights
> Perform thine odoriferous rites,
> While clouds of incense half divine
> Involve thy disappearing shrine,
> And so may smoke-inhaling Bull
> Be always filling, never full.[56]

Cowper's summer house, where he wrote, can still be seen at *Orchard Side*, with Newton's vicarage and the steeple of St. Peter and St. Paul in the background.

Cowper kept up a correspondence with Newton, "this scribbling employment"[57], which covers a wide range of topics, from world affairs to the escape of his pet hares. One letter with the local news begins,

"MY VERY DEAR FRIEND,

I am going to send, what when you have read, you may scratch your head, and say, I suppose there's nobody knows, whether what I have got, be verse or not .... For Mr. Scott we have seen him not, except as he pass'd, in a wonderful haste, to see a friend in Silver End..."

The letter is entirely in verse concluding, "from your humble me – W. C.

P.S. – When I concluded, doubtless you did not think me right, as well you might, in saying what I said of Scott; and then it was true, but now it is due, to him to note, that since I wrote, himself and he has visited we."[58]

In some of his letters to Newton Cowper described his feelings of melancholy: "In such a situation of mind, encompassed by the midnight of absolute despair, and a thousand times filled with unspeakable horror, I first commenced as an author. Distress drove me to it, and the impossibility of subsisting without some employment still recommends it. I am not, indeed, so perfectly hopeless as I was; but I am equally in need of an occupation, being often as much, and sometimes even more, worried than ever."[59]

"When January returns, you have your feelings concerning me, and such as prove the faithfulness of your friendship. I have mine also concerning myself, but they are of a cast different from yours. Yours have a mixture of sympathy and tender solicitude, which makes them, perhaps, not altogether unpleasant. Mine, on the contrary, are of an unmixed nature, and consist, simply and merely, of the most alarming apprehensions. Twice has that month returned upon me, accompanied by such horrors as I have no reason to suppose ever made part of the experience of any other man. I accordingly look forward to it, and meet it, with a dread not to be imagined. I number the nights as they pass, and in the morning bless myself that another night is gone, and no harm has happened. This may argue, perhaps, some imbecility of mind, and no small degree of it; but it is natural, I believe, and so natural as to be necessary and unavoidable. I know that God is not governed by secondary causes, in any of his operations, and that, on the contrary, they are all so many agents in his hand, which strike only when he bids them. I know consequently that one month is as dangerous to me as another, and that, in the middle of summer, at noonday, and in the clear sunshine, I am in reality, unless guarded by him, as much exposed as when fast asleep at midnight, and in midwinter. But we are not always the wiser for our knowledge, and I can no more avail myself of mine, than if it were in the head of another man, and not in my own. I have heard of bodily aches and ails, that have been particularly troublesome when the season returned in which the hurt that occasioned them was received. The mind, I believe (with my own, however I am sure it is so) is liable to similar periodical affection. But February is come, my terror is passed, and some shades of the gloom that attended his presence have past with him. I look forward with a little cheerfulness to the buds and the leaves that will soon appear, and say to myself, till they turn yellow I will make myself easy. The year will go round, and January will approach. I shall tremble again, and I know it; but in the meantime I will be as comfortable as I can. "[60]

Cowper died on 25 April 1800. Preaching a funeral sermon for him a few days later, Newton is recorded as having said, "I don't know a person upon earth I consult upon a text of scripture or any point of conscience so much to my satisfaction as Mr. Cowper. He could give comfort though he could not receive any himself."[61] Newton took his text from Exodus 3:2-3, *And the angel of the LORD appeared unto him in a flame of fire out of the midst of a bush: and he looked, and behold, the bush burned with fire and the bush was not consumed. And Moses said, I will now turn aside and see this great sight, why the bush is not burnt.*

"I know of no text in the whole book of God's Word more suited to the case of my dear friend than that I have read. He was indeed a bush in flames for 27 years but he was not consumed. And why? Because the Lord was there.

"The last sermon he ever heard preached was on New Year's Day 1773. He drank tea with me in the afternoon. The next morning a violent storm overtook him which caused a very great shyness. I used to visit him often but no argument could prevail with him to come and see me. He used to point with his finger to the church and say: you know the comfort I have had there and how I have seen the glory of the Lord in His House and until I can go there I'll not go anywhere else. He was one of those who came out of great tribulation. He suffered much here for twenty-seven years, but eternity is long enough to make amends for all. For what is all he endured in this life, when compared with the rest which remaineth for the children of God."

The last hymn that Cowper composed for the *Olney Hymns* was *God moves in a mysterious way*.[62] It was written on the eve of his sudden onslaught of oppression in January 1773. It seems he had a premonition of the attack while walking alone in the fields and composed this hymn.

> *Light shining out of darkness*
>
> God moves in a mysterious way
> His wonders to perform;
> He plants his footsteps in the sea,
> And rides upon the storm.
>
> Deep in unfathomable mines
> Of never-failing skill,
> He treasures up his bright designs,
> And works his sovereign will.
>
> Ye fearful saints, fresh courage take,
> The clouds ye so much dread
> Are big with mercy, and shall break
> In blessings on your head.
>
> Judge not the Lord by feeble sense,
> But trust him for his grace:
> Behind a frowning providence
> He hides a smiling face.
>
> His purposes will ripen fast,
> Unfolding every hour;
> The bud may have a bitter taste,
> But sweet will be the flower.

Blind unbelief is sure to err,*
And scan his work in vain:
God is his own interpreter,
And he will make it plain.

Samuel Greatheed, preaching a Funeral Sermon in memory of Cowper to "a numerous congregation of different denominations" at the Independent Meeting House in Olney on 18 May 1800, referred to this hymn as being "so expressive of that faith and hope which he retained as long as he possessed himself". He preached from the text Isaiah 55:8-9, *For my thoughts are not your thoughts, neither are your ways my ways, saith the Lord. For as the heavens are higher than the earth, so are my ways higher than your ways, and my thoughts than your thoughts.*[63]

The curacy of Olney
Newton sought fellowship and support from his friends in caring for his parishioners. He invited George Whitefield to come and preach and received this reply:

"Rev. and dear Sir
With great pleasure I this day read your kind letter. The contents gladdened my heart. Blessed be God, not only for calling you to a saving knowledge of Himself, but sending you forth also to proclaim the Redeemer's unsearchable riches amongst poor sinners. 'God,' says Dr. Goodwin, 'had but one Son, and he made a minister of him.' Gladly shall I come whenever bodily strength will allow to join my testimony with yours in Olney pulpit, that God is love. As yet I have not recovered from the fatigues of my American expedition. My shattered bark is scarce worth docking any more. But I would fain wear, and not rust out...."[64]

Newton wrote to Clunie, "Tell dear Mr. Brewer that I beg one book out of his study towards furnishing my new den. His name must be in it, and I leave the choice entirely to him: I make the same request to you and to Mr. West, whatever you please to pitch upon; for I doubt not but you will, without my telling you, give the preference to those books that can say something to me about Jesus, or give me some direction towards stirring me up to faith and communion with him."[65]

* John 13:7 [*Olney Hymns*]

In addition to the church services, there were other meetings. At the beginning of 1765 he noted in his diary, "We have a fixed little company who come to my house on sabbath evening after tea. We spend an hour or more in prayer and singing, and part between 6 and 7."[66]

While the number of hearers in the church grew, it was really the growth of heart knowledge that he was after, taking unusual steps to promote this. To Clunie he wrote, "The prayer meeting I lately set up on Tuesday evenings is likely to thrive and be comfortable. Our number is about 40. We might easily enlarge it; but I choose to have none but such as I hope are downright in earnest; however it increases every time."[67]

One Sunday he recorded, "In the evening we had a full house. I have lately sent tickets to those who I hope are serious, to exclude some who only come to look about them. Upon these occasions I have reckoned about 70 persons of both sexes, of whom I have good hope the Lord has touched their hearts."[68]

He started a prayer meeting on Tuesday evenings and a lecture on Thursday evenings. The congregation also began meeting at 6 o'clock on Sunday mornings, "to pray for their poor minister and for a blessing on the ordinances."[69]

When the need arose, they held special prayer meetings. "Since we heard of the commencement of the hostilities in America, we have had a prayer meeting extraordinary, on a national account. It is held on Tuesday morning, weekly, at five o'clock, and is well attended. We are not politicians at [Olney]; but we wish to be found among those described, Ezekiel 9:4 [*And the* LORD *said unto him, Go through the midst of the city, through the midst of Jerusalem, and set a mark upon the foreheads of the men that sigh and that cry for all the abominations that be done in the midst thereof*]. We pray for the restoration of peace and a blessing upon our public counsels."[70] When it began, this meeting had an attendance of between 150 and 200.

There were a number of prayer meetings, including one in Molly Mole's house (the Mole-Hill, Newton called it). When the Sunday afternoon prayer meeting moved to Lord Dartmouth's Great House next to the church in 1769, Newton and Cowper both wrote a hymn (see next page) for the occasion. Cowper's became well known.[71]

To know how Cowper's hymn came to be written is very moving, seeing the reassurance and encouragement being given at a time of a

William Cowper
On Opening a Place for Social Prayer

John Newton
Another

JESUS, where'er thy people meet,
There they behold thy mercy-seat;
Where'er they seek thee thou art found,
And ev'ry place is hallowed ground.

For thou, within no walls confined,
Inhabitest the humble mind;
Such ever bring thee, where they come,
And going, take thee to their home.

Dear Shepherd of thy chosen few!
Thy former mercies here renew;
Here, to our waiting hearts, proclaim
The sweetness of thy saving name.

Here may we prove the power of prayer,
To strengthen faith, and sweeten care;
To teach our faint desires to rise,
And bring all heav'n before our eyes.

Behold! at thy commanding word,
We stretch the curtain and the cord (a);
Come thou, and fill this wider space,
And help us with a large increase.

LORD, we are few, but thou art near;
Nor short thine arm, nor deaf thine ear;
Oh rend the heav'ns, come quickly down,
And make a thousand hearts thine own!

(a) Isaiah 54:2
Olney Hymns, Book 2, Hymn 44

O LORD, our languid souls inspire,
For here, we trust, thou art!
Send down a coal of heav'nly fire,
To warm each waiting heart.

Dear Shepherd of thy people, hear,
Thy presence now display;
As thou hast giv'n a place for prayer,
So give us hearts to pray.

Show us some token of thy love,
Our fainting hope to raise;
And pour thy blessings from above,
That we may render praise.

Within these walls let holy peace,
And love, and concord dwell;
Here give the troubled conscience ease,
The wounded spirit heal.

The feeling heart, the melting eye,
The humble mind bestow;
And shine upon us from on high,
To make our graces grow!

May we in faith receive thy word,
In faith present our prayers;
And, in the presence of our LORD,
Unbosom all our cares.

And may the gospel's joyful sound
Enforced by mighty grace,
Awaken many sinners round,
To come and fill the place.

Olney Hymns, Book 2, Hymn 43

break with familiar surroundings, looking to the future. Who can tell what answers came in response to this little prayer meeting, their simple faith and obedience, the plea of the last line of Cowper's hymn, *And make a thousand hearts thine own*? How many thousands since, throughout the world, have gained fresh hope and encouragement or perhaps their first spiritual longings through the words of Cowper's and Newton's hymns written for the spiritual encouragement of the

people of this little market town? Hymns such as *Amazing grace;
Approach, my soul, the mercy seat; Begone unbelief; Be still my heart,
these anxious cares; Glorious things of thee are spoken; God moves
in a mysterious way; Hark, my soul! it is the Lord; How sweet the
name of Jesus sounds; Let us love and sing and wonder; Oh! for a
closer walk with God; Sometimes a light surprises; There is a fountain
filled with blood; What various hindrances we meet; Why should I
fear the darkest hour?*

Newton looked for instruction in everything he saw. Josiah Bull,
in *John Newton of Olney*, quotes from Newton's diary for 1776:

"July 30th. Tonight I attended an eclipse of the moon. How great,
O Lord, are Thy works! With what punctuality do the heavenly bodies
fulfil their courses and observe the seasons to a moment! All things
obey Thee but fallen angels and fallen man. My thoughts would have
taken a serious turn, but I was not alone. I thought, my Lord, of
Thine eclipse. The horrible darkness which overwhelmed Thy mind
when Thou saidst, 'Why hast Thou forsaken Me?' Ah, sin was the
cause – my sins – yet I do not hate sin nor loathe myself as I ought."

He expressed these thoughts as a hymn.[72]

On the eclipse of the moon	July 30, 1776.
The moon in silver glory shone,	Thy people's guilt, a heavy load!
And not a cloud in sight;	(When standing in their room)
When suddenly a shade begun	Deprived thee of the light of GOD,
To intercept her light.	And filled thy soul with gloom.
How fast across her orb it spread,	How punctually eclipses move,
How fast her light withdrew!	Obedient to thy will!
A circle, tinged with languid red,	Thus shall thy faithfulness and love,
Was all appeared in view.	Thy promises fulfil.
While many with unmeaning eye	Dark, like the moon without the sun,
Gaze on thy works in vain;	I mourn thine absence, LORD!
Assist me, LORD, that I may try	For light or comfort have I none,
Instruction to obtain.	But what thy beams afford.
Fain would my thankful heart and lips	But lo! the hour draws near apace,
Unite in praise to thee;	When changes shall be o'er;
And meditate on thy eclipse,	Then shall I see thee face to face,
In sad Gethsemane.	And be eclipsed no more.

Many of Newton's hymns were expositions of scripture passages. So for 1 Kings 17:6, *Elijah fed by the ravens*:[73]

Nor is it a singular case,	Thus Satan, that raven unclean,
The wonder is often renewed;	Who croaks in the ears of the saints;
And many can say, to his praise,	Compelled by a power unseen,
He sends them by ravens their food:	Administers oft to their wants:
Thus worldlings, though ravens indeed,	God teaches them how to find food
Though greedy and selfish their mind,	From all the temptations they feel;
If God has a servant to feed,	This raven, who thirsts for my blood,
Against their own wills can be kind.	Has helped me to many a meal.

In times of hardship and difficulty, Newton sought to learn something from them. He wrote to Joshua Symonds,[74] "I think I may say without vanity that if you had heard me preach last Sunday in the afternoon, you would have been edified. You have seemed to think I have such a facility in speaking, that I am in no danger of appearing to any considerable disadvantage in the pulpit. I hope I never seriously thought so myself, but the Lord only knows the deceitfulness of my heart, and how prone I am to give way to the temptations of Satan, who would *willingly* persuade me to pride and presumption. I hope it was in mercy, that he was pleased at the time I have mentioned to give both me and the people a proof how little I can do without him. I found myself very much straightened before I had got to the middle of my sermon, and was at length brought to a full stop. I had only power to make a public confession of my weakness, and that I was utterly unable to proceed. The Lord gave me however at the same time to hope that it might be good for me and for my people that I should be thus humbled, so that I was not much disconcerted, nor has it given me a moment's uneasiness ever since. Only I hope it will be an abiding *memento* to me to be afraid of leaning to my own understanding, and make me go up the pulpit steps for the future, with a deeper conviction both of my unworthiness and my inability. When I had prayed and given out a hymn, I spoke for a few minutes and told the people what I thought might be the meaning of such a dispensation, namely, that I might not think too highly of myself, and that they might not think too highly of me, as if I have anything of my own, and that both they and I might be encouraged to hope that if I had more liberty at any time, it was not because I had words at will, but because the Lord was graciously pleased to afford me his promised assistance. As to myself I had no right to complain, having been conscious of so much deadness and evil in my heart, and such a disparity between what I seemed in the pulpit and what I felt myself at other times, that I have often wondered my mouth has not been stopped before. O my friend we often pray that the Lord would make us sensible that we are nothing and can do nothing of ourselves and keep us in a humble and dependent spirit, let us not then be grieved if he is pleased to answer our prayers, though he does it by such methods as are not pleasing to flesh and blood. I hope I can thank him for what has happened. And I see he dealt gently with me in permitting it to be at home. It might have been at Everton, or some of the places where he has opened me a door abroad. And perhaps my foolish heart would have made a harder struggle, to have had my poverty exposed amongst strangers. Here I had many to pray for me, and many more to pity me, and I hardly think there was a single person in the congregation disposed to triumph over me. We had a comfortable prayer meeting that evening, another on Tuesday, and last night the Lord permitted me to preach with my usual liberty. Help me to praise him."

Next to his sermon notes on Genesis 11:1, which was probably the sermon he described to Joshua Symonds, Newton wrote, "Almost silenced in the delivery of this discourse and did not finish the subject."[75]

In Liverpool, Olney and London, Newton got the local ministers together for their mutual encouragement. "It is my judgment," he wrote from Liverpool, "that Societies formed on this view will, by divine blessing, be abundantly useful in promoting a spiritual and vital Godliness. I pray that I may always see it my duty to attempt the forming of such or frequenting them when I have opportunity to do so."[76]

Within a month of being ordained priest at Olney he wrote to Clunie, "I hope to have a meeting here of six or seven clergymen who preach the gospel in this and the adjoining counties, on the first Thursday in August. I shall be sorry if your business will not permit you to join us. If you cannot come, help us with your prayers, that the Lord may bless us together, and enable us happily to enter upon an association, which we propose to keep up monthly, sometimes at one place, sometimes at another, to strengthen each other's hands, and refresh the people by a variety and communication of gifts and counsels."[77]

He sometimes closed down his own church meetings in order to go and hear the Independents or the Baptists. He explained, "I am glad of such opportunities at times, to discountenance bigotry and party spirit, and to set our dissenting brethren an example, which I think ought to be our practice towards all who love the Lord Jesus Christ and preach the gospel without respect to forms or denominations."[78]

Cowper wrote to his aunt in 1768, "We have had a Holiday Week at Olney. The Association of Baptist Ministers met here on Wednesday. We had three sermons from them that day, and one on Thursday, besides Mr. Newton's in the evening. One of the preachers was Mr. Booth, who has lately published an excellent work called *The Reign of Grace*.... It was a comfortable sight to see gospel ministers together. Most of them either preached or prayed, and all that did so approved themselves sound in the Word and Doctrine, whence all good presumption arises in favour of the rest. I should be glad if the partition wall between Xtians of different Denominations would every where fall down flat as it has done at Olney. The Dissenters here, most of them at least who are serious, forget that our Meeting House has a steeple to it, and we that theirs has none. This shall be the case universally, may the Lord hasten it in his time!"[79]

Incidentally, Polly didn't share Newton's enjoyment of the Baptists. She wrote to him from Kent, "I know you will not scold me now I am so far off, and you will forget it by the time I come home, but I would much rather be a Methodist than a Baptist."[80] He teased her over this, writing back, "Yesterday was a meeting of Baptist ministers. Brother Thompson, a young man newly sent out, opened it with an excellent prayer and (which I hope will not displease you) he prayed warmly for me." With some reassurance, perhaps, he described the Brother who concluded the meeting in prayer, "He likewise prayed for a minister in the town, to whom he wished much comfort and prosperity in his work, though, as he said, we could not see exactly eye to eye in all things."[81]

A couple of weeks later he told her, "Last post brought me an affecting letter from Mr. Hall. Baptist as he is, I am sure you will like it." The same day, he preached in Olney from Galatians 4:19, with the hymn, *What strange contradictions meet in ministers' employ*, (used on the contents page of this book) which was presumably prompted by his reflections on the Baptist Association Meeting he had just attended. [82]

On 7 August 1776 Newton attended the ordination of John Sutcliff, the new pastor of the Baptist church in Olney. That year there were forty-six ministers at the Baptist Association Meeting, including Sutcliff, Andrew Fuller of Kettering, John Ryland senior and John Ryland junior, both of Northampton. The public meetings were held in the orchard between Cowper's and Newton's houses, for several hundred people attended. Some of the ministers stayed over to hear Newton preach from Zechariah 2:10 on the last evening. In fact, some had stayed with him at the vicarage throughout the conference. From this group of men was to come Sutcliff's call to prayer once a month for the spread of the gospel, followed by William Carey's challenge to expect great things from God, attempt great things for God, leading to the foundation of the Baptist Missionary Society in 1792, with Fuller as its secretary. Both Sutcliff and Fuller had modified their personal views considerably by this time, from high-Calvinism to a missionary concern. It is thought likely that Newton had a significant influence in this. Fuller continued as secretary of the BMS until his death in 1815. Robert Hall said of Fuller, that he had "laid the world under lasting obligations."[83] The birth of the BMS was followed by the London Missionary Society, the Church Missionary Society and the British and Foreign Bible Society, Newton having some involvement with each of these.

William Bull
Newton's association with dissenter William Bull was a great comfort to them both. They were able to share the burdens and joys of ministry together freely, often exchanging sermon outlines, though Newton made Bull promise he would not divulge any secrets before the day of his preaching.

In 1788 he wrote to him, "At present it is January with me, both within and without. The outward sun shines and looks pleasant, but his beams are faint, and too feeble to dissolve the frost. So it is in my heart. I have many bright and pleasant beams of truth in my view, but cold predominates in my frost-bound spirit, and they have but little power to warm me. I could tell a stranger something about Jesus that would perhaps astonish him: such a glorious person, such wonderful love, such humiliation, such a death. And then, what He is now in Himself, and what He is to His people. What a Sun! what a Shield! what a Root! what a Life! what a Friend! My tongue could

run on upon these subjects sometimes; and could my heart keep pace
with it, I should be the happiest fellow in the country. Stupid creature,
to know these things so well, and yet be no more affected with them!
Indeed, I have reason to be upon ill terms with myself. It is strange
that pride should ever find anything in my experience to feed upon;
but this completes my character for folly, vileness, and inconsistence,
that I am not only poor but proud; and, though I am convinced I am
a very wretch, as nothing before the Lord, I am prone to go forth
among my fellow-creatures as though I were wise and good.

"You wonder what I am doing, and well you may. I am sure you
would, if you lived with me. Too much of my time passes in busy
idleness, too much in waking dreams. I aim at something, but
hindrances from within and without make it difficult for me to
accomplish anything. I dare not say I am absolutely idle, or that I
wilfully waste my time; but I have seldom one hour free from
interruption. Letters come that must be answered, visitants that must
be received, business that must be attended to. I have a good many
sheep and lambs to look after, sick and afflicted souls dear to the
Lord; and therefore, whatever stands still, these must not be neglected.
Amongst these various avocations night comes before I am ready for
noon, and the week closes when, according to the state of my business,
it should not be more than Tuesday. O precious irrecoverable time!
O that I had more wisdom in redeeming and improving thee! Pray
for me that the Lord may teach me to serve Him better."[84]

In November 1765 Lord Dartmouth called him to London. Newton wrote
home to his wife, "My Lord is the prime manager in Georgia. Mr.
Whitefield's orphan-house is to be converted into a seminary, college
or university; and Mr. N. is desired to be the president thereof, with
the annexed living of Savannah, the chief town. My love to Olney
and your hatred of the water are the chief reasons which moved me
to say I would not accept it, otherwise it is a most important service."[85]

Children's meetings
Newton began meetings for the children on a Thursday afternoon.
One of his notebooks commences:[86]

"Thursday 17 January [1765]. Held my first meeting with the
children at the Great House. Took their names down, forty-nine boys
and forty girls. Called one of them out to read Matt. 19:13-15 from

whence I took occasion to speak of the condescension and love of the Lord Jesus, his gracious attention even to young children, having been once (for our sakes) an infant and a child himself."

He handed out catechisms and explained a few of the questions and answers at the beginning. "Cautioned them against those proofs of depravity, which too soon appear in children, disobedience, lying, bad words, petty thefts, breach of the Sabbath etc."

He proposed prizes for the best boy and girl by Whitsuntide. "Amongst other things I directed them to attend constantly at church. Accordingly the chief part of them came at the lecture and seated themselves before the pulpit in the middle aisle. It was a pleasing and affecting sight, and moved me to pray for them before the congregation."

The following Thursday more children came and they had to move across into the chancel. He had one of them read Matthew 27:29-31. "From this passage I spoke to them:

"1) of the love of Jesus in submitting to all these indignities for our sakes.

"2) the wickedness of man, in treating him who did nothing but good in this manner. I made them observe progress in wickedness. These ungodly men who crucified Christ, were once children – began with little things, and so grew hardened as they grew old – from hence I showed them,

"3) the necessity of praying to God to keep us, for if he should leave us to ourselves, we know not what we may come to.

"Afterwards explained a little of the catechism, and proposed the Lord's prayer and six questions to be learnt by heart against next meeting. Then to be repeated by one boy and girl (to be called by lot) which, if they did well, they should have 6 pence each. I began this meeting with prayer with which several seemed affected. I commended their attendance at church and promised prayer books to such as could read well. Little donatives of this kind will, I hope, be a means of spurring them up to diligence in learning. I have a considerable number of the Dissenters' children, and it is partly to avoid discouraging them, that I begin with Mason's *Catechism*." [*A Little Catechism, with Little Verses and Little Sayings, for Little Children*, by John Mason, rector, in the 17th century, in the village of Water Stratford, not far from Olney.][87]

His next week's entry has, "I have since found that some of my young folks were displeased, because two of the rewards fell upon the children of Dissenters. This will give me an occasion next time to show them the nature and evil of party spirit, which begins to show itself very early, even in children.... The readiness and good behaviour of most, with the particular attention and seriousness of some, encourages me to hope that the Lord will favour me with some usefulness, from this attempt."

Next week he had one of them read the parable of the Good Samaritan, "which I explained to them with a reference to their little prejudices about Church and Meeting." Perhaps the following hymn was written specially for this occasion:[88]

The good Samaritan
Luke 10:33-35

How kind the good Samaritan,
To him who fell among the thieves!
Thus Jesus pities fallen man,
And heals the wounds the soul receives.

Oh! I remember well the day,
When sorely wounded, nearly slain;
Like that poor man I bleeding lay,
And groaned for help, but groaned in vain.

Men saw me in this helpless case,
And passed without compassion by;
Each neighbour turned away his face,
Unmoved by my mournful cry.

But he whose name had been my scorn,
(As Jews Samaritans despise)
Came, when he saw me thus forlorn,
With love and pity in his eyes.

Gently he raised me from the ground,
Pressed me to lean upon his arm;
And into ev'ry gaping wound,
He poured his own all-healing balm.

Unto his church my steps he led,
The house prepared for sinners lost;
Gave charge I should be clothed and fed,
And took upon him all the cost.

Thus saved from death, from want secured,
I wait till he again shall come,
(When I shall be completely cured)
And take me to his heav'nly home.

There through eternal boundless days,
When nature's wheel no longer rolls;
How shall I love, adore and praise,
This good Samaritan to souls!

Olney Hymns, Book 1, Hymn 99

By 14 February, Mr. Hull had come to assist in teaching them to sing. "They sung two hymns very prettily for beginners. Thus the promise fulfilled. Praise to God from the mouths of children. Lord, enable them to praise thee from the heart." He was encouraged by a "remarkable alteration" in one of the boys.

His records for the first week of March show that he taught them about Joseph from Genesis 37, speaking for about twenty minutes, then went on to the catechism. They began and ended the meeting with a hymn. By the end of the month the numbers had risen to 219. Of these he thought he could pick out "at least two thirds that are orderly and teachable". He explained Genesis 41 but added, "I often find myself under remarkable dullness and unwillingness to this service when the day returns but I endeavour to press on against it, and for the most part when I get among them, I find it pleasant. Lord, do thou strengthen my hands, and water my poor endeavours, and grant that some of these little ones may look back with thankfulness to thee for these opportunities, when I am laid low in the dust."

One of his hymns from Genesis draws lessons from the occasion when Joseph made himself known to his brothers, summoned, trembling with fear, into his presence. Newton's desire to search for Christ in the Scriptures is shown clearly in this extract (verses 4-6):[89]

Joseph made known to his Brethren
Genesis 45:3,4

Thus dragged by my conscience, I came,
And laden with guilt, to the Lord;
Surrounded with terror and shame,
Unable to utter a word.

At first he looked stern and severe,
What anguish then pierced my heart!
Expecting each moment to hear
The sentence, "Thou cursed, depart!"

But oh! what surprise when he spoke,
While tenderness beamed in his face;
My heart then to pieces was broke,
O'erwhelmed and confounded by grace:
"Poor sinner, I know thee full well,
By thee I was sold and was slain;
But I died to redeem thee from hell,
And raise thee in glory to reign.

I am Jesus, whom thou hast blasphemed,
And crucified often afresh;
But let me henceforth be esteemed,
Thy brother, thy bone, and thy flesh:
My pardon I freely bestow,
Thy wants I will fully supply;
I'll guide thee and guard thee below,
And soon will remove thee on high.

Olney Hymns, Book 1, Hymn 12

By 11th April there were twenty children who could say the whole catechism. The attendance list increased to 233, "of whom I suppose I have 200 that will constantly attend."

Then followed a gap in time, with the next entry, "I went to London in May, returned in June, met the children but twice afterwards, till we were interrupted by the building of a new gallery in the church, and before that was finished smallpox came into the town, which continued till February or March. These and other hindrances have caused a long interruption – but now (3 July 1766) by the grace of God I propose to begin again. But I see cause to make some alteration in my plan and particularly not to make a point of having a great number, but only such as I have good hope will behave well and orderly, for there was much rudeness amongst the boys, and too many came, not with a view to instruction, but for the sake of money and books. O Lord, I am both unskilful and unfaithful; do thou graciously pardon all my mistakes and teach me to do better – Amen."

By 1798, Newton was passing on advice at the Eclectic Society to Cecil, who was uncertain how to manage the children during his own services:[90]

Question: What may be done towards the interests of the children of a congregation?

Cecil: I collected mine on benches, but they tattled and were troublesome...

Newton: What is agreeable to children is agreeable to children six feet high. Particularly the Apostle's method among children – *I determined to know nothing amongst you save Jesus Christ and him crucified.* Talk to children about God abstractly, and it is all in vain. But they can think on One who is now in heaven, though once a child. Go through the life of Christ, and all the historical parts of Scripture.

Thomas Scott

Scott's son, John, relates how his father came to hear Newton for the first time when the apothecary of Olney came to see his brother, owner of the house where Scott was boarding.[91] He quotes from *Force of Truth*. "He gave Mr. N. full credit for blameless and benevolent conduct, and for diligence as a minister: but he was 'a methodist and an enthusiast to a very high degree. I cannot,' said the apothecary, 'tell what judgment to form of his preaching; it is like nothing I ever heard: I wish you would come and hear him, and give me your opinion. He preaches on a Thursday evening: come and dine with me and we will go to church together.' This was accordingly settled and executed. I sat fronting the pulpit, and verily thought that Mr. N. looked full on me when he came into the desk: and, when he named his text, to my great astonishment it was this, *Then Saul, (who also is called Paul,) filled with the Holy Ghost, set his eyes on him, and said, O full of all subtlety and all mischief, thou child of the devil, thou enemy of all righteousness, wilt thou not cease to pervert the right ways of the Lord?* (Acts 13:9,10) As I knew that he preached *extempore*, I took it for granted that he had chosen the text purposely on my account. He observed, indeed, that ministers in the present day, not being under any immediate or infallible influence of the Holy Spirit, ought not to imitate the decided and severe language of the apostle; and he then undertook to show what were the right ways of the Lord, and to point out the wickedness and danger of persisting in endeavours to prevent or oppose them. But I thought his doctrine abstruse, imaginative and irrational; and his manner uncouth; and the impression, that, though Elimas was named, I was intended, abode with me for a long time: nor was it wholly effaced till I discovered, some years afterwards, that he was regularly expounding the Acts of the Apostles, and that this passage came in course that evening; and that, in fact, he neither saw nor thought of me."

Newton saw the potential in Scott and became concerned when he seemed to be going down with a severe fever. "He is but just entering upon a scene of great usefulness, and I am willing to hope there is much for him yet to do. But I know the Lord has no need of sinful man, and he sometimes suddenly calls away instruments from whom we expect great things – to teach us all not to presume that because he is pleased to employ us, we are therefore necessary to the accomplishment of his purposes."[92]

When Newton later moved to London and Scott was ministering at Olney, Newton wrote to him, "Methinks I see you sitting in my old corner in the study. I will warn you of one thing. That room – (do not start) – used to be haunted. I cannot say I ever saw or heard anything with my bodily organs, but I have been sure there were evil spirits in it and very near me – a spirit of folly, a spirit of indolence, a spirit of unbelief, and many others – indeed their name is legion. But why should I say they are in your study when they followed me to London, and still pester me here?"[93]

Scott became chaplain at the Lock Hospital Chapel in London in 1785, where his gifts in Biblical teaching were recognised and appreciated by men such as William Wilberforce and Henry Thornton, though he encountered some difficulties unfortunately common to many committed pastors. "I had at this time many instructors as to my style of preaching; and some at the Lock board assumed rather a higher tone of authority: while others were disposed to counsel me as the messengers of Ahab did Michaiah (I Kings 22:13,14). But I disposed of the dictating instruction very shortly. 'Gentlemen,' I said, 'you possess authority sufficient to change me *for* another preacher, whenever you please; but you have no power to change me *into* another preacher.' The vexations, however, which I continually experienced, often overcame for a time my patience and fortitude. On one occasion they led me to say to my wife, 'Whatever be the consequence, I will quit this situation; for I shall never have any peace in it.' She promptly answered, 'Take heed what you do: if you leave your station in this spirit, you will perhaps soon be with Jonah in the whale's belly.' The check was seasonable, and procured my acquiescence."[94]

Wilberforce gave this testimony to Scott's significance in his own life:

"It was in the winter of 1785-6 that the late Mr. Newton informed me that the Rev. Mr. Scott, a clergyman of a very superior understanding and of eminent piety, more peculiarly remarkable for his thorough acquaintance with the Holy Scriptures, was about to settle in London, having been appointed to the Lock Hospital.

That was a period of my life when it was peculiarly important to me habitually to attend the ministrations of a sound and faithful pastor, and I willingly assented to Mr. Newton's earnest recommendations of Mr. Scott. I soon found that he fully equalled the strongest expectations that I had formed of him; and from that time for many years I attended him regularly, for the most part accompanied by my dear friends (the Hon. Edward James Elliot and Mr. Henry Thornton). We used to hear him at the Lock in the morning; Mr. Thornton and I often gladly following him for the afternoon service into the city, where he had the lectureship of Bread Street Church. All objections arising from an unfavourable manner were at once overruled by the strong sense, the extensive acquaintance with Scripture, the accurate knowledge of the human heart, and the vehement and powerful appeals to the conscience, with which all his sermons abounded in a greater degree than those of any minister I ever attended. Indeed the substantial solidarity of his discourses made those of ordinary clergymen, though good and able men, appear comparatively somewhat superficial and defective in matter.

"Were I required to specify the particular Christian principles which shone most conspicuously in his character, I should mention his simplicity of intention, his disinterestedness and his generous contempt of this world's wealth in comparison with those heavenly treasures on which his heart was supremely set."[95]

Richard Cecil would occasionally ask Scott to preach in his pulpit and would "involuntarily give vent in a whisper to bursts of admiration of the profundity of his knowledge of Holy Scripture, and of the human heart, and of his surprising power of applying this knowledge to all the varied concerns of men in all their relations in life."[96]

Scott had a strong influence in the formation of the British and

Foreign Bible Society in 1804. He had earlier been asked for some Welsh Bibles and had written, "I have got upon a new scent, but know not how I shall succeed.... As far as I can with propriety procure either the sale or gift of Welsh Bibles I shall count it a privilege to send them."[97] He managed to obtain a few hundred from the SPCK, but eventually exhausted their supplies. They were persuaded to do a reprint of 10,000 in 1799, but although Scott personally redirected 1,000 of those, the demand was so great that stocks were soon finished. Charles of Bala (who had spent his long vacation, while an undergraduate, at Newton's vicarage in Olney shortly after Newton had met Scott) approached the Religious Tract Society, telling them the story of young Mary Jones who had saved hard for her own Bible, walking 30 miles barefoot to buy one, only to discover that the supply had run out months before. It was decided to print more Bibles, not just in Welsh but in every language throughout the world.

Scott's practical Commentary on the Bible was very well received. Andrew Fuller's opinion was echoed by many, "I believe it exhibits more of the mind of the Spirit in the scriptures, than any other work of the kind extant."[98]

His contribution to the training of ministers and missionaries was highly valued. Asked one day by Josiah Pratt to teach missionaries Susoo and Arabic, neither of which he knew, he "felt very uncomfortable about this for a day or two," and then began studying the languages with them.[99]

Scott played a major role in putting shoemaker William Carey's feet on solid ground when he was almost caught in William Law's mysticism. Scott had told him the story of how he had led an aunt of his late employer's into assurance of faith. He noted at the time Carey's intentness and his apt, modest questions. They had further conversations, with Scott referring to Carey's Hackleton workshop as *Carey's College*. He predicted that Carey "would prove no ordinary man." Years later Carey wrote to a friend about Scott , "If there be anything of the work of God in my soul, I owe much of it to his preaching when I first set out in the ways of the Lord." [100]

Scott's son, John, writes in his biography, "I well remember the late Rev. Andrew Fuller reporting, in my father's house, in the year 1792, the impression which had been made upon an association meeting of his own denomination [Northamptonshire Baptist Association], by Mr. Carey's sermon on the address to the church,

(Isaiah 54:2) *Lengthen thy cords, and strengthen thy stakes*; from which he pressed the two following propositions, that we should *expect* great things, and *attempt* great things. Hence originated the Baptist Missionary Society. The London Missionary Society followed; then the Church Missionary Society; then the [British and Foreign] Bible Society; and, in succession, various other institutions."[101]

(Cardinal) John Henry Newman acknowledged his debt to Scott. As an undergraduate, his thoughts on the Trinity were clarified by reading Scott's *Essays*. He thought then of visiting the man, "to whom (humanly speaking) I almost owe my soul."[102] Newman wrote in his *Apologia*, "That Scripture contains an inexhaustible mine of divine treasures, cannot be better proved than by the case of Scott, who though for near forty years engaged in studying it, found something new to his dying day. 'It is delightful,' he beautifully said, 'to have the whole body of Scripture *revolving*, as it were, before one day after day.'"[103]

The Bible Societies

The British and Foreign Bible Society, formed in 1804, is sometimes referred to as 'the Bible Society'. However, there already was a Bible Society in Aldersgate which was formed in 1780. The 1780 Bible Society still exists, as the Naval, Military and Air Force Bible Society. Newton preached for them on 22 September 1782, from Judges 5:18, urging concern for those who risk their lives for us, that they might hear the name of Jesus, not in blasphemy but in dignity, coming to know of His great love, power and grace.

"Furnish them with the means of this knowledge. Procure them Bibles and accompany your gift with your prayers. Whenever you succeed you will be instrumental in saving a soul from death... Can you estimate the value of a soul?"[104]

Early supporters included John Bacon, Lord Dartmouth, Henry Foster, William Goode, Samuel Greathead, Zacharay Macaulay, John Owen (Chaplain General to HM Forces), Josiah Pratt, William Romaine (the first secretary), John, Robert, Henry and Samuel Thornton, John Venn, William Wilberforce and Newton's niece, Betsy Smith.

CHAPTER 8

RECTOR OF ST. MARY WOOLNOTH, LONDON
1779–1807

From Olney Mr. N. was removed to the Rectory of the United Parishes of St. Mary Woolnoth and St. Mary Woolchurch-Haw, Lombard Street, on the presentation of his friend Mr. THORNTON.

These parishes had been favoured with two very eminent Pastors before Mr. N. appeared; namely, the Rev. Josias Shute, B.D. Archdeacon of Colchester, and Rector of St. Mary Woolnoth, who died 1643 – and the Rev. Ralph Robinson, who died in 1655. There is a well-written account of Mr. Shute in the *Christian Observer*, for January 1804;[1] from which it appears, that his piety, ministerial talents, and moderation, in those difficult times, were very much distinguished, during the thirty-three years which he continued Rector.* Mr. Robinson died young, but has left a Volume of truly evangelical discourses, preached at St. Mary's.[2]

Some difficulty arose on Mr. N.'s being presented, by Mr. Thornton's right of presentation being claimed by a nobleman: the question was, therefore, at length brought before the House of Lords, and determined in favour of Mr. Thornton. Mr. N. preached his first sermon in these parishes, Dec. 19, 1779, from Ephesians 4:15, *Speaking the truth in love.*[3] It contained an affectionate address to his parishioners, and was immediately published for their use.

Here a new and very distinct scene of action and usefulness was set before him. Placed in the centre of London – in an opulent neighbourhood – with connections daily increasing, he had now a

---

* Granger, in his *Biographical History of England*, says, that "his learning in divinity and ecclesiastical history was extensive, indeed almost universal." And Walker, in his *Account of the Clergy*, says, that "In the beginning of the troubles he was molested and harassed to death, and denied a funeral sermon to be preached for him by Dr. Holdsworth, as he desired;" and that he was "a person of great piety, charity, and gravity, and of a most sweet and affable temper." It further appears, that, like his successor Mr. N. he preached twice on the Sunday, and had a lecture in his church every Wednesday.

course of service to pursue, in several respects different from his former at Olney. Being, however, well acquainted with the word of God and the heart of man, he proposed to himself no new weapons of warfare, for pulling down the strongholds of sin and Satan around him. He perceived, indeed, most of his parishioners too intent upon their wealth and merchandise to pay much regard to their new minister: but, since they would not come to him, he was determined to go, so far as he could, to them; and therefore, soon after his institution, he sent a printed address to his parishioners: he afterwards sent them another address, on the usual prejudices that are taken up against the Gospel. What effects these attempts had then upon them does not appear: certain it is, that these, and other acts of his ministry, will be recollected by them, when the objects of their present pursuits are forgotten or lamented.

I have heard Mr. N. speak with great feeling on the circumstances of his last important station. "That one," said he, "of the most ignorant, the most miserable, and the most abandoned of slaves, should be plucked from his forlorn state of exile on the coast of Africa, and at length be appointed Minister of the parish of the first magistrate of the first city in the world – that he should go there, not only testify of such grace, but stand up as a singular instance and monument of it – that he should be enabled to record it in his *history, preaching,* and *writings,* to the world at large – is a fact I can contemplate with admiration, but never sufficiently estimate." – This reflection indeed, was so present to his mind, on all occasions and in all places, that he seldom passed a single day any where, but he was found referring to the strange event in one way or other.

It may be necessary to add, that the latter part of these Memoirs leads me to speak so personally of my friend, that any further inspection from his own eye was deemed improper.

When Mr. N. came to St. Mary's, he resided for some time in Charles' Square, Hoxton. Afterwards he removed to Coleman-Street Buildings, where he continued till his death. Being of the most friendly and communicative disposition, his house was open to Christians of all ranks and denominations. Here, like a father among his children, he used to entertain, encourage, and instruct his friends; especially the younger ministers, or candidates for the ministry. Here also the poor, the afflicted, and the tempted found an asylum and a sympathy, which they could scarcely find, in equal degree, any where besides.

His timely hints were often given with much point and profitable address, to the numerous acquaintance which surrounded him in this public station. Some time after Mr. N. had published his *Omicron*, and described the three stages of growth in religion, from the *blade*, the *ear*, and the *full corn* in the ear, distinguishing them by the letters A. B. and C. a conceited young Minister wrote to Mr. N. telling him that he read his own character accurately drawn in that of C. Mr. N. wrote in reply, that in drawing the character of C. or full maturity, he had forgotten to add, till now, one prominent feature of C.'s character, namely, that C. *never knew his own face*.

"It grieves me," said Mr. N., "to see so few of my wealthy parishioners come to church. I always consider the rich as under greater obligations to the preaching of the Gospel than the poor. For, at church the rich *must* hear the whole truth as well as others. *There* they have no mode of escape. But let them once get home, you will be troubled to get at them; and when you are admitted, you are so fettered with *punctilio* – so interrupted and damped with frivolous conversation of their friends, that, as Archbishop Leighton says, 'It is well, if your visit does not prove a blank or a blot.'"

Mr. N. used to improve every occurrence which he could with propriety bring into the pulpit. One night he found a bill put up at St. Mary Woolnoth's, upon which he largely commented when he came to preach. The bill was to this effect: – "A young man having come to the possession of a very considerable fortune, desires the prayers of the congregation, that he may be preserved from the snares to which it exposes him." – "Now if the man," said Mr. N., "had lost a fortune, the world would not have wondered to have seen him put up a bill; but *this* man has been better taught."

Coming out of his church on a Wednesday, a lady stopped him on the steps, and said, "The ticket, of which I held a quarter, is drawn a prize of ten thousand pounds. I know you will congratulate me upon the occasion." – "Madam," said he, "as for a friend under temptation, I will endeavour to *pray* for you."

Soon after he came to St. Mary's, I remember to have heard him say, in a certain company, "Some have observed, that I preach shorter sermons on a Sunday morning, and with more caution: but this I do upon principle. – I suppose I may have two or three bankers present, and some others of my parish, who have hitherto been strangers to my views of truth. I endeavour to imitate the Apostle. *I became*, says he, *all things to all men:* but observe the END; it was in order to *gain some.*[4] – The fowler must go cautiously to meet shy birds, but he will not leave his powder shot behind him. *I have fed you with milk,*[5] says the Apostle: but there are some, that are not only for forcing strong meat, but *bones* too, down the throat of the child. – We must have patience with a single step in the case of an infant; and there are *one-step* books and sermons, which are good in their place. Christ taught his disciples, *as they were able to bear:*[6] and it was upon the same principle that the Apostle accommodated himself to prejudice. Now," continued he, "what I wish to remark on these considerations is, that this apostolical principle, steadily pursued, will render a Minister *apparently* inconsistent: superficial hearers will think him a trimmer. On the other hand, a Minister, destitute of the apostolical principle and intention, and directing his whole force to preserve the appearance of consistency, may thus *seem* to preserve it; but, let me tell you, here is only the *form* of faithfulness, without the *spirit.*"

I could not help observing, one day, how much Mr. N. was grieved with the mistake of a Minister, who appeared to pay too much attention to politics. "For my part," said he, "I have no temptation to turn politician, and much less to inflame a party, in these times. When a ship is leaky, and a mutinous spirit divides the company on board, a wise man would say, 'My good friends, while we are debating, the water is gaining on us. We had better leave the debate, and go to the pumps.' I endeavour," continued he, " to turn my people's eyes from instruments to God. I am continually attempting to show them, how far they are from knowing either the matter of *fact* or the matter of *right.* I inculcate our great privileges in this country, and advise a discontented man to take a lodging for a little while in Russia or Prussia."

Though no great variety of anecdote is to be expected in a course so stationary as this part of Mr. N.'s life and ministry; for sometimes the course of a single day might give the account of a whole year; yet that *day* was so benevolently spent, that he was found in it not only *rejoicing with those that rejoiced,* but literally *weeping with those that wept.*[7] The portrait, which Goldsmith drew from imagination, Mr. N. realised in fact, insomuch, that, had Mr. N. sat for his picture to the poet, it could not have been more accurately delineated than by the following lines in his *Deserted Village*:[8]

"Unskilful he to fawn, or seek for power,
By doctrines fashion'd to the varying hour:
Far other aims his heart had learn'd to prize,
More bent to raise the wretched than to rise.
Thus to relieve the wretched was his pride,
And e'en his failings lean'd to Virtue's side;
But, in his duty prompt at every call,
He watch'd and wept, he pray'd and felt, for all:
And, as a bird each fond endearment tries,
To tempt its new-fledg'd offspring to the skies,
He tried each art, reprov'd each dull delay,
Allur'd to brighter worlds, and led the way."

I remember to have heard him say, when speaking of his continual interruptions, "I see in this world two heaps of human happiness and misery: now if I can take but the smallest bit from one heap and add to the other, I carry a point. – If, as I go home, a child has dropped a halfpenny, and if, by giving it another, I can wipe away its tears, I feel I have done something. I should be glad, indeed, to do greater things; but I will not neglect this. – When I hear a knock at my study door, I hear a message from God. It may be a lesson of instruction; perhaps a lesson of patience: but, since it is *his* message, it must be interesting."

But it was not merely under his own roof that his benevolent aims were thus exerted: he was found ready to take an active part in relieving the miserable, directing the anxious, or recovering the wanderer, in whatsoever state or place he discovered such: of which take the following instance.

Mr. ******** [Dr. Buchanan], who is still living, and who holds a post of great importance abroad, was a youth of considerable talents, and had received a respectable education. I am not informed of his original destination in point of profession: but, certain it is, that he left his parents in Scotland, with a design of viewing the world at large: and that, without those pecuniary resources which could render such an undertaking convenient, or even practicable. Yet, having the sanguine expectations of youth, together with its inexperience, he determinately pursued his plan. I have seen an account from his own hand, of the strange, but by no means dishonourable, resources to which he was reduced in the pursuit of this scheme: nor can romance exceed the detail. But the particulars of his long journey, till he arrived in London, and those which have since occurred, would not be proper, at present, for any one to record except himself; and I cannot but wish he would favour the world with them, on the principle which led Mr. N. to write his *Narrative*. To London, however, he came; and then he seemed to *come to himself*. He had heard Mr. N.'s character, and on a Sunday evening he came to St. Mary Woolnoth, and stood in one of the aisles, while Mr. N. preached. In the course of that week he wrote Mr. N. some account of his adventure, and state of mind. Such circumstances could be addressed to no man more properly. Mr. N.'s favourite maxim was often in his mouth, more often in his actions, and always in his heart;

Haud ignara mali, miseris succurrere disco.
Not ignorant of suffering I hasten to succour the wretched.

Mr. N. therefore gave notice from the pulpit on the following Sunday evening, that, if the person was present who had sent him such a letter, he would be glad to speak with him.

Mr. B[uchanan] gladly accepted the invitation, and came to Mr. N.'s house, where a friendship began which continued till Mr. N.'s death. Mr. N. not only afforded this youth the instruction which he, at this period, so deeply needed; but marking his fine abilities and corrected inclination, he introduced him to Henry Thornton, Esq. who, inheriting his father's unbounded liberality and determined adherence to the cause of real religion, readily patronised the stranger. By the munificence of this gentleman, he was supported through a university education, and was afterwards ordained to the curacy of [St. Mary Woolnoth]. It was, however, thought expedient that his talents should be employed in an important station abroad, which he readily undertook, and in which he now maintains a very distinguished character.

It ought not to be concealed, that, since his advancement, he has not only returned his patron the whole expense of his university education; but has also placed in his hands an equal sum, for the education of some pious youth, who might be deemed worthy of that assistance once afforded to himself!

Mr. N. used to spend a month or two annually, at the house of some friend in the country. He always took an affectionate leave of his congregation before he departed; and spake of his leaving town as quite uncertain of returning to it, considering the variety of incidents which might prevent that return. Nothing was more remarkable than his constant habit of regarding the hand of God in every event, however trivial it might appear to others. On every occasion – in the concerns of every hour – in matters public or private, like Enoch, he *walked with God.*[9] Take a single instance of his state of mind in this respect. In walking to his church he would say, *"The way of man is not in himself,*[10] nor can he conceive what belongs to a single step. When I go to St. Mary Woolnoth, it seems the same whether I turn down Lothbury or go through the Old Jewry; but the going through one street and not another may produce an effect of lasting consequences. A man cut down my hammock in sport; but had he cut it down half an hour later, I had not been here; as the exchange of crew was then making. A man made a smoke on the sea shore at the time a ship passed, which was thereby brought to, and afterwards brought me to England."

Mr. N. had experienced a severe stroke soon after he came to St. Mary's, and while he resided in Charles' Square, in the death of his niece, Miss Eliza Cunningham. He loved her with the affection of a parent, and she was, indeed, truly lovely. He had brought her up; and had observed, that, with the most amiable natural qualities, she possessed a real piety. With every possible attention from Mr. and Mrs. Newton and their friends, they saw her gradually sink into the arms of death: but fully prepared to meet him, as a messenger sent from a yet kinder Father; to whom she departed, October 6th, 1785, aged fourteen years and eight months. On this occasion Mr. N. published some brief memoirs of her character and death.[11]

In the years 1784 and 1785, Mr. N. preached a course of sermons, on an occasion, of which he gives the following account in his first discourse: – "Conversation, in almost every company, for some time past, has much turned upon the commemoration of the 'Messiah'. I mean to lead your meditations to the language of the oratorio; and to consider, in their order, (if the Lord, on whom our breath depends, shall be pleased to afford life, ability, and opportunity) the several sublime and interesting passages of Scripture, which are the basis of that admired composition." In the year 1786, he published these discourses, in two volumes octavo.[12]

There is a passage so original, at the beginning of his fourth sermon, from Malachi 3:1-3, *The Lord whom ye seek, shall suddenly come to his temple,* etc. that I shall transcribe it for the use of such as have not seen these discourses: at the same time, it will, in a few words, convey Mr. N.'s idea of the usual performance of this oratorio, or attending its performance, in present circumstances.

"*Whereunto shall we liken the people of this generation, and to what are they like?*[13] I represent to myself a number of persons of various characters, involved in one common charge of high treason. They are already in a state of confinement, but not yet brought to their trial. The facts, however, are so plain, and the evidence against them so strong and pointed, that there is not the least doubt of their guilt being fully proved, and that nothing but a pardon can preserve them from punishment. In this situation, it should seem their wisdom to avail themselves of every expedient in their power for obtaining mercy. But they are entirely regardless of their danger, and wholly taken up with contriving methods of amusing themselves, that they may pass away the term of their imprisonment with as much cheerfulness as possible. Among other resources, they call in the assistance of music. And, amidst a great variety of subjects in this way, they are particularly pleased with one: they choose to make the solemnities of their impending trial, the character of their Judge, the methods of his procedure, and the awful sentence to which they are exposed, the ground-work of a musical entertainment: and, as if their attention is chiefly fixed upon the skill of the composer, in adapting the style of his music to the very solemn language and subject with which they are trifling. The King, however, out of his great clemency and compassion towards those who have no pity for themselves, prevents [provides for] them with his goodness: undesired by them, he sends them a gracious message: he assures them, that he is unwilling they should suffer: he requires, yea, he entreats them to submit: he points out a way in which their confession and submission shall be certainly accepted: and, in this way, which he condescends to prescribe, he offers them a free and a full pardon. But, instead of taking a single step towards a compliance with his goodness, they set his message likewise to music: and this, together with a description of their present state, and of the fearful doom awaiting them if they continue obstinate, is sung for their diversion; accompanied with the sound of cornet, flute, harp, sackbut, psaltery, dulcimer, and all kinds of instruments. Surely, if such a case as I have supposed could be found in real life, though I might admire the musical taste of these people, I should commiserate their insensibility!"

But, *clouds return after the rain*:[14] a greater loss than that of Miss Cunningham was to follow. Enough has been said in these Memoirs already to show the more than ordinary affection Mr. N. felt for her who had been so long his idol, as he used to call her; of which I shall add but one more instance, out of many that might easily be collected.

Being with him at the house of a lady at Blackheath, we stood at a window which had a prospect of Shooter's Hill. "Ah," said Mr. N. "I remember the many journeys I took from London to stand at the top of that hill, in order to look towards the part in which Mrs. N. then lived: not that I could see the spot itself, after travelling several miles, for she lived far beyond what I could see, when on the hill; but it gratified me even to look *towards* the spot: and this I did always once, and sometimes twice a week." – "Why," said I, "this is more like one of the vagaries of romance than of real life." – "True," replied he: "but real life has extravagancies that would not be admitted to appear in a well-written romance – they would be said to be *out of nature.*"

In such a continued habit of excessive attachment, it is evident how keenly Mr. N. must have felt, while he observed the progress of a threatening indication in her breast. This tumour seemed to have arisen from a blow she received before he left Liverpool. The pain it occasioned at the time soon wore off, but a small lump remained in the part affected. In October, 1788, on the tumour's increasing, she applied to an eminent surgeon [Mr. Warner, of Guy's Hospital], who told her it was a cancer, and now too large for extraction, and that he could only recommend quiet. As the spring of 1789 advanced, her malady increased: and though she was able to bear a journey to Southampton, from which she returned, in other respects tolerably well, she grew gradually worse with the cancer, till she expired December 15th, 1790.

Mr. N. made this remark on her death: – "Just before Mrs. N.'s disease became so formidable, I was preaching on the waters of Egypt being turned into blood. The Egyptians had idolised their river, and God made them loath it. I was apprehensive it would soon be a similar case with me." – During the very affecting season of Mrs. N.'s dissolution, Mr. N., like David, *arose from the earth, and came into the temple of the Lord, and worshipped*;[15] and that, in a manner which surprised some of his friends.

I must own I was not one of those who saw any thing that might not be expected from *such* a man, surrounded with such circumstances. I did not wonder at his undertaking to preach Mrs. N.'s Funeral Sermon, on the following Sunday, at St. Mary's: since I always considered him as an original; and his case was quite an exception to general habits, in many respects. There could be no question as to the affection he had borne to the deceased: it had even prevailed, as he readily allowed, to an eccentric and blameable degree; and, indeed, after her removal, he used to observe an annual seclusion, for a special recollection of her, whom through the year he had never forgotten, and from which proceeded a sort of little elegies or sonnets to her memory. But he clearly recognised the will of God in the removal of his idol, and reasoned as David did on the occasion: *While* she *was yet alive, I fasted and wept: for I said, Who can tell whether God will be gracious to me, that* she *may live? But, now* she *is dead, wherefore should I fast? Can I bring* her *back again? I shall go to* her, *but* she *shall not return to me.*[16]

Besides which, Mr. N. had a favourite sentiment, which I have heard him express in different ways, long before he had so special an occasion of illustrating it in practice. "God in his providence," he used to say, "is continually bringing about occasions to demonstrate characters." He used to allege the case of Achan and Judas among *bad* men; and that of St. Paul, Acts 27, among *good* ones. "If any one," said he, "had asked the Centurian who Paul the prisoner was, that sailed with them on board the ship, it is probable he would have thus replied: 'He is a troublesome enthusiast, who has lately joined himself to a certain sect. These people affirm that a Jewish malefactor, who was crucified some years ago at Jerusalem, rose the third day from the dead; and this Paul is mad enough to assert that Jesus, the leader of their sect, is not only now alive, but that he himself has seen him – *Poor crazy creature!*' But God made use of this occasion to discover the real character of Paul; and taught the Centurian, from the circumstances which followed, to whom it was he owed his direction in the storm, and for whose sake he received his preservation through it."

In all trying occasions, therefore, Mr. N. was particularly impressed with the idea of a Christian; and especially of a Christian minister being called to stand forward as an example to his flock – to feel himself placed in a post of honour – a post, in which he may not only glorify God, but also forcibly demonstrate the peculiar supports of the Gospel. More especially, when this could be done (as in his own case) from no doubtful motive; then it may be expedient to leave the path of ordinary custom, for the greater reason of exhibiting both the doctrines of truth and the experience of their power.

Though I professedly publish none of Mr. N.'s letters, for reasons hereafter assigned; yet I shall take the liberty to insert part of one, with which I am favoured by J. Forbes, Esq. of Stanmore-Hill, written to him while at Rome, and dated December 5th, 1796. It shows the interest which the writer took in the safety of his friend; and his address in attempting to break the enchantments with which men of taste are surrounded when standing in the centre of the Fine Arts.

"The true Christian, in strict propriety of speech, has no home here: he is, and must be, a stranger and a pilgrim upon earth: his citizenship, treasure, and real home are in a better world; and every step he takes, whether to the east or to the west, is a step nearer to his Father's house. – On the other hand, when in the path of duty, he is always at home; for the whole earth is the Lord's: and, as we see the same sun in England or Italy, in Europe or Asia: so wherever he is, he equally sets the Lord always before him; and finds himself equally near the throne of grace, at all times and in all places. – God is every where; and, by faith in the Great Mediator, he dwells in God, and God in him. To him that line of Horace may be applied, in the best sense,

> Cælum, non animum mutant, qui trans mare currant.
> They change their sky, not their mind, who scour across the sea.
>
> [Horace, *Epistles*]

"I trust, my dear sir, that you will carry out, and bring home with you, a determination similar to that of the patriarch Jacob, who vowed a vow, saying, *If God will be with me, and will keep me in the way that I go, and will give me bread to eat and raiment to put on, so that I come again to my father's house in peace, then shall the Lord be my God!*[17] – May the Lord himself write it on your heart!

"You are now at Rome, the centre of the Fine Arts; a place abounding with every thing to gratify a person of your taste. Athens had the pre-eminence in the Apostle Paul's time: and I think it highly probable, from many passages in his writings, that he likewise had a taste capable of admiring and relishing the beauties of painting, sculpture, and architecture, which he could not but observe during his abode in that city: but then he had a higher, a spiritual, a divine taste, which was greatly shocked and grieved by the ignorance, idolatry, and wickedness which surrounded him, insomuch that he could attend to nothing else. – This taste, which cannot be acquired by any effort or study of ours, but is freely bestowed on all who sincerely ask it of the Lord, divests the vanities which the world admire of their glare; and enables us to judge of the most splendid and specious works of men who know not God, according to the declaration of the prophet, *They hatch cockatrice eggs, and weave the spider's web.*[18] Much ingenuity is displayed in the weaving of a cobweb; but, when finished, it is worthless and useless. Incubation requires close diligence and attention: if the hen is too long from her nest, the egg is spoiled; but why should she sit at all upon the egg, and watch it, and warm it night and day, if it only produces a cockatrice at last? Thus vanity or mischief are the chief rulers of unsanctified genius; the artists spin webs; and the philosophers, by their learned speculations, hatch cockatrices, to poison themselves and their fellow-creatures: few of either sort have one serious thought of that awful eternity, upon the brink of which they stand for a while, and into the depth of which they successively fall.

"A part of the sentence denounced against the city which once stood upon seven hills, is so pointed and graphical that I must transcribe it: *And the voice of harpers, and musicians, and pipers, and trumpeters, shall be heard no more at all in thee; and no craftsman, of whatsoever craft he be, shall be found any more in thee; and the light of a candle shall no more be seen in thee.*[19] – Now, I am informed, that upon certain occasions, the whole cupola of St. Peter's is covered with lamps, and affords a very magnificent spectacle: if I saw it, it would remind me of that time when there will not be the shining of a single candle in the city; for the sentence must be executed, and the hour may be approaching – *Sic transit gloria mundi.*[20]

"You kindly enquire after my health: myself and family are, through the divine favour, perfectly well: yet, healthy as I am, I labour under a growing disorder for which there is no cure; I mean Old Age. I am not sorry it is a mortal disease, from which no one recovers: for who would live always in such a world as this, who has a scriptural hope of an inheritance in the world of light? I am now in my seventy-second year, and seem to have lived long enough for myself. I have

known something of the evil of life, and have had a large share of the good. I know what the world *can* do, and what it *cannot* do: it can neither give nor take away that *peace of God, which passeth all understanding*:[21] it cannot soothe a wounded conscience, nor enable us to meet death with comfort. – That you, my dear sir, may have an abiding and abounding experience that the Gospel is a catholicon adapted to all our wants and all our feelings, and a suitable help when every other help fails, is the sincere and ardent prayer of
    "Your affectionate friend,
     "JOHN NEWTON."

But, in proportion as Mr. N. felt the vanity of the pursuits which he endeavoured to expose in the foregoing letter, he was as feelingly alive to whatever regarded eternal concerns. Take an instance of this, in a visit he paid to another friend. This friend was a minister, who affected great accuracy in his discourses; and who, on that Sunday, had nearly occupied an hour in insisting several laboured and nice distinctions made in his subject. As he had a high estimation of Mr. N.'s judgment, he enquired of him, as they walked home, whether he thought the distinctions just now insisted on were full and judicious. Mr. N. said he thought them not *full*, as a very important one had been omitted. – "What can that be?" said the minister: "for I had taken more than ordinary care to enumerate them fully." – "I think not," replied Mr. N., "for when your congregation had travelled several miles for a meal, I think you should not have forgotten the important distinction which must ever exist between MEAT and BONES."

In the year 1779, Mr. N. had the honorary degree of D.D. conferred upon him by the University of New Jersey in America, and the Diploma sent to him. He also received a work in two volumes, dedicated to him with the above title annexed to his name.[22] Mr. N. wrote the author a grateful acknowledgement for the work, but begged to decline an honour which he never intended to accept. "*I am*," said he, "*as one born out of due time.**[23] I have neither the pretension nor

---

* In a MS note, dated Dec. 15th, 1797, on a Letter in the collection before referred to, Mr. N. writes: – "Though I am not so sensibly affected as I could wish, I hope I am truly affected by the frequent reviews I make of my past life. Perhaps the annals of thy church scarcely afford an instance in all respects so singular. Perhaps thy grace may have recovered some from an equal degree of apostasy, infidelity, and profligacy: but few of them have

wish to honours of this kind. However, therefore, the University may over-rate my attainments, and thus show their respect, I must not forget myself: it would be both vain and improper were I to concur in it."

But Mr. N. had yet another storm to weather. While we were contemplating the long and rough voyage he had passed, and thought he had only now to rest in a quiet haven, and with a fine sunsetting at the close of the evening of his life; clouds began to gather again, and seemed to threaten a wreck at every entry of the port.

He used to make excursions in the summer to different friends in the country; endeavouring to make these visits profitable to them and their neighbours, by his continual prayers and the expositions he gave of the Scriptures read at their morning and evening worship. I have heard of some, who were first brought to the knowledge of themselves and of God, by attending his exhortations on these occasions; for, indeed, besides what he undertook in a more stated way at the church, he seldom entered a room, but something profitable and entertaining fell from his lips.

After the death of Miss Cunningham and Mrs. N., his companion in these summer excursions was his other niece, Miss Elizabeth Catlett. This young lady had also been brought up by Mr. and Mrs. N. with Miss Cunningham; and, on the death of the two latter, she became the object of Mr. N.'s naturally affectionate disposition. She also became quite necessary to him by her administrations in his latter years: she watched him, walked with him, and visited wherever he went: when his sight failed, she read to him, divided his food, and was unto him all that a dutiful daughter could be.

But in the year 1801, a nervous disorder seized her, by which Mr. N. was obliged to submit to her being separated from him. During the twelve month it lasted, the weight of the affliction, added to the weight of years, seemed to overwhelm him. I extracted a few of his

---

been redeemed from such a state of misery and depression as I was in, upon the coast of Africa, when thy unsought mercy wrought for my deliverance. But, that such a wretch should not only be spared and pardoned, but reserved to the honour of preaching thy gospel, which he had blasphemed and renounced, and at length be placed in a very public situation, and favoured with acceptance and usefulness, both from the pulpit and the press; so that my poor name is known in most parts of the world, where there are any who know thee – This is wonderful indeed! – The more thou hast exalted me, the more I ought to abase myself."

reflections on the occasion, written on some blank leaves in an edition of his *Letters to a Wife*, which he lent me on my undertaking these Memoirs, and have subjoined them in a note.* It may give the reader pleasure to be informed that Miss Catlett returned home; gradually recovered; and afterwards married a worthy man of the name of Smith.

It was with a mixture of delight and surprise, that the friends and hearers of this eminent servant of God beheld him bringing forth such a measure of fruit in extreme age. Though then almost eighty years old, his sight nearly gone, and incapable through deafness, of joining in conversation; yet his public ministry was regularly continued, and maintained with a considerable degree of his former animation. His memory, indeed, was observed to fail, but his judgment in divine things still remained: and, though some depression of spirits was observed, which he used to account for from his advanced age; yet his perception, taste, and zeal for the truths which he had long received and taught were evident. Like Simeon, having seen the salvation of the Lord, he now only waited and prayed to depart in peace.

---

* August 1st, 1801. "I now enter my 77th year. I have been exercised this year with a trying and unexpected change; but it is by thy appointment, my gracious Lord, and thou art unchangeably wise, good, and merciful. Thou gavest me my dear adopted child. Thou didst own my endeavours to bring her up for thee. I have no doubt that thou hast called her by thy grace. I thank thee for the many years' comfort (ten) I have had in her; and for the attention and affection she has always shown me, exceeding that of most daughters to their own parents. Thou hast now tried me, as thou didst Abraham, in my old age; when my eyes are failing, and my strength declines. Thou hast called for my Isaac, who had so long been my chief stay and staff; but it was thy blessing that made her so. A nervous disorder has seized her, and I desire to leave her under thy care; and chiefly pray for myself, that I may be enabled to wait thy time and will, without betraying any signs of impatience or despondency unbecoming my profession and character. Hitherto thou hast helped me; and to thee I look for help in future. Let all issue in thy glory, that my friends and hearers may be encouraged by seeing how I am supported: let thy strength be manifested in my weakness, and thy grace be sufficient for me, and let all finally work together for our good: Amen! I am to say from my heart, *Not my will but thine be done.*[26] But, though thou hast in a measure made my spirit willing, thou knowest, and I feel, that the flesh is weak. *Lord, I believe: help thou my unbelief.*[27] Lord, I submit: subdue every rebellious thought that dares arise against thy will. Spare my eyes, if it please thee; but, above all, strengthen my faith and love."

After Mr. N. was turned of eighty, some of his friends feared he might continue his public ministry too long. They marked not only his infirmities in the pulpit, but felt much on account of the decrease of his strength and of his occasional depressions. Conversing with him in January 1806, on the latter, he observed that he had experienced nothing which in the least affected the principles he had felt and taught; that his depressions were the natural result of *fourscore years;* and that, at any age, we can only enjoy that comfort from our principles which God is pleased to send. "But," replied I, "in the article of public preaching, might it not be best to consider your work as done, and stop before you evidently discover you can speak no longer?" "I cannot stop," said he, raising his voice, – *"What! shall the old African blasphemer stop while he can speak?"*

In every future visit, I perceived old age making rapid strides. At length his friends found some difficulty in making themselves known to him: his sight, his hearing, and his recollection exceedingly failed; but, being mercifully kept from pain, he generally appeared easy and cheerful. Whatever he uttered was perfectly consistent with the principles which he had so long and so honourably maintained. Calling to see him a few days before he died, with one of his most intimate friends, we could not make him recollect either of us; but, seeing him afterwards when sitting up in his chair, I found so much intellect remaining, as produced a short and affectionate reply, though he was utterly incapable of conversation.

Mr. N. declined in this very gradual way, till at length it was painful to ask him a question, or to attempt to arouse faculties almost gone: still his friends were anxious to get a word from him, and those friends who survive him will be as anxious to learn the state of his mind in his latest hours. – It is quite natural thus to enquire, though it is not important *how* such a decided character left this world. I have heard Mr. N. say, when he has heard particular enquiry made about the last expressions of an eminent Christian, "Tell me not how the man died, but how he lived."

Still I say, it is natural to enquire: and I will meet the desire; not by trying to expand uninteresting particulars, but so far as I can collect encouraging *facts*; and I learn from a paper, kindly sent me by his family, all that is interesting and authentic.

About a month before Mr. N.'s death, Mr. Smith's niece was sitting by him, to whom he said, "It is a great thing to die; and when our flesh and heart fail, to have God for the strength of our heart, and our portion for ever – *I know whom I have believed, and he is able to keep that which I have committed against that* great *day. Henceforth there is laid up for me a crown of righteousness, which the Lord, the righteous Judge, shall give me at that day.*"

When Mrs. Smith came into the room, he said, "I have been meditating on a subject, *Come, and hear, all ye that fear God, and I will declare what he hath done for my soul.*"[24]

At another time he said, "More light, more love, more liberty. – Hereafter I hope, when I shut my eyes on the things of time, I shall open them in a better world. What a thing it is to live under the shadow of the wings of the Almighty! – I am going the way of all flesh." And when one replied, "The Lord is gracious," he answered, "If it were not so, how could I dare to stand before him?"

The Wednesday before he died, Mrs. G– asked him, if his mind was comfortable: he replied, "I am satisfied with the Lord's will."

Mr. N. seemed sensible to his last hour, but expressed nothing remarkable after these words. He departed on the 21st, and was buried in the vault of his church the 31st of December, 1807, having left the following injunction in a letter for the direction of his executors.

"I propose writing an epitaph for myself if it may be put up, on a plain marble tablet, near the vestry door, to the following purport:

JOHN NEWTON, CLERK,

Once an Infidel and Libertine,
A servant of slaves in Africa,
Was, by the rich mercy of our Lord and Saviour
JESUS CHRIST,
Preserved, restored, pardoned,
And appointed to preach the Faith
He had long laboured to destroy,
Near 16 years at Olney in Bucks;
And [28] years in this church.

On Feb. 1, 1750, he married
MARY,
Daughter of the late George Catlett,
Of Chatham, Kent.
He resigned her to the Lord who gave her,
On 15th December, 1790.

And I earnestly desire that no other monument, and no inscription but to this purport, may be attempted for me."

The following is a copy of the exordium of Mr. Newton's will,[25] dated June 13, 1803.

"In the name of God, Amen. I, JOHN NEWTON, of Coleman Street Buildings, in the parish of St. Stephen Coleman Street, in the city of London, Clerk, being through mercy in good health, and of sound and disposing mind, memory, and understanding, although in the seventy-eighth year of my age, do, for the settling of my temporal concerns, and for the disposal of all the worldly estate which it hath pleased the Lord in his good providence to give me, make this my last Will and Testament as follows. I commit my soul to my gracious God and Saviour, who mercifully spared and preserved me, when I was an Apostate, a Blasphemer, and an Infidel, and delivered me from that state of misery on the coast of Africa into which my obstinate wickedness had plunged me; and who has been pleased to admit me (though most unworthy) to preach his Glorious Gospel. I rely with humble confidence upon the atonement and mediation of the Lord Jesus Christ, God and Man, which I have often proposed to others as the only Foundation whereon a sinner can build his hope; trusting that he will guard and guide me through the uncertain remainder of my life, and that he will then admit me into his presence in his Heavenly Kingdom. I would have my Body deposited in the Vault under the Parish Church of Saint Mary Woolnoth, close to the coffins of my late dear Wife and my dear niece Elizabeth Cunningham; and it is my desire that my Funeral may be performed with as little expense as possible, consistent with decency."

Appendix to Chapter 8

St. Mary Woolnoth
Newton's arrival at St. Mary Woolnoth took some adjustment on the part of the "regulars". He wrote to his wife shortly after beginning his new ministry:[26]

"A churchwarden came to me yesterday in the vestry extremely civil, and gave me to understand he spoke in the name of the principal parishioners, who were very respectable, and disposed to be very obliging. They believed I would do anything in my power to oblige them. Then followed the Complaint – that some of them found their pews possessed by strangers before they came to church and others, though their seats were vacant, could not get to them for the crowd in the middle aisle. I answered that the latter inconvenience was unavoidable, if the church doors stood open; the former I was very sorry for, but knew not how it was in my power to remedy it. He proposed with many apologies, my letting another clergyman preach now and then for me, hinted that it should be no expense to me and thought that if it was uncertain whether I preached or no, the people would not throng the church so much. I could not but admire the scheme. I thought it would exactly answer the design. But I said I could not possibly comply with it. If he pleased I would speak to the people from the desk. He wished I would – therefore I shall, and add a word to the parishioners to dispose them to be good humoured to the strangers. Some little difficulty upon this head must be expected, but I hope it will subside by degrees."

Charles Square

By April they had both settled in Charles Square, but it was still a wrench to have left friends in Olney. Newton had recently fallen and had his arm in a sling, which gave expression to the pain of separation when next he wrote to Cowper, "Indeed, a removal from two such dear friends is a dislocation, and gives me at times a mental feeling, something analogous to what my body felt when my arm was forced from its socket. I live in hopes that this mental dislocation will one day be happily reduced likewise, and that we shall come together again *as bone to its bone*. The connexion which the Lord himself formed between us, was undoubtedly formed for *eternity*, but I trust we shall have more of the pleasure and comfort of it *in time*. And that I shall yet hear you say, 'Come, *magnify the Lord with me, and let us exalt his name together*, for he hath turned my mourning into joy, and he hath taken off my sackcloth, and girded me with gladness.'"[27]

There is an interesting account of life in Charles Square in the diary of William Herbert.[28] His father, John Wilderspin, was a leading member of the Tabernacle. He died from an accident at work leaving a wife and four children, of whom William, in his tenth year, was the eldest. Although the church showed kindness to the family, the one who kept an eye on them was John Newton. William writes, "After my father's death I was taken into the family of the Revd John

Newton. To this providential early patronage I owe much of my succeeding good fortune in life." He ran errands for Mrs. Newton and describes his first one, which he thought "a most auspicious beginning of this line!"

"Mrs. Newton (or "*Madam Newton*") as I was so taught to call her, sent for me one day to *Charles Square*, where the family then lived, to carry a small present of game with a letter to a Mr. Shoolbread, a large merchant of their acquaintance in Mincing Lane; and strictly cautioned me before setting off – not to take any *money*, if it should be offered – as being too insignificant a present! – and that I should thereby be no loser, – gave me *a shilling* from her own pocket. I promised not – and really meant to keep my word! – The present was delivered by me to a groom or livery servant – taken upstairs, and some tart with wine and water set before me in a lobby, where I was told to wait. This, of itself pleasing enough, was followed when the servant came down by his slipping a *shilling* into my hand – As told to do, I softly whispered I was told not to take anything: the servant who knew the reason and had his lesson, – stoutly protested that he dared not take the shilling upstairs again, and that I must put it into my pocket and say nothing about it. I did as told: – And hasting gladly back – with a letter in answer to Charles Square. Mr. Newton opened the door to me! '*Well! Bill,* where have you been?' – 'To Mr. Shoolbread Sir with a letter and a present.' 'And have you safely left them?' 'Yes, Sir, And brought a letter back.' 'That's a good boy. Here's a shilling for you!' I thus got 3 shillings – and undesignedly for my first errand."

His next errand was for Sally Johnson, the Newtons' servant, who sent him to her brother, a large confectioner next door to Savile House, Leicester Square, where he was invited to eat as much as he liked. With the money he earned from running errands for the Newtons and others he gradually bought himself a Boys' Library. However, it was not the same every day. "One swallow does not make a summer. And so I found it."

Again it was Newton who came to his rescue and found him work with his friend Eli Bates, the ex-secretary of Sir George Savile. He was to read to him and generally wait on him. He was given a closet under his master's room, but Bates snored and William had to buy thruppence worth of straw from the Angel Inn, Islington, and stuff it up the chimney to get any sleep.

When he resigned from this post he turned to Newton again, who employed him as a messenger between their home and the German Dr. Benamore of Milman Place, Bedford Row, who was attending their niece Eliza Cunningham. William would fetch her medicines from Apothecary's Hall where they were guaranteed to be genuine. At other times Betsy Catlett set him lessons in arithmetic so as not to neglect his education, "in which I was greatly deficient".

He helped the Newtons move to Coleman Street Buildings, where one morning he "had the high gratification ... of opening the door ... to the great poet of *The Task*, Cowper – a plain, meek, unassuming man."

Yet again Newton became involved in procuring him employment. While his new and blind employer, Mr. Atkins, was consulting Newton for a character reference, William remained "on the listen" after he had opened the parlour door for him, but found to his dismay that nothing particularly good was said of him, except, "but I could do very well if I wanted to." After he had seen Mr. Atkins to the door and was "lurking about the Hall," William was briefly addressed by Newton, "I'll thank you *Bill*, another time when you listen at the door, to make less noise."

This young man whose first pocket-money went on books and whose adolescent struggles drew Newton's patient guidance and compassion, went on to become the first Librarian of the Guildhall. His biography has recently been written by one of his successors.

Coleman Street Buildings

When the Newtons moved to 6 Coleman Street Buildings, a short walk from St. Mary Woolnoth, they entered the noise and clamour of city life. The only similarity John could find with Olney was that the bustle of Lombard Street was like the bleating of lambs. What was previously the official parsonage house had for a long time been part of the Post Office. A vivid description of this area of Lombard Street in 1805 was given in the *City Press* by "Aleph".[29]

"The whole wall-surface was of smoke-blacked brick; its colour seemed to imitate the mud in the road, and as coach, or wagon, or mail-cart toiled or rattled along, the basement storeys were bespattered freely from the gutters. The glories of gas were yet to be. After three o'clock p.m. miserable oil lamps tried to enliven the foggy street with their 'ineffectual light,' while through dingy, greenish squares of glass you might observe tall tallow candles dimly disclosing the mysteries of bank or counting house. Passengers needed to walk with extreme caution; if you lingered on the pavement, woe to your corns; if you sought to cross the road, you had better beware of the flying postmen or the letter-bag express. As six o'clock drew near, every court, alley, and blind thoroughfare in the neighbourhood echoed to the incessant din of letter-bells. Men, women, and children were hurrying to the chief office, while the fiery-red battalion of postmen, as they neared the same point, were apparently pleased to balk the diligence of the public, anxious to spare their coppers. The mother post-office for the United Kingdom and Colonies was then in Lombard Street, and folk thought it was a model establishment. Such armies of clerks, such sacks of letters, and countless consignments of newspapers! How could those hard-worked officials ever get through their work? The entrance, barring paint and stucco, remains exactly as it was fifty years ago. What crowds used to besiege it! What a strange confusion of news-boys! The struggling public, with late letters; the bustling red-coats, with their leather bags, a scene of anxious life and interest seldom exceeded. And now the letter boxes are all closed; you weary your knuckles in vain against the sliding door in the wall. No response. Every hand within is fully occupied in letter-sorting for the mails; they must be freighted in less than half an hour. Yet, on payment of a shilling for each, letters were received till ten minutes to eight, and not unfrequently a post-chaise, with the horses in a positive lather, tore into the street, just in time to forward some important despatch. Hark! The horn! The horn! The mail-guards are the soloists, and very pleasant music they discourse; not a few of them are first rate performers. A long train of gaily got-up coaches, remarkable for their light weight, horsed by splendid-looking animals, impatient at the curb, and eager to commence their journey of ten miles (at least) an hour; stout 'gents,' in heavy coats, buttoned to the throat, esconce themselves in 'reserved seats.' Commercial men contest the right of a seat with the guard or coachman; some careful mother helps her pale, timid daughter up the steps; while a fat old lady already occupies two-thirds of the seat – what will be done? Bags of epistles innumerable stuff the boots; formidable bales of the daily journals are trampled small by the guard's heels. The clock will strike in less than five minutes; the clamour deepens, the hubbub seems increasing; but ere the last sixty seconds expire, a sharp winding of warning bugles begins. Coachee flourishes his whip, greys and chestnuts prepare for a run, the reins move, but very gently, there is a parting crack from the whipcord, and the brilliant cavalcade is gone – *exeunt omnes*!"

[A small section of blackened brick has been preserved in the wall of Coleman Street, at the entrance to Coleman Street Buildings.]

After living in London for several years, Newton was able to write to friends, "Though I love the country, I may be thankful I live in London; for God makes me acceptable, and I hope useful, in my ministry. And your prospect from the highest hill in your neighbour-hood is not to be compared with mine from St. Mary's pulpit on a Sunday. God has blessed me with many friends, many endeared connexions; and therefore I need not envy you your mountains; for though I meet with riot and disorder in the streets, through mercy, we have *love* and *peace* at home."[30]

Encouraging younger ministers and friends

Those who enjoyed Newton's company at his prayer breakfasts at home and sought out his wise counsel included William Wilberforce, MP, through whose lengthy efforts the slave trade was finally abolished; John Clayton, Independent minister of Weighhouse Chapel; Claudius Buchanan, who prepared the way for the gospel in India and became Vice-Provost of Fort William College in Bengal; Charles Simeon, whose teaching ministry at Cambridge became the launching pad for so many missionaries; Richard Cecil, the author of these Memoirs; Hannah More, whose writings were so popular and led to the formation of the Religious Tract Society; Henry Martyn, Bible translator and missionary to Bengal; William Carey, the shoemaker whose zeal led to the formation of the Baptist Missionary Society, and who spent his life as a missionary to India, becoming professor of Sanskrit at Fort William College; Daniel Wilson, later Bishop of Calcutta; William Jay, who was to be pastor of Argyle Independent Chapel in Bath for more than sixty-two years; and James Moody.

James Moody

James Moody was pastor of the Independent meeting in Warwick where Newton had begun his ministry. (The first minister of the original Presbyterian source of this church, in the seventeenth century, was John Wilson, on whose death his friend Matthew Henry, the Bible commentator, wrote "He was a great loss; and I should say irreparable, did I not know that God has the residue of the Spirit.") Moody used to go up to London for six weeks a year to preach at the Tabernacle in Moorfields and Spa-fields chapel in Tottenham Court Road. He wrote home to his wife during one of these visits, saying that he had just spent "a sweet hour with dear Mr. Newton" adding how much it had helped him.[31] It was a meeting in Moody's house in Warwick in June 1793 that led to the formation of the London Missionary Society.

William Jay

William Jay writes in his autobiography[32] that after he had taken a service in London for Rowland Hill at Surrey Chapel, Newton came and introduced himself and asked to speak privately with him. Jay writes, "I led him into the study; and I have never forgotten the condescension and kindness with which he addressed me. Taking me by the hand, he said, 'Some of us are going off the stage, but we rejoice to see others rising up, and coming forward. But, my young friend, you are in a very trying situation, and I am concerned for your safety and welfare. I have been so many years in the ministry, and so many years a minister in London; and if you will allow me to mention some of the snares and dangers to which you are exposed, I shall be happy to do it.' How could I help feeling, not only willing to receive, but grateful for, such a seasonable warning? And how useful might the aged servants of God be to the younger, if they would privately and freely communicate of their experiences and observations! Some of the things he mentioned seemed for the moment rather strange and needless; but I confided in his wisdom, and time has fully shown me that they were all words in season.

"Mr. Newton also invited me to call upon him, and to his kind of open breakfast I soon repaired; and for years afterward, whenever I was in town, I availed myself as often as it was in my power of this invaluable privilege. On these occasions I met with ministers and Christians of all denominations; for he loved all who loved the Saviour, and all, while they were with him, felt themselves to be 'one in Christ Jesus.'

"In the family worship, after reading a chapter, he would add a few remarks on some verse or sentence, very brief, but weighty and striking, and affording some sentiment for the day. Whoever was present, he always prayed himself; the prayer was never long, but remarkably suitable and simple. After the service and the breakfast, he withdrew to his study with any of his male friends who could remain a while, and there, with his pipe (the only pipe I ever liked, except Robert Hall's), he would converse in a manner the most easy, and free, and varied, and delightful, and edifying."

During one of these occasions, "a forward young man said, 'Pray, Mr. Newton, what do you think of the entrance of sin into our world?' 'Sir,' said he, 'I never think of it. I know there is such a thing as moral evil, and I know there is a remedy for it; and there my knowledge begins, and there it ends.'"

Charles Simeon

From time to time Newton had contact with Charles Simeon. He wrote of him, "There is good going on at Cambridge. Mr. Simeon is much beloved and very useful; his conduct has almost suppressed the spirit of opposition which was once very fierce against him."[33]

On another occasion he commented, "Mr. Simeon preached for me last Wed. from Rev. 5, 11th, 12th and 13th verses. He spoke of the company, the object of their worship, and their song; I was going to say, as if he had just come down from among them. I think he had a favoured peep within the veil; and there was such a visible impression on his hearers as is not common."[34]

John Ryland, jnr.

John Ryland, Newton's young friend from Northampton whom he had first met in Olney when attending the Northampton Baptist Association meetings, was undecided about accepting a call to Broadmead Baptist, Bristol. He consulted Newton who thought it right for him to decline, but added that he thought they would ask him again. They did, twice more.

Newton discussed the call with Abraham Booth, pastor of Prescott Street Baptist Church, and passed on his advice, "Mr. Booth says, that if you consult only your personal ease and comfort you will stay where you are, for you will probably meet with more difficulties and exercises at Bristol, but if you regard the good of the whole [denomination], and the fairest opportunity of preventing evil and promoting the common cause, you must and will go. Of this, he is a better judge than I, but you must at least judge for yourself."[35]

The decision to leave Northampton took him almost two years to reach, during which time College Lane struggled to fend off the approaches of Broadmead, letting them know that the application for them to release their pastor "causes in us somewhat very opposite to pleasure" and that they were "more inclined to excuse your request, than to comply with it."

However, both churches were prepared to commit the matter to prayer. It was finally agreed that his place would be filled by a suitable alternative and Ryland prepared for the move. At the last moment the person expected to fill the Northampton pulpit declined. Ryland again turned to Newton for advice, who wrote back this time saying, "You have already passed the Rubicon and I see not how you can retreat," adding later, "Had I been one of your church I should have voted for nailing your ear to the door of College Lane Meeting House [Northampton]. If I could have stopped you, you should not have gone to Bristol, but I am a short sighted creature."[36]

Ryland went on to become president of the Baptist College in Bristol.

William Wilberforce
William Wilberforce's Christian beginnings are fascinating. His mother placed him in the care of his aunt Hannah Wilberforce in Wimbledon after his father died. As she was the (half) sister of John Thornton, young William saw quite a bit of John Newton, both in London and in Olney and came to regard him as a father figure. Newton saw the potential in him and prayed earnestly for his conversion. Wilberforce's mother hastily brought him back home to Hull when she realised the influence of these "Methodists" on her son.

In an undated letter from "Mr. N. to Mrs. W." quoted in *Gleanings*, Newton writes, "I hope your nephew engages good bodily health, and his soul nourished and refreshed; and though he lives in a barren land, I trust he finds that the Lord can open springs and fountains in the wilderness. The word of grace and the throne of grace afford wells of salvation, from which he cannot be debarred; from thence, I hope, he will daily draw with joy the water of life, and, like a tree of the Lord's planting, strike root downwards, and bear fruit upwards, and experience that the Lord is able to keep, establish, and comfort him, though for a season he is deprived of the public ordinances of the Gospel."[37]

Some years later, when William was a Member of Parliament he went on holiday touring Europe with a friend Isaac Milner (brother of Joseph). Their discussions on religion and on reading Philip Doddridge's book, *The Rise and Progress of Religion in the Soul of Man,* convinced him in theory of Biblical truth (the particular copy he read had been passed on from William Unwin, son of the family that Cowper stayed with). But it was some time before he finally decided to put Luke 11:13 to the test. Reading it, the same thought occurred to him as this very verse had prompted in Newton's mind during the storm at sea, "If these things be so – if there be any truth in all this – and if I set myself to seek the blessings thus promised – I shall certainly find a sensible effect and change wrought within me, such as is thus described. I will put the matter to the proof: I will try the experiment: I will seek, that I may find the promised blessings."[38] He did so and found peace in believing. He was uncertain, however, about his future. Perhaps the following passage from *Rise and Progress*[39] influenced his next move:

"But there are difficulties in the way. And what then? Have those difficulties never been cleared? Go to the living advocates for Christianity, to those of whose abilities, candor, and piety, you have the best opinion, if your prejudices will give you leave to have a good opinion of any such. Tell them your difficulties; hear their solutions; weigh them seriously, as those who know they must answer it to God. And while doubts continue, follow the truth as far as it will lead you, and take heed that you do not imprison it in unrighteousness (Romans 1:28)."

He sought a secret meeting with Newton, apprehensive of being seen to associate with a "Methodist". Newton encouraged him to stay in politics and directed him to Thomas Scott's ministry at the Lock.

Hannah Wilberforce shed tears of joy when she heard of his Christian commitment.[40] Henry Venn wrote excitedly to a friend, "Mr. Wilberforce has been at the chapel, and attends the preaching constantly. Much he has to give up! And what will be the issue, who can say?"[41]

Wilberforce was very touched when Newton told him that, from the time he first met him when he was a young boy in the care of his aunt Hannah, he had not failed constantly to pray for him.[42] Newton kept up a very supportive correspondence with Wilberforce, as the following extracts show:

18 May [1786?]
"My heart is with you, my dear sir. I see, though from a distance, the importance and difficulties of your situation. May the wisdom that influenced Joseph and Moses, and Daniel rest upon you. Not only to guide and animate you in the line of Political Duty – but especially to keep you in the habit of dependence upon God, and communion with him, in the midst of all the changes and bustle around you."[43]

He recommended the following books to Wilberforce, though he made it plain he had hoped he would rely for his direction on giving "attention to the Word of God, and the throne of His grace.... There is none teacheth like God, but He teaches us gradually and in the school of experience":[44] Augustine's *Confessions*, Bunyan's *Jerusalem Sinner Saved, Come and Welcome to Jesus Christ, Grace Abounding to the Chief of Sinners*, Baxter's *Call*, Alleine's *Alarm to the Unconverted*, Flavel "on *Providence*, on *The Keeping of the Heart*, and any of his works, most of which have been published in small books, his *Spiritual Navigation*".[45]

5 July 1788
"I have had no particular information concerning you of late, but that you were much better when you left Cambridge, and are now somewhere among the Mountains and Lakes of Westmoreland. I can honestly say, that were it practicable, I should not be unwilling to travel on foot, for the sake of spending two or three days with you in your present retreat.... But I must content myself with imaging the scene, and the pleasure – and in this way am often with you. What a difference between the magnificent solitudes of Westmoreland and the noisy hurry and pageantry which surround and pervade Westminster Hall!"[46]

Wilberforce to Newton   6 September 1788
"I believe I can truly declare, that not a single day has passed in which you have not been in my thoughts, and at those seasons too when the mind abstracts itself from the little cares and little concerns to which it is, alas, too apt to addict itself, and fixes its consideration on what it most esteems and loves – I trust I occupy a distinguished place in your regards at the times to which I am alluding: and in truth 'tis often matter of solid comfort to me, and of gratitude to the bountiful Giver of all mercies, to reflect that the prayers of many of the well beloved of the Lord are offered up for me: O my dear Sir, let

not your hands cease to be lifted up, lest Amalek prevail [Exodus 17:11-16] – entreat for me that I may be enabled by divine grace to resist and subdue all the numerous enemies of my salvation. My path is peculiarly steep and difficult and dangerous, but the prize is a crown of glory and 'celestial panoply' is offered me and the God of Hosts for my ally.

"This place wherein I looked this summer for much solitude and quiet, has proved very different from a retirement. The tour to the Lakes has become so fashionable that the banks of the Thames are scarcely more public than those of Windermere and you little knew what you were doing when you wished yourself with me in Westmoreland."[47]

When Wilberforce's *Practical View of the Prevailing Religious System of Professed Christians in the Higher and Middle Classes in this Country Contrasted with Real Christianity*[48] was published, Newton wrote, "I can scarcely talk or write without introducing Mr. Wilberforce's book. It revives my hope that, ripe as we seem for judgment, while the Lord raises up such witnesses for His truth, He will not give us up, as we justly deserve, for a prey to our enemies. His situation is such that this book *must* and *will* be read by many in high circles, to whom we little folks can get no access. If we preach they will not hear us; if we write they will not read. May the Lord *make it useful* to the great men both in Church and State."[49]

Newton expressed to Wilberforce his thoughts on the group operating from Clapham, later referred to as the Clapham Sect, "But when I think of you, Mr. Thornton and a few of your friends, I am ready to address you in the words of Mordecai – who knoweth but God has raised you up for such a time as this!"[50]

He felt that Wilberforce had a very significant contribution to make in advancing missionary causes. Once when writing to him,[51] his thoughts were blocked for a while by discordant sounds. It led him into meditation on his own nature and into a pertinent expression of Wilberforce's role in the future spread of the gospel.

"At present while I write a harpsichord is tuning in my ears which does not at all help my invention [imagination]. Methinks I may compare myself to a harpsichord, how often in tuning, how seldom in tune, and how soon put out of tune again. My imagination, in particular, is as an instrument, which seems not in my own power. Happy am I, when it is under a gracious influence. But at times, it seems as if an evil genius had command of the keys. Then I am tortured with a medley of folly, discord and confusion, from which I cannot run, nor can I stop my ears against it, for it is within me. Wonderful is the grace that can cause the voice of joy and melody to be heard, when but a little before, all was disorder and distress. If the Lord appears, the storm is hush, and calm succeeds....

"To you, as the instrument, we owe the pleasing prospect of an opening for the propagation of the gospel in the Southern Hemisphere. Who can tell what important consequences may depend upon Mr. Johnson's going to New Hollands! It may seem but a small event at present. So a foundation stone, when laid, is small compared with the building to be erected upon it; but it is the beginning and earnest of the whole. This small beginning, may be like the dawn, which advances to a bright day, and leads on to a happy time, when many nations, which now sit in darkness and in the region of the shadow of death, shall rejoice in the light of the Sun of Righteousness."

Richard Johnson (CMS)

Through Wilberforce's efforts, permission was granted for Richard Johnson to sail as chaplain of the first shipment of convicts to Botany Bay, New South Wales, opening the way for the CMS into Australia.

William Bull had written to Newton the previous month enquiring about "Mr. Johnson's Botany Bay scheme" adding, "It filled me with a thousand thanks that the Lord did not call me to that cross. A call to be bound to the stake does not seem to me more painful.... However, I can easily believe it possible his call may be from God; and if it is, I have no doubt but He will fit him for it, and support him under it. I am glad it was not in my way to tell him what I thought of it, and you have too much humanity to let him know."[52]

Newton replied, "A minister who should go to Botany Bay without a call from the Lord, and without receiving from Him an apostolic spirit, the spirit of a missionary, enabling him to forsake all, to give up all, to venture all, to put himself into the Lord's hands without reserve, to sink or swim, had better run his head against a brick wall. I am strongly inclined to hope Mr. Johnson is thus called, and will be thus qualified. I should not advise him to consult you upon this point. Your appointment is to smoke your pipe quietly at home, to preach, and to lecture to your pupils. You are not cut out for a missionary; and nothing, perhaps, would have been done either in the Danish

West Indian Islands, or in Greenland, if the attachments and feelings of all men had been like yours and mine. I must have my tea, my regular hours, and twenty little things which I can have when my post is fixed. I should shrink upon the thought of living upon seals and train oil. I have not zeal to sell myself to be a slave for the opportunity of preaching to the slaves while I was working with them; but the Lord inspired the Moravian missionaries with the resolution to court hardships like these, so that they might win souls, and He gave them success. Oh, if Johnson is the man whom the Lord appoints to the honour of being the first to carry the glad tidings into the southern hemisphere, he will be a great and honoured man indeed! Let the world admire Columbus, Drake, and Cook, Johnson in my view will be unspeakably superior to them all. I believe, with his simple views, the Lord will not permit him to mistake His will in an affair of such vast importance; therefore, if he does go, I shall hope for a happy event. If I am not mistaken, sooner or later the gospel must be preached in the South Seas; if so, there must be a beginning. We hope this is the time. Perhaps this is the final cause of our attempting a settlement in New Holland. Often when the politicians have one thing in view, the Lord has another; and their plans succeed in order to the accomplishment of His."[53]

William Carey (BMS)

William Carey was another who found encouragement from Newton. Once a member of John Sutcliff's Baptist Church in Olney, he approached Newton in London with an introduction from the minister of St. Mary's in Leicester, where Carey had become the Baptist pastor. Newton in turn wrote a letter to introduce him to Wilberforce, "I expect that a Mr. Cary [sic] will shortly wait upon you, and will probably bring an introductory line from me. Though I do not personally know him, his character and business are such that I could not refuse him this request.

"He was the Baptist Minister at Leicester, well known to Mr. Robinson, and much respected by him. Mr. Robinson has often mentioned him to me in terms of strong approbation. He has for some time had a strong desire of preaching the Gospel among the heathen, and the accounts he received from Mr. Thomas (of whom I know nothing but from Mr. Grant) determined his choice to Bengal. Mr. Cary wishes to know if it be practicable to procure the Company's leave for his passage thither, or if he might be permitted to stay, if he could find his way by a foreign ship. He thought, if you and Mr. [Henry] Thornton approved of his character, motives and ends, your patronage might probably enable him to go. However this may be, if you could afford him a short audience, you could perhaps give him such advice in a quarter of an hour, as might put him in a right path, and be useful to him through life.

"I believe what he heard from Mr. Thomas (how true I know not) chiefly determined him to think of India. He said he was ready to go any where, to the ends of the earth, so that he might preach the Gospel to the ignorant. I mentioned America, that there was an open door to Canada and Nova Scotia, particularly to New Brunswick; whether he considers himself too far engaged for Bengal, to think of any other place I know not, but perhaps a word from you might have weight. From what Mr. Robinson has said of him, I believe he may be depended upon as a faithful man; and that his zeal to be a Missionary is not the flight of a warm fancy, but the desire of a man who is willing to give up, and to hazard everything for the glory of God and the good of souls."[54]   *27 May 1793*

In his last week in England, Carey, blocked by uproar at India House over Wilberforce's success in paving the way in parliament for missionaries to India, and refused a licence to allow his entry into Bengal, called on "good old father Newton" to ask what to do if he got to India and was turned back. Newton told him, "Conclude that your Lord has nothing there for you to accomplish. If He have, no power on earth can prevent you."[55] Carey's eccentric friend Thomas, with whom he was going out to Bengal, "happened" to meet a ship's captain for whom he had previously been ship's surgeon, and was persuaded to take the risk of allowing them to sail with him. However, they had more delays and Providential interventions before finally reaching India.

Once in Bengal, Carey felt the pressure keenly. "My soul is a jungle, when it ought to be a garden.... I can scarce tell whether I have the grace of God or no.... How shall I help India, with so little godliness myself?" He wrote to Newton in December 1779, "I know God can use weak instruments, but I often question whether it would be for His honour to work by such as me."[56]

He greatly appreciated Newton's response and replied to him from

Mudnabatty, "Yours [Newton's letter] of last year I received and must say that it not only afforded me much pleasure, but profit also: the justice of your remarks upon disappointments, and want of success, was such as struck me very forcibly, and contributed much to my support and encouragement and I feel myself determined to go on in the name of the Lord, even till death, depending on him to give success in his own time, and in his own method."[57]

Newton's opinion was, "Such a man as Carey is more to me than a bishop or an archbishop: he is an apostle."[58]

When William Ward, the printer, was due to join Carey in India, a party including Andrew Fuller, John Sutcliff and Abraham Booth gathered to bid the missionaries farewell. Ward was delighted to discover that the Captain of the ship was an elder in an American church whose pastor was known to Newton. In a letter to Samuel Pearce, pastor of Cannon Street, Birmingham, he added, "We breakfasted at Mr. Newton's the other morning, and the old man was truly excellent. Mentioning his age he said he was one of the old 74s falling to pieces."[59]

At home

Bateman recorded in his *Life of Daniel Wilson*,[60] "It was the custom of that excellent clergyman to open his house for religious purposes on Tuesday and Saturday evening. On Saturday evenings, several of the London clergy regularly met there: on Tuesday evenings, he received (to use his own words) 'Parsons, Parsonets, and Parsonettas.' On these occasions some religious subject was freely discussed and conversed upon, and the meeting closed with prayer.

"Mr. Newton has also his breakfast parties, open to friends by invitation. They were perhaps the most edifying; for the good old man, in his velvet cap and damask dressing-gown, was then fresh and communicative, always instructive, always benevolent. His expositions of Scripture with his family, which consisted of niece, some aged servants, and some poor blind inmates of his house, were peculiarly simple and devout."

Wilson wrote to Mr. Eyre, "I this morning breakfasted with Mr. Newton. I hope the conversation I had with him will not soon be effaced from my mind. He inculcated that salutary lesson you mentioned in your letter, of 'waiting patiently upon the Lord'. He told me, God could, no doubt, if He pleased, produce a full-grown oak in an instant on the most barren spot; but that such was not the ordinary working of His providence...."

Introduced at one of these breakfasts to a young man from the country who "had expressed a desire to see him," Newton replied, "Ah, I was a wild beast once, on the coast of Africa, and the Lord tamed me; and there are many people now who have a curiosity to see me!"[61]

Claudius Buchanan

Cecil's hopes for Buchanan's autobiography were met. His *Memoirs*[62] gave full details of his journey down from Scotland to London. Having been disappointed in not being eligible for a certain young lady "superior to himself in birth and fortune", he set out for Europe on foot, following Dr. Goldsmith's example, intending to support himself by playing his violin. But he told his parents he had employment as a tutor. Things didn't work out. He only got as far as London before poverty and distress stopped him, but in his pride he wrote back to his family as if from Europe. He was reduced to starvation before he finally found work. A colleague invited him to church where he came under deep conviction of sin. He subsequently came across a copy of Doddridge's *Rise and Progress* that had been left at a public bath. Reading this helped him. He wrote back to his mother, admitting his position and asking for her prayers. She suggested he got in touch with John Newton if at all possible.

Buchanan's note to Newton describes his response, "On receipt of my mother's letter I immediately reflected that I had heard there was a crowded audience at a church in Lombard Street. Thither I accordingly went the next Sunday evening, and when you spoke, I thought I heard the words of eternal life. I listened with avidity, and wished that you had preached till midnight.... You say many things that touch my heart deeply, and I trust your ministry has been in some degree blessed to me: but your subjects are generally addressed to those who are already established in the faith, or to those who have not sought God at all. Will you then drop one word to me? If there is any comfort in the word of life for such as I am, O shed a little of it on my heart. And yet I am sensible that I am not prepared to receive that comfort. My sins do not affect me as I wish. All that I can speak of is a strong desire to be converted to my God. O sir, what shall I do to inherit eternal life? I see clearly that I cannot be happy in any degree, even in this life, until I make my peace with God; but how shall I make that peace? If the world were my inheritance, I would sell it, to purchase that pearl of great price. How I weep when I read of the prodigal son as described by our Lord! I would walk many miles to hear a sermon from the 12th and 13th verses of the 33rd chapter of the 2nd book of Chronicles....

"Tomorrow is the day you have appointed for a sermon to young people. Will you remember *me* and speak some suitable word, that by the act of the blessed Spirit may reach my heart?"

Buchanan took up Newton's invitation to the anonymous letter writer to speak to him. "I called on him on the Tuesday following, and experienced such a happy hour as I ought never to forget. If he had been my father, he could not have expressed more solicitude for my welfare. Mr. N. engaged me much. He put into my hands the narrative of his life, and some of his letters; begged my careful perusal of them before I saw him again, and gave me a general invitation to breakfast with him when and as often as I could."

After qualifying at Cambridge under Henry Thornton's sponsorship Buchanan became Newton's curate. When John Venn needed a replacement at Clapham while he was away, Newton offered him Buchanan, adding, "As to myself, if well, I can either make shift without him (though not cleverly on Sacrament days) or I want him always alike. For now it is known that I have a curate, my kind friends who used to help me, will of course think of me no longer. But I have cause to be thankful, that at my time of life [aged 70], I can go through the whole service of the day if needful without help, and without much inconvenience."[63]

A few months later Buchanan was appointed one of the chaplains to the East India Company. The important station abroad that Cecil wrote of was Vice Provost of the College of Fort William in Bengal. Presumably he was a little uncertain of associating with the Baptist missionaries, for Newton had to write to him, "It is easy for you (little as yet tried in character, and from your superior and patronized station), to look down upon men who have given themselves to the Lord, and are bearing the burden and heat of the day. I do not look for miracles; but if God were to work one in our day, I should not wonder if it were in favour of Dr. Carey."[64] Buchanan's work in India prepared the way for the Gospel there, with support from William Wilberforce in Parliament, the backing of the Church Missionary

Society and others such as Andrew Fuller. William Carey wrote home
of the great privilege that Calcutta had in Claudius Buchanan and his
colleague Brown.[65]

Henry Martyn

Another missionary to call on Newton on the way out to Bengal was
Henry Martyn, Charles Simeon's curate at Holy Trinity, Cambridge.
His *Journals* have a number of references to Richard Cecil, who,
known for a commanding preaching style, was intent on improving
Martyn's delivery. "Mr. Cecil has been taking a great deal of pains
with me," he wrote, "My insipid, inanimate manner in the pulpit, he
says, is intolerable."[66]

However, he found a more gentle form of encouragement in
Newton, as his notes for 25th April 1805 show: "Breakfasted with
the venerable Mr. Newton, who made several striking remarks in
reference to my work. He said he had heard of a clever gardener,
who would sow seeds when the meat was put down to roast, and
engage to produce a salad by the time it was ready, but the Lord did
not sow oaks in this way. On my saying that perhaps I should never
live to see much fruit; he answered I should have a bird's-eye view
of it, which would be much better. When I spoke of the opposition
that I should be likely to meet with, he said, he supposed Satan would
not love me for what I was about to do. The old man prayed afterwards
with sweet simplicity."[67]

Once in India Martyn wrote, "I have hitherto lived to little purpose,
like a clod upon the earth. Now let me burn out for God!"[68] Henry
Martyn died from a fever at the age of thirty-one, having accomplished
translations of the New Testament and Prayer Book into Hindustani,
the New Testament and Psalms into Persian, and the Gospels into
Judaeo-Persic.

Utopian Dissenting Academy

When Newton moved to London he remained in regular contact with
Bull. Bull naturally turned to Newton for advice some years later
when was considering starting an academy for dissenting ministers in
Newport Pagnell. John Clayton asked Newton on his behalf to come up
with an outline for them. Newton replied to Bull that he was "quite a
stranger to what passes within the walls of colleges and academies"
but that the proposal to educate young men for the ministry was so
important that he would offer his thoughts as if "in Utopia, where I

could have the modelling of everything to my own mind."[69]

"Though I have filled seven sheets of note paper with very close writing, I have a good hope there will hardly be found a single period which will meet your disapprobation. Your good opinion is of more consequence to me than that of others, because you are a nearer neighbour to me; for you live, or frequently reside, in Utopia, as well as myself. Though you and I are both originals in our way, have our separate and distinct peculiarities, and consequently cannot be exactly alike, yet, it appears to me (*absist invidia*)[70] that I have the honour to think more with you upon the whole circle of our professional subjects than any minister I know; accordingly, I expect that you will approve in a manner of the whole and every part of my plan; whereas I can hardly think of any other friend of mine who may not find something to object to here and there."[71]

On Bull's approval of the plan, Newton wrote to him, "This will seem an awkward business all round to some persons. What apology can Mr. Clayton make to many dissenters for applying to a clergyman for the plan of an academy? And what can the poor cleric say to some people in his line, for chalking out the lines of a dissenting, methodistical academy? How will some of the staunch tabernacle-folks like his innuendoes against some of their popular, loud, powerful preachers? I think this poor speckled bird will be pecked at by fowls of every wing. But it is well, that though he does not wish to offend any of them, he is mighty indifferent as to their censures. If we act with a single eye, and are desirous to serve and please the Lord, we may be easy as to consequences. When the conscience is clear, and the heart simple, neither the applauses nor the anathemas of worms are worth two-pence a bushel."[72]

He warned him of what might lie ahead,[73] "If there is good to be done at Newport, Satan will not stand and look on with the indifference of a mere spectator: he will do what he can to disturb the peace of the academy within doors, and to misrepresent it abroad. The tutor and pupils too had need be angels to keep quite out of the reach of his malice and influence. And as his own name is Legion, so he has a legion of instruments of various talents in his service: some to invent; some who would not go so far as to invent a falsehood, are yet very well pleased to circulate it; and if they can say *I was told so*, they think they are quite safe and right. The skill of others lies in exaggerating; others in colouring and misrepresenting, which they do so cleverly, that though the substance of what they say be truth, it shall have all the effects of a lie. Others are masters in the way of surmise and insinuation; they will not say, *It is so*, but, *It is well if it be not so*, or *I wish it may not prove so*, which with weak and credulous folks, answers the purpose no less than if they had proved *it certainly was so*. Again, others, when a word or action is capable of two constructions, have an admirable dexterity in taking it by the wrong handle. No wonder, if the combined effort of so many acts and so much industry, should make a great noise abroad, and be sensibly felt at home. But simplicity, and integrity, under the Lord's blessing, though they be sometimes jostled, cannot be overthrown. *Magna est veritas, et prevalebit.*[74] If the Lord gives you grace and wisdom to do your part, you may depend on it he will do his, and fulfil that promise: *no weapon that is formed against thee shall prosper.*"[75]

A little more than fifty years later, the Academy had educated over eighty young men for the ministry in the British Isles and overseas as missionaries in Jamaica, the West Indies, Calcutta, the East Indies and America.

Eliza Cunningham
Eliza Cunningham was Mary Newton's niece, the daughter of her sister Elizabeth. She lost her brother, her father, her sister and finally her mother. In 1783 she came to live with the Newtons, who were then in Charles Square. She arrived with a fever, a cough and sweats. At times she recovered temporarily and was taken on holiday to bathe at the seaside at Southampton and Lymington. As her body grew weaker, her faith grew stronger. She died two years later at the age of fourteen. Newton was constantly asked to repeat her testimony. He eventually wrote a short account of her life, mainly of the last few months spent with them. *A Monument to the Praise of the Lord's Goodness and to the Memory of Dear Eliza Cunningham* is amongst Newton's *Works*.[76]

The British Library has a copy of the 3rd edition of this, to which is added an account of her brother John, written by his mother, Elizabeth Cunningham. From this it appears that John spent a year with the Newtons in Olney when he was just three. His mother wrote, "Soon after he came home to us, he asked why we had not prayer as often as at his uncle's, and expressing his liking their way best. I think this early impression upon his mind of a holy life, was, with God's blessing, owing to their good example and instructions." He maintained a strong faith, delighting in reading the Bible and withdrawing for private prayer for an hour every evening. He died just before his thirteenth birthday.

Newton's wife's death

Mary Newton's death was something John had dreaded for years. It had been difficult to watch her fade away in the last few months. He described his pain to Wilberforce:

"My dear Mrs. Newton is in dying circumstances. We have expected her dismission almost daily for about a month past. She is still living, but is so low and weak, that she can neither move nor be moved, can hardly bear to speak, or to hear my voice, if I attempt to speak to her. It has been a long time of trial with me, for I am touched in a tender point. But the Lord is very gracious to me. I am supported. I eat, sleep and preach as usual. I see much reason to be thankful that she has been spared to me so long (more than forty years) and none to think it hard that I am to part with her at last. For could we desire or expect to live always here? Oh he is Wise and Good. He does all things well. I am enabled with some consciousness of sincerity to say, Not my will but thine be done! How little does the world ... appear to me now!"   *23 November 1790*[77]

There is a more detailed account of Mary Newton's illness and death in Newton's *Works*.[78]

He had long since chosen the text for her funeral sermon – Habakkuk 3:17,18 – and deliberately never preached from it until then. Thomas Frognall Dibdin, author of *Bibliomania*, recalled being at the funeral. "I remember, when a lad of about fifteen, being taken by my uncle to hear the well-known Mr. Newton (the friend of Cowper the poet) preach his wife's funeral sermon in the church of St. Mary's Woolnoth in Lombard Street. Newton was then well stricken in years, with a tremulous voice, and in the costume of the full-bottomed wig of the day. He had, and always had, the entire possession of the ear of his congregation. He spoke at first feebly and leisurely, but as he warmed, his ideas and periods seemed mutually to enlarge: the tears trickled down his cheeks, and his action and expression were at times quite out of the ordinary course of things. It was as the *mens agitans moleum et magno se corpore miscens*.[79] In fact, the preacher was *one* with his *discourse*. To this day I have not forgotten his text, Habakkuk 3:17-18, *Although the fig tree shall not blossom, neither shall fruit be in the vines; the labour of the olive shall fail, and the fields shall yield no meat; the flock shall be cut off from the fold, and there shall be no herd in the stalls: Yet I will rejoice in the LORD, I will joy in the God of my "salvation"*.[80]

Cowper wrote to offer comfort to his old friend: "The years that we have seen together will never be out of our remembrance; and, so long as we remember them, we must remember you with affection. In the pulpit, and out of the pulpit, you laboured in every possible way to serve us; and we must have a short memory indeed for the kindness of a friend, could we by any means become forgetful of yours.

"You speak of your late loss in a manner that affected me much; and when I read that part of your letter, I mourned with you and for you. But surely, I said to myself, no man had ever less reason to charge his conduct to a wife with any thing blameworthy. Thoughts of that complexion, however, are no doubt extremely natural on the occasion of such a loss; and a man seems not to have valued sufficiently, when he possesses it no longer, what, while he possessed it, he valued more than life. I am mistaken, too, or you can recollect a time when you had fears, and such as became a Christian, of loving too much; and it is likely that you have even prayed to be preserved from doing so. I suggest this to you as a plea against those self-accusations, which I am satisfied that you do not deserve, and as an effectual answer to them all. You may do well to consider, that had the deceased been the survivor she would have charged herself in the same manner, and I am sure you will acknowledge, without any sufficient reason. The truth is, that you both loved at least as much as you ought, and, I dare say, had not a friend in the world who did not frequently observe it. To love just enough, and not a bit too much, is not for creatures who can do nothing well. If we fail in our duties less arduous, how should we succeed in this, the most arduous of all?"[81]

Newton described the mixture of pain and peace he experienced in Polly's absence in a letter to Captain and Mrs. Hansard.[82] Speaking first of the death of others close to him, including his niece Eliza, he wrote, "But I still had *one* left, that seemed to make amends for all! The will of the Lord was declared by the event, and I acquiesced; but how often have I thought, if *she* should be taken from me, though

His grace might enable me to submit, the flesh *must* sink under the blow, and I should never wear a cheerful look again. Yet *He* has been better to me than my deserts or fears; *He* helps me to do very tolerably well without her. I still live in the same house, where every room, and every chair, seems to say, 'she is not here!' I sleep in the same bed where she long languished, and where I saw her draw her last breath, and I have never felt a wish to change the scene. Though no object appears quite the same to me, and a sort of sombre cast hangs over them all, yet I can relish in my many memories, and smile and chat with my friends as formerly. I know not that I am more or less affected than I was the first day after she left me. I write this for your encouragement. Imagination is a busy painter, and disposed at times to draw frightful pictures of what *may* happen: but we may depend upon it, that nothing *shall* happen, to which *His* promises of strength, according to the day, and 'grace sufficient for us,' shall not render those who trust in *Him* fully equal."

When Samuel Palmer referred to her, Newton wrote back, "I would spend half an hour at the church-door to see a person whom I should think so nearly resembled my late dear Mary, as it seems you did; but I do not expect it. I account it a great mercy, that through life, from my partiality to her, she always appeared to me *Sans pareil*."[83]

Betsy Catlett

Elizabeth Catlett (Betsy) was the daughter of Mary's younger brother George. When Elizabeth's mother died Mary went down to Kent, sending word back to John, "When I came here, my sister's house all in confusion, beds down and drawers and chests and things all about. One can hardly stir about.... and seeing my poor brother in such a way is very distressing. He never eats but by himself, and is afraid of everybody that comes, lest they come to cheat him."[84]

They adopted their niece in 1774 when George died and while they were still in Olney. Betsy went to a boarding school in Northampton run by Mrs. Trinder, whose husband was a deacon at John Ryland's Baptist church. Thomas Trinder had for a while attended White Row Independent Meeting in London, where he had met George Flower, a wealthy stationer of Canon Street. George's daughter, Jane, came to the Trinders' school and became a good friend of Betsy's. When Newton went across to Northampton he often preached at the Trinders' school and later maintained a correspondence with Jane, some of which was published in *Cardiphonia.*

Betsy later followed the Newtons up to London, going to school in Highgate.

For the year she was in Bedlam Newton would get help to walk there every day, his eyesight having nearly gone by this time. He would wait outside until told that she had seen him and had waved her handkerchief.

Betsy married Joseph Smith in St. Mary Woolnoth on 2nd May 1805. Newton's shaky hand signed the register entry.[85] Her husband was an optician who kept a shop outside the Royal Exchange. The three of them lived together at No. 6 Coleman Street Buildings.

Honorary Degree
Newton's unwillingness to be awarded a doctorate prompted him to write to John Campbell, then in Edinburgh, "I have been hurt by two or three letters directed to Dr. Newton. I beg you to inform my friends in Scotland, as they come in your way, that, after a little time, if any letters come to me, addressed to Dr. Newton, I shall be obliged to send them back unopened. I know no person. I never shall, I never will, by the grace of God."[86] Drawing attention to his youthful years spent in Africa, he added, "Shall such a compound of misery and mischief, as I then was, be called DOCTOR? Surely not." However, he was pleased with the honourary degree in so far as it showed a regard for the Gospel truths he professed.

Old Age and Death
Newton's eyesight and hearing were fading, but his heart was strong. Speaking of an interview with Mr. Newton at the house of a mutual friend, Bull said, "Before we parted, we made him speak, which he did for fifty minutes on *I, if I be lifted up from the earth, will draw all men unto me.* But his understanding is in ruins. Yet its very ruins are precious, and the bits you pick up retain their intrinsic value, beauty and riches."[87]

When Newton died, William Bull wrote to Betsy, "My dear and very highly-esteemed friend, When I heard of the removal of the dear departed, I wished to have written to you directly; but feeling grieved, as I was exceedingly, and very much agitated, I dare not trust a pen in my hand, lest I should widen the wound I wished to heal, and set it bleeding afresh. It seemed best to wait till my spirits were a little more composed.

"Very, very dear indeed was the departed to my heart! He sought me, he owned me as a brother in the year 1764, and to this day always carried himself as a tender, faithful, affectionate friend. How many things has he done to serve me; how often has he exerted himself to vindicate my character, or to soften down the offence my foibles have given occasion to. How pointedly did he manifest a most endearing partiality to my person and ministry, and even before my face has reproved others who have said things that he thought might hurt my prejudices or wound my feelings. With what assiduity did he labour to serve me! With how excellent a spirit did he converse with me and write to me! Oh, how much I loved him, and how richly did he merit my love! Since his removal, many, many things recur to my memory which I had forgotten. There is no man living (my son excepted) so dear to my heart."[88]

In his will Newton left money to his sister Thomasina Nind, his nephews Benjamin and Henry Nind, his sister-in-law Ann Newton (wife of his brother Henry), his servants (as a token of his "gratitude for their fidelity and affection and particularly for their attention and kindness during the long illness of my late dear wife") Elizabeth Crabb, Sarah Hodges and Mary Walker (the niece of Elizabeth Crabb) and his clerk at St. Mary Woolnoth, Thomas Batt. Everything else he possessed he bequeathed to his "dear adopted child Elizabeth Catlett". A codicil was added with gifts to the Sunday School Society and the Society for the Relief of Poor Clergymen in the Country. It also relieved Betsy of the responsibility of acting as executrix.

Richard Cecil preached Newton's funeral sermon in St. Mary Woolnoth on 3 January 1808 from Luke 12:42, 43 – *Who then is that faithful and wise steward whom his Lord shall make ruler over his household, to give them their portion in due season? Blessed is that servant when his Lord, when he cometh, shall find so doing* (see Appendix 9).

CHAPTER 9

REVIEW OF
MR. NEWTON'S CHARACTER

There seems to be little need of giving a general character of Mr. N. after the particulars which appear in the foregoing Memoirs. He unquestionably was a child of peculiar providence, in every step of his progress; and the deep sense of the extraordinary dispensation through which he had passed, was the prominent topic in his conversation. Those, who personally knew the man, could have no doubt of the probity with which his *Narrative* (singular as it may appear) was written. They, however, who could not view the subject of these Memoirs so nearly as his particular friends did, may wish to learn something further of his character with respect to his LITERARY ATTAINMENTS – his MINISTRY – his FAMILY HABITS – his WRITINGS – and his FAMILIAR CONVERSATION.

Of his LITERATURE, we learn from his *Narrative* what he attained in the learned languages; and that, by almost incredible efforts. Few men have undertaken such difficulties under such disadvantages. It, therefore, seems more extraordinary, that he should have attained so much, than that he should not have acquired more. Nor did he quit his pursuits of this kind, but in order to gain that knowledge which he deemed much more important. Whatever he conceived had a tendency to qualify him, as *a scribe well instructed in the kingdom of God, bringing out of his treasury things new and old* [1] – I say, in pursuit of *this* point, he might have adopted the Apostle's expression, *One thing I do.* [2] By a principle so simply and firmly directed he furnished his mind with much information: he had consulted the best old divines; he had read the moderns of reputation with avidity; and was constantly watching whatever might serve for analogies or illustrations in the service of religion. "A Minister," he used to say, "wherever he is, should be always in his study. He should look at every man, and at every thing, as capable of affording him some instruction." – His mind, therefore, was ever intent on his calling – ever extracting something even from the basest materials, which he could turn into gold.

In consequence of this incessant attention to this object, while many (whose early advantages greatly exceeded his) might excel Mr. N. in the knowledge and investigation of some curious abstract, but very unimportant points; he vastly excelled them in points of infinitely higher importance to man: In the knowledge of God, of his word, and of the human heart in its wants and resources, Newton would have stood among mere scholars, as his name-sake the philosopher stood in science among ordinary men. I might say the same of some others, who have set out late in the profession; but who, with a portion of Mr. N.'s piety and ardour, have greatly outstripped those who have had every early advantage and encouragement: men with specious titles and high connexions have received the *rewards*; while men, like Newton, without them have done the *work*.

With respect to his MINISTRY, he appeared, perhaps, to least advantage in the pulpit; as he did not generally aim at accuracy in the *composition* of his sermons, nor at any *address* in the delivery of them. His utterance was far from clear, and his attitudes ungraceful. He possessed, however, so much affection for his people, and so much zeal for their best interests, that the defect of his manner was of little consideration with his constant hearers; at the same time, his capacity and habit of entering into their trials and experience, gave the highest interest to his ministry among them. Besides which he frequently interspersed the most brilliant allusions, and brought forward such happy illustrations of his subject, and those with so much unction on his own heart, as melted and enlarged theirs. The parent-like tenderness and affection, which accompanies his instruction, made them prefer him to preachers, who, on other accounts, were much more generally popular.

It ought also to be noted, that, amidst the extravagant notions and unscriptural positions which have sometimes disgraced the religious world, Mr. N. never departed, in any instance, from soundly and seriously promulgating the *faith once delivered to the saints*;[3] of which his writings will remain the best evidence. His doctrine was strictly that of the Church of England, urged on the consciences of men in the most practical and experimental manner. "I hope," said he one day to me, smiling, "I hope I am upon the whole a SCRIPTURAL preacher; for I find I am considered as an Arminian among the high Calvinists, and as a Calvinist among the strenuous Arminians."

I never observed any thing like bigotry in his ministerial character; though he seemed at all times to appreciate the beauty of order, and its good effects in the ministry. He had formerly been intimately connected with some highly respectable Ministers among the Dissenters, and retained a cordial regard for many to the last. He considered the strong prejudices which attach to both Churchmen and Dissenters, as arising more from education than from principle. But, being himself both a Clergyman and an Incumbent in the Church of England, he wished to be consistent. In public, therefore, he felt he could not act with some Ministers, whom he thought truly good men, and to whom he cordially wished success in their endeavours; and he patiently met the consequence. They called him a *bigot*; and he, in return, prayed for them, that they might not be *really* such.

He had formerly taken much pains in composing his sermons, as I could perceive in one MS which I looked through; and, even latterly, I have known him, whenever he felt it necessary, produce admirable plans for the pulpit. I own I thought his judgment deficient, in not deeming such preparation necessary at *all* times. I have sat in pain, when he has spoken unguardedly in this way before young Ministers; men, who, with but comparatively slight degrees of his information and experience, would draw encouragement to ascend the pulpit with but little previous study of their subject. A Minister is not to be blamed, who cannot rise to qualifications which some of his brethren have attained; but he is certainly bound to improve his own talent to the utmost of his power: he is not to cover his sloth, his love of company, or his disposition to attend a wealthy patron, with the *pretence* of depending entirely on *divine influence.* Timothy had as good ground, at least, for expecting such influence, as any of his successors in the ministry; and yet the Apostle admonishes him to *give attendance to reading, to exhortation,* and *to doctrine* – to *neglect not the gift that was in him* – to *meditate upon these things* – to *give* himself WHOLLY *to them, that* his *profiting* might *appear to all.*[4]

Mr. N. regularly preached on the Sunday morning and evening at St. Mary Woolnoth, and also on the Wednesday morning. After he was turned of seventy he often undertook to assist other clergymen; sometimes even to the preaching of six sermons in the space of a week. What was more extraordinary, he continued his usual course of preaching at his own church after he was fourscore years old, and that, when he could no longer see to read his text! His memory and voice sometimes failed him; but it was remarked, that at this great age, he was no where more recollected or lively than in the pulpit. He was punctual as to time with his congregation. Every first Sunday evening in the month he preached on relative duties. Mr. Alderman Lea regularly sent his carriage to convey him to the church, and Mr. Bates sent his servant to attend him in the pulpit; which friendly assistance was continued till Mr. N. could appear no longer in public.

His ministerial visits were exemplary. I do not recollect one, though favoured with many, in which his general information and lively genius did not communicate instruction, and his affectionate and condescending sympathy did not leave comfort.

Truth demands it should be said, that he did not always administer consolation, nor give an account of characters, with sufficient discrimination. His talent did not lie in *discerning of spirits.*[5] I never saw him so much moved, as when any friend endeavoured to correct his errors in this respect. His credulity seemed to arise from the consciousness he had of his own integrity; and from that sort of parental fondness which he bore to all his friends, real or pretended. I knew one, since dead, whom he thus described while living – "He is certainly an odd man, and has failings; but he has great integrity, and I hope he is going to heaven:" whereas, almost all who knew him thought the man should go first into the pillory!

In his FAMILY Mr. N. might be admired more safely than imitated. His excessive attachment to Mrs. N. is so fully displayed in his *Narrative*, and confirmed in the two volumes he thought it proper to publish, entitled, *Letters to a Wife*, that the reader will need no information on this subject. – Some of his friends wished this violent attachment had been cast more into the shade; as tending to furnish a spur, where human nature generally needs a curb. He used, indeed, to speak of such attachments, in the abstract, as *idolatry*; though his own was providentially ordered to be the main hinge on which his preservation and deliverance turned, while in his worst state. Good men, however, cannot be too cautious how they give sanction, by their expressions or example, to a passion, which, when not under sober regulation, has overwhelmed not only families, but states, with disgrace and ruin.

With his unusual degree of benevolence and affection, it was not extraordinary that the spiritual interests of his servants were brought forward, and examined severally every Sunday afternoon; nor that, being treated like children, they should grow old in his service. In short, Mr. N. could *live* no longer than he could *love*: it is no wonder, therefore, if his nieces had more of his heart than is generally afforded to their own children by the fondest parents. It has already been mentioned that his house was an asylum for the perplexed or afflicted. – Young Ministers were peculiarly the objects of his attention: he instructed them: he encouraged them: he warned them: and might truly be said to be a father in Christ, *spending and being spent*,[6] for the interest of his Church. In order thus to execute the various avocations of the day, he used to rise early: he seldom was found abroad in the evening, and was exact in his appointments.

Of his WRITINGS, I think little needs to be said here: they are in wide circulation, and best speak for themselves. An able editor is now employed in adding some posthumous pieces, left for publication by the author. After which, the whole will appear in a complete set,[7] with a reduced copy of the admirable portrait of Mr. N. lately published by Mr. Smith, engraved by J. Collyer, A.R.A., from an original painting by J. Russell, R.A. This was the *only* reason why no portrait was published in these Memoirs,* as had been done in the Memoirs of the Hon. and Rev. Mr. Cadogan, and of John Bacon, Esq. – I hope to see a fuller and more accurate account of these writings published by the editor, should the executors deem it necessary. At present, therefore, what I shall observe upon them will be but general and cursory.

The *Sermons* which Mr. N. published at Liverpool, after being refused on his first application for orders, were intended to show what he would have preached, had he been admitted: they are highly creditable to his understanding and to his heart. The facility with which he attained so much of the learned languages seems partly accounted for, from his being able to acquire so early a neat and natural style in his own language, and that under such evident disadvantages. His *Review of Ecclesiastical History*, so far as it proceeded, has been much esteemed; and, if it had done no more than excite the Rev. Joseph Milner[8] (as that most valuable and instructive author informs us it did) to pursue Mr. N.'s idea more largely, it was sufficient success. Before this, the world seems to

---

* To render the three Memoirs uniform, a portrait of Mr. N. has been given in the last 8vo. edition, reduced, for the purpose, by Collyer, from the larger portrait above-mentioned. J.P.

have lost sight of a history of real Christianity; and to have been content with what, for the most part, was but an account of the ambition and politics of secular men, assuming the Christian name.

It must be evident to any one who observes the spirit of all his Sermons, Hymns, Tracts, etc. that nothing is aimed at which should be met by critical investigation. In the preface to his Hymns, he remarks, "Though I would not offend readers of taste by a wilful coarseness and negligence, I do not write professedly for them. – I have simply declared my own views and feelings, as I might have done if I had composed hymns in some of the newly-discovered islands in the South Sea, where no person had any knowledge of the name of Jesus but myself."

To dwell, therefore, with a critical eye on this part of his public character, would be absurd and impertinent: it would be to erect a tribunal to which he seems not amenable. He appears to have paid no regard to a nice ear, or an accurate reviewer; but, preferring a style at once neat and perspicuous, to have laid out himself entirely for the service of the Church of God, and more especially for the tried and experienced part of its members.

His chief excellence, as a writer, seemed to lie in the easy and natural style of his epistolary correspondence. His Letters will be read while real religion exists; and they are the best draught of his own mind.

He had so largely communicated with his friends in this way, that I have heard him say, he thought, if his Letters were collected, they would make several folios. He selected many of these for publication; and expressed a hope that no other person would take that liberty with the rest, which were so widely spread abroad. In this, however, he was disappointed and grieved; as he once remarked to me: and for which reason I do not annex any letters that I received from him. He esteemed that collection published under the title of *Cardiphonia* as the most useful of his writings, and mentioned various instances of the benefits which he heard they had conveyed to many.

His *Apologia*,[9] or defence of conformity, was written on occasion of some reflections (perhaps only jocular) cast on him at that time. – His *Letters to a Wife*, written during his three voyages to Africa, and published in 1793, have been received with less satisfaction than most of his other writings. While, however, his advanced age and inordinate fondness may be pleaded for this publication, care should

be taken lest men fall into a contrary extreme; and suppose *that* temper
to be their *wisdom*, which leads them to avoid another, which they
consider as his *weakness*. But his *Messiah*, before mentioned, his
Letters of the Rev. Mr. Vanlier, Chaplain at the Cape[10] – his *Memoirs
of the Rev. John Cowper*,[11] (brother to the poet,) and those of the
Rev. Mr. Grimshaw, of Yorkshire,[12] together with his single *Sermons
and Tracts*,[13] have been well received, and will remain a public benefit.

I recollect reading a MS which Mr. N. lent me, containing a
correspondence that had passed between himself and the Rev. Dr.
Dixon, Principal of St. Edmund Hall, Oxford; and another MS of a
correspondence between him and the late Rev. Martin Madan. They
would have been very interesting to the public, particularly the latter;
and were striking evidences of Mr. N.'s humility, piety, and
faithfulness; but reasons of delicacy led him to commit the whole to
the flames.

To speak of his writings in the mass, they certainly possess what
many have aimed at, but very few attained, namely, *originality*. They
are the language of the heart: they show a deep experience of its
religious feelings; a continual anxiety to sympathise with man in his
wants, and to direct him to his only resources.

His CONVERSATION, and familiar habits with his friends, were more
peculiar, amusing, and instructive, than any I ever witnessed. It is
difficult to convey a clear idea of them by description. I venture,
therefore, to add a few pages of what I may call his *Table Talk*, which
I took down at different times, both in company and in private, from
his lips. Such a collection of printed remarks will not have so much
point, as when spoken in connection with the occasions that produced
them; they must appear to a considerable disadvantage, thus detached;
and candid allowance should be made by the reader, on this account.
They, however, who had the privilege of Mr. N.'s conversation when
living, cannot but recognise the speaker in most of them, and derive
both profit and pleasure from these remains of their late valuable
friend; and such as had not, will (if I do not mistake) think them the
most valuable part of this book.

Appendix to Chapter 9

Ministry

Newton gave his preference for preaching extempore as: "When we read to the people, they think themselves less concerned in what is offered than when we speak to them point blank."[14]

But he defended his position in a letter written to his friend Henry Venn,[15] who felt he might be neglecting sermon preparation. Though reluctant to justify himself, Newton was concerned that he should not be thought to "rush into pulpit service *without preparation or prayer*," or to have been careless or slothful.

"I think you will not wonder that I am so unwilling a person whom I so justly esteem, should harbour so hard a thought of me, which my conscience bears me witness that vile as I am before the Lord, I do not deserve this judgment from my fellow creature. Till of late that Mrs. Newton's repeated illnesses abridged my time, and broke in a little upon my plan, I believe I may say that for more than 20 years, very few single days passed when I was at home and had the dispersal of my own time, in which I did not spend from six to ten hours daily in subjects and employments, which had a direct suitableness to pulpit service. I have written several perhaps I may say many reams of paper in the forms of discourses, and for about ten or twelve years after I came to Olney, I seldom preached upon any text on which I had not previously written to some extent. And to this hour I bless God, I know no other method of employing myself when alone, but in attempting to maintain communion with my Lord in prayer and by his word, except some times recently while smoking my pipe, with some light reading such as history or the like. And though I wish not to be servilely bound to rules of my own, the day seems rather lost and tedious, if I have not opportunity of spending some hours with my pen in my hand, and the Bible open before me.

"It is however true, that of late years I have been generally led to speak with little premeditation on the particular subject – and am very often at a loss how to fix upon a subject – not for want of *any* subject I hope, but I find it difficult to choose from among 2 or 3 which offer. I often spend whole days in determining beforehand, and was often undetermined at last. Till at length I found liberty to give it up, and leave it more with the Lord. So far as I can judge, but who can judge it in his own case, I do not generally speak with less precision and coherence, in this way than I did formerly – sometimes perhaps I do – yet upon the whole I cannot repent it, believing that the Lord is not displeased – and that my ministry is not less acceptable. As to many of the questions you propose, I can only briefly answer, that the Lord who knows our different turns, and our different snares, is pleased to lead us in different paths – and that in incidental matters the methods best suited and own'd to one, may not so well suit another. My shoes fit me – but I would not wish every person to have his made upon my last, because the size and form of his foot may be different. The substance of your advice is good, I thank you for it, and hope the Lord will enable me to attend to it, whether I live in town or country, for I would not dare to preach at Olney with less preparation than I would venture upon in London."

9 November 1779

An example of his careful preparation can be seen in *The Searcher of Hearts*,[16] a section of his series of lectures given in Olney in 1765/6 from Romans 8, recently published by Christian Focus.

Newton, Cecil, Henry Foster and Eli Bates had formed the Eclectic Society in 1783 for discussion of religious truths and "mutual improvement". This Society consisted of clergy from the established church, dissenting ministers and laymen. Some, like Charles Simeon of Holy Trinity, Cambridge, were "country visitors". Josiah Pratt, secretary of the Church Missionary Society, was a member from 1798 to 1814. His son John published records of the discussions for this period as *Eclectic Notes* (reprinted in 1978 by Banner of Truth Trust as *The Thoughts of the Evangelical Leaders*). Newton and Thomas Scott gave their views on preaching in answer to a question posed by John Bacon,[17] *"What constitutes what is termed effect in Preaching?"*

Scott: Many would have Whitefield's spirit if they could catch it. If we cannot get a sword, let us go with a sling and a stone. Let the Minister do what he can, and go with simplicity. If he has none of the imagination with which some are gifted, still God will bless him. The greatest hindrance to effect is the want of the apostolic spirit.

Newton: Effect, I believe, has been produced in my preaching by a solemn determination to bring forth Jesus Christ as the GREAT SUBJECT in all my discourses.

I try, moreover, to leave this impression on the people – that I *wish them well.*

... no general rule can be laid down for all. There are two grand arguments which we must constantly put forth:

(1) *I beseech you by the mercies of God.*

(2) I warn you by *the terrors of the Lord.*

Similarly, in a letter to an American friend, Dr. Robbins, Newton stated that his chief points that he aimed at in preaching were, "First, To set forth the glory and grace of God in the person of the Saviour – Second, To show the danger and folly of a form of godliness without the power, of a mere talking, speculative profession – Third, To persuade, if possible, those that love the Lord Jesus Christ to love one another, to lay much stress upon the things in which we are agreed, and but little upon those in which we differ."[18]

Quoting the aim of Newton and Cecil in forming the Eclectic Society, John Stott invited a similar group of like-minded people in 1955 to relaunch "the same kind of thing". The fellowship and stimulus which came from this group helped prepare the groundwork for and give the confidence to convene the First National Evangelical Anglican Congress in Keele in 1967. This marked the resurgence of an evangelical generation with the introduction of Family Services, a focus on evangelism in the cities and an increase in youth work. The whole music field was transformed. Youth groups throughout the country enlivened their worship from the new Youth Praise music books. Many went forward from this and later Eclectic fellowships into strong positions of leadership and influence – Michael Baughn, Richard Bewes, Michael Botting, George Carey, Timothy Dudley-Smith, Michael Green, George Hoffman, James Jones, Dick Lucas, Gavin Reid, Michael Saward, David Shepherd, Norman Warren (*Journey Into Life*) and others.

Newton's concern for punctuality is shown in the following couple of letters, the first of which is again to Henry Venn:[19]

"I am pleased and obliged greatly by your ready acceptance of my invitation to St. Mary Woolnoth on the 23rd. And tho' there be nothing particularly tempting in the occasion, I will just put you in mind, that it would be a pretty exploit if the Lord should enable you to catch a Lord Mayor, and a sheriff or two in the Gospel net. And who can tell? Grace has long and strong arms, the τοα δυνατον [the impossible] with men is easy to him who says, I will work and none shall let it. But if the rich and the little great folks of the world should refuse to hear – the Lord may appoint you to be a messenger of grace and peace to some others, whose obscurity may prevent you knowing the good you have done, at present, but you shall know it and hear of it hereafter, in the great day when he shall appear to gather up his jewels. For I take it for granted that his truth can never be preached in dependence upon his Spirit, in vain.

"Our time of beginning service is half past ten. I am punctual to a minute in general. But when the Chief Magistrate comes in form, he must be waited for, and his entrance announced by the Organ – this will probably make us a quarter of an hour later at least (Sir Watkin Lewes kept us near a whole hour). But I will be in the Vestry about ten o'clock and wait for your coming.

"After Sermon the preacher and Rector are usually invited to dine at the Mansion House – an honour which I have hitherto found means to decline. If you choose to accept it, I will readily accompany you. If otherwise you had better be previously engaged – then you stand excused."

15 March 1783

When Wilberforce asked him to change the time of his evening lecture so that he could hear Thomas Scott in the afternoon as well, Newton replied, at the age of seventy-five,[20] "I expressed in my note, how very painful it was for me, even to hesitate for a moment, upon complying with any proposal that comes from *you*. But indeed in this case I could not hesitate. To alter the time of my Evening Lecture is not practicable. It would throw us into confusion, it would be against my judgment, and therefore would hurt my conscience. It would likewise deprive me of the comfort and liberty with which the Lord usually favours me in the service.

"My church is so full before 6, that they who are not there before the clock strikes, can with difficulty obtain a seat and by a quarter after 6 is so crowded, that many cannot get within the door. The hour suits the bulk of my hearers, and we have been accustomed to it for more than twenty years. I could not I durst not attempt an alteration for the few, I believe they are but few, who come from Mr. Scott's lecture.

"But there is another objection. Begin when I will, I must dismiss the people by a quarter before eight – so that as it is, I am often straitened for time. It has pleased the Lord to give to me, the most Unworthy, much acceptance with his people. Many of my evening hearers come from far, from most of the villages round the Metropolis: Some from Chelsea, from Camberwell, Newington Butts, Stoke Newington, and eastward from Limehouse and Bow, etc; If I do not dismiss them in time for the Stage Coaches at eight o'clock, they might have to walk perhaps 3 or 4 miles home. They depend upon my punctuality in this respect, and I am thankful that I have never once disappointed them. I rather choose when it is necessary, to shorten the sermon.

"*Sed hactinus haec.*[21] My feelings that I cannot joyfully comply with your desire, have made me say, more than you will perhaps think needful, but indeed it gives me great pain, to say, I cannot do it. I have sometimes almost wished we could begin at a quarter before six. But I never attemptes to alter what has been so long established."

23 March 1801

Family
Polly's father, George Catlett, came to live with them in Olney in his last years. In 1777 Newton wrote to his sister-in-law, Elizabeth Cunningham, "Father died Saturday. Romaine prayed with him. One of the last to whom he spoke on Friday evening. I thought it providential, that the only Gospel Minister, whom he came to know and had formerly, should be sent as it were on purpose to close his eyes, and to receive his dying testimony of his faith in Jesus, and his assured hope of immortality."[22]

When Polly died, Mary Unwin wrote to Mrs. Cowper, "The long continued illness of Mrs. Newton without (in our judgment) the least hope of her recovery, prepared both Mr. Cowper and me for the event that lately took place. I had no fear on account of the safety of her future state, yet I sincerely rejoiced that she was enabled to give so pleasant a token of the certainty of it. Her illness to be sure, was long and distressing; and yet I do think it was graciously designed by the Lord, as a gradual loosening of the bands our affections are too apt to draw more closely than they ought. I speak freely on this head, as I have been a sufferer on that account. Mr. Newton by this trying dispensation has had opportunity of illustrating in his own particular, the truths that he has always inculcated; the duty of, and (what is a still greater honour) the practicability in his own path, of submission to the will of the Almighty; the power of grace has shone gloriously on this occasion!"[23]

Newton made a special point of showing kindness to domestic servants, no doubt remembering the degradation to which he had been subjected as a slave. After the successful but trying operation on his thigh, referred to on page 114, he wrote to Mary Unwin, Cowper's friend, with a special mention for his own servant, Sally Johnson. Mary Unwin replied that Sally's "sincere love for you created many fears and misgivings on your account. Mr. Cowper and I did what we could to persuade her to believe that every circumstance seemed to bear a favourable aspect. By her desire she kept the letter till yesterday afternoon; by the frequent reading of it, as she was obliged to do to all the Mollys and Bettys and Sallys and Nannys that came to enquire after you, she almost got it by heart, and believes now that she may indulge a hope that you are in a fair way of recovery. I thank God Mr. Cowper is well. I am middling." She adds, "My Sally was so affected by your remembrance of her that she could testify her gratitude no other way than by tears, and a wish that she could pray for you as she ought."[24]

Writings

Cardiphonia

When Newton was about to print some of his correspondence he asked Cowper's assistance.[25] "I shall be obliged to your ingenuity to hammer me out a title and a motto – my name is not to be prefixed. Can you compound me a nice Greek word as pretty in sound and as scholastically put together as *Thelyphthora* (see page 209), and as much more favourable import as you please, to stand at the top of the title page, and to serve as a handle for an inquirer?" Cowper came up with *Cardiphonia* – the utterance of the heart.

John Aikman, a Congregational minister in Edinburgh, told of the influence of Newton's writings on him. "I was returning to Jamaica, where I was engaged upon one of the plantations, and wishing to take out some books for the use of the people there, amongst others I selected was Newton's *Cardiphonia*. Its title struck me, and I supposed it was a novel. Looking over the books on the voyage I took up this, and soon found it something very different from what I had thought; and *that book* was, in God's providence, the means of my conversion."[26]

Newton understood the importance of his letter-writing ministry, drawing from the example of James Hervey in reaching this conclusion. "Hervey, who was so blessed as a writer, was hardly able to mention a single instance of conversion by his preaching, and nothing could exceed the lifelessness of his audience; and I rather reckoned upon doing more good by some of my other works than by my 'Letters,' which I wrote without study, or any public design; but the Lord said, 'You shall be most useful by *them*;' and I learned to say, 'Thy will be done! Use me as Thou pleasest, only *make* me useful.' " [27]

He received many letters of thanks from around the country, from Scotland, America, India, France, Holland and elsewhere, for the encouragement and spiritual growth received through his writings.

A Review of Ecclesiastical History
Cowper wrote to Newton regarding his *Review*, "I have always regretted that your ecclesiastical history went no further: I never saw a work that I thought more likely to serve the cause of truth, nor history applied to so good a purpose. The facts incontestable, the grand observation upon them all irrefragable, and the style, in my judgement, incomparably better than that of Robertson or Gibbons. I would give you my reasons for thinking so, if I had not a very urgent one for declining it. You have no ear for such music, whoever may be the performer. What you added, but never printed, is quite equal to what has appeared, which I think might have encouraged you to proceed, though you missed that freedom in writing which you found before. While you were at Olney, this was at least possible; in a state of retirement you had leisure, without which I suppose Paul himself could not have written his epistles."[28]

The Messiah
Newton wrote to Bull, "The *Messiah* is nearly printed off; I think it will be finished this week, but we must wait awhile for an index, without which I do not think a book complete. I suppose about the time that you are published in London, the *Messiah* will be published in Paternoster Row in St. Paul's churchyard. Here again I entreat your prayer that the Lord may be pleased to breathe his blessing upon a series which I trust he himself put into my heart.

"Indeed, if it had not been much impressed upon my mind, I should hardly have had firmness and perseverance to finish it in the midst of the many engagements and avocations which call upon me daily.

"Considering that I have greatly lost my habit of rising early I almost wonder that besides other writing, visiting and being visited, I should be able to write for the press, so much as will fill nearly a thousand octavio pages in print in less than ten months.

"If the Lord is pleased to make it useful it would be foolishness in me to be much concerned what my fellow worms may think of the performance.

"I expect to appear as I am, a speckled bird, in the eyes of the religious world, and in some places I have expressed myself with a freedom which will not be very pleasing to some of my superiors. I have not designed to give offence but some truths will offend some people.

"I hope simplicity has been my aim but I know my heart is deceitful. However I would be very thankful that the Lord has enabled me to finish this work which I consider as my most important publication and it will probably be my last, except a fugitive paper for a magazine or two.

"I certainly could not leave the press with a more noble subject. It will likewise have some novelty and much variety to recommend it."[29]

Bull had his Academy students reading the work three times a week, writing to Newton, "I always expected more from your *Messiah* than from your other works, and am not at all disappointed." He had one complaint though, "There was one sentiment in the first sermon I did not like, about not applying passages in the Old Testament to Jesus, unless they are expressly quoted in so many words in the New. I think I could advance a solid and scriptural argument against it; but I love the author, and I love the book – indeed, am highly delighted with it; and I think you said more than you intended."[30]

The reply came in full,[31] "Mon Cher Taureau, I believe what you disapprove about not applying passages in the Old Testament to the Messiah, without express authority from the New, is in the 23rd sermon of vol. 2. I have met with such trash from some who pretend to *spiritualize*, and obtruded with so much confidence, that I thought it right to enter my protest against the practice, especially as I think it obtains most amongst rash and injudicious preachers. And though sometimes wise and good men give a little in to it, I think it is rather countenanced than justified by their example. For instance I remember to have heard Mr. Bull preach a sermon, and a very good one, from Exodus 4:14; but though the sermon was a good one, I thought the points enlarged upon were no more deducible from the text than from the first verse in Genesis. Mr. Bull, however, knew what he was about; but when such men as Mr. Page [the curate at Olney] attempt to preach from Genesis 30:8 that Deborah is the law, the oak under which she was buried the cross, &c., &c., they make wild work of it. I have allowed the propriety of preaching by way of accommodation, and *I think I have not said that we should apply no passages to Jesus, unless quoted in so many words in the New Testament*; but that when we propose our own sentiments, which are not so supported, we should do it under great modesty, which perhaps you will readily allow. After all, if in this point the observation that doctors differ should apply to you and me, I have still the comfort of thinking that there are not many doctors who differ less, or in fewer particulars, than we do.

"*I* like to have the proofs of the subject lie plainly in the text; but if another preaches solid scriptural truth from *Higgaion, Selah*, I am content. My censure is only intended against those who affect to please, and to show their superior sagacity by the singularity, quaintness, and novelty of their conceits; and who think they can discover mysteries in a text, when, perhaps, they do not understand even the literal sense of it."

The passage Cecil quotes earlier in this chapter, from Newton's *Messiah*, was quoted by Robert Murray M'Cheyne to illustrate his exposition of Revelation 2:18-29 at his weekly Prayer Meeting at St. Peter's, Dundee. McCheyne's expositions on *The Seven Churches of Asia* have been published by Christian Focus.[32]

Olney Hymns

Newton acknowledged Dr. Watts's hymns as the "admirable patterns" for his own and stressed that they were designed for public worship and for the use of "plain people", rather than for any poetic value. In the preface he stated his aims and prayers for the hymns, which we now see have been met more abundantly than he could have anticipated:

"As the workings of the heart of man, and of the Spirit of GOD, are in general the same, in all who are the subjects of grace, I hope most of these hymns, being the fruit and expression of my own experience, will coincide with the views of real Christians of all denominations.

"This publication, which, with my humble prayer to the LORD for his blessing upon it, I offer to the service and acceptance of all who love the LORD JESUS CHRIST in sincerity, of every name and in every place, into whose hands it may come."

Olney, Bucks, Feb. 15 1779

Memoirs of the Rev. John Cowper
Published in 1802 as *Adelphi*, this sketch of the Rev. John Cowper's character and account of his last illness was written by his brother William Cowper. Newton transcribed the original manuscript and had it published.

Dr. Dixon
Dr. Dixon was the principal of St. Edmund Hall, Oxford. Six students were expelled in 1768 for Methodism, though Dr. Dixon himself warmly supported their cause.

"The six students, Benjamin Kay, Thomas Jones, Thomas Grove, Matthews, Erasmus Middleton and Joseph Shipman, used to meet at the house of Mrs. Durbridge, where Dr. Stillingfleet, then a fellow of Merton College, would expound and pray. A tutor at St. Edmund complained to the principal, Dr. Dixon, that they were 'enthusiasts, who talked of inspiration, regeneration, and drawing nigh to God.' Dr. Dixon knew and approved of their character, and defended their actions from the Thirty-Nine Articles. However the Vice-Chancellor, Dr. Durrell, expelled them on March 11 1768 'for holding Methodistical tenets, and taking upon them to pray, read and expound the Scriptures, and singing hymns in private houses.' The report in the St. James's Chronicle adds, 'One of the Heads of Houses present observed that, as these six gentlemen were expelled for having too much religion, it would be very proper to enquire into the conduct of some who had too little'."[33]

They had also been accused of having associated with men such as Stillingfleet, Fletcher, Haweis, Venn and Newton. Whitefield wrote to the Vice-Chancellor in strong support of the students and Lady Huntingdon took an active interest in their future.

Thomas Jones had previously spent some time studying at the

vicarage in Olney with Newton, who had instructed him in Hebrew and Greek. He was later ordained and made curate of Clifton, a village next to Olney. He married the sister of Lady Austin, who was a friend of William Cowper's.

Thelyphthora
(by Cowper's cousin Martin Madan, chaplain at the Lock Hospital, who had shown great kindness to Newton in the early stages of his Christian life)

Madan's book advocating polygamy caused dismay in Christian circles. Newton felt it was "well calculated to convince those who have hitherto felt a conflict between their passions and their consciences. They are now at liberty. The violations of the seventh commandment, according to this writer, are few indeed."[34] With his legal training, Madan had been able to present many apparently plausible arguments, interspersed with so many Scripture quotes, that though most believers would strongly disapprove of it, few would have the sharpness of mind to present their arguments against it in writing.

Newton wrote to Cowper, "Heaps of folk would persuade me that I can attempt nothing so seasonable, needful, and with equal probability of usefulness, as an answer to *Thelyphthora*. I am not yet of this mind, and besides that I am not satisfied with the expediency of an answer. Mr. Indolence uses all his influence with me, which is considerable, to keep me quiet; Mr. Prudence cautions me against meddling with one above my match; and Mr. Delicacy says, Surely you would not write against your friend. However, this triumvirate may prevent my writing; notwithstanding all that Prudence and Delicacy urge, and whether they are pleased or not, I must bear my testimony against *Thelyphthora* tomorrow night *viva voce*. I shall not so much mind Indolence, except he should actually follow me into the pulpit, which he seldom does, though I am pestered with him everywhere else. But in the course of sermons I recently began on relative duties I must enter on the relation of husband and wife tomorrow night; and it would be high treason, or at least misprision of treason against the truth, when expressly preaching on the subject of marriage, to leave the dangerous and novel doctrine of the present lawfulness of polygamy unnoticed, because I love the person who presumed to broach it."[35]

Cowper sent Newton the following verses:[36]

M quarrels with N because M wrote a book
And N did not like it, which M could not brook,
So he called him a bigot, a wrangler, a monk,
With as many hard names as would line a good trunk.
And set up his back and clawed like a cat,
But N liked it never the better for that.

Now N had a wife, and he wanted but one,
Which stuck in M's stomach as cross as a bone;
It had always been reckoned a just cause of strife,
For a man to make free with another man's wife,
But the strife is the strangest that ever was known,
If a man must be scolded for loving his own.

Conclusion

Let Newton have the last word on his ministry in this quote from his own notes of the Eclectic Society meeting on 26 January 1795.[37] In answer to the question, "What do we now see were our principal errors when we first set out as Ministers?" he wrote:

"This was a fruitful subject and I could contribute my quota. I have not seemed to want zeal and diligence for Pulpit Service – yet in some respects irresolution and indolence have made me too passive. I am thankful for the love of peace, but this sometimes has bribed me to be simply silent. I have been too systematic and have not sufficiently kept the Saviour in the foreground of my discourses. O Lord, Thou only knowest what are my faults and errors to this; pardon them I beseech Thee, show them unto me as I am able to bear and teach me to avoid and correct them! Ah! Who can understand his errors! If Thou wert strict to mark what is amiss, who could stand? Shame and humiliation become me!"

CHAPTER 10

REMARKS
MADE BY
MR. NEWTON
IN FAMILIAR CONVERSATION.

"While the mariner uses the loadstone, the philosopher may attempt to investigate the cause; but, after all, in steering through the ocean, he can make no other use of it than the mariner."

"If an angel were sent to find the most perfect man, he would probably not find him composing a body of divinity, but perhaps a cripple in a poor-house, whom the parish wish dead; a man humbled before God with far lower thoughts of himself than others have of him."

"When a Christian goes into the world, because he sees it his *call*, yet, while he feels it also his *cross*, it will not hurt him."

"Satan will seldom come to a Christian with a gross temptation: a green log and a candle may be safely left together; but bring a few shavings, then some small sticks, then larger, and you may soon bring the green log to ashes."

"If two angels came down from heaven to execute a divine command, and one was appointed to conduct an empire, and another to sweep a street in it, they would feel no inclination to choose employments."

"The post of honour in an army, is not with the baggage, nor with the women."

"What some call providential openings are often powerful temptations. The heart, in wandering, cries, 'Here is a way opened before me;' but, perhaps, not to be *trodden*, but *rejected*."

"I should have thought mowers very idle people; but they work while they whet their scythes. Now devotedness to God, whether it mows or whets the scythe, still goes on with the work."

"Young people marry as others study navigation, by the fire-side. If they marry unsuitably, they can scarcely bring things to rule; but, like sailors, they must sail as near the wind as they can. I feel myself like a traveller with his wife in his chaise and one: if the ground is smooth, and she keeps the right pace, and is willing to deliver the reins when I ask for them, I am always willing to let her drive."

"A Christian should never plead spirituality for being a sloven: if he be but a shoe-cleaner, he should be the best in the parish."

"My course of study, like that of a surgeon, has principally consisted in walking the hospital."

"In divinity, as well as in the other professions, there are *little* artists. A man may be able to execute the buttons of a statue very neatly, but I could not call him an able artist. There is an air, there is a taste, to which his narrow capacity cannot reach."

"My principal method of defeating heresy is, by establishing truth. One proposes to fill a bushel with *tares*: now if I can fill it first with *wheat*, I shall defy his attempts."

"When some people talk of religion, they mean they have heard so many sermons, and performed so many devotions; and thus mistake the *means* for the *end*. But true religion is a habitual recollection of God and intention to serve him; and this turns every thing into gold. We are apt to suppose that we need something splendid to evince our devotion, but true devotion equals things – washing plates, and cleaning shoes, is a high office, if performed in a right spirit. – If three angels were sent to earth, they would feel perfect indifference who should perform the part of prime-minister, parish-minister, or watchman."

"When a ship goes to sea, among a vast variety of its articles and circumstances there is but one object regarded, namely, doing the business of the voyage; every bucket is employed with respect to *that*."

"Many have puzzled themselves about the origin of evil: I observe there *is* evil, and that there is a way to escape it; and, with this, I begin and end."

"Consecrated things, under the Law, were first sprinkled with blood, and then anointed with oil, and thenceforward were no more common. Every Christian has been a common vessel for profane purposes; but, when sprinkled and anointed, under the Gospel, he becomes separated and consecrated to God."

"I would not give a straw for that assurance which sin will not damp. If David had come from his adultery, and had talked of his assurance at that time, I should have despised his speech."

"A spirit of adoption is the spirit of a child: he may disoblige his father, yet he is not afraid of being turned out of doors. The *union* is not dissolved, though the *communion* is. He is not well with his father, therefore must be unhappy, as their interests are inseparable."

"We often seek to apply cordials when the patient is not prepared for them; and it is to the patient's advantage, that he cannot take a medicine when prematurely offered. When a man comes to me, and says, 'I am quite happy,' I am not sorry to find him come again with some fears, – I never saw a work of grace stand well without a check. 'I only want,' says one, 'to be sure of being safe, and then I will go on.' – No; perhaps, then you will *go off.*"

"For an old Christian to say to a young one, 'Stand in my evidence,' is like a man, who has with difficulty climbed a ladder or scaffolding to the top of the house, and cries to one at the bottom, 'This is the place for a prospect – come up at a step.'"

"A Christian in the world, is like a man who has had a long intimacy with one whom at length he finds to have been the murderer of a kind father: the intimacy, after this, will surely be broken."

"*Except a man be born again, he cannot see the kingdom of God.*[1] – A man may live in a deep mine in Hungary, never having seen the light of the sun: he may have received accounts of prospects, and, by the help of a candle, may have examined a few engravings of them; but, let him be brought out of the mine, and set on the mountain – what a difference appears!"

"Candour will always allow much for inexperience. I have been thirty years forming my own views; and, in the course of this time, some of my hills have sunk, and some of my valleys have risen: but, how unreasonable would it be to expect all this should take place in another person; and that, in the course of a year or two!"

"Candour forbids us to estimate a character from its accidental blots. Yet it is thus that David, and others, have been treated."

"Apollos met with two candid people in the Church: they neither ran away because he was *legal*, nor were carried away because he was *eloquent*."

"There is the analogy of faith: it is a master-key, which not only opens particular doors, but carries you through the whole house. But an attachment to a rigid system is dangerous. – Luther once turned out the Epistle of St. James, because it disturbed his system. I shall preach, perhaps, very usefully upon two opposite texts, while kept apart; but, if I attempt nicely to reconcile them, it is ten to one if I do not begin to bungle."

"I can conceive a living man without an arm or a leg, but not without a head or a heart: so there are some truths essential to vital religion, and which all awakened souls are taught."

"Apostacy, in all its branches, takes its rise from atheism. *I have set the Lord always before me*,[2] etc."

"We are surprised at the fall of a famous professor; but, in the sight of God, the man was gone before: *we*, only, have now first discovered it. *He that despiseth small things, shall fall little by little*."[3]

"There are critical times of danger. After great services, honours, and consolations, we should stand upon our guard. Noah – Lot – David – Solomon, fell in these circumstances. Satan is a robber: a robber will not attack a man *going* to the bank, but in returning with his pocket full of money."

"A Christian is like a young nobleman, who on going to receive his estate, is at first enchanted with its prospects; this, in a course of time, may wear off: but a sense of the value of the estate grows daily."

"When we first enter into the divine life, we propose to *grow rich*: God's plan is to make us *feel poor*."

"Good men have need to take heed of building upon groundless impressions. Mr. Whitefield had a son, whom he imagined born to be a very extraordinary man: but the son soon died, and the father was cured of his mistake."

"I remember, in going to undertake the care of a congregation, I was reading as I walked in a green lane, *Fear not, Paul, I have much people in this city.*[4] But I soon afterwards was disappointed in finding that Paul was not John, and that Corinth was not Warwick."

"Christ has taken our nature into heaven, to represent *us*; and has left us on earth, with his nature, to represent *him*."

"Worldly men will be true to their principles; and if we were as true to ours, the visits between the two parties would be short and seldom."

"A Christian in the world is like a man transacting his affairs in the rain. He will not suddenly leave his client, because it rains; but, the moment the business is done, he is gone: as it is said in the Acts, *Being let go, they went to their own company.*"[5]

"God's word is certainly a restraint; but it is such a restraint as the irons, which prevent children from getting into the fire."

"The Scriptures are so full, that every case may be found in them. – A rake went into a church, and tried to decoy a girl, by saying, 'Why do you attend to such stuff as these Scriptures?' – 'Because,' said she, 'they tell me, that, *in the last days, there shall come* such *scoffers*[6] as you.'"

"God deals with us as we do with our children: he first *speaks*; then, gives a gentle *stroke*; at last, a *blow*."

"The religion of a sinner stands on two pillars; namely, what Christ did for us in his flesh, and what he performs in us by his Spirit. Most errors arise from an attempt to separate these two."

"Man is not taught any thing to purpose till God becomes his teacher: and then the glare of the world is put out, and the value of the soul rises in full view. A man's present sentiments may not be accurate, but we make too much of sentiments. We pass a field with a few blades: we call it a field of wheat; yet here is no wheat in perfection; but wheat is sown, and full ears may be expected."

"The word Temperance, in the New Testament, signifies *self-possession*: it is a disposition suitable to one who has a race to run, and therefore will not load his pockets with lead."

"One reason why we must not attempt to pull up the tares which grow among the wheat is, that we have not skill for the work; like a weeder, whom Mrs. N. employed in my garden at Olney, who for weeds pulled up some of Mrs. N.'s favourite flowers."

"Contrivers of systems on the earth, are like contrivers of systems in the heavens; where the sun and moon keep the same course, in spite of the philosophers."

"I endeavour to walk through the world as a physician goes through Bedlam: the patients make a noise, pester him with impertinence, and hinder him in his business; but he does the best he can, and so gets through."

"A man always in society, is one always on the spend: on the other hand, a mere solitary is, at his best, but a candle in an empty room."

"If we were upon the watch for improvement, the common news of the day would furnish it: the falling of the tower in Siloam, and the slaughter of the Galileans, were the news of the day; which our Lord improved."

"The generality make out their righteousness, by comparing themselves with some others whom they think worse. A woman of the town, who was dying of disease in the Lock Hospital, was offended at a minister speaking to her as a sinner, because she had never picked a pocket."

"Take away a toy from a child and give him another, and he is satisfied; but if he be hungry, no toy will do. As new-born babes, true believers desire the sincere milk of the word; and the desire of grace, in this way, is grace."

One said that the great Saints in the Calendar were many of them poor Sinners. Mr. N. replied, "They were poor Saints indeed, if they did not feel they were great Sinners."

"A wise man looks upon men as he does upon horses, and considers their comparisons of title, wealth, and place, but as harness."

"The force of what we deliver from the pulpit is often lost by a starched, and what is frequently called a correct style; and, especially, by adding meretricious ornaments. – I called upon a lady who had been robbed, and she gave me a striking account of the fact; but had she put it into heroics, I should neither so well have understood her, nor been so well convinced that she had been robbed."

"When a man says he received a blessing under a sermon, I begin to enquire the character of the man who speaks of the help he has received. The Roman people proved the effect they received under a sermon of Antony, when they flew to avenge the death of Cæsar."

"The Lord has reasons far beyond our ken, for opening a wide door, while he stops the mouth of a useful preacher. – John Bunyan would not have done half the good he did, if he had remained preaching in Bedford, instead of being shut up in Bedford prison."

"If I could go to France, and give every man in it a right and peaceable mind by my labour, I should have a statue: but to produce such an effect in the conversion of one soul, would be a far greater achievement."

"Ministers would over-rate their labours, if they did not think it worth while to be born and spend ten thousand years in labour and contempt, to recover one soul."

"Don't tell me of your feelings. A traveller would be glad of fine weather; but, if he be a man of business, he will go on. – Bunyan says, you must not judge of a man's haste by his horse; for when the horse can hardly move, you may see, by the rider's urging him, what a hurry he is in."

"A man and a beast may stand upon the same mountain, and even touch one another; yet they are in two different worlds: the beast perceives nothing but grass; but the man contemplates the prospect, and thinks of a thousand remote things. – Thus a Christian may be a solitary at a full exchange: he can converse with the people there upon trade, politics, and the stocks; but they cannot talk with him upon *the peace of God which passeth all understanding.*"[7]

"It is a mere fallacy to talk of the sins of a short life. The sinner is always a sinner. – Put a pump into a river, you may throw out some water, but the river remains."

"Professors, who own the doctrines of free grace, often act inconsistently with their own principle when they are angry at the defects of others. – A company of travellers fall into a pit: one of them gets a passenger to draw him out. Now he should not be angry with the rest for falling in; nor because they are not yet out, as he is. He did not pull himself out: instead, therefore, of reproaching them, he should show them pity. He should avoid, at any rate, going down upon their ground again; and show how much better and happier he is upon his own. – We should take care that we do not make our profession of religion a receipt in full for all other obligations. A man, truly illuminated, will no more despise others, than Bartimeus, after his own eyes were opened, would take a stick and beat every blind man he met."

"We much mistake in supposing that the removal of a particular objection would satisfy the objector. – Suppose I am in bed, and want to know whether it be light, it is not enough if I draw back the curtain; for though there be light, I must have eyes to see it."

"Too deep a consideration of eternal realities might unfit a man for his present circumstances. – Walking through St. Bartholomew's Hospital, or Bedlam, must deeply affect a feeling mind; but, in reality, this world is a far worse scene. It has but two wards: in the one, men are miserable; in the other, mad."

"Some preachers near Olney dwelt on the doctrine of Predestination: an old woman said – 'Ah! I have long settled that point: for, if God had not chosen me before I was born, I am sure he would have seen nothing in me to have chosen me afterwards.' "

"I see the unprofitableness of controversy in the case of Job and his friends: for, if God had not interposed, had they lived to this day, they would have continued the dispute."

"It is pure mercy that negatives a particular request. – A miser would pray very earnestly for gold, if he believed prayer would gain it; whereas, if Christ had any favour to him, he would take his gold away. – A child walks in the garden in spring, and sees cherries: he knows they are good fruit, and therefore asks for them. 'No, my dear,' says the father, 'they are not yet ripe: – Stay the season.' "

"If I cannot *take pleasure in infirmities*,[8] I can sometimes feel the profit of them. – I can conceive a king to pardon a rebel, and take him to his family, and then say 'I appoint you, for a season, to wear a fetter. At a certain season, I will send a messenger to knock it off. In the mean time, this fetter will serve to remind you of your state: it may humble you, and restrain you from rambling.' "

"Some Christians at a glance, seem of a superior order; and are not: they want a certain quality. – At a florist's feast the other day, a certain flower was determined to wear the bell; but it was found to be an artificial flower: there is a quality called GROWTH, which it had not."

"Doctor Taylor of Norwich said to me, 'Sir, I have collated every word in the Hebrew Scriptures seventeen times; and it is very strange if the doctrine of atonement, which you hold, should not have been found by me.' – I am not surprised at this: I once went to light my candle with the extinguisher on it: now, prejudices from education, learning, etc. often form an extinguisher. – It is not enough that you bring the candle: you must remove the extinguisher."

"I measure ministers by square measure. I have no idea of the size of the table, if you only tell me how *long* it is; but, if you also say how *wide*, I can tell its dimensions. – So, when you tell me what a man is in the pulpit, you must also tell me what he is out of it, or I shall not know his size."

"A man should be *born* to high things not to lose himself in them. Slaters will walk on the ridge of a house with ease, which would turn our heads."

"Much depends on the way we come into trouble. – Paul and Jonah were both in a storm, but in very different circumstances."

"I have read of many wicked Popes, but the worst Pope I ever met with is Pope SELF."

"The men of this world are children. – Offer a child an apple and a bank note, he will doubtless choose the apple."

"The heir of a great estate, while a child, thinks more of a few shillings in his pocket than of his inheritance. – So a Christian is often more elated by some frame of heart than by his title to glory."

"A dutiful child is ever looking forward to the holidays, when he shall return to his father: but he does not think of running from school before."

"The Gospel is a proclamation of free mercy to guilty creatures – an act of grace to rebels. Now, though a rebel should throw away his pistols, and determine to go into the woods, and make his mind better before he goes to court and pleads the act; he may, indeed, not be found in *arms*, yet, being taken in his reforming scheme, he will be hanged."

"Man is made capable of three births: by nature, he enters into the present world; by grace, into spiritual light and life; by death, into glory."

"In my imagination, I sometimes fancy I could make a perfect minister. I take the eloquence of —, the knowledge of —, the zeal of —, and the pastoral meekness, tenderness, and piety of —: then, putting them altogether into one man, I say to myself, *'This* would be a perfect minister.' Now there is one, who, if he chose it, could actually *do* this; but he never did. He has seen fit to do otherwise, and *to divide these gifts to every man severally as he* will."[9]

"I feel like a man who has no money in his pocket, but is allowed to draw for all he wants upon one infinitely rich: I am, therefore, at once both a beggar and a rich man."

"I went one day to Mrs. G—'s, just after she had lost all her fortune. I could not be surprised to find her in tears: but she said, 'I suppose you think I am crying for my loss, but that is not the case; I am now weeping to think I should feel so much uneasiness on the account.' After that, I never heard her speak again upon the subject as long as she lived. – Now this is just as it should be. – Suppose a man was going to York to take possession of a large estate, and his chaise should break down a mile before he got to the city, which obliged him to *walk* the rest of the way; what a fool we should think him if we saw him wringing his hands, and blubbering out all the remaining mile, 'My chaise is broken! My chaise is broken!'"

"I have read many books that I cannot sit down to read: they are, indeed, good and sound; but like halfpence, there goes a great quantity to a little amount. There are *silver* books; and a very few *golden* books: but I have one book worth more than all, called the Bible: and that is a book of *bank-notes*."

"Sometimes I compare the troubles which we have to undergo in the course of the year to a great bundle of fagots, far too large for us to lift. But God does not require us to carry the whole at once; he mercifully unties the bundle, and gives us first one stick, which we are to carry today, and then another which we are to carry tomorrow, and so on. This we might easily manage, if we would only take the burden appointed for us each day; but we choose to increase our troubles by carrying yesterday's stick over again today, and adding tomorrow's burden to our load, before we are required to bear it."

I conclude these remarks, not because my memorandum-book is exhausted, but lest the reader should think I forgot the old maxim, *ne quid nimis.*[10] No undue liberty, however, has been taken in publishing Mr. N.'s private conversation, since all the above remarks were submitted to him as intended for this publication, and were approved.

CHAPTER 11

GENERAL OBSERVATIONS

The difference of mental improvement among men, seems very much to depend on their capacity and habit of gathering instruction from the objects which are continually presented to their observation. Two men behold the same fact: one of them is in the habit of drawing such remarks and inferences as the fact affords, and learns somewhat from every thing he sees: while the other sees the same fact, and perhaps with a momentary admiration, but lets it pass without making so much as one profitable reflection on the occasion. – The excursions of the *bee* and the *butterfly* present an exact emblem of these two characters.

I have present to my mind an acquaintance, who has seen more of the outside of the world than most men: he has lived in most countries of the civilised world; yet I scarcely know a man of a less improved mind: with every external advantage, he has learned nothing to any useful purpose: he seems to have passed from flower to flower without extracting a drop of honey; and now, he tires all his friends with the frivolous garrulity of a capricious, vacant, and petulant old age.

I wish the reader of these Memoirs may avoid such an error, in passing over the history here laid before him. An extraordinary train of facts is presented to his observation; and if

"The proper study of mankind is man,"[1]

the history before us will surely furnish important matter of the kind to the eye of every wise, moral traveller.

I would here call the attention of three classes of men to a single point of prime importance; namely, the EFFICACY AND EXCELLENCE OF REAL CHRISTIANITY as exhibited in the principles and practice of the subject of these Memoirs.

I. Suppose the reader to be so unhappy (though his misfortune may be least perceived by himself) as to be led astray by bad society, in conjunction with *an evil heart of unbelief.* I will suppose him to be *now* in the state in which Mr. N. describes himself formerly to *have been*, and in which the writer of these Memoirs once was. I will suppose him to be given up to *believe his own lie*; and that he may be in the habit of thinking that God, when he made man, left him to find his way without any express revelation of the mind and will of his Maker and Governor: or, at most, that he is left to the only rule in morals, which Nature may be supposed to present. – What *that* way is, which such a thinker will take, is sufficiently evident from the general course and habits of unbelievers.

But there is a conscience in man. Conscience, in sober moments, often alarms the most stout-hearted. When such an unbeliever meets an overwhelming providence, or lies on a death-bed, he will probably awake to a strong sense of his real condition. He will feel, if not very hardened indeed, in what a forlorn, unprovided, and dangerous state he exists. Life is the moment in which only this sceptical presumption can continue; and when it is terminating, where is he to set the sole of his foot? He wildly contemplates the book of nature, in which he may have been persuaded that man may read all he needs to know: but the forlorn outcast sees nothing there to meet his case as a sinner. Infinite power, wisdom, contrivance, general provision, alone appear: but nothing of that *further* and *distinct* information which a dying offender needs. He wants footing, and finds none. He needs the hand of a friend to grasp, but none is seen. Possibilities shock his apprehension. He may, perhaps, discern that the present system has a moral government, which frowns upon guilt; and, for ought he knows to the contrary, the next scene may present a Judge upon his throne of justice, – this world, his present idol, vanished like smoke, and quick and dead called to give their account. Where then is he? – an atom of guilt and wretchedness. All this I say may be, for aught he knows to the contrary. But the express and well-authenticated revelation, which that Judge has sent to man, tells us plainly, that all this *shall* be, and that every eye shall behold it!

"Be it so," such a reader may reply: "still I am what I am. My habits of thinking are fixed; and I perceive my habits of life can only be decently borne out by my profession of unbelief. Both are now inveterate. Nor do I see, all things considered, what can be done in my case. How can *I* adopt the Christian Revelation? – and what could it do for me, if I could?"

I answer, by calling your attention to the fact before us. What was the case of John Newton? Could any one be more deeply sunk in depravity, in profligacy, in infidelity than he? Can you even conceive a rational creature more degraded, or more hardened in his evil habits? Would you attempt to recover such a mind, by arguments drawn from the advantage which virtue has over vice? or by rousing his attention to the duties of natural religion, or to the possible consequences of a future retribution? He would have gone on thinking he had made the most of his circumstances, in his practice of catching fish, and eating them almost raw. – He would sullenly have proceeded to sleep through the drying of his one shirt, which he had just washed on the rock, and put on wet. – He would, with a savage ferocity, have watched an opportunity for murdering his master. – He would have drowned all reflection in a drunken revel; and would have overwhelmed all remonstrance, by belching out new-invented blasphemies; and then sought to rush headlong, in a drunken paroxysm, into the ocean.*

Here is, certainly, presented the utmost pitch of a depraved and degraded nature: nor does it seem possible for Satan to carry his point further with a man – EXCEPT in one single instance, namely, by *the final disbelief of a remedy.*

Now, by God's help, this divine remedy was applied, and its efficacy demonstrated; of which there are thousands of living witnesses. A plain matter of fact is before us. It pleased God, that, by a train of dispensations, this prodigal should *come to himself.* – He is made to feel his wants and misery: he follows *the light shining in a dark place:* he calls for help: he is made willing to follow his guide: he proceeds with implicit confidence. And now let us examine to what, at length, he is brought; and by what *means?*

I speak of a matter of fact. Whither is he brought? He is brought from the basest, meanest, under-trodden state of slavery – from a state of mind still more degraded, being *foolish, disobedient, deceived, serving divers lusts and pleasures, living in malice and envy, hateful and hating* – wanting nothing of a complete devil but his powers. This man is brought, I say, to be a faithful and zealous servant of his God – an able and laborious minister of Christ – a useful and benevolent friend to his neighbour – wise to secure the salvation of his own soul, and wise to win the souls of others.

Consider also the MEANS by which he was brought. It was not by the arguments of philosophists, or the rational considerations of what

* See these Memoirs, pages 30, 38, 39, 46

is called natural religion. Mr. N.'s own account informs us, that the peculiar discoveries of Revealed Truth gradually broke in upon his mind; till, at length, he was made sensible that *there was a remedy provided in the Gospel*, and which was fully sufficient to meet even *his* case; and he found *that*, and that *only*, to be *the power of God unto salvation.*

The result, therefore, which should be drawn from these premises, is the following. There exists a desperate disorder in the world, called *Sin*. Heathens, as well as Christians, have marked its malignant influence: they have tried various expedients, which have been prescribed for its cure; or its mitigation, at least: but no means have been discovered, except God's own appointed means, which have availed to the relief of so much as a single individual. Yet, strange to say, this *medicina mentis*[2] of God's own appointment, to which only he has promised a peculiar blessing, and by which he is daily recovering men in the most desperate circumstances who actually employ it – strange to say, this remedy remains a stumbling block – is counted foolishness – insomuch that many will rather dash this cup of salvation from the lips of a profligate, like Newton, when *disposed* to receive it, than that he should obtain relief in *that* way. – Their conduct seems to say, "Rather let such a wretch go on in his profligacy, than the Gospel be acknowledged to be the wisdom and the power of God."

Not that the case of Mr. N., here presented to the consideration of an unbeliever, is brought forward as if the Gospel *needed* any further evidence, or has occasion for facts of our own time to give it additional authenticity: but we are directed to regard the *cloud of witnesses*, among which our departed brother was distinguished; *and, though now dead, yet speaketh*. May the reader have ears to hear the important report!

Does, therefore, the question return, as to what the unbeliever should do? Let him, after seriously considering what is here advanced, consider also what conduct is becoming a responsible, or at least a rational creature. Surely it becomes such an one, to avoid all means of stifling the voice of conscience, whenever it begins to speak – to regard the voice of God, yet speaking to him in the revelation of his grace; and that, much more humbly and seriously than such persons are wont to do. – It becomes him, if he have any regard to the interest of his own soul, or the souls of his fellow-creatures, to give no countenance by his declarations or example, to the senseless cavils and indecent scoffs, by which the profligate aim to cloak the disorders of their hearts – by which vanity aims at distinction, and half-thinkers affect depth. – The person I am now speaking to, cannot but observe how much the judgment becomes the dupe of the passions. If *the veil be upon the heart*, it will be upon every thing. We need not only an *object* presented, but an *organ* to discern it. Now the Gospel alone affords both these. Mr. N. becomes an instructive example in this respect, to the unbeliever. – "One of the first helps," says he, "which I received," in consequence of a determination to examine the New Testament more carefully, "was from Luke 11:13, *If ye then, being evil, know how to give good gifts unto your children, how much more shall your heavenly Father give the Holy Spirit to them that ask him?* I had been sensible, that to profess faith in Jesus Christ, when, in reality, I did not believe his history, was no better than a mockery of the heart-searching God; but here I found a *Spirit* spoken of, which was to be communicated to those who ask it. Upon this I reasoned thus: If this book be true, the promise in this passage must be true likewise: I have need of that very Spirit by which the whole was written, in order to understand it aright. He has engaged here, to give that Spirit to those who ask: and, if it be of God, he will make good his own word."

A man, therefore, who is found in this unhappy state, but not judicially hardened in it, should mark this stage of Mr. N.'s recovery, and attend to the facts and evidences of the power and excellency of real religion, such as this before him. – He should appreciate that Gospel, which it has pleased God to employ as his instrument for displaying the wonders of his might in the moral world. He should pray that he may experience the power of it in his own heart, and thus not lose the additional benefit of the cases presented to him in Memoirs like these: a case, probably, far exceeding his own in the malignity of its symptoms. Let him also consider, that, while such convictions can produce no real loss to him, they may secure advantages beyond calculation. He may not be able, at present, to comprehend how *Godliness is profitable for all things*, in *having* not only *the promise of life that now is*, but *of that which is to come;* but he may see, as a rational creature, that, at the very lowest estimation, he has taken the safe side, by embracing the only hope set before him: and, on this ground, it is clearly demonstrable, that not only the grossest *folly* must attach to the rejecter of a revelation attended with such accumulated evidences; but actual guilt also, and the highest ingratitude and presumption.

II. But there is another class of men, to whom I would recommend a serious consideration of Mr. N.'s religious character and principles.

The persons whom I am now addressing are convinced of the truth of revelation, and some of them ably contend for it against unbelievers. They are also conscientious: they are often useful in society: and are sometimes found amiable and benevolent: they are even religious, according to their views of religion; and some of them are exact in their devotions. Yet, from certain morbid symptoms, they appear not to receive the grace of God in truth, nor to be cordially disposed to the spirit of the Gospel. – So much apparent right intention and exemplary conduct seems, indeed, to demand respect; and a respect, which some who possess more zeal than judgment do not duly pay them.

ARDELIO despises his neighbour EUSEBIUS's religious views and habits; and not only deems him a blind pharisee, but has sometimes expressed the sentiment in the rudest terms. This reminds me of the old story of Diogenes' walking on the costly carpet of his brother philosopher, saying, "I trample on the pride of Plato." "Yes," said Plato, "but with greater pride, Diogenes."

If it be asked, "Why should any one judge unfavourably of such a character as Eusebius?" I answer, we may charitably seek to convince one whom we have reason to think under fatal mistakes without any disposition to judge or condemn him. I meet a traveller who is confidently pursuing a path, which I have reason to believe is both wide of his mark, and dangerous to his person: I may charitably attempt to direct his steps, without thinking ill of his intention. – It is recorded of our Lord, that he even loved a young man, who went away sorrowful on having his grand idol exposed.

"But why," it is asked, "should you suspect any thing essentially wrong in such characters as you describe?" I reply, for the following reasons: I have observed with much concern, when God hath wrought a mighty operation of grace in the heart of a man, like NEWTON, that this man has not, upon such a saving change being wrought, suited the religious taste of the persons just mentioned. They will, indeed, commend his external change of conduct: but will by no means relish

his broken and contrite spirit, or his ascription of the change to free
and unmerited favour, and his *counting all things but loss for the
excellency of the knowledge of Christ Jesus*, as that Lord who hath
thus called him *from darkness to light, and from the power of Satan
to God*. They will not relish the zeal and evangelical strain of his
preaching; his endeavour to alarm a stupid, sleeping conscience, to
probe a deceitful heart, to expose the wretchedness of the world, and
to rend the veil from formality and hypocrisy; nay, they will rather
prefer some dry moralist, or mere formalist, who, instead of having
experienced any such change of heart, will rather *revile* it.

Again, I have observed a lamentable *disposition* of mind in such
persons to form false and unfavourable associations. They will pay
too much attention to injurious representations, true or false, of a
religious class of mankind, whom the world had branded with some
general term of reproach. – Two or three ignorant or extravagant
fanatics shall be admitted to represent the religious world at large; it
not being considered how much such offensive characters are actually
grieving those, whose cause I am pleading. No one, indeed, can have
lived long in society, but he must needs have met the counterfeit of
excellence. – In the article of property, for instance, who is not on
the watch lest he should be imposed on? And, while the love of
property is so general, who is not studious to discover the difference
between the true and the false? It will be so in religion, wherever
there is the attention which its worth so imperiously demands. Love
has a piercing eye, which will discover its object in a crowd. But, if
there be this disposition to confound in the lump the precious with
the vile, it is symptomatic of something morbid in the heart. We
have reason to fear a latent aversion, in the persons offended, from
vital and spiritual religion; notwithstanding all the allowance that
can be made for the prevailing prejudices of their education and
circumstances.

And here also, we cannot but lament the effect of such a disposition
in those *perverse conclusions* which these persons are often observed
to draw from a sermon. Of the two handles which attach to every
thing, what must we think of that mind which is ever choosing the
wrong? Our Lord, for instance, shows how much the *farm*, the *oxen*,
and the *wife* become impediments in the way of those who refuse his
invitation: but a *perverse conclusion* would infer that he was,
therefore, an enemy to lawful engagements. Candour, however, sees,

at a glance, that this was not his design in speaking the parable. His drift was evidently to mark the state and *spirit* of recusants [those who refuse to attend]; and not to discountenance their lawful occupations. He meant to show that even lawful pursuits may be unlawfully pursued, when they become *sole* objects, and are thus preferred to his inestimable proposal. It is thus the well-disposed hearer will mark the *design* of his minister; and draw wholesome nourishment from that discourse, which another will turn to poison, by stopping to cavil at the letter.

Another objection arises from the affinity which characters of this class have with *a world which lieth in wickedness.* In this instance of their worldly attachments, their *charity will* readily *cover a multitude of sins,* and form excuses for serious breaches of both tables of the Law, in their worldly friends. They appear in their element while in the society of these friends, especially if wealthy and accomplished. If any person's ear is wounded with a profane expression of their rich or fashionable acquaintance, they are ready to whisper that "notwithstanding his unguarded language, he has yet upon the whole one of the best hearts." Yet an infallible monitor has said, *Know ye not that the friendship of the world is enmity with God?* If the old maxim does not always hold good, that "a man is known by the company he *keeps,*" it will infallibly stand good if we add one word to it, namely, that "a man is known by the company he *chooses* to keep." – The physician may be detained in an infectious chamber, and the lawyer be found conversing with his client in a shower of rain; but nobody will infer from thence, that the one *chooses* to breathe foul air, or that the other *chooses* to be wet to his skin. While the true Christian, therefore, will avoid inurbanity [courseness], fanaticism, or becoming the dupe of any religious party, he will also join the Psalmist in declaring, *I am a companion of all them that fear thee, and of them that keep thy precepts.*

Again, these moral and religious characters, whom I am labouring to convince of their errors, have been observed to be more disposed to nurse, than to examine their prejudices against a minister of Mr. N.'s principles. "His teaching," say they, "tends to divide a parish, or a family." But why do they not examine the reason? Why do they not consider, that introducing *good* has ever been the occasion of disturbing *evil*? I recollect a great family, whose servants were in a ferment, because one truly conscientious man was found among them.

"*He will spoil the place*," was their term, because he would not connive at their iniquity. But let me ask, what was to be blamed in this affair? his integrity, or their corruption? The Master understood the case, and valued his servant in proportion as he marked the division. And thus it is in religion, while moving in a blind and corrupt world. Christ, though the Prince of Peace, expressly declared that his doctrine would be the occasion of much division in the world; that he *came not to send peace, but a sword*; that he should be the occasion of family variance, &c. Matthew 10:34,35; and warns his disciples of what they must expect, while they endeavoured faithfully to conduct his interests. – Plain matter of fact declares, that, to maintain truth, has been the occasion of the suffering state of the true Church in all ages, and that often unto the death of its innumerable martyrs. But, should a man who reads his Bible, or has any regard for the interests of truth, need to have this explained?

Another mistake might be exposed, in the state of objection, that such principles as Mr. N.'s tend to injure the interests of morality, from his strictly adhering to the doctrine of our eleventh Article, on Justification by Faith. I would hope that this objection arises, in many, from a very slight acquaintance with the subject. It requires, indeed, but little attention to mark how expressly the Scriptures maintain our justification on the sole merit of our Redeemer, while they as fully maintain the necessity of our sanctification or holiness by his Spirit. It has been repeatedly proved, by sound and incontestable arguments, that these two grand fundamentals of our religion are so far from opposing each other, either in Scripture or in experience, that, when *real*, they are found *inseparable*. But, because this is not the place to either state or defend this doctrine at large, it may help such as have hitherto stumbled respecting it, to observe an illustration and proof of this position, in the matter of fact just now presented to their view.

To one willing to learn, I would say, What proof would you require of the practical tendency of principles like Mr. N.'s? We bring you, in his history, a most deplorable instance of human depravity and moral disorder. What experiment should be tried to recover this wretched creature to God and to himself? – Regard, I say, the fact in this man's history. You will find that his recovery was not brought about by such considerations as are urged in what are termed moral or rational discourses; but, on the contrary, by such truths as he laboured throughout his ministry to establish, not only from the

Scriptures, but from his own experience of their efficacy. He dwelt on truths which are essential and peculiar to Christianity: – such as the guilt and utter depravity of our fallen human nature, whereby man is become an alien and apostate from his God; his inability to recover himself without the grace of the Holy Spirit; the necessity of regeneration by the same Spirit; and of faith in the Redeemer, not only as the alone ground of his justification before God, but as the root and motive of all acceptable obedience and good works. "If I wanted a man to fly," said Mr. N., "I must contrive to find him wings; and, thus, if I would successfully enforce moral *duties*, must advance evangelical *motives*." He preached truths like these, constantly and fervently; and he lived a consistent example of them.

Thus in all things approving himself a true disciple and minister of Christ, those, who knew him, know that, without making any odious comparison, it might be literally affirmed of Mr. N. that "*by pureness, by knowledge, by long-suffering, by kindness, by the Holy Ghost, by love unfeigned, by the word of truth, by the power of God, by the armour of righteousness on the right hand and on the left*, his mouth was opened and his heart enlarged towards men."

I trust it is from a pure motive, that I am endeavouring to convince persons of the class which I am addressing, of their mistake. And I am the more induced to bring a case in point before them, because I think it cannot be paralleled as an instance of the power of religion, among those who labour to keep up prejudices against Ministers of Mr. N.'s character; or who, by unfair or partial statements, strive to subvert the doctrines which he preached, and the great end to which all his labours were directed, namely, *the life of God in the soul of man*.

If indeed any one *is* WILLING *to be deceived, let him be deceived.* At least such an one will not be addressed here. But, if a man has any serious sense of the value of his soul, of its lost condition by sin, and of the necessity of recovering the friendship of his God; if he feels the express declaration in the Scriptures of an eternity of happiness or misery to be of infinite importance, and one to which the weightiest concern in this perishing world is but as the *dust on the balance* – let such an one consider these things. Let him enquire whether those, who object to the character and views of such a minister as Mr. N., labour first to probe the state of their own hearts deeply, as he did. When he was no longer an infidel, had renounced his grosser habits, and was to all appearance a new man, "Yet," says he, "though I cannot doubt that this change, so far as it prevailed, was wrought by the Spirit and power of God, still I was greatly deficient in many respects. I was in some degree affected with a sense of my enormous sins, but I was little aware of the innate evils of my heart. I had no apprehension of the spirituality and extent of the Law of God. The hidden life of a Christian, as it consists in communion with God by Jesus Christ, and a continual dependence upon him for hourly supplies of wisdom, strength, and comfort, was a mystery of which I had as yet no knowledge. I acknowledged the Lord's mercy in pardoning what was past, but depended chiefly upon my own resolution to do better for the time to come."

Let the honest enquirer also consider, whether the objectors just spoken of, are observed to be as anxious as Mr. N. was in their endeavours to serve God and propagate his will, to glorify his Son, and to save the souls of men: whether they have experienced the force of truth, in the conversion of their own hearts and lives. *Conformed to the world*, as he once was, have they been since *transformed by the renewing of their minds*, as he at length became? A few such questions as these, well considered, would lead to important discoveries. Such an enquiry would show, that, however some persons may be able to treat of the outworks of revelation, as they may of any other science which they have studied; yet, for such to dogmatize on religion, as it consists in a vital, spiritual, and experimental principle, would be as absurd as for a man originally deprived of one of the five senses, to deny the perceptions of those who possess them all. In short, it is as ridiculous as it is profane, for men rashly to assert on religious points, who evidently appear to have nothing so little at heart as the real influence and actual interests of religion.

Lastly, let nominal Christians seriously consider whether our immortal interests are not much too important to be staked upon a mere *prejudice of education* – an old, unrevised *habit of thinking* – a taking it for granted that they are right, when the event may awfully prove the reverse; and that too, when such errors can never be rectified. The persons with whom I have been pleading would pity the Jew or the Pagan in such an error: I earnestly pray that they may be enabled to see as clearly their own mistake, and not resent the admonition of a real friend now seeking to prevent it.

III. But there yet remains a class of persons, found in the religious world, who entertain a high regard for Mr. N.'s character, and who should gather that instruction from it of which they appear to stand in great need. "They should all take care," as he expresses it, "that they do not make their profession of religion *a receipt in full for all other obligations*." I do not regard this class as hypocrites, so much as *self-deceivers*. They have a zeal for the Gospel; but without a comprehensive view of its nature. They do not consider, that, in avoiding error on the one hand, they are plunging into a contrary mistake. Like a child crossing a bridge, they tremblingly avoid the deep water which they perceive roaring on one side; and recede from it, till they are ready to perish from not perceiving the danger of that which lies on the other side.

The persons of whom I am here speaking, are defective in the grand article of AN HUMBLE AND CONTRITE SPIRIT. I remember Mr. N. used to remark, that, "if any one *criterion* could be given of a real work of grace begun in the heart of a sinner, it would be found in his *contrite spirit*." Nothing is more insisted on in Scripture, as essential to real religion. I never knew any truly serious Christian, who would not readily join in acknowledging that "the religion of a sinner," as Mr. N. expresses it, "stands on two pillars, namely, what Christ did *for* us in his flesh, and what he performs *in* us by his Spirit: most errors," he adds, "arise from an attempt to separate these two." But the enemy still comes and sows tares among the wheat: a sort of loose profession has obtained, which has brought much reproach on religion; and has become a cause of stumbling to many, who perceive a class of Christians contending for only *part* of Christianity.

You can prevail little with a professor of this description, in exhorting him by *the meekness and gentleness of Christ*, to self-denying, patient, or forbearing habits. If you state the genius of Christ's religion as it relates to the returning *good for evil* – in *blessing them that curse*, and *praying for such as revile and persecute* – in *showing, out of a good conversation, their works with meekness of wisdom* – or, in *having a fervent charity towards all men*, &c. he is ready to take fire; and to cover his conduct by maintaining a crude system of mere doctrinal points ill understood. Your well-intended remonstrance may perhaps lead him to ask, whether you mean to bring him back to the "*Whole Duty of Man*,"[3] or to "*Nelson's Fasts and Festivals*".[4] He will lament that you yourself are not *clear* in the

Gospel; because, in fact, you maintain the *whole* of it: that you are not *faithful*; because you maintain the whole of it in a patient forbearing spirit.

The views of such persons, and the evil tempers to which they give place in their spiritual warfare, have often reminded me of the shrewd answer which our Richard the First sent to the Pope; who was angry because a certain warlike bishop had fallen by Richard in battle, and whom, being an ecclesiastic, the Pope called his *son*. Richard sent the Bishop's armour to the Pope, with the words of Joseph's brethren – *"Know now whether this be thy son's coat or not."*

Nothing, however, could be more opposed to the spirit and character of our departed friend, than the temper that has just been described. His zeal in propagating the truth, the whole truth, and nothing but the truth, was not more conspicuous, than the tenderness of his spirit as to the manner of his maintaining and delivering it. He was found constantly *speaking the truth in love; and in meekness instructing those that oppose themselves, if God peradventure would give them repentance to the acknowledging of the truth.* There was a gentleness, a candour, and a forbearance in him, that I do not recollect to have seen in equal degree among his brethren; and which had so conciliating an effect, that even the enemies of truth often spoke loudly in praise of his character. On the other hand, this generated such an affection in his friends, that, had he attempted to preach longer than he did, a great part of his congregation would have assembled, were it only for the pleasure they had in seeing his person.

That this account is not panegyric [praise], is known to all who were personally acquainted with Mr. N. But, as many who may read these Memoirs had not that pleasure, I will add the testimony of one whose nice discernment of character will admit of no question.

"A people will love a minister, if a minister seems to love his people. The old maxim, *simile agit in simile*,[5] is in no case more exactly verified: therefore you were beloved at Olney; and, if you preached to the Chickesaws and Chactaws, would be equally beloved by them."*

As the spirit of Christian benevolence and charity seems not to have been sufficiently cultivated among us, while a furious and often abusive zeal for certain points, as Cowper remarks, has been

---

* See, in Hayley's *Life of Cowper*, the twenty-seventh Letter, which is addressed by Cowper to Mr. Newton.

substituted for the whole truth, I am led to dwell longer than I intended in exhibiting this amiable feature of Mr. N.'s character; especially on account of those Christians who have imbibed a false taste in their religion from such teachers or books as have fallen in their way. I therefore, earnestly request such persons to weigh well the enquiries which follow.

Have you sufficiently considered the evil divisions and heart burnings in a church; and what interest that enemy, who comes to sow tares among the wheat, takes in promoting them? – Do you reflect that another Christian may be doing God's work, though his mode of doing it may not meet your taste, any more than your taste meets his? – Do you consider how much greater evil a wrong spirit and temper produce, than the things you object against? – Do you weigh the consequences of your haste in weakening the hands, and grieving the heart of any godly minister, whom you constantly or occasionally attend; and in actually laying a stumbling block in the way of the ungodly, while you depreciate him and his services? Nothing affected that eminent character, Mr. Cadogan, like what he met from some religious persons of this kind, as I have related from his own lips, in his Memoirs.*

Let me further exhort such as are in danger from this unchastised spirit to consider, how much corrupt nature is *at the bottom of this error*. Corrupt nature frets and rages at any supposed contradiction or restraint: it would substitute the work of the *tongue* for that of the *heart*. In the mean time, *real* religion is scorned by the world; which cannot distinguish between a thing so deformed, and the thing as it ought to appear.

Consider, also, whether there needs any grace at all, in order to maintain such a sort of profession. Are we only to *christen* the evil passions of corrupt nature, and then call names, hate, boast, and give ourselves the preference, as much as any ungodly man whatever? A zealot at an election can fight and strive for his favourite candidate: with inflamed zeal he can cause divisions, exhibit pride, self-will, and impatience of subordination; but, let me ask, will the same evil tempers change their nature because they are employed about spiritual objects?

Much blame attaches, too, respecting certain disputable points for which such persons strive. It seems as if some, who are otherwise

---

* See Mem. of Cadogan, Cecil's *Works*, 2nd ed. vol.1. p. 196.

good men, did not relish the Bible till they had garbled and selected it; and that, if the whole were not of acknowledged authority, they would condemn it as it now stands. They speak as if it were not accurate in its terms, or sufficiently express or decisive in confirming their fond opinions. This leads them to be *shy* of some parts of Revelation; and to distort others, in order to fit them for their system. While contending for that system, they appear to forget the stress which the Apostle lays upon the holy, humble, self-denying, affectionate spirit of Christianity, in 1 Corinthians 13. How gentle it is! How easy to be entreated; how it hopeth and endureth all things, &c. while, on the contrary, they who can speak with the tongues of men and of angels, who have all knowledge, who can work miracles, and even die martyrs, would, without this distinguishing characteristic of Christianity, be considered of God as NOTHING. The Old Testament dispensation, it is granted, had a severe aspect; and special occasions may be pleaded for special expressions of holy indignation, under any dispensation: but when the Prophet describes the brighter day, he foretells that then *the wolf shall dwell with the lamb*, as emblematical of the prevalence of that grace described by the Apostle in the chapter just quoted. Hold, therefore, the faith once delivered to the saints as *firmly* as possible; but hold it in *love*. *Buy the truth, and sell it not* – rather die for it, than part with it – but, *speak it in love*; and walk in it *as Christ also walked*; ever remembering that *the wrath of man worketh not the righteousness of God*.

I feel conscious that it is simply with a view to convince many well-meaning Christians of their error (and I have found more or less of this class in almost every place where I have been) that I thus speak. If a gross superstition arising in the Church perverted the Christianity of former ages; I wish I may mistake in supposing, that a loose and unscriptural profession is widely spreading as the bane of our age. Against such a departure from the true genius of Christianity, I certainly, as a minister of Christ, ought to bear my feeble testimony. Consider, therefore, that what is said is said with a single view to your best interests; and *the Lord give you understanding in all things!*

As I referred the Christians who were last addressed to the character of Mr. N. as an example, so I never knew a more perfect one to my purpose. When any person depreciated the ministry of a good man, who, by advancing important truths, was opposing the reigning errors of the times; but who, from timidity or prejudice, was shy of Mr. N. he would imitate his Divine Master, by saying, "Let him alone: he that is not against us is on our side. – Make no man an offender for a word. – He is doing good, according to his views. – Let us pray for him, and by no means weaken his hands. – Who knows but God may one day put him far above our heads, both in knowledge and usefulness?"

His grand point, in a few words, as he used to express it, was, "TO BREAK A HARD HEART, AND TO HEAL A BROKEN HEART." – To implant the life of God in the soul of man, he would sacrifice every subordinate consideration; he felt every other to be comparatively insignificant. He saw the spirit of ancient Pharisaism working among those who cry the most against it – who exact to a scruple, in the tythe of mint, anise, and cummin of their own peculiarities, while they pass over the weightier matters of unity and love – straining out the gnat of a private opinion, and swallowing the camel of a deadly discord. On the contrary, so far as order and circumstances would admit, Mr. N. clave to every good man, and endeavoured to strengthen his hands, in whatever denomination of Christians he was found. His character well illustrated the Scripture, that though *scarcely for a righteous* (or just) *man would one die, yet for a good man* (i.e. one eminent for his candour and benevolence) *some would even dare to die*. However they *admired* some ministers, they all *loved* him; and saw exemplified in him that *wisdom which is from above, – which is first pure, then peaceable, gentle and easy to be entreated, full of mercy and good fruits, without partiality, and without hypocrisy.*

I conclude these Memoirs with a word to such as are endeavouring to follow the steps of their late faithful friend as he followed Christ. We cannot but lament the errors just described. We cannot, if we have any zeal for the Gospel, but protest against them. But let us recollect that they are not the *only* errors which are found in the Church; and therefore let us watch lest any other *root of bitterness spring up to trouble us, and defile many*. When you lament with me the removal of ministers like Mr. N., let us recollect that ETERNAL FRIEND, who will never leave his Church without witness to the truth; and who, among other reasons for removing earthly helps, teaches us thereby to rest only on that help which cannot be removed. Let us take comfort too in recollecting, that, spotted as the Church may appear from the inconsistencies of many of its members, yet all the real good in this corrupt world is to be found in that Church. – God saw seven thousand true believers in Israel, while his prophet could see but one. – Where some Jehu is sounding a trumpet before him, many are quietly passing to heaven without any such clamour. As a great writer remarks, "Because half a dozen grasshoppers under a fern make the field ring with their importunate chink, while thousands of great cattle chew the cud and are silent, pray do not imagine that those that make the noise are 'the only inhabitants of the field.'"

But I must remark, that nothing has been more profitable to myself in considering Mr. N.'s life, than the exhibition which it makes of a Particular Providence. If the Church be not conducted by such *visible* signs now, as formerly, it is found to be *actually* conducted. We read of a divine hand concerned in *the fall of the sparrows*, in numbering *the hairs of our head*, and in raising *our dust to life;* but with what little interest we read this, appears by our distrust in the first trial we meet. If we do not dare to join the sentiments of some, who regard such expressions as purely figurative and hyperbolical; yet our imagination is so overwhelmed with the difficulty of the performance, that we are apt to turn from the subject, with some general hope, but with a very indistinct and vague idea of *a God at hand*, faithful to his promise, and almighty to deliver. Yet, how many cases occur in the history of every one of us, where nothing short of an Almighty Arm could prove *a present help in the time of trouble!*

Now this short history before us is admirably calculated to encourage our faith and hope, when we are called to pass through those deep waters that seem to bid defiance to human strength and contrivance. What, for instance, but a divine interference caused Mr. N. to be roused from sleep on board the *Harwich* at the moment of exchanging men, and thereby affected his removal? – What placed him in a situation so remarkably suited to his recovering the ship which had already passed the place of his station in Africa, and brought him back to his country? – What kept him from returning in the boat that was lost at Rio Cestors? – or from putting off to the ship that was blown up near Liverpool? – Not to mention many other of his special deliverances.

"*I am a wonder unto many,*" says he, in the motto of his *Narrative*: and, if we as distinctly considered the strange methods of mercy which have occurred in our own cases, we should at least be *a wonder to ourselves*. But my aim is to point out the use we should make of these Memoirs in this respect. We should, as Christians, mark the error of despair. – We should see that the case of a praying man *cannot* be desperate – that if a man be out of the pit of hell, he is on the ground of mercy. We should recollect that God sees a way of escape when we see none – that nothing is too hard for him – that he *warrants* our dependence, and invites us to call on him in the day of trouble, and gives us a promise of deliverance. We should, therefore, in every trial adopt the language of Mr. N.'s favourite HERBERT:[6]

> *Away, despair: my gracious Lord doth hear;*
> *Though winds and waves assault my keel,*
> *He doth preserve it: he doth steer,*
> *Ev'n when the boat seems most to reel:*
> *Storms are the triumph of his art:*
> *Well may he close his eyes, but not his heart.*

From these facts we should see that Christ is able, not only *to save to the uttermost all that come unto God by him;* but that he is able to bring the most hardened blasphemer and abject slave from his chains of sin and misery, to stand in the most honourable and useful station, and proclaim to the wretched and to the ruined the exceeding riches of his grace. I have observed from my own experience as well as from that of others, how strong a hold Satan builds by *despair*. The pressing fascinations of the world, the secret invitations of sensuality, and the distant prospect of eternal things, form a powerful current against vital religion. The heart of a Christian is ready to sink whenever these proud waters rise. Let him, therefore, recollect, that his hope, his only hope, is in pressing right onward through a world of lies and vanity – that his present dispensation is the walk of *faith*, and not of *sight* – and that *by two immutable things in which it is impossible for God to lie, he has given strong consolation to such as flee for refuge to the hope set before them.*

One could, indeed, scarcely conjecture that cases like Mr. N.'s should be so perverted by any of our children, as that they should take confidence in their sins from his former course of life; but, because such facts, as I am credibly informed, do exist, let us be upon the watch to counteract this deep device of the great enemy.

MY DEAR YOUNG FRIENDS, who may have read these Memoirs merely, perhaps, for your amusement, consider with what a contrary design St. Paul states his former unrenewed condition: *I was*, says he, *before, a blasphemer, a persecutor, and injurious – but for this cause I obtained mercy.* For what cause? Was it that men should continue in sin because a miracle of special grace has been wrought? To do *evil that good may come*, is the black mark of a reprobate mind. – But *for this cause*, saith the Apostle, *I obtained mercy, that in me first Jesus Christ might show forth all long-suffering, for a pattern to them who should hereafter believe in him to life everlasting.* The same caution is necessary whenever you may be tempted to hope for such a recovery as Mr. N.'s after erring like him. To proceed upon such a hope is a gross presumption. Thousands perish in wrong courses for one who escapes from their natural consequences. Pray, therefore, that you may be enabled to resist the temptation of *perverting* such extraordinary cases. God affords them to be *a savour of life unto life*, while Satan would employ them to be *a savour of death unto death.* One, Almighty to save, affords you here, indeed, an instance of special mercy, which gives you the strongest encouragement in setting your faces towards his kingdom: and this is the proper use to be made of such a case.

Your parents, your most disinterested friends, are anxiously watching for your good; and they, perhaps, have put this book into your hand with a view of promoting it. The author has cause to thank God who put it into the heart of *his* pious parent to make a similar attempt, and bless it with success; and he could tell of more such instances. May it please God that you may be added to the number!

Worldly prosperity would rather hurt than help you, before your minds become rightly directed. Mr. N, shows us, (p. 56) that his firmest friend could not have served him, had not God first prepared his mind for the advancement. An enemy would occupy your minds with perishing objects; but God calls you to cultivate nobler feelings. He proposes glory, honour, immortality, and eternal life, by the Gospel. –SEEK, therefore, FIRST THE KINGDOM OF GOD AND HIS RIGHTEOUSNESS, AND ALL OTHER THINGS SHALL BE ADDED UNTO YOU.

THE END.

REFERENCES

Abbreviations used in REFERENCES and WHO'S WHO

ALS   A Letter Signed
BOD   Bodleian Library, Oxford
BFBS British and Foreign Bible Society
BL   British Library
BMS   Baptist Missionary Society
C&N   Cowper & Newton Museum, Olney
CMJ   Christian Mission to the Jews
CMS   Church Mission Society
CUL   Cambridge University Library
DWL   Dr Williams's Library, London
ECR   Essex County Records Office, Chelmsford
FRO   Family Records Office, London
GL   Guildhall Library, Corporation of London
LMS   London Missionary Society
LPL   Lambeth Palace Library, London
LSPCJ London Society for Promoting Christianity amongst the Jews
MS/S Manuscript/s
NMM   National Maritime Museum, Greenwich
TH   Tower Hamlets Local History Library and Archives

Preface
1. Richard Cecil, *The Memoirs of the Hon. and Rev. William Bromley Cadogan*, 1798
2. Richard Cecil, *The Memoirs of John Bacon*, 1801
3. John Newton, *An Authentic Narrative*, 1764. Published with some additional material for Cecil's *Life of Newton* in 1990 as *Out of the Depths.*

Appendix to Preface
4. John Newton, *The Christian Correspondent*, 1790, Newton to Alexander Clunie, 11 December 1764

Chapter 1
1. Dates given in the Old Style refer to the Julian Calendar. The New Style, the Gregorian Calendar, was adopted in Britain by omitting the eleven days from 3rd to 13th of September, 1752. From then on, Newton regarded his birthday as being on 4th August.
2. *The Westminster Shorter Catechism*, 1647
3. Dr. Isaac Watts wrote several catechisms which are listed in the

bibliography. Also in catechetical form was *A Short View of the Whole of Scripture History*, 1732, which Watts says in his preface was originally intended "for persons of younger years, and the common ranks of mankind".

4. Dr. Isaac Watts, *Divine Songs Attempted in Easy Language for the use of Children*, 1715. A facsimile was published by the Oxford University Press in 1971.

5. John Newton, *Letters to a Wife*, 1793; also in *The Works of John Newton*, vol. 5, 1808

6. Benjamin Bennett, *The Christian Oratory, or the Devotion of the Closet*, 1726-28

7. [Daniel Defoe], *The Family Instructor*, 1715

8. Acts 26:5

9. Lord (Anthony Ashley Cooper) Shaftesbury, *Characteristicks of Men*, 1711. The Rhapsody refers to the second of his two treatises, The Moralists: A Philosophical Rhapsody.

Appendix to Chapter 1

10. John Stow, *A Survey of London*, 1598, revised by Strype, 1720; facsimile edition by Alan Sutton Publishing Ltd., 1994

11. John Newton, *Letters to a Wife*, 1793, from Antigua, 4 July 1751

12. *Independent Church Meeting Book*, FRO. There is a note opposite the page of entry of Elizabeth Newton's name as a member on 30 March 1727 confirming her identity as the mother of John. Opposite the page recording John's baptism on 26 July 1725 is a note, "This was the celebrated John Newton whose early history is so full of awful depravity – but who was at length arrested by the Almighty – say[ing], "thus far shalt thou go but no farther" [a ref. to Job 38:11]. Both notes were by William Kelly.

13. *Land Tax Records* for Wapping 1730-32, Guildhall Library (GL)

14. David Jennings, *Sermons to Young People,* 1730

15. Newton to David Jennings, January 1753, ALS, DWL

16. *Aveley Parish Records,* ECR

17. Newton to John Thornton, 16 July 1776, ALS, CUL

18. Newton, *The Aged Pilgrim's Triumph*, 1825, Newton to Walter Taylor, 20 July 1784

CHAPTER 2

1. Isaiah 49:24

2. Andrew Baxter, *An Enquiry into the Nature of the Human Soul*, 1733, p.6. He writes of a resistance which makes it appear "that matter never acts, or effects a change of state in itself, but resists action, and all possible change of its present state, whether of motion or rest. It is a kind of

positive, or stubborn inactivity... a *vis inertiae*, as it were a negative activity; something receding farther from action than bare inactivity." John Bacon was a subscriber to this book.

3. Daniel 2:45
4. Job 33:24
5. Psalm 23:1
6. Psalm 103:1

Appendix to Chapter 2
7. Josiah Bull, *Letters of John Newton*, 1869, Newton to John Catlett, 8 February 1763
8. Newton to Polly, 24 January 1744/5, ALS, LPL
9. John Newton, *Cardiphonia*, 1781, Newton to John Ryland, 31 July 1773

CHAPTER 3
1. Luke 15:16
2. Isaac Barrow, *Euclidis Elementa*, 1655, Book 6
3. Genesis 32:10

Appendix to chapter 3
4. John Newton, *Letters to a Wife*, 1792, from Bananas, 21 November 1750
5. William Wordsworth, *The Prelude*, 1805 edtn., Book 6, Cambridge and the Alps, lines 160-174 (142-154 in 1850 edtn.) are quoted from Jonathan Wordsworth, M.H. Abrams & Stephen Gills, *The Prelude 1799, 1805, 1850 Authoritative Text, Context and Reception, Recent Critical Essays*, 1979, p.194.
6. Isaac Newton, *Principia*, 1687
7. John Newton, *Cardiphonia*, 1781, Five Letters to Mr. C[ollins]: March 1776
8. William Jowett, *A Memoir of the Rev. W. A. B. Johnson*, 1852, pp.268-269

CHAPTER 4
1. George Stanhope, Dean of Canterbury, *The Christian's Pattern: or, A Treatise of the Imitation of Jesus Christ written originally in Latin by Thomas-a-Kempis*, 1698
2. William Beveridge, *Sermons on several subjects*, 12 vol., 1708-15, probably vol. 2, The Being, Love and other Attributes of God; as our Creator, Redeemer, and Sanctifier. Illustrated in 12 sermons. Sermon 3, The Merits of Christ's Passion, John 1:29, *Behold the Lamb of God, which taketh away the sin of the world.*

Other related sermons by Beveridge are: *Good Friday to be kept by all Christians and the Manner of keeping it, Zechariah 12:10, And they shall look upon me whom they have pierced*, published in 1709, and in his *Works* two more Good Friday Sermons: John 19:30, *And he bowed his head* and Philippians 2:8, *And being found in fashion as a man, he humbled himself, and became obedient unto death, even the death of the cross.*

3. 1 Timothy 3:16; 2 Corinthians 5:19
4. Psalm 119:25
5. Hebrews 3:12, 13
6. Judges 16:20

Appendix to Chapter 4

7. Josiah Bull, *John Newton of Olney*, 1868, Newton to Thornton, 4 August 1773
8. John Newton, Annotated copy of *Letters to a Wife*, MSS, C&N [to be published by Christian Focus], a note written on 21 March 1803. Newton's comment of, "Why me, O Lord, Why me?" was one he often uttered, in echo partly of David in 1 Chronicles 17:16, *Who am I, O Lord God ... that thou hast brought me hitherto?* [the verse above *Amazing Grace* in *Olney Hymns*] and partly of the fourth verse from Isaac Watt's hymn, *How sweet and awful is the place*, which begins, "Why was I made to hear thy voice, And enter while there's room...?"
9. John Newton, *The Aged Pilgrim's Triumph*, 1825, Newton to Mrs. Taylor, 1 October 1785

CHAPTER 5

1. A reference to William Law, author of *Serious Call*, a book which had influenced a number of leading evangelicals in their search for God. Newton later rejected Law's work owing to his increasing emphasis on mysticism and his doctrine of Inner Light. In a letter to Mrs. Dawson (p.87 of *Life and Writings*) he explains, "I cannot recommend any of Mr. Law's writings in the gross, and perhaps there are none of them in which some excellent things are not to be found. But in his *Serious Call* particularly, he shows the folly and vanity of a worldly life in a very striking and masterly manner. I wish he had been as happy in delineating the nature and effect of true religion, as he has been in showing the misery of those who live without God in the world."
2. perfectly (lit. to a fingernail), Horace, *Satires*
3. 1 Thessalonians 5:22
4. George Buchanan, *Psalmorum Davidis Paraphrasis Poetica*, 1566
5. [Henry Scougal], *Life of God in the Soul of Man*, 1677
6. James Hervey, *Meditations among the Tombs, Reflections on a Flower-Garden, and a Descant on Creation*, 1746. *Meditations* and *Reflections* were written while Hervey was curate at Bideford. *Meditations* was

suggested to him by a ride to Kilkhampton, Cornwall, and *Reflections* was partly composed in the garden summer-house of the family he lodged with. During his curacy at Bideford, Hervey's generosity was so unbounded that his friends devised a way of helping him by asking for a loan when they knew he had just received his salary, and returning it when they saw he was almost penniless.

7. Philip Doddridge, *Some Remarkable Passages in the Life of Colonel James Gardiner*, 1747
8. Hebrews 7:25
9. 2 Timothy 2:19

Appendix to Chapter 5
10. Newton to his father, 16th March 1749, ALS, LPL
11. John Campbell, *Letters and Conversational Remarks of John Newton*, 1808
12. Log of John Newton while master of the *Duke of Argyle* and the *African* on voyages to Africa and the West Indies between 1750 and 1754, NMM
13. Newton's contributions in evidence against the slave trade may be seen in *Reports of the House of Lords of the Committee of Council...*, 1789 [524.K.14 British Library] and in *Evidence to a Committee of the House of Commons, 11th and 12th May 1790,* [State Papers, British Library, vol. 88 pp.137ff] [Martin's ref.]
14. John Newton, *Thoughts upon the African Slave Trade*, 1788
15. Money first (lit. virtue after money] Horace
16. Josiah Bull, *Memorials of the Rev William Bull*, 1864
17. Josiah Woodward, *The Seaman's Monitor*, 1703, 3rd edtn. enlarged
18. John Flavel, *Navigation Spiritualiz'd*: or, a *New Compass for Seamen*, 1682
19. Newton to David Jennings, 29 August 1752, ALS, DWL
20. Newton to David Jennings, 8 September 1753, ALS, DWL
21. Newton to David Jennings, 7 June 1754, ALS, DWL
22. Newton's Diary, 1752-56, MSS, LPL [a transcript of his autograph diary held in Firestone Library, Princeton University]
23. *Stepney Meeting Church Book*, MSS, TH
24. John Newton, *The Christian Correspondent*, 1790
25. John Newton, *Sixty-Eight Letters to a Clergyman*, 1845; Newton to Mrs. Coffin, 22 June 1791

CHAPTER 6
1. Edward Young, *The Complaint, a Night Thought on Life, Death and Immortality*, 1742. The quote is from Night the Sixth, The Infidel Reclaimed, Part the First, referring to having to watch the suffering of a loved one dying a slow death, Young's own experience.

2. in the open air
3. 1 Corinthians 2:2
4. 1 Timothy 1:15

Appendix to Chapter 6

5. The Life of the Rev. Samuel Brewer, B.D. *Evangelical Magazine,* January 1797
6. George Ford, *The Good Man, and a faithful Minister, made eminently useful, A Funeral Sermon preached at Stepney meeting June 19 1796, occasioned by the death of the Rev. Samuel Brewer, B.D.,* 1796
7. Newton to Polly, undated, ALS, LPL
8. Newton's Diary, 1752-56, MSS, LPL
9. Newton's Diary, 1752-56, MSS, LPL
10. John Newton, *Letters to a Wife,* 1792: Appendix No. 3, *Ebenezer: A Memorial of the unchangeable goodness of God, under changing dispensations,* No. 5, Third Anniversary of the 15th December, 1793
11. Newton's Diary, 1752-56, MSS, LPL
12. John Newton, *Letters to a Wife,* 1792: 12 September 1755
13. John Newton, *Letters to a Wife,* 1792: 16 September 1755
14. Newton's Diary, 1752-56, MSS, LPL
15. Newton's Diary, 1752-56, MSS, LPL
16. John Newton, *The Christian Correspondent,* 1790
17. John Gadsby, *Memoirs of the Principal Hymn-Writers and Compilers of the 17th, 18th & 19th Centuries,* 1882, 5th edtn
18. Aaron Crossley Hobart Seymour, *The Life and Times of Selina, Countess of Huntingdon,* 1840, vol. 1, p.271
19. Josiah Bull, *John Newton of Olney,* 1868, p.98
20. Josiah Bull, *John Newton of Olney,* 1868, p.106
21. Newton to Henry Venn, 31 March 1792, ALS, CMS
22. John Newton, *Memoirs of the Life of the Late Rev. William Grimshaw, in Six Letters to the Late Rev Henry Foster, Minister of St. James, Clerkenwell,* 1799. This was not included in Newton's *Works* as the copyright was given to the Society for Relieving Poor Pious Clergymen of the Established Church. The copy which Newton inscribed to his friend William Bull was recently sold by an Oxford bookshop.
23. Josiah Bull, *John Newton of Olney,* 1868, Newton to John Wesley, 14 November 1760
24. Thomas Kemp, *A History of Warwick and its People,* 1905, p.169
25. Josiah Bull, *John Newton,* 1868, p.104
26. John Wesley, *The Journal of John Wesley,* Standard Edition, edited by Nehemiah Curnock, 1909, 8 vols
27. William T. Goodwin, *The Baptists of Warwick 1640–1955,* 1955 (shortened from *Baptist Quarterly*)

28. Newton to his wife, 28 July 1760, ALS, LPL
29. Newton to his wife, 5 August 1760, ALS, LPL
30. John Newton, *The Christian Correspondent*, 1790, 16 May 1767, p.163
31. Samuel Palmer, *A Brief Sketch of the character of the late Rev. John Newton being an extract from a Sermon preached to a Dissenting Congregation, January 3 1808*. His text was Acts 11:24, *He was a good man, and full of the Holy Ghost and of faith: and much people was added unto the Lord*. Taken from Newton, *Correspondence with a Dissenting Minister*, 1809, pp.19-20.
32. Bruce Hindmarsh, *John Newton and the Evangelical Tradition*, 1996, p.94n, quoting from the *Private Journals and Literary Remains of John Byrom*, ed. Richard Parkinson, 2 vols, 1854-7, vol. 2 p.636
33. Josiah Bull, *John Newton of Olney*, 1868, May 1759, p.102
34. Josiah Bull, *John Newton of Olney*, 1868, p.113
35. Newton to his wife, 5 April 1764, ALS, LPL
36. Josiah Bull, *John Newton of Olney*, 1868, 10 March 1763, p.117
37. Josiah Bull, *John Newton of Olney*, 1868
38. John Newton, *Sixty-Eight Letters to a Clergyman*, 1845, Newton to Mr. Coffin, 31 July, 1792
39. Newton, *Lectures on the Church Catechism*, 1765, MSS, C&N

CHAPTER 7

1. This was mistakenly printed as "the following year" in the original edition and the error repeated in Newton's *Works*. The Lincoln Episcopal Register No. 39, fo. 32r/33r, records his ordination as Sunday, June 17th, 1764. Newton's diary and letters to his wife (14 June 1764) and Clunie (21 June 1764) also refer to this event.
2. John Newton, *Cardiphonia*, 1781
3. Moses Browne, *Sunday Thoughts*, 1752
4. 1 Kings 4:29
5. Revelation 3:1
6. 2 Timothy 3:5
7. let it stand for what it's worth
8. 1 Chronicles 29:14
9. *Memoir of the Early Life of William Cowper, Esq., written by himself*, MSS, C&N
10. William Hayley, *Life of Cowper*, 1803
11. Matthew 18:3; Mark 10:15; Luke 18:17
12. Newton to John Thornton, 18 November 1777, ALS, CUL
13. 2 Corinthians 2:16
14. Acts 19:8, 9
15. Luke 11:21
16. Psalm 13:3

248 THE LIFE OF JOHN NEWTON

17. 1 Timothy 4:16
18. 2 Timothy 3:12
19. Matthew 5:44
20. 2 Timothy 2:24, 25
21. John Newton, *Six Discourses, as intended for the pulpit*, 1760
22. A new edition of *Omicron* with *Vigil* letters annexed, 1793 (appears as *Forty-One letters on religious subjects* in *The Works of John Newton*, 1808). Cecil originally stated 1762 as the publication date of *Omicron*.
23. John Newton, *Sermons preached in the parish-church of Olney*, 1767
24. John Newton, *A Review of Ecclesiastical History*, 1769
25. John Newton, *Olney Hymns*, 1779

Appendix to Chapter 7
26. Newton to his wife, 16 April 1764, ALS, LPL
27. Newton to his wife, 3 April 1764, ALS, LPL
28. Newton to his wife, 19 April 1764, ALS, LPL
29. Newton to his wife, 26 April 1764, ALS, LPL
30. Josiah Bull, *John Newton of Olney*, 1868, p.122
31. John Newton, *The Christian Correspondent*, 1790
32. John Newton, *The Searcher of Hearts*, 1997
33. William Cowper, *Memoir of the Early Life of William Cowper*, MSS, C&N
34. John Newton, *Olney Hymns*, 1779, Book 3, Hymn 44
35. William Cowper to Judith Madan, 10 July 1767, ALS, C&N
36. William Cowper to Judith Madan, 10 July 1767, ALS, C&N
37. William Cowper to Judith Madan, 18 July 1767, ALS, C&N
38. William Cowper to Judith Madan, 10 August 1767, ALS, C&N
39. William Cowper to Judith Madan, 26 September 1767, ALS, C&N
40. Newton's diary for 1767, MSS, LPL
41. William Cowper to Judith Madan, 1 March 1768, ALS, C&N
42. The quote is from Virgil's *Aeneid*, Book 4, 291:
> *Sese interea ...*
> *Temptaturum aditus et quae mellissma fandi*
> *Tempora*

"Himself meanwhile ... would assay to find access and watch what hour might be the smoothest for his tale.' [Perhaps also from Horace (favourable opportunities for speaking), Newton's *Sixty-Eight Letters*, 1845, p.83]
43. *Works*, 1820, vol. 6, John Newton to Cowper, 22 February 1770
44. William Cowper, *Adelphi. A Sketch of the Character, and an Account of the Last Illness, of the late Rev. John Cowper, A.M., written by his brother, faithfully transcribed from his original manuscript by John Newton*, 1802
45. *Works*, 1820, vol. 6, John Newton to Cowper, March 8 1770
46. *Works*, 1820, vol. 6, John Newton to Cowper, March 15 1770

47. T. S. Grimshawe, *Life and Works of William Cowper*, 1849, William Cowper to Thomas Park, 3 January, 1793, p.408

48. T. S. Grimshawe, *Life and Works of William Cowper*, 1849, p.654

49. *Unfinished memoir of William Cowper by John Newton*, 1800, Mills Memorial Library, McMaster University, Hamilton, Canada [quoted from Hindmarsh's bibliography]

50. Judith Madan to Newton, 13 May 1773, ALS, LPL

51. Josiah Bull, *Letters by the Rev. John Newton*, 1869, John Newton to Hannah Wilberforce, July 1764, p.69

52. Mary Newton to John Newton, undated, ALS, CMS

53. T. S. Grimshawe, *The Life and Works of William Cowper*, 1849, William Cowper to Mary Newton, 2 June 1780, p.47

54. T. S. Grimshawe, *The Life and Works of William Cowper*, 1849, William Cowper to Mary Newton, 4 March 1780, p.41

55. 'Nothing is an unmixed blessing,' Horace, *Odes*; letter quoted from T. S. Grimshawe, *The Life and Works of William Cowper*, 1849, William Cowper to William Unwin, 8 June 1783, p.133

56. T. S. Grimshawe, *The Life and Works of William Cowper*, 1849, William Cowper to William Bull, 22 June 1782, p.114

57. T. S. Grimshawe, *The Life and Works of William Cowper*, 1849, William Cowper to John Newton, 3 May 1780 [perhaps also an allusion to Ashley Cowper's pseudonym of 'Timothy Scribble' in his *Poems and translations*, 1767]

58. T. S. Grimshawe, *The Life and Works of William Cowper*, 1849, William Cowper to John Newton, 12 July 1781 (known as the hop o' my thumb letter), p.77

59. T. S. Grimshawe, *The Life and Works of William Cowper*, 1849, William Cowper to John Newton, 20 May 1786, p.236

60. T. S. Grimshawe, *The Life and Works of William Cowper*, 1849, William Cowper to John Newton, 5 February 1790, p.321

61. Notes taken by Hannah Jowett, daughter of Newton's friend John Jowett, during Newton's Funeral Sermon for William Cowper in St. Mary Woolnoth, 1800, MSS, C&N, [see Appendix 4: Newton's text, from Exodus, has been mistakenly quoted elsewhere as from Ecclesiates]

62. John Newton, *Olney Hymns*, 1779, Book 3, Hymn 15

63. Samuel Greatheed, *A Practical Improvement of the Divine Counsel and Conduct, a sermon occasioned by the decease of W. Cowper*, 1800

64. Josiah Bull, *John Newton of Olney*, 1868, George Whitefield to Newton, 8 August 1765, p.125

65. John Newton, *The Christian Correspondent*, 1790, 27 September 1767

66. Josiah Bull, *John Newton of Olney*, 1868, 27 January 1765

67. John Newton, *The Christian Correspondent*, 1790, 23 February 1765

68. Josiah Bull, *John Newton of Olney*, 1868, 13 September 1765

69. John Newton, *The Christian Correspondent*, 1790, 16 March 1765
70. Newton's *Works*, vol. 6, p.280, Newton to James Stillingfleet, 26 July 1775
71. Newton, *Olney Hymns*, 1779, Book 2, Hymns 43 and 44
72. Newton, *Olney Hymns*, 1779, Book 2, Hymn 85
73. Newton, *Olney Hymns*, 1779, Book I, Hymn 35, verses 3 and 4
74. Newton to Josiah Symonds, 29 September 1769, ALS, C&N
75. Newton, *Sermon Notebook* N.6, MSS, C&N
76. Newton's Diary, 1752-56, MSS, LPL
77. John Newton, *The Christian Correspondent*, 1790: 3 July 1764, p.33
78. Josiah Bull, *John Newton of Olney*, 1868, p.142
79. William Cowper to Judith Madan, 18 June 1768, ALS, C&N
80. Mary Newton to John, 13 November 1775, ALS, CMS
81. Newton to his wife, 7 December 1775, ALS, LPL
82. Newton to his wife, 23 December 1775, ALS, LPL
83. Arthur Kirby, *Andrew Fuller*, 1961
84. Josiah Bull, *Letters of John Newton*, 1869, Newton to William Bull, 27 January 1778, p.302
85. Josiah Bull, *John Newton of Olney*, 1868, p.141
86. John Newton, *A List of Children*: The meetings for the children at the Great House until January 1765, MSS, C&N
87. John Mason, *A Little Catechism, with Little Verses and Little Sayings, for Little Children*, 1692
88. John Newton, *Olney Hymns,* 1779, Book 1, Hymn 99
89. John Newton, *Olney Hymns,* 1779, Book 1, Hymn 12
90. John Henry Pratt, *Eclectic Notes*, 1856, question discussed on 22 January 1798
91. John Scott, *The Life of the Rev. Thomas Scott*, 1822, p.63
92. Newton to John Thornton, 22 May 1779, ALS, CUL
93. John Scott, *The Life of the Rev. Thomas Scott*, 1822, Newton to Scott, 31 March, 1781, p.185
94. John Scott, *The Life of the Rev. Thomas Scott*, 1822, p.236
95. John Scott, *The Life of the Rev. Thomas Scott*, 1822, William Wilberforce to John Scott, 16 April 1822, pp.615-9
96. John Scott, *The Life of the Rev. Thomas Scott*, 1822
97. John Scott, *The Life of the Rev. Thomas Scott*, 1822, p.266
98. John Scott, *The Life of the Rev. Thomas Scott*, 1822, p.635
99. John Scott, *The Life of the Rev. Thomas Scott*, 1822, p.381
100. John Scott, *The Life of the Rev. Thomas Scott*, 1822, p.173
101. John Scott, *The Life of the Rev. Thomas Scott*, 1822, p.174
102. Lee, Sir Sidney (ed), *Dictionary of National Biography*, 1921
103. John Scott, *The Life of the Rev. Thomas Scott*, 1822, p.483, and John Henry Newman, *Apologia*, 1864
104. John Newton, Sermon Notebook N.42, MSS, C&N

CHAPTER 8

1. Some Account of the Rev. Josias Shute, *The Christian Observer*, January 1804, p.4

2. Ralph Robinson, *Christ All and in All. Or, several significant similitudes by which the Lord Jesus is described in the Holy Scriptures. Being the substance of many sermons.* Edited by S. Ashe, E. Calamy and W. Taylor, 1656

3. Ephesians 4:15, *Speaking the truth in love*, was published in 1800 under the title *The Subject and Temper of the Gospel Ministry* and appears in Newton's *Works*, vol. 5

4. 1 Corinthians 9:22

5. 1 Corinthians 3:2

6. John 16:12 is implied

7. Romans 12:15

8. Oliver Goldsmith (1728-1774), *Deserted Village*, 1770. The quote refers to a village parson.

9. Genesis 5:22

10. Jeremiah 10:23

11. John Newton, *A Monument to the praise of the Lord's goodness and to the memory of dear Eliza Cunningham*, 1785, MSS, C&N

12. John Newton, *Messiah,* 2 vols, 1786 [also in *Works*, Vol. 4]

13. Luke 7:31

14. Ecclesiastes 12:2

15. 2 Samuel 12:20

16. 2 Samuel 12:22, 23

17. Genesis 28:20, 21

18. Isaiah 59:5

19. Revelation 18:22, 23

20. So passes away earthly glory (from Thomas a Kempis's *Imitation of Christ*, used in Latin at the coronation of a pope)

21. Philippians 4:7

22. David Williamson, *Lectures on Civil and Religious Liberty; with reflections on the Constitution of France and England; and on the violent writers, who have distinguished themselves in the controversy about their comparative goodness; and particularly on Mr. Burke and Mr. Paine. To which are added, two sermons, on the "Influence of religion on the death of good men"*, [1792?]; the sermons at the end of this book were dedicated to the Rev. Doctor Newton of St. Mary Woolnoth, and Mr. Bonar,of Scotland. Newton commented, "I think my politics do not go beyond the Apostle's direction, Titus 3:1 [*Put them in mind to be subject to principalities and powers, to obey magistrates, to be ready to every good work*]." His reply to Dr. Williamson is the last letter in Vol. 6 of his *Works*.

23. 1 Corinthians 15:8
24. Psalm 66:16
25. Newton's Will, FRO & LPL

Appendix to Chapter 8

26. Newton to his wife, 22 January 1780, ALS, LPL
27. Josiah Bull, *Letters of John Newton*, 1869, Newton to William Cowper, 29 April 1780, p.157
28. William Herbert, *Memoir of my own Life*, MSS, GL
29. William Harvey, *London Scenes and London People*, 1863, a collection of articles written for the *City Press* under his pseudonym, *Aleph*
30. Rebecca Warner, *Original Letters from Richard Baxter, Matthew Prior [and others]*, 1817, Newton to Capt. and Mrs. Hansard, May 17-, p.253
31. James Moody, *Pious Remains of the Rev. James Moody*, 1809, Letter 3, p.37
32. William Jay, *The Autobiography of William Jay*, edited by George Redford and John Angell James, 1854, repr. 1974
33. John Newton, [ed. Walter Taylor, William Cadogan, et al.], *The Aged Pilgrim's Triumph over Sin and the Grave*, 1825, p.205
34. Josiah Bull, *Letters of John Newton*, 1869, Newton to Mrs. Ring, 16 September 1794, p.405
35. Grant Gordon, The Call of John Ryland jnr., *Baptist Quarterly*, vol. 34, 1991-92, p.215
36. John Newton to John Ryland jnr., 28 March 1793, *Baptist Quarterly*, vol. 34, 1991-92, p.220
37. [ed. E. Powell] *Gleanings*, 1824, Mr. N. to Mrs. W., p.391
38. William Wilberforce, *A Practical View of the Prevailing Religious System of Professed Christians in the Higher and Middle Classes in this Country Contrasted with Real Christianity*, 1836 edtn: Memoir by Thomas Price, p.14
39. Philip Doddridge, *Rise and Progress*, 1812 edtn., p.133
40. Newton to William Wilberforce, 22 December 1785, ALS, BOD [MS Wilberforce c. 49 fol. 1]
41. Henry Venn, Letters, 1993 ed: May/June 1786, p.435
42. William Wilberforce, *Practical View*, 1836 edtn: Memoir by Thomas Price, p.7
43. Newton to William Wilberforce, 18 May [1786?], ALS, BOD [MS Wilberforce c. 49 fol. 9]
44. Newton to William Wilberforce, 1 November 1787, ALS, BOD [MS Wilberforce c. 49 fols. 14-15]
45. Newton to William Wilberforce, 26 March 1786, ALS, BOD [MS Wilberforce c. 49 fol. 3]
46. Newton to William Wilberforce, 5 July 1788, ALS, BOD [MS Wilberforce c. 49 fols. 17-18]
47. William Wilberforce to Newton, 6 September 1788, ALS, BOD [MS Wilberforce c. 49 fols. 19-20]

48. William Wilberforce, *A Practical View,* 1797

49. Josiah Bull, *John Newton of Olney,* 1868, p.335

50. Newton to William Wilberforce, [31 July 1799], ALS, BOD [MS Wilberforce c. 49 fols. 93-94]

51. Newton to William Wilberforce, 15 November 1786, ALS, BOD [MS Wilberforce c. 49 fols. 12-13]

52. Josiah Bull, *Memorials of the Rev. William Bull,* 1865 edtn: William Bull to John Newton, 25 October 1786, p.157

53. Josiah Bull, *Memorials of the Rev. William Bull,* 1865 edtn: John Omicron [Newton] to William Bull, 27 October 1786, p.160

54. Newton to William Wilberforce, 27 May 1793, ALS, BOD [MS Wilberforce c. 49 fol. 46]

55. S. Pearce Carey, *William Carey,* 1923, p.119

56. S. Pearce Carey, *William Carey,* 1923, p.175

57. William Carey to Newton, 5 December 1798, ALS, LPL

58. S. Pearce Carey, *William Carey,* 1923, p.134

59. William Ward to Samuel Pearce, 13 May 1799, *Northamptonshire Biographical Notices,* ed. John Taylor, 1901, p.11

60. Josiah Bateman, *The Life of the Right Rev. Daniel Wilson,* 1860, p.13

61. Erasmus Middleton, *A Dictionary of Evangelical Biography,* 1807, vol 3, p.453

62. Hugh Nicholas Pearson, *Memoirs of the Life and Writings of the Rev. Dr. Claudius Buchanan,* 1817

63. John Newton to John Venn, 17 October 1795, ALS, CMS

64. Hugh Nicholas Pearson, *Memoirs of the Life and Writings of the Rev. Dr. Claudius Buchanan,* 1817, Newton to Claudius Buchanan

65. William Carey to Newton, 19 November 1802, ALS, LPL

66. Henry Martyn, *Journals and Letters,* 1837, vol 1, p.269

67. Henry Martyn, *Journals and Letters,* 1837, vol 1, p.247

68. Henry Martyn, *Journals and Letters,* 1837, vol 1, p.447

69. John Newton, *A plan of academical preparation for the ministry, in a letter [signed Omicron],* 1784 [written 14 May 1782]

70. no offence intended

71. Josiah Bull, *Memorials of the Rev. William Bull,* 1865 edtn: John Newton to William Bull, May 1782, p.104

72. John Watson, *A Discourse on the studies of Newport Pagnell College,* delivered October 26 1842, p. 41 of Appendix, Newton to William Bull, April 1784

73. ibid

74. Truth is mighty, and will prevail.

75. Isaiah 54:17

76. John Newton, *A Monument to the Praise of the Lord's Goodness and to the Memory of Dear Eliza Cunningham,* 1785; 3rd edtn. To which is

added some account of her brother, John Cunningham, who died January 22, 1777, in his twelfth year of age. Written by his mother, 1811.

77. Newton to William Wilberforce, 23 November 1790, ALS, BOD [MS Wilberforce c. 49 fol. 32]

78. John Newton, *Letters to a Wife*, 1793: Appendix No. 1, *A Relation of some Particulars respecting the Cause, Progress, and Close, of the last Illness of my late dear Wife*

79. The quote is from Virgil's *Aeneid*, Book 6, 726:

> *Spiritus intus alit, totamque infusa per artus*
> *Mens agitat molem et magno se corpore miscet.*

"An indwelling spirit sustains, and a mind fused throughout the limbs sways the whole mass and mingles with the giant frame."

80. John Timbs, *Curiosities of London*, 1855, p.149, quoting from Thomas Frognall Dibdin, *Reminisces of a Literary Life*, 1836, vol. 1, p.162

81. Thomas Shuttleworth Grimshawe, *The Life and Works of William Cowper*, 1849: William Cowper to John Newton, 24 June 1791, p.357

82. Rebecca Warner, *Original Letters*, 1817, Newton to Captain and Mrs. Hansard, p.151

83. John Newton, *Correspondence with a dissenting minister*, 1809, p.104

84. Mary Newton to John Newton, 27 April 1774, ALS, CMS

85. Marriage Register entry of Joseph Smith to Elizabeth Catlett, 2 May 1805, MF, GL

86. John Campbell, *Letters and Conversational Remarks*, 1808, Newton to Campbell, 2 June 1792

87. Josiah Bull, *Memorials of the Rev. William Bull*, 1865 edtn, 1802, p.288

88. Josiah Bull, *Memorials of the Rev. William Bull*, 1865 edtn, William Bull to Elizabeth Smith, 29 December, 1807

CHAPTER 9

1. Matthew 13:52
2. Philippians 3:13
3. Jude 3
4. 1 Timothy 4:13-15
5. 1 Corinthians 12:10
6. 2 Corinthians 12:15
7. *The Works of the Rev. John Newton, 6 volumes,* 1808. The 1824 edition (a reprint of 1820) was reprinted by Banner of Truth Trust in 1985, 1988
8. Joseph Milner, *The History of the Church of Christ*, edited by Isaac Milner, 5 vols, the first three volumes published 1794-97, the last two edited after Joseph's death by his brother Isaac Milner, 1803-1809
9. John Newton, *Apologia: Four Letters to a Minister of an Independent Church, by a Minister of the Church of England*, 1784. The letters were

written to Samuel Palmer, minister of the Independent Congregation at Mare Street, Hackney, London. Palmer had been a member of Bunyan Meeting in Bedford, fifteen miles from Olney. He left there to be ordained in 1764, the same year that fellow member William Bull was ordained pastor of Newport-Pagnell and Newton was ordained to Olney, five miles from Newport-Pagnell.

10. John Newton, *Letters of the Rev. Mr. Helperus Ritzema van Lier: The Power of Grace Illustrated*, 1792
11. William Cowper, *Adelphi, edited by John Newton*, 1802
12. John Newton, *Memoirs of the Life of the Late Rev. William Grimshaw, in Six Letters to the Late Rev. Henry Foster*, 1799
13. The Bodleian Library, Oxford, has a tract of Newton's which is a well argued dialogue on Matthew 11:28. [see Appendix 4]

Appendix to Chapter 9

14. John Newton, *Works*, 1808, vol. 2, Newton to Mr. Collins, 18 May 1776
15. Newton to Henry Venn, 9 November 1779, ALS, CMS
16. John Newton, *The Searcher of Hearts*, 1997
17. John Henry Pratt, *Eclectic Notes*, 1856, question discussed on 5 March 1798
18. Erasmus Middleton, *A Dictionary of Evangelical Biography*, 1807, vol. 3, p.452, Newton to the Rev. Dr. Robbins of Plymouth, America, 19 April 1794
19. Newton to Henry Venn, 15 March 1783, ALS, CMS
20. Newton to William Wilberforce, 23 March 1801, ALS, BOD [MS Wilberforce c. 49 fol. 109]
21. But enough of this
22. Newton to Elizabeth Cunningham, 4 August 1777, ALS, LPL
23. Mary Unwin to Mrs. Cowper, 22 December 1790, ALS, C&N
24. Mary Unwin to John Newton, 15 October, 1776, ALS, C&N
25. Josiah Bull, *John Newton of Olney*, 1868, p.252
26. Josiah Bull, *John Newton of Olney*, 1998 edtn., p. 323
27. William Jay, *The Autobiography of William Jay*, 1974 edtn., p. 280
28. T. S. Grimshawe, *The Life and Works of William Cowper*, 1849, Cowper to Newton, 13 June 1783
29. Josiah Bull, *Letters of John Newton*, 1869, Newton to William Bull, 13 March 1786
30. Josiah Bull, *Memorials of the Rev. William Bull*, 1868, Bull to Newton, 25 October 1786, p.157
31. Josiah Bull, *Memorials of the Rev. William Bull*, 1868, Newton to Bull, 27 October 1786, p.158
32. Robert Murray M'Cheyne, *The Seven Churches of Asia*, 1986, p.31n

33. Aaron Crossley Hobart Seymour, *The Life and Times of Selina Countess of Huntingdon*, 1840, vol. 1, p.422
34. Josiah Bull, *John Newton of Olney*, 1868, Newton to William Cowper, 2 July 1780
35. Josiah Bull, *Letters of John Newton*, 1869, Newton to William Cowper, 39 September 1780, p.162
36. Bernard Martin, *John Newton, a biography*, 1950, William Cowper to Newton, p.299
37. Newton's *Eclectic Society* Notes, MSS, C&N

CHAPTER 10
1. John 3:3
2. Psalm 16:8
3. alludes to Zechariah 4:10
4. Acts 18:9, 10
5. Acts 4:23
6. 2 Peter 3:3
7. Philippians 4:7
8. 2 Corinthians 12:10
9. 1 Corinthians 12:11
10. nothing in excess

CHAPTER 11
1. Alexander Pope, *Essay on Man*, 1733
2. medicine for the mind
3. [Richard Allestree] *The Whole Duty of Man*, 1657
4. Robert Nelson, *Companion for the Festivals and Fasts for the Church of England, with Collects and Prayers for each Solemnity*, 1704
5. like gives rise to like
6. George Herbert, *The Temple,* 1633, quote from The Church: The Bag

WHO'S WHO

As one or two of the people mentioned in the book could be confused with others of that period with the same or similar names, especially as spellings tended to vary at times, occasionally a new person is mentioned here to clarify who really was who. For abbreviations, see page 241.

William Jarvis Abdy 1755-1823
Rector of St. John's Horsley Down, Southwark. An early member of the Eclectic Society and of the CMS.

Sir Thomas Abney 1640-1722
A former Lord Mayor, MP for the city of London, one of the original promoters and directors of the Bank of England, president and benefactor of St. Thomas's Hospital, he was a wealthy dissenter who lived at Stoke Newington and Theobalds, near Cheshunt, Hertfordshire. Isaac Watts visited the Abneys for a week in 1712, needing to recover from poor health, and stayed on for thirty-six years, becoming chaplain to the family and tutor to his three daughters.

John Aikman d.1834
Converted through reading Newton's *Cardiphonia* en route to Jamaica. He became the minister of College Street Chapel in Edinburgh.

Aleph 1795-1873
William Harvey, a journalist who wrote for the *City Press*. His descriptions of London in the early 19th century are particularly interesting.

Joseph Alleine 1634-1668
When his brother died, Alleine set his mind to take his place in the ministry. He studied in Oxford under John Owen and Thomas Goodwin, becoming Chaplain to Corpus Christi College, then assistant to George Newton in Taunton. He was a diligent worker. He began each day at 4 a.m. with 4 hours of prayer, meditation and singing psalms. He was twice imprisoned for his faith. His book, *An*

Alarm to the Unconverted, was the means of stirring up many to faith, including Whitefield and Spurgeon. His wife, Theodosia, wrote his life.

Philip Astley 1742-1814

A retired sergeant-major who performed feats of horsemanship for public entertainment. He began his equestrian events in a field near the Halfpenny Hatch, Lambeth, about 1765, also travelling through the country performing at fairs and markets. In 1770 he opened a wooden amphitheatre with sheltered seats around an open circus in a timberyard at the foot of Westminster Bridge. He and his wife appeared on horseback at Drury Lane at the Shakespeare Jubilee. Astley also performed before George III by royal command.

Thomas Atkins c.1744-1812

Came to Newton for a character reference of William Herbert. Atkins had an eventful life. Orphaned at eight, shipwrecked en route to Jamaica, attacked with a knife, regained consciousness from a fever to find he was being buried alive, taken prisoner by the Spaniards on the way back to England and left to die on a desert island. At one point he was in a fire close to a quantity of gunpowder which, his biographer adds, had it exploded, "would have been of the most destructive tendency". Atkins returned home blind. His sister took him to hear Romaine at Blackfriars. Young William Herbert's duties were to pray with him, read the Bible to him and generally accompany him throughout the day attending to his needs, more as a companion than as a servant. Atkins lived in Charles Square.

John Bacon 1740-1799

Bacon started his career at 14 as an apprentice to a china manufacturer and went on to become a highly talented sculptor, specialising in funeral monuments. The statues of Pitt in Westminster Abbey and Dr. Johnson in St. Paul's Cathedral are Bacon's work. William Cowper admired his skill and referred to Bacon's monument of William Pitt, Prime Minister and 1st Earl of Chatham, in *The Task.* A foundation student of the Royal Academy, Bacon was the first to receive its gold medal for sculpture. Bacon was the first layman to become a member of the Eclectic Society and was also on the CMS committee. Archdeacon Pratt said of him, "He was a man of imagination; a quick discerner of the points of men's characters. Genius was more conspicuous in his own than solidarity of judgment." His son, John Bacon [1777-1859], also became a celebrated sculptor. He designed the funeral plaque for James Moody, pastor of the Independent Meeting in Warwick where Newton first began his ministry. Bacon senior was buried at Whitefield's Tabernacle, having written his own epitaph:

> *What I was as an artist*
> *Seemed to me of some importance*
> *While I lived:*
> *BUT*
> *What I really was as a believer*
> *in Christ Jesus,*
> *Is the only thing of importance*
> *to me now.*

Isaac Barrow 1630-1677

It was Barrow's *Euclid* which Newton read as a slave on the island in Guinea. Professor of Mathematics at Cambridge, Barrow resigned in favour of his pupil Isaac Newton, whose *Principia* John Newton left as he found it, "a sealed book."

Eli Bates d. 1812

A founder member of the Eclectic Society and friend of Newton's. He was Secretary to Sir George Savile [1726-1784]. Newton recommended the young William Herbert into his service in 1784 when Bates was at Savile House, Leicester Square, to read to him and run errands. Many of the books read were from Sir George Savile's Library. Bates later moved to 3 Hermes Street, off Pentonville Road in Islington. Herbert was given a closet under his master's room, but Bates snored and William had to buy thruppence worth of straw from the Angel Inn and stuff it up the chimney to get any sleep. Bates married Elizabeth Mary Morgan in 1788.

Bates's father was a tenant of Sir George Savile. His intellect appealed to Savile, who undertook his education and provided for him. He wrote several books, *Rural Philosophy*, *Christian Policies*, *Chinese Fragments* and *Selections from the Works of Baxter*. When he married Elizabeth they settled at Blackheath in Montpellier-row.

Elizabeth Mary Bates (née Morgan) d. 1835

Wife of Eli. Her father was a great antiquarian. When the gate at Aldersgate was taken down he bought it and built it up in his own garden. As a child Elizabeth was concerned about the scripture describing judgment and the separation of the sheep on the right and the goats on the left. She used to ask her maid every morning to put something into her right hand so that she would learn which it was and know which side to go on. She was friendly with Wesley's sister. After Bates's death she married Joseph Wilson who, like Bates, was one of the first subscribers to the British and Foreign Bible Society.

Benjamin Beddome 1717-1795

Pastor of Bourton on the Water, in the Cotswolds, for over 50 years. John Collett Ryland was converted through his preaching. Beddome often preached at Warwick (Baptist). He was in Olney the day Sutcliff was ordained. Newton heard him speak that evening from Zechariah 11:12 and wrote in his diary, "He is an admirable preacher; simple, savoury, weighty."

Dr. Benamore

Of Milman Place, Bedford Row. One of the first subscribers to the British and Foreign Bible Society. Doctor to Newton's niece, Eliza Cunningham. The young William Herbert was sent by the Newtons to fetch him and to go for medicines from the apothecary. William Bull was also attended by Benamore in London. Newton wrote of Benamore to Thomas Mitchell in Shearness, "His son, James, was my curate; an excellent young man, who bid fair to be one of the First Three, if his life had been prolonged – but it pleased the Lord to remove him to a better world, when he had been with me little more than a month [Michaelmas 1796]. His sudden removal, by the bursting of a blood vessel, was a great trial to myself and to my people, but we know the Lord did it, and that He does all things well." To Campbell Newton wrote of James: "He was able and ready as a preacher, humble, spiritual, and devoted as a Christian, beyond the common standard at his years. I was ready to call him *Seth*, and thought the Lord had given him to me in the room of Buchanan." James had only recently lost his wife. Of his four children only one, a boy of four, was left alive. The child had small-pox and so couldn't see his dying father. Newton added that though all his earthly expectations had been crossed, James's last words were, "'The Lord has done all things well,' and from there I preached his funeral sermon last Sabbath evening. I thank the Lord I can say and believe He does all things well; but I have had my feelings, for I hoped I had found a person on whom I might fully depend, and whom my people would hear with pleasure in case I should be laid aside. Perhaps I am to live and preach a little longer. If it be so, *well*, if otherwise, *well*, He does all things well; and when He sees I really need assistance, He can provide it. My part is, to live today, and to leave tomorrow with Him." Father and son were both buried on 9 September 1796.

Another of Dr. Benamore's sons, Fell, was the Master of a gun boat. His conduct, conversation and correspondence changed for the better after his brother's death.

Benjamin Bennett 1674-1726
Non-conformist minister and author of the *Christian Oratory*, a product of shared devotion with his pastor, James Janeway, of Jamaica-Row, Rotherhithe. This church had come under considerable persecution. It was pulled down by soldiers and there were several attempts to shoot the pastor. Janeway's own work, *A Token for Children*, an account of the conversion of several young children, was very popular. Newton requested it when he started teaching the children at Olney.

William Beveridge 1637-1708
Bishop of St. Asaph. Newton had a volume of his sermons on board *The Greyhound* during the voyage back from Guinea when he was converted. Beveridge's sermon on Christ's Passion was a particular help to him.

William Bligh 1754-1817
Made famous by the film, *Mutiny on the Bounty*. In 1772 Bligh accompanied Captain Cook as sailing master on one of his voyages. From 1785 Bligh stayed in Broad Street, Wapping, which was virtually a continuation of Red Lyon Street where Newton had been born 60 years earlier and lived as a child. By now Newton was rector of St. Mary Woolnoth. The Blighs attended the church of St. George in the East, Wapping. Bligh's mutineer, Fletcher Christian, was a family friend and often visited him in Broad Street. As a Lieutenant,

Bligh was in command of the *Bounty* when Fletcher Christian rebelled, seizing the ship and casting Bligh, and those loyal to him, adrift with scanty provisions. He managed to reach land and returned to England. In 1814 Bligh was promoted to Vice-Admiral.

Josiah Blunt
Mate on the *Pegasus*, who became Captain after the death of Penrose. It was this change in leadership which prompted Newton to rather take his chances working for Clow in the Plantanes than risk being transferred to a Man-of-War for his disregard for authority.

Abraham Booth 1734-1806
Pastor of the Particular Baptist Church, Little Prescott Street, Goodman's Fields, 1769-1806. An off-shoot from an Independent Church which existed in Southwark in 1616, this Baptist Church was officially founded in 1638, while several of its members were still in prison (literally in the Clink) for their faith. It then met in Wapping, between Old Gravel Lane and Broad Street, a block away from Newton's birthplace. The main church moved to Little Prescott Street in 1730 (some dissidents remained, but their meetings soon ceased). When Booth came to Olney, Cowper wrote to his aunt, "He was bred a weaver and has been forced to work with his hands hitherto for the maintenance of himself and a large family. But the Lord who has given him excellent endowments has now called him from the small congregation he ministered to in Nottinghamshire, to supply Mr. Burford's place in London." Cowper and Newton attended the Baptist Association meetings in Olney in 1768, hearing Booth preach from Acts 11:26. Booth had just written *Reign of Grace*, promoting evangelical Calvinism.

Typical of the good fellowship between believers of other denominations, it was a member of the Established Church, Henry Venn, who wrote the preface to Booth's sermons on salvation available for all. Newton enjoyed fellowship with Booth in London, seeking his advice for his Baptist friends in the country. Booth was instrumental in founding the Baptist Society in London for the Encouragement and Support of Itinerant Preaching, later called the Home Missionary Society. He took a keen interest in raising support for an academy to assist young men in training for the ministry. Shortly after his death this was realised in the building of the Stepney Academy, later renamed Regent's Park College and now in Oxford.

David Bradberry 1735-1803

Converted in the North Ridings of Yorkshire by George Whitefield's preaching, he attended the Stepney Academy at Mile End. He was ordained by Samuel Brewer. In 1764 he ministered at Wellingborough. When he came to preach at John Drake's Independent Meeting in Olney, Newton cancelled his regular prayer meeting that Tuesday night and took the church across to hear him.

Thomas Bradbury 1677-1759

A dissenting minister whom Newton first heard preaching in London. He had been an Assistant at Stepney Meeting from 1703 to 1707. Bradbury was known for having a catholic spirit, enjoying fellowship with all who confessed Christ as Lord. During one of his lectures at Salter's Hall he was hissed at whilst proving our Lord's divinity. An account in the *Dictionary of Evangelical Biography* says, "Mr. Bradbury's friends were much affected with this insolent abuse, and expressed their grief on account of it; to which, with his usual vivacity and ingenuity, he replied, 'You need not be concerned about this, it is quite natural. You know we have been bruising the head of the old serpent, and no wonder you heard the hisses of the generation of vipers.'"

John Brekell 1697-1769

Known to both David Jennings and Newton. Brekell was the Presbyterian pastor of the church meeting in Kaye Street in Liverpool during Newton's period there as Surveyor of Tides. He published "a sort of comment upon St. Paul's voyage" which Newton felt put its readers off reaching the most constructive part of it. The sermon referred to quotes 2 Corinthians 11:26, *In journeyings often, in perils of waters, ... in perils in the sea*, in its appeal "to Merchants and those persons who trade to the sea to remember the necessary dependence you have upon the God of Nature and Providence for the prosperous issue of your voyage." Its title *Euroclydon* is from Acts 27:14, a reference to *Euros*, the east wind, and *Aquilo*, the north wind, i.e. a "north-easter" [John Stott, *The Message of Acts*, 1990]. Newton heard him preach once on Romans 12:2, "a florid declamation upon or against conformity to the world... nothing within the prayer or sermon by which I could have guessed the speaker to have been a minister of Jesus, rather than a disciple of Zeno or Aristotle."

Samuel Brewer 1723-1796
Minister of the Stepney Meeting and lecturer. He was ordained on 23 October 1746, when David Jennings gave him his charge from 2 Timothy 4:5 (the service began at 10 and closed at 3). He lived in Mile End. Spitalfields Trust is currently refurbishing a couple of houses very similar to one of Brewer's homes. Stepney Meeting House was in the garden of the Samuel Jones family, who were Directors of the Hudson Bay Company. Their neighbour was Captain James Winter, Governor of the East India Company. Captain Clunie was a member of Stepney Meeting and suggested to Newton that he contact Brewer on his return to London. Brewer was a great encouragement to Newton in establishing him in the faith. When he visited Olney, he preached at Newton's church, the Baptists and the Independents, and was greatly appreciated by all (all four pastors dined together at Newton's vicarage). His son, Thomas, attended John Ryland's Boarding School in Northampton.

Patrick Brontë 1777-1861
Later known as the father of the Brontë sisters, Ann, Charlotte and Emily Jane. Patrick left Ireland to train for the ministry at St. John's, Cambridge. He received financial support in his last years there from William Wilberforce and Henry Thornton, who were approached on his behalf by Henry Martyn, then curate at Charles Simeon's church in Cambridge. In 1820 Brontë became the perpetual curate of Haworth, the same church where William Grimshaw had exercised such a fruitful ministry. He gave the top deck of Grimshaw's pulpit (still extant) to the chapel of ease at Stanbury.

Lancelot Brown 1715-1783
'Capability' Brown, the master landscape designer who transformed gardens such as Kew, Blenheim Palace, Nuneham Courtney and the Belhus estate in Aveley. He began work as a gardener's boy at Stowe, Buckinghamshire, under the direction of William Kent (the pioneer of creating "informal" English gardens). He acquired his nickname by assuring potential clients that their grounds had "great capabilities". Cowper wrote of him in *The Task:*

Lo! he comes!
The omnipotent magician, Brown appears.
Down falls the venerable pile, the abode
Of our forefathers, a grave whiskered race,

But tasteless. Springs a palace in its stead,
But in a distant spot; where more exposed
It may enjoy the advantage of the north,
And aguish east, till time shall have transformed
Those naked acres to a sheltering grove.
He speaks. The lake in front becomes a lawn;
Woods vanish, hills subside, and valleys rise;
And streams, as if created for his use,
Pursue the track of his directing wand,
Sinuous or straight, now rapid and now slow,
Now murmering soft, now roaring in cascades –
E'en as he bids! The enraptured owner smiles.
'Tis finished, and yet, finished as it seems,
Still wants a grace, the loveliest it could show,
A mine to satisfy the enormous cost.

Moses Browne 1704-1787

Browne was the vicar of Olney when Newton was invited to become its curate. He had been James Hervey's curate at Collingtree in 1753 and whilst vicar of Olney also became chaplain of Morden College, Blackheath to help finance his large family. He had been so hard up in 1745 that he had applied for the post of messenger or doorkeeper to the Royal Society. Cowper's impression was that he had "10 or a dozen children." He occasionally assisted Martin Madan at the Lock and Thomas Jones at St. Saviour's. His publication of *Sunday Thoughts*, a translation of work by Professor Zimmerman, was well known in its time. In a letter to Robert Jones, a merchant in Hull, Newton gives some further details: "The Gospel seed was first sown in Olney by Mr. Whitefield and his brethren, about the year '39. We have several precious souls of so long standing in the kingdom of God. Soon after a little place was built, a society formed, and Mr. Whitefield's preachers came frequently. But, in the year '54, the Lord brought Mr. Moses Browne to be vicar. By him the Gospel was preached in the church; and then the Methodist preachers withdrew, and went where they were more wanted. The gentleman who gave Mr. Browne the living resided in the parish, and soon became his open enemy. With such a head, the spirit of opposition and enmity exerted itself with great courage. Mr. Browne went through a great deal – was often abused to his face – put in the spiritual court; but, in the interim, the old gentleman sold his estate, with the advowson, to

Lord Dartmouth. By the favour of such a patron, Mr. B. was held up; and at last the Lord gave him the victory, and put his enemies to shame."

Thomas Bryan
A trader on the Guinea coast, Bryan wrongly accused Newton of adultery with the sister of another trader, Harry Tucker. Just before this, Newton had dreamt that he had been stung by a scorpion, but, while in pain and danger, an unknown person had applied oil to the wound; he felt it a prediction that although something unexpected and disagreeable was about to happen to him, no real harm would come of it. He sent Bryan a written declaration of his innocence before the Searcher of Hearts, adding in his personal diary, "nay I think a scorpion sting would have been preferable if I might have chosen." In one of his *Letters to a Wife* Newton added a footnote emphasising his regard for Tucker, "Henry Tucker, a Mulatto, at Shebar, was the man with whom I had the largest connexion in business, and by whom I was never deceived."

Claudius Buchanan 1766-1815
He left Scotland at the age of twenty-one to travel Europe on foot, supporting himself playing the violin, but got no further than London, by which time he had run out of money and hope. He was converted, much encouraged by Newton, entered the ministry under the sponsorship of Henry Thornton, became Newton's curate and in 1796 was appointed to the chaplaincy of the East India Company in Bengal. He set sail in 1797. Surviving the long journey was not all that was needed: writing home from Calcutta in July he described one of the hazards. "On the morning of our arrival, a young man, looking out anxiously at the land, and hailing with joy the end of his voyage, fell into the sea, and rose no more! Think of this a little, before you read further."

When Buchanan had left Cambridge to be Newton's curate he had expressed to him the hope that he would learn from him first humility, second humility and third humility. It was not surprising therefore that when Newton wrote to encourage him to meet with the Baptists, comparing his unproven appointment as a fresh arrival with their hard labours, that Buchanan took his gentle admonition in good spirit and sought their fellowship.

George Buchanan 1506-1562

A contemporary of John Knox and Moderator of the Reformed Church of Scotland, a satirist and historian. He wrote his much acclaimed Latin paraphrase of the Psalms while imprisoned in a Portuguese dungeon in a monastery, circumstances which one of his biographers, MacMillan, felt gave him particular empathy with David's cries from the heart.

Josiah Bull 1807-1885

Third generation Pastor of the Independent Church at Newport Pagnell, grandson of William Bull and son of Thomas Palmer. He published books on Newton and on his father. Recalling the last day of his grandfather William he wrote, "About half-past six (I can well remember it) he desired that his three grandchildren might be brought into the room. When we entered, he sent for three Bibles, and desired that one might be given to each of us as his dying bequest. But he had no strength to speak to us." William died at seven o'clock, what he called his canonical hour, or time of evening prayer.

Thomas Palmer Bull 1773-1859

Son of William Bull and father of Josiah. Newton took a fatherly interest in him. When Tommy was ill, Newton wrote and asked Bull to send his love and assure him that he would often be with him in spirit. Newton insisted that Tommy came with him when William visited London. He used to make paper boats for him. Newton was asked to conduct Thomas's marriage service in St. Luke's Church, Old-street Road. This was in 1803, when his eyesight, hearing and memory were all fading. He had to sit for the entire time, losing his attention in the middle, asking, "What do I here?" Thomas was co-pastor (1800) then pastor of the Independent Church at Newport Pagnell. At his ordination Samuel Greatheed gave the introductory discourse, John Sutcliff, Olney Baptist pastor, the ordination prayer and Thomas Hillyard, pastor of the Independent Church in Olney, the address.

In his history of their church, Thomas relates how Philip Doddridge, when a student, was once caught in pouring rain and interrupted his journey to ask for help from one of their predecessors. This pastor, Hunt, was criticised by his mother for giving the unknown man his coat, but Hunt replied, "I am sure he is a gentleman and a scholar!" Doddridge overheard this comment and never forgot it. Some years later the owner of the ground on which the church had been built died, the absence of any provision in his will threatening the continuing existence of the church. When Doddridge heard of this he bought the land to enable them to continue. The new young minister at Newport-Pagnell then was Humphrey Gainsborough, brother of the Royal Academy painter, Thomas. Humphrey was a mechanical genius: he designed the locks on the River Thames at Henley and a sun-dial which pointed the time "to a second in every part of the globe" (later kept in the British Museum).

William Bull 1738-1814

As a young boy, William was thrown out of church for sniggering when the preacher who had announced his text as *Write, Blessed are the dead that die in the Lord* [Rev. 14:13], went on to preach about those who were *right* blessed and those who were *wrong* blessed.

He was very talented academically. Though he lost some of his exceptional abilities after an illness, he retained a very sharp mind. He studied at Daventry Academy under Dr. Ashworth, Doddridge's successor. He was sent out by Bunyan Meeting to Newport-Pagnell in June 1764, where he was ordained Pastor in October, a few months after Newton had arrived in Olney. He used to ride over to Olney to see Newton, who felt he could converse on equal terms with this deep thinker. One of Newton's letters to him ends with "you will be as welcome to us here, if you will trot over, as a new guinea to a miser's pocket." They exchanged sermon outlines and shared a similar sense of humour. Bull sometimes spoke at Newton's meetings at the Great House. His health was not as good as he wished. He often felt low, but Newton encouraged him: "I hope you will preach away all your cough and pain and come to us lusty and strong as an eagle" – and Polly enjoyed making him laugh to cheer him up.

On a journey south with Thornton, Bull once wrote from Exmouth, "I am told many are coming from Exeter on the Sabbath-day to hear me. Alas! alas! if they knew me as much as I know myself, I think they would keep at home." John Thornton supported Bull financially, assuring him, "When you want money, remember I am your banker, and draw freely." He wrote to Bull at least twice a week and sought his advice in all his evangelical efforts. "I had rather hear you set forth Jesus than any man I know," he wrote.

Bull's grandson writes, "Once in the pulpit he quoted the words, 'About the ninth hour, Jesus cried with a loud voice, saying, *Eli, Eli, lama sabacthani.*' He covered his face with his hands, and burst into tears. Unable to conclude the sentence, he said, 'You know the rest.'"

He spoke at Newton's Tuesday evening meetings at the Great House in Olney. Newton's diary for 25th April 1779 states, "It was the first time of his appearance there, but I hope it will not be the last." Newton added that Bull had spoken excellently on *Thou wilt have compassion.*

William's son, Thomas Palmer, described the friendship between his father and Newton as "an evangelical alliance which lasted unbroken between the parties till death did them part."

The news of Newton's pending departure from Olney to London drew warm expression from William, "Sometimes I think nobody loves me, and it makes me very low. But I know you do, and I am sure Jonathan did not love David more than I do you."

In old age, the friendship between Bull and Newton continued as strong as ever, as Newton's letters to him illustrated. "My dear old friend.... Though the flame of our affection is not much supported by the fruit of frequent letters and converse, I trust it still burns brightly, for it is fed from a secret, invisible, and inexhaustible source. If two needles are properly touched by a magnet, they will retain their sympathy for a long time. But if two hearts are properly united to the Heavenly Magnet, their mutual attraction will be permanent in time and to eternity. Blessed be the Lord for a good hope that is thus betwixt you and me. I could not love you better if I saw you or heard from you every day."

John Bunyan 1682-1688

Born at Elstow, near Bedford, John Bunyan was the son of a tinker. He fought in the Civil War, though more out of anger at his father's remarrying so soon after his mother's death. Overhearing some poor women speaking of their spiritual birth he entered into a great struggle over his own state of unbelief. He was invited into their pastor's home to join with others receiving instruction in the scriptures and some years later was himself preaching and teaching at the invitation of the church, who recognised his gifts in this area. It led to his imprisonment for preaching as a non-conformist. A short sentence was extended further as he refused to discontinue public preaching.

In his autobiographical *Grace Abounding to the Chief of Sinners*, written from prison twelve years after he had been arrested, Bunyan could write, "I never had in all my life so great an inlet into the Word of God as now; those scriptures that I saw nothing in before, are made in this place and state to shine upon me; Jesus Christ also was never more real and apparent than now; here I have seen Him and felt Him indeed". He wrote also of temptations, oppression, prayerlessness, coldness of heart and weakness – but found that in the wisdom of God these kept him from trusting in himself and moved him "to look to God, through Christ, to help me, and carry me through this world." He wrote sixty books, the best known being *Pilgrim's Progress*. This was a particular favourite of Newton's, who wrote the preface for an edition of it (see Appendix 6), providing notes also (together with Scott and others). Newton's letters to Alexander Clunie often included an update on how far they had read at their Tuesday prayer meetings in Olney – "reached the wicket gate last Tuesday." Many of Bunyan's thoughts and attitudes became evident in Newton's own life.

John Bunyan became the pastor of his church in 1672. Bedfordshire Historical Record Society have published the Church Minutes, edited by Tibbutt. This church later provided two of Newton's clergy friends – William Bull, who became pastor at Newport Pagnell, and Samuel Palmer, author of *The Protestant Dissenters' Catechism* and *The Non-Conformists' Memorial*, who became pastor of Hackney Independent Church (and the recipient of Newton's *Apologia*).

William Bromley Cadogan 1751-1797
Cadogan was Rector of St. Luke's, Chelsea, Vicar of St. Giles's, Reading and Chaplain to the Right Hon. Lord Cadogan, his father, who was Master of the Mint. He was converted through the letters, prayers and example of Mrs. Talbot, the widow of his predecessor in Reading (nephew of Lord Chancellor Talbot). She frequently invited clergy to prayer meetings in her home. The Talbots had been a great source of strength to Newton in his early days of ministry in Warwick, when they lived at Kineton. Newton published four of his letters to Mrs. Talbot in *Cardiphonia*. In the last of these he used an illustration of our hearts being "all alike, destitute of every good, and prone to every evil. Like money from the same mint, they bear the same impression of total depravity."

Newton wrote to Cadogan, "Your birth, early habits, connexions and prospects in life, and I suppose your character also, were such bars in the way of happiness and usefulness, as nothing less than the power of God could break through. I suppose you are the only person in the kingdom so closely related to a noble family who is able or willing to preach the gospel of Christ and to glory in the cross of our Lord. Thus that line, 'Oh, to grace how great a debtor,' is applicable to us both; and you, as well as I can declare, not merely from heresay, but from experience, that the grace of our Lord Jesus Christ is exceeding abundant." Newton preached for Cadogan occasionally. Charles Simeon preached his Funeral Sermon.

John Campbell 1766-1840

As a layman Campbell started a tract society in Edinburgh and established "Sabbath evening schools". An orphan himself, he was particularly concerned for the abandoned and underprivileged, and for visiting those in prison. On entering the ministry he became pastor of the Congregational Church in Kingsland, London, which gave him much opportunity to enjoy the fellowship, advice (and breakfasts) of Newton. His deep interest in mission took him twice to South Africa to visit stations of the LMS as its Director. He wrote *Travels in South Africa* and toured England to encourage support for the mission. He edited *The Youth's Magazine*, writing especially for young people.

Canaletto (Giovanni Antonio Canal) 1697-1768

The painting of *The Bucintoro Returning to the Molo on Ascension Day*, depicting the ritual described by Newton which involved throwing a gold ring into the sea, is dated about 1730. Newton's first voyage across the Mediterranean as a young lad of eleven years old was in 1736. He may well have been taken to see this painting, in Venice, shortly after it was completed.

William Carey 1761-1834

A shoemaker, Carey became a member of John Sutcliff's church in Olney in 1785 (five years after Newton had left). He had been baptised by John Ryland junior. His passion for evangelism had been triggered off by reading the journals of Captain James Cook. He was invited to be the pastor in the village of Earls Barton, but Sutcliff advised him to rather join a church which could give solid support for his missionary work. By 1786 he had the Olney Baptists' recognition of his ministerial gifts and was sent out "to preach the Gospel wherever God in His providence might call him." His last sermon at Olney was on Romans 12:1, *Present your bodies as a living sacrifice*, after which he announced the hymn as *And must I part with all I have...*, with great emphasis on the first four words of the second verse, *Yes, let it go...*

He was first pastor in Moulton, Northamptonshire and later in Leicester. In 1792 he preached at the Baptist Association Meeting at Nottingham from Isaiah 54:2,3 urging all to "Expect great things from God, attempt great things for God." In response The Particular Baptist Society for Propagating the Gospel among the Heathen (the Baptist Missionary Society) was formed a few months later. Thomas Robinson, vicar of St. Mary's in Leicester, commended him to Newton (as also John Ryland had already done some time earlier), who introduced him to Wilberforce, who sponsored his passage to India. Carey became known as the father of modern Bengali. He worked in Calcutta and Serampore, became Professor of Sanskrit at Fort William College, translated the New Testament into Bengali, supervised many other translations and produced grammars and dictionaries. He founded the Agricultural Society of India and worked successfully for the abolition of widow-burning.

Philip Carteret d. 1796
Captain of HMS *Harwich* when Newton was press-ganged. If Newton had found a way to put his thoughts into action, he would have murdered Carteret. Newton's father had tried to get him transferred to a merchant ship by the request of Admiral Medley, but Carteret had refused. It was from this ship that Newton was eventually exchanged at Madeira and began his voyage to Sierra Leone and slavery. Carteret sailed as lieutenant of the *Dolphin* in John Byron's voyage, 1764-6. He retired in 1794 as Rear Admiral.

Elizabeth Catlett (née Churchill) 1707-1773
Wife of George (snr.), born in Chatham, baptised at St. Mary's. She was a cousin or distant relation of Elizabeth Newton's. They had attended the same school. The register of St. Mary-le-Bow, London, records the marriage of George Catlett to Elizabeth Churchill (both of Chatham) on 2 November 1727. They had six children. Mary

(Polly), who married John Newton, Elizabeth, who married James Cunningham, Jack (John Churchill), Sarah (b. 1738), Susanna (b. 1741) and George jnr., who married Sarah Kite. John Newton's mother, Elizabeth, died in the Catlett's home.

Elizabeth (Betsy) Catlett (later Smith) 1769-1834

Daughter of George (jnr.), Polly's younger brother. The Newtons adopted her as an orphan in 1774. Newton added in his diary, "Oh may He by His grace adopt her into His chosen family." In September 1779 they took her to Martha Trinder's boarding school, Market Hill, Northampton, while they were at Olney and later to school in Highgate. Newton loved her as his own child, writing to her at Highgate, "I have no news to tell you; but one thing I can assure you, I mean, that I am your very affectionate friend, and feel for you as if I was really and truly your father." After the death of Polly, Betsy cared for him in his old age.

By 1801, a long illness had left Betsy's mind affected. She felt deserted by God. Newton wrote to his friends the Coffins, "She is always under the immediate apprehension of death, which is very terrible in her state of despondency. I seldom leave her but she says I shall find her a corpse on my return." He struggled to write with poor eyesight, adding, "She was indeed my *factotum*." He took her down to Reading to stay with a medical friend, Thomas Ring, hoping the change would also do her good. William Bull saw Newton during this period and remarked, "He is almost overwhelmed with this most awful affliction. I never saw a man so cut up. He is almost broken-hearted."

It became necessary to send her to Bethlehem Hospital, where she gradually recovered and was able to return to Coleman Street Buildings. She continued to live there with Newton and her husband, Joseph Smith, whom she married in 1805. The couple were buried in St. Mary Woolnoth, but re-interred in the City of London Cemetery near the St. Mary Woolnoth Memorial (plot 271). Betsy left money to the Moravian Missionary Society, the CMS, the BFBS and the LSPCJ, amongst others. She bequeathed "the arm chair called Mr. Newton's" to John Scott.

George Catlett (snr.) 1701-1777

Father of Newton's wife Mary (Polly). George was born in Chatham, baptised at St. Mary's. He married Elizabeth Churchill. He was

Customs Officer in Chatham, Kent (where Nelson's ship, HMS *Victory*, was laid down in 1759 and launched in 1765). In 1776 he went to live with John and Mary in Olney. The following year he died and was buried in Olney churchyard.

George Catlett (jnr.) 1742-1774
Mary's youngest brother, who married Sarah Kite at St. Mary's, Dover, on 3 February 1767. Their daughter Elizabeth (Betsy) was adopted as an orphan by the Newtons in 1774.

John (Jack) Churchill Catlett 1731-1764
One of Polly's brothers. Newton struck up a firm friendship with him from the beginning. Jack became a solicitor at Mr. Gaunter's in St. Olave's Street, Southwark.

Richard Cecil 1748-1810
Author of this book, rector of St. John's Bedford Row, a founder member of the Eclectic Society and the CMS. Jay says his preaching was striking and powerful and recalls the forcefulness with which he expressed his feelings, 'I *must* be heard.' Daniel Wilson wrote, 'Mr. Cecil possessed an unusual power of impressing a congregation and riveting their attention. Sometimes a sentence, or even a single word, sufficed.' In later years Cecil suffered a paralysis of his right side and was subsequently much in pain. He would sit in his pulpit to preach. His thoughts then were, "The dying words of Mr. Hervey are much on my mind, 'If I had my life to live again, I would spend more of it on my knees.'"

Thomas Charles [of Bala] 1755-1814
Methodist minister at Bala, North Wales. His concern for the provision of Welsh Bibles contributed to the founding of the British and Foreign Bible Society.

The Clapham Sect
A group of evangelicals whose influence of Christian standards on social issues was extensive.

A memorial in the wall of Clapham Parish Church (Holy Trinity) states:

LET US PRAISE GOD
for the memory and example of all faithful departed who have
worshipped in this Church, and especially for the undernamed
Servants of Christ sometime called
"THE CLAPHAM SECT"
who in the latter part of the 18th and the early part of the 19th
centuries laboured so abundantly for the increase of National
Righteousness and the Conversion of the Heathen and rested not
until the curse of slavery was swept away from all parts of the
British Dominions –

CHARLES GRANT	HENRY THORNTON
ZACHARY MACAULAY	JOHN THORNTON
GRANVILLE SHARP	HENRY VENN (Curate of Clapham)
JOHN SHORE (Lord Teignmouth)	JOHN VENN (Rector of Clapham)
JAMES STEPHEN	WILLIAM WILBERFORCE

"O God, we have heard with our ears, and our fathers
have declared to us, the noble works that thou didst in their days,
and in the old time before them."

The National Celebration of the Bicentenary of the Church Mission
Society was held on Clapham Common in May 1999. John Venn
was chairman of its first meeting.

John Clayton 1754-1843

John was converted through Romaine's preaching. He trained at
Trevecca College, becoming a preacher in the Countess of Huntingdon's chapel at Tunbridge Wells, then Presbyterian minister of
Weighhouse Chapel from 1778 to 1826. The only church member to
oppose his appointment there was Mary Flower, whom he later
married. A man of discipline, he started each day with devotions
from 5 a.m. to 8 a.m., for part of which he gradually read through
Owen, Baxter, Watts, Doddridge and others. One of Newton's
breakfast guests, he was invited to join the Eclectic Society. His sons
John, George and William each became pastors. It was Clayton who
approached Newton to draw up plans for the proposed academy in
Newport Pagnell "for preparing young men for the ministry, in which
the greatest stress might be laid upon truth, life, spirituality, and the
least stress possible upon modes, forms, and non-essentials."

Amos Clow
The trader with whom Newton decided to enter employment on arriving at Sierra Leone. His mistress was PI, who mistreated Newton in Clow's absence and made a slave of him, discrediting him on Clow's return.

Alexander Clunie d. 1770
Captain Clunie met up with Newton at St. Kitts in 1754 and spent much time in fellowship with him, teaching him from the Bible and encouraging him to pray extempore. Newton was always grateful for this foundation. He kept in touch with Clunie regularly, his letters later being published as *The Christian Correspondent*. Whenever he could he saw him in London and invited him down to Olney. Clunie had become a member of Brewer's Stepney Meeting on 3 January 1754, when his address was given as Bird Street, Wapping, very close to Newton's childhood home in Red Lyon Street. Mary Newton often mentioned the Clunies in her letters home to John when staying in London. After Clunie's death, his widow, Jane, stayed on in their new house on the east side of Stepney Green until 1785.

Joseph Collyer (jnr.) 1748-1827
Associate of the Royal Academy who engraved Newton's portrait. This engraving is kept in the National Portrait Gallery.

John Colquitt (jnr.) 1746-1807
Collector of Customs when Newton was Tide Surveyor. He succeeded his father in this post. He was also Recorder of Liverpool for many years.

Richard Conyers 1725-1786
Brother-in-law of John Thornton. On Christmas Day 1758 Conyers read John 1:7 and Hebrews 9:20; suddenly understanding what he had read he rushed around the house shouting, "I have found Him!" The Archbishop of York warned him not to preach such stuff or he would drive the congregation mad. He poured himself out for his parish. Henry Venn wrote to a friend, "And now you will grieve with us, to hear that this our dear fellow-labourer has quite impaired his constitution by his excessive fatigues in preaching to different congregations, in his most extensive parish, twenty-one times each week."

Conyers married Thornton's widowed sister Mrs. Knipe in 1765. After her death he accepted a living in Deptford from Thornton, leaving Helmsley at midnight to avoid scenes from his anguished parishioners who had threatened to lie in the path of his carriage. T. S. Grimshawe described his death, "He had ascended the pulpit of St. Paul's, Deptford, of which he was rector, and had just delivered his text, *Ye shall see my face no more*, when he was seized with a sudden fainting and fell back in the pulpit: he recovered, however, sufficiently to proceed with his sermon, and to give the concluding blessing, when he again fainted away, was carried home, and expired without a groan, in his sixty-second year of his age."

Newton held a high opinion of him. When he heard of his death, he wrote to William Wilberforce that he expected to be preaching to the largest congregation ever when he preached his funeral sermon at Deptford. He preached from 1 Thessalonians 2:8, *So being affectionately desirous of you, we were willing to have imparted unto you, not the gospel of God only, but also our own souls, because ye were dear unto us*. He told how Conyers, though described in his early years at Helmsley as " the most exemplary, indefatigable, and successful parochial minister in the kingdom," had been convicted of his need by reading Paul's reference to "the unsearchable riches of Christ." He apologised to his congregation for having misled them. From then on, he preached Christ crucified. Vulnerable to pressure, "a continued hurry and flutter upon his spirits", in his later years, he preached only in his own pulpit or his own home. The one exception was when he preached at the archdeacon's visitation at Dartford. He was extremely agitated during the weeks leading up to it; on entering the pulpit he lost his eyesight for several minutes. Newton described Dr. Conyer's compassion for his congregation as resembling that of a nursing mother for her child, being "exceeding dear" to him. "When I thought of preaching to you this day, and of mingling my tears with yours, the occasion suggested the choice I have made of a text; and the countenances of many of you convince me that I have not made an improper choice."

James Cook 1728-1779
Cook came to Wapping in 1746 as an apprentice to a local shipowner and volunteered for the Navy in 1755. He would have been in the area when Newton returned home from sea and frequently visited

his home ground to meet with Jennings and Brewer. Captain Cook circumnavigated the world, contributing also to health improvements for seamen.

Nathaniel Cotton 1705-1788
Dr. Cotton was a GP, a scholar and a poet. He ran a private asylum, Collegium Insanorum, at St. Alban's, to which William Cowper was sent when he came under extreme pressure at the House of Lords. Cotton was considered a man of spiritual compassion and professional skill. He was a friend of Dr. Edward Young and attended him at his deathbed. Although his poetry was popular some thought he should have been more evangelical in his expression.

Ann Cowper (née Donne) 1703-1737
William Cowper's mother, daughter of Roger Donne of Ludham Hall, Norfolk; she married the Rev. Dr. John Cowper. She died at the age of thirty-four, when William was six. When he received a picture of his mother from a cousin many years later, it moved him deeply. He wrote a poem which included these lines:

> My Mother! when I learn'd that thou wast dead,
> Say, wast thou conscious of the tears I shed?
> Hover'd thy spirit o'er thy sorrowing son,
> Wretch even then, life's journey just begun?
> Perhaps thou gavest me, though unfelt, a kiss;
> Perhaps a tear, if souls can weep in bliss –
> Ah, that maternal smile! it answers – Yes.
> I heard the bell toll'd on thy burial day,
> I saw the hearse that bore thee slow away,
> And turning from my nursery window, drew
> A long, long sigh, and wept a last adieu!
>
> Thy maidens, grieved themselves at my concern,
> Oft gave me promise of thy quick return.
> What ardently I wish'd, I long believed,
> And disappointed still, was still deceived.
> By expectation every day beguiled,
> Dupe of tomorrow even from a child.
> Thus many a sad tomorrow came and went,
> Till, all my stock of infant sorrows spent,
> I learn'd at last submission to my lot,
> But, though I less deplored thee, ne'er forgot.

Ashley Cowper 1702-1788

William Cowper's uncle, who lived at 30 Southampton Row. He was the father of Theodora, whom William was forbidden to marry. Letters from William on Ashley's death show no bitterness borne towards him:

To Joseph Hill, June 8 1788

"While our friends yet live inhabitants of the same world with ourselves, they seem still to live to *us*; we are sure that they sometimes think of us; and however improbable it may seem, it is never impossible that we may see each other again. But the grave, like a great gulf, swallows all such expectations, and, in the moment when a beloved friend sinks into it, a thousand tender recollections awaken a regret that will be felt in spite of all reasonings, and let our warnings have been what they may. Thus it is I take my last leave of poor Ashley, whose heart towards me was ever truly parental, and to whose memory I owe a tenderness and respect that will never leave me."

To Lady Heskith, June 10 1788

"My dear uncle's death awakened in me many reflections, which for a time sunk my spirits.... I will add no more at present than a warm hope, that you and your sister will be able effectually to avail yourselves of all the consolatory matter with which it abounds. You gave yourselves, while he lived, to a father, whose life was doubtless prolonged by your attentions, and whose tenderness of disposition made him always deeply sensible of your kindness in this respect, as well as in many others. His old age was the happiest I have ever known, and I give you both joy of having had so fair an opportunity, and of having so well used it, to approve yourselves equal to the calls of such a duty in the sight of God and man."

This last letter had a very rare reference to Theodora, William's unattainable love, who was Lady Heskith's sister. Her other sister, Elizabeth Charlotte, married Sir Archer Croft.

John Cowper (snr.) 1694-1756

William's father, the son of Judge [Spencer] Cowper. He was Chaplain to King George II and lived at the Rectory of Great Berkhampstead, Hertfordshire. His wife Ann died in childbirth, leaving him with two young sons, John and William.

John Cowper (jnr.) 1737-1770

The brother of William. John had been considered one of the best classic scholars at Cambridge. He was Fellow of Bennett and had been ordained for ten years before his death in 1770. William had tried earlier to share his personal faith with him, but John had gradually withdrawn from these discussions and maintained a liberal view of religion. In his final illness, caused by an abscess in the liver, he allowed William to pray with him. His last days are recorded in *Adelphi,* written by William and transcribed by Newton.

John was helped by William to come to a personal knowledge of gospel truths. He longed to see Newton and have an hour's conversation with him, but he did not recover and died on 20th March 1770. The emotional strains of this time were thought to have contributed to William's breakdown three years later.

Maria Frances Cecilia Cowper (née Madan) 1726-1797

William Cowper's cousin, wife of Major Cowper and sister of Martin Madan. Her mother was a Wesley convert as was her brother. Letters addressed by Newton and Cowper to "Mrs. Cowper" were to her. The Cowper and Newton Museum has her *Commonplace Book*, her autograph journal. Her poems were published, revised by William. She was buried at South Audley Chapel. On her tomb is the inscription, "A sinner saved by grace".

Spencer [Judge] Cowper 1669-1728

William's grandfather. His sons were William, John (father of the poet William) and Ashley. Judith Madan was his daughter.

Theodora Jane Cowper d. 1824

Daughter of Ashley, she was in love with William Cowper the poet. They wanted to marry but her father forbade it. After her death, James Croft, her nephew, edited twenty-five love poems from William Cowper to her. In this one Cowper refers to her as "Delia":

> Bid adieu, my sad heart, bid adieu to thy peace,
> Thy pleasure is past, and thy sorrows increase;
> See the shadows of evening, how far they extend,
> And a long night is coming, that never may end;
> For the sun is now set that deliver'd the scene,
> And an age must be past e'er it rises again.

Already deprived of its splendour and heat,
I feel thee more slowly, more heavily beat;
Perhaps overstrain'd with the quick pulse of pleasure,
Thou art glad of this respite to beat at thy leisure;
But the sigh of distress shall now weary thee more
Than the flutter and tumult of passion before.

The heart of a lover is never at rest,
With joy overwhelm'd, or with sorrow oppress'd:
When Delia is near, all is ecstasy then,
And I even forget I must lose her again:
When absent, as wretched, as happy before,
Despairing I cry, I shall see her no more.

William Cowper 1731-1800

Son of John, rector of Berkhampstead. His mother died when he was
six. He attended Westminster School from 1742 to 1749. Cowper
was in love with his cousin, Theodora Jane Cowper, sister of Lady
Heskith, and wanted to marry her. Her father, Ashley, objected on
the grounds of the near relationship and William's inadequate fortune.
Neither William nor Theodora ever married. He was called to the bar
as a member of the Middle Temple in 1754 and offered the clerkship
of the journals of the House of Lords in 1763. Overwhelmed, he
became seriously depressed. His cousin, Martin Madan, tried to give
him some spiritual help before he was referred to Dr. Cotton's asylum
in St. Alban's in December. While there, he became a Christian and
deliberately stayed on longer than necessary in order to receive
spiritual help from Dr. Cotton. When he left he moved to Huntingdon,
where he met the Unwins and moved in with them. He considered
entering the ministry in 1766. After Rev. Morley Unwin's death he
and Mary Unwin moved to Olney at the invitation of Newton.

Cowper and Newton were inseparable, Cowper becoming in effect
"the Curate's curate." Newton recognised Cowper's literary talents
and had his individual poems published. He wrote the preface to the
first edition of his collection, *Poems*. Cowper acknowledged, "The
honour of your preface prefixed to my poems will be on my side; for
surely to be known as the friend of a much-favoured minister of
God's word is a more illustrious distinction, in reality, than to have
the friendship of any poet in the world to boast of."

When Cowper showed signs of returning depression Newton
suggested they work together on providing hymns for the weekly

meetings. This gesture of friendship resulted in many hymns grounded in prayer and scripture which still give much encouragement and incentive to worship today, two hundred years later, all over the world.

Cowper visited the sick and took a special interest in the welfare of the lace-makers. He sometimes led at the church prayer meetings. Samuel Teedon, the village schoolmaster, considered, "Of all the men I ever heard pray, no one equalled Mr Cowper." Newton's testimony to him in his *Incomplete Memoirs* was, "He loved the poor. He often visited them in their cottages, conversed with them in the most condescending[obliging] manner, sympathised with them, counselled and comforted them in their distresses; and those who were seriously disposed were often cheered and animated by his prayers!"

Cowper was fiercely defendant of Newton. His personal copy of *An Apology for Protestant Dissenters* shows his spontaneous reaction, in scribbled verse (p.427), to reading this written criticism of Newton: "In reply to Mr. Newton's fourth argument (in which in the usual *cant of these Reformers*, he pleads, that the Lord...)".

> These critics who to faith no quarter grant,
> But call it mere hypocrisy and cant
> To make a just acknowledgement of praise
> And thanks to God for governing our ways,
> Approve Confucius more and Zoroaster
> Than Christ's own servant or that servant's Master.

After Cowper's death, some unjustified blame was put on Newton for his depression. Jay comments on this, "Some have thought the divine was hurtful to the poet. How mistaken were they! He was the very man, of all others, I should have chosen for him. He was not rigid in his creed. His views of the Gospel were most free and encouraging. He had the tenderest disposition; and always judiciously regarded his friend's depression and despondency as a physical effect, for the removal of which he prayed, but never reasoned or argued with him concerning it."

When Cowper and Mary Unwin moved from Weston Underwood in their final years to stay with his cousin Johnson, he wrote these lines in pencil on the window shutter of a bedroom overlooking the garden of the Lodge,

> "Farewell, dear scenes, for ever closed to me,
> Oh, for what sorrows must I now exchange ye!"

The shutter was closed up for twenty years to save paying the window tax. It is now kept at the Cowper and Newton Museum, Olney. "Oh! with what a surprise of joy," wrote Newton a few days after Cowper's death, "would he find himself immediately before the throne, and in the presence of his Lord! All his sorrows left below, and earth exchanged for heaven."

Elizabeth Crabb d. 1807
One of Newton's servants in London. He was deeply grateful to her for her "fidelity and affection" and assistance when his wife was dying. Crabb's orphaned niece, Mary Walker, came to work for Newton after the death of another servant, Phoebe. Newton was delighted when one of their frequent visitors made provision for Crabb in her old age, by appointing an almshouse for her on family property in Buckinghamshire. However, she died a few months before Newton.

Sir Herbert Croft 1751-1816
Wrote Young's Memoirs for Dr. Johnson's *Lives of the Poets* (and a satirical collection of epitaphs based on Hervey's *Meditations*).

Harry [Henry] Crook 1708-1770
Harry Crook, Vicar of Hunslet, Yorkshire, previously curate at Huddersfield. Newton accepted an offer of the curacy of Kippax from him in 1758 but was unable to obtain a licence from the Archbishop of York.

Croxton (jnr.) d. 1755
Newton's predecessor as Surveyor of Tides in Liverpool. When Croxton's father died there was a rumour that he would retire and enjoy the inheritance. Joseph Manesty applied to the local MP on Newton's behalf for this impending post. While the reply was on its way back that it was not going to be vacated, Croxton was found dead. Although the Mayor immediately applied for his nephew, Newton's application was accepted as having been the first.

William Cunneigh [Coney]
Midshipman on the *African*, 1752. Informed Newton of the mutinous plot against him.

Eliza (Elizabeth) Cunningham 1771-1785

The daughter of Elizabeth and James and the niece of Mary Newton, Eliza came to live with the Newtons in London a couple of months before her mother, the last surviving member of her family, died. Eliza was constantly ill, but her faith grew stronger. She died at the age of 14 and was buried on 12 October 1785 at St. Mary Woolnoth's. Newton preached her funeral sermon to a crammed church. She had chosen the text for herself: Revelation 14:13.

Elizabeth Cunningham (née Catlett) 1730-1783

Elizabeth Catlett, Mary Newton's sister, married James Cunningham in St Mary's, Chatham in 1764. For a while they lived in Five Bell Lane, Rochester, moving to his estated Lairdship at Anstruther, Fifeshire, in 1773. By this time the Newtons had decided that there should always be one of them on hand in Olney for William Cowper's sake, so it was Mary, who was very close to her sister, who went to see them off. A few months later Newton wrote to Elizabeth, "Your removal led my thoughts to the subject of the following hymn, and therefore you ought to have a copy."

JACOB'S ladder

Genesis 28:12

If the LORD our leader be,
We may follow without fear;
East or West by land or sea,
Home, with him, is ev'ry where:
When from Esau Jacob fled,
Tho' his pillow was a stone,
And the ground his humble bed,
Yet he was not left alone.

Kings are often waking kept,
Rack'd with cares on beds of state;
Never king like Jacob slept;
For he lay at heaven's gate:
Lo! he saw a ladder reared,
Reaching to the heav'nly throne;
At the top the LORD appeared,
Spake and claimed him for his own.

"Fear not, Jacob, thou art mine,
And my presence with thee goes;
On thy heart my love shall shine,
And my arm subdue thy foes:

From my promise comfort take,
For my help in trouble call;
Never will I thee forsake,
'Till I have accomplished all."

Well does Jacob's ladder suit
To the gospel throne of grace;
We are at the ladder's foot,
Ev'ry hour, in ev'ry place:
By assuming flesh and blood,
JESUS heav'n and earth unites;
We by faith ascend to GOD (i),
GOD to dwell with us delights.

They who know the Saviour's name,
Are for all events prepared;
What can changes do to them,
Who have such a Guide and Guard?
Should they traverse earth around,
To the ladder still they come;
Ev'ry spot is holy ground,
GOD is there – and he's their home.

(i) 2 Cor. 6:16
Olney Hymns, Book 1, Hymn 9

Newton wrote to Thornton that Elizabeth knew the Gospel and, like Jacob, was happy in any place. The Cunninghams had three children, Jackie (John), Susie and Eliza. One by one the family died early in life leaving just Elizabeth and Eliza, who were both invited to live with the Newtons. Only Eliza survived to do so.

Lord Dartmouth (William Legge) 1731-1801

2nd Earl of Dartmouth, President of the Board of Trade and Foreign Plantations, Colonial Secretary, Lord Keeper of the Privy Seal, High Steward of Oxford University, a friend of the Countess of Huntingdon. He took up Haweis's suggestion that Newton be appointed at Olney, which was in his patronage. He ended Newton's seven years of attempting to be accepted into the ministry of the Church of England by convincing the Bishop of Lincoln that he was worthy of ordination. It was most timely and generous assistance and an insight for Newton into the life of the nobility. He wrote home to his wife from London, "Besides him [Lord Dartmouth] and my Lady – I think I am acquainted with near half a score persons who ride in their own coaches, and are as humble and simple as Yorkshire cottagers, and at the same time both cheerful and entertaining." It was Dartmouth who sponsored Newton's *Narrative* being printed, on which Cecil based most of this book. A number of Newton's personal letters to Lord Dartmouth were published in *Cardiphonia*.

Daniel Defoe 1661?-1731

Journalist and novelist, prolific writer of political, religious and social works. Imprisoned in 1703 for publishing his satirical *The Shortest way with the Dissenters*. Defoe had just four years' education, which were at a Non-conformist seminary in Islington at the same time as John Wesley's father was there. His *Family Instructor* guided Newton's early Christian thinking.

Thomas Frognall Dibdin 1776 -1847

Author of *Bibliomania*, rector of St Mary's, Bryanston Square from 1824, nephew of Charles Dibdin the dramatist and songwriter, who took him as a young boy of fifteen to hear Newton preaching at Mary's funeral. Thomas wrote briefly of his memories of this.

George Dixon 1709-1787

The Principal of St. Edmund Hall, Oxford, when six students were expelled for holding "methodistical tenets". Fourteen of Newton's letters to Dr. Dixon are in Vol. 6 of his *Works*.

Philip Doddridge 1702-1751

20th child of Daniel, he was the pastor of the Independent Congregation at Castle Hill, Northampton, Principal of the Dissenters' Academy, a friend of David Jennings and Isaac Watts, author of *The Family Expositor* (a paraphrase of Bible portions with notes), and the composer of hymns such as *O God of Bethel by whose hand Thy people still are fed* and *Ye servants of the Lord*. A leading dissenter with a wide influence. His *Rise and Progress* was instrumental in the conversion and spiritual growth of William Wilberforce and Claudius Buchanan amongst many others. Newton particularly valued his *Life of Colonel Gardiner*.

John Drake d. 1775

Dissenting minister at the Independent Church in Olney. The Independents, Baptists and Established Church held combined New Year's services for their youth and sometimes attended each other's midweek meetings. The church had been brought back to life a few years earlier through the interest and efforts of Isaac Watts and Thomas Gibbons (his friend and biographer, who had worshipped here in his youth when his father was the minister).

John Edwards 1714 - 1785

Dissenting minister in Leeds whose first invitation to Newton to preach resulted in some embarrassment for the latter. Edwards had been brought to a strong faith through hearing George Whitefield preach. He was initially a methodist preacher, but left to join the Independents at the same time as John Whitford did.

Writing to Newton in 1771 he reminded him "that your name is still mentioned with pleasure at Leeds, and that you and yours are remembered at the throne of grace, especially on our Wednesday evening meetings." He regretted that though a recent trip to London had meant he came within 20 miles of seeing Newton, he had had to pass by "highly-favoured Olney".

Jonathan Edwards 1703-1758
Leader of the Great Awakening in Northampton, Massachusetts. Associate Pastor of the Congregational Church at Northampton and Tutor at Yale (then the Collegiate School of Connecticut). He experienced a fresh awareness of God's sovereignty, which was the beginning of the Awakening. His two main works were his *Personal Narrative*, 1739 and *Freedom of the Will*, 1754. He became President of the College of New Jersey at Princeton in January 1758, but died in March after a smallpox inoculation. Newton's and Ryland's doctorates came from Princeton.

Mrs. Eversfield
When Newton was forbidden to contact Polly in his youth, he corresponded with her via an aunt. This may have been Susanna Eversfield (née Churchill, Polly's mother's maiden name), who married William at St. Mary's Chatham in 1725. They had a daughter Mary, in 1726.

John Eyre 1754-1803
Editor of the *Evangelical Magazine*. His father turned him out of the house for preaching in the town hall. He received training for the ministry at Trevecca. He then held various posts including being Cecil's curate at Lewis and Cadogan's at St. Giles, Reading and St. Luke's, Chelsea. He became the minister at Homerton (Romaine's chapel). Daniel Wilson was one of his pupils. John was a founder member of the LMS.

John Fawcett 1740-1817
Pastor of Wainsgate Baptist Church near Hebdon Bridge, converted under Whitefield (preaching from John 3:14), shaped as a young Christian by William Grimshaw (he walked the nine miles to Haworth on Communion Sundays), friendly with Henry Venn and Henry Foster, actively supported the BMS (he raised £200 towards Carey's voyage) and the Bible Society. He wrote a devotional commentary on the Bible and founded a nonconformist Academy. The hymn *Blest be the tie that binds,* was written by him.

Newton's *Narrative* originated from a series of letters written to him which he showed to Haweis. Though he was the instrument of bringing to light such an uplifting testimony, his own experience was painful, as he described to a friend, "I am continually bowed down under a sense of my own weakness and foolishness. I spend my days in pain and anguish of mind on these accounts.... In attempting to make preparation for the pulpit, I sit for hours together, and can do little or nothing." He was invited to be pastor of Broadmead Baptist in Bristol, but declined.

John Flavel 1627-1691
Presbyterian, ejected from Dartmouth in 1622 but continued to minister there secretly, holding services on a rock in the Kingsbridge estuary at low tide. While Newton recommended particular books of other authors to his friends he advised reading "anything by Flavel." He wrote simply and perceptively in plain, straightforward language. His *Works* were reprinted by Banner of Truth Trust in 1968.

Jane Flower 1760-1826
She was the daughter of Martha (née Fuller) and George Flower, a stationer of Cannon Street and a deacon at White Row Independent under the Rev. Edward Hitchen. Jane attended Martha Trinder's school in Northampton with Betsy Catlett. Her fellow-pupil John Ryland jnr. writes, "Miss Flower now being at Northampton and hearing of our Society desired her brother [Benjamin] might meet with us although she did not say he was truly serious but hoped this might be of use to him: we consented thereto, and he professed to be under concerns about his soul, which we are not without hopes was the case." About this time Newton was preaching his series of lectures on Genesis. I have wondered whether Jane took notes on his sermon on Jacob's ladder (he used to lend his notebooks around) and later passed them on to Benjamin's daughters, Sarah Fuller (Flower) Adams and Eliza Flower, who, between them, wrote the words and music to the hymn *Nearer My God To Thee* (based on Genesis 28), so recently brought to our attention as the last hymn to be played as the *Titanic* sank. Jane's sister, Mary, married John Clayton (snr.), pastor of Weighhouse Chapel and a member of Newton's Eclectic Society. Her brother, Richard, was a brewer. His son, Edward Fordham Flower, founded Flower's Brewery in Stratford-on-Avon. One of his sons, Charles Edward, was the founder of the Shakespeare Memorial Theatre in Stratford. Another, Sir William Henry, was Director of the Natural History Museum in London. Jane's brother

Benjamin lost his fortune in property speculation and started up a weekly newspaper, *The Cambridge Intelligencer*. He was imprisoned for libel. Some of Newton's letters to Jane were published in *Cardiphonia*. Her *Life and Writings* contain some of his letters. She married John Dawson of Aldcliffe Hall near Lancaster. He died in May 1804.

George Ford 1766? -1821
Congregational minister and a director of the (London) Missionary Society. He preached Samuel Brewer's funeral sermon at Stepney Independent Meeting. He continued as minister of Stepney Meeting for the next twenty-five years.

John Ford 1740-1806
He came from a long line of faithful Gospel ministers, including his great-great-grandfather, John Vincent, mentioned in Calamy for his steadfastness under persecution. John's father, William, was pastor at Castle Hedingham in Essex, where he was reputed never to have preached twice from the same text during forty years of ministry. John was apprenticed to a surgeon in Ipswich where he began to think seriously about religion after receiving a letter from his father. He was greatly helped by reading a Christian book which lay in the shop to be used as waste paper. Moving to London, he first worshipped under his brother William's ministry, then at the Tabernacle, eventually moving to Jewin Street under Hart, the hymn writer, attending Romaine's lectures on Tuesday mornings at Blackfairs. Romaine taught him Hebrew and he entered the ministry with the Countess of Huntingdon's Connection.

Thomas Ford 1742-1821
Newton first met the Fords when they lived in London at 25 Old Jewry. He and Mary often stayed with them when passing through from Olney to Kent. In turn the Fords spent time at Olney vicarage. In 1774 Thomas was instituted vicar of Melton Mowbray, with the oversight of neighbouring hamlets. On Sundays he took four full services and one without the hour-long sermon. He was not averse to reading out other people's sermons, telling his congregation that they were better than his own. He was witty and somewhat eccentric, but dedicated to the gospel. Newton was terribly upset to hear from

Thomas Robinson of Leicester that after twenty years of faithful service Dr. Ford had lost his zeal. He wrote prayerfully to him, "My dear friend, can you ever think you were too frequent or too earnest in the most active part of your ministry? Are the souls of men, the cause of truth, the honour of our Lord, become of less importance than formerly? Have the world or the devil beaten a parley, made a truce, withdrawn their snares, or discontinued their assaults, so that it is no longer needful for you to be earnest and frequent in warning every one, night and day, publicly and from house to house, as you once did? Ah! my friend, truth and facts remain in themselves just as they were. While I weep for you I may tremble for myself. The snare in which you have been entangled has been spread for me, and it is not by any power, or wisdom, or goodness of my own that I have escaped it." He pleaded with Ford to break off damaging connections with one mighty Samson-like effort and to humble himself before the Lord, praying for the return of His Spirit. Dr. Ford made public confession of his backsliding, asked forgiveness of his congregation and resumed his earlier work.

William Ford (jnr.) 1736-1783
Brother of Dr. John Ford and husband of Elizabeth [1730-1781]. He was assistant at Old Gravel Lane and ordained pastor of Miles-Lane in 1757. His father and David Jennings both spoke at the service. Ford junior was not a popular preacher, "due to an extreme heaviness in the pulpit", though Dr. Gibbons benevolently said of him that he had "heard much worse sermons at Pinner's Hall lecture, than those made by Mr. Ford."

Joseph Forrester
Sailed before the mast in Newton's ship *The African* in 1752. Intended to seize the ship. His attempts to get the crew to sign a round robin were exposed just in time. He was put in irons and transferred to the *Earl of Halifax* "to be put on board the first Man of War for his misdemeanour."

Henry Foster 1745-1844
Rector of St. James Clerkenwell, lecturer and a founder member of the Eclectic Society and the CMS. His first serious thoughts came from overhearing one of his father's workmen at family prayers. He assisted Romaine at St. Ann's, Blackfriars. Newton had wanted him

to join him as a curate at Olney. He was associated with Cecil for many years as minister of Long-Acre Chapel, preaching the alternate Sunday morning lectures at St Margaret's, Lothbury, and in the evenings at Spitalfields. Pratt writes that he was "a plain and deeply pious man; without any peculiar decoration of task, style or eloquence in his general preaching; his ministrations were much valued, chiefly on account of their heart-searching and experiential character. On certain subjects, so great was his solemnity of manner, especially when discoursing upon death and eternity, that the late Mr. W[ilberforce?] used to say he was on these occasions the most eloquent man he knew." His days began with a walk in Spafields before breakfast and ended with a supper of bread and cheese. He conducted Newton's funeral service at St. Mary Woolnoth.

Andrew Fuller 1754-1815
Baptist pastor at Kettering, secretary of the Baptist Missionary Society. He attended the Baptist Association Meetings in Olney. Fuller, Sutcliff and Ryland formed a firm friendship. Together with William Carey they were at the heart of the founding of the Baptist Missionary Society. His *Gospel Worthy of All Acceptation* stimulated a missionary concern. In 1798 he received a doctorate from Princeton, but, like Newton, he declined to use the title.

James Gardiner 1688-1745
Colonel of the Dragoons, deserted by most of his men at Prestonpans and mortally wounded.

Doddridge preached a funeral sermon at Northampton for him from Revelation 2:10, *Be thou faithful unto death*, and published his *Life of Colonel Gardiner* two years later. His widow was Lady Frances Gardiner.

To kill time while waiting for "an unhappy assignment with a married woman", Gardiner had picked up a copy of *The Christian Soldier* and was reading it when he saw a blaze of light and a vision of the Lord Jesus Christ upon the cross reproaching him for the way in which he was responding to his sufferings. Gardiner felt deeply convicted. Although his life changed immediately, it was three months before he found forgiveness and peace through Romans 3:25, 26 (the same verses which brought such relief to Cowper). Newton aligned himself closely with his experience, writing to Jennings, "I cannot read the latter part of Luke 7 without blessing the life of Colonel G., as related by Dr. Doddridge, which I think has affected me more frequently and sensibly than all the books I ever read. I allow the manner of his conversion was most extraordinary, yet I think mine was not less awful and then as to the measure of iniquity from which we were reclaimed, I must incur the unhappy pre-eminence, not only from him, but from every person in the present age." His diary records that reading the *Life of Colonel Gardiner* reduced him to tears.

Henry Gauntlett 1762-1833
Curate at Olney 1811-15, vicar 1815-33. The church music then consisted of trombone and bassoon. Gauntlett suggested using an organ, intending that his daughters would learn to play it. But his young son of nine, Henry John, thought it unfitting for girls to take such a prominent part in the service and offered to play if his mother would teach him. He was ready to do this when the organ was installed six months later.

Henry John Gauntlett 1805-1876
Son of Henry. He came to Olney at the age of six. For more than ten years he was the organist, until leaving to become a solicitor. He designed the first Bach organs ever made in England, installed in Christchurch Newgate Street and St. Peter's Cornhill. He received a Lambeth Doctorate, acquiring the title of "the father of church music". Mendelssohn chose him to play *Elijah*. Amongst the tunes he wrote were *Irby* for *Once in Royal David's City*, *Braylesford* for *Lead us Heavenly Father* and *St. Albinus* for *Jesus Lives!*

John Gilbert 1693-1761
Archbishop of York, known for being inflexible, he refused to ordain Newton as he hadn't been to university. Pollock refers to him as "the elderly idle Dr. Gilbert." He began the practice of laying hands on each candidate at confirmation.

John Goode 1754?-1831
Brother of William (snr.), from Potter's Pury. He was a pupil of William Bull's before the academy was established in Newport Pagnell. He became pastor of White Row, London. Pratt wrote in 1856 that John Clayton and John Goode were "more like Watts and

Doddridge than like Dissenters of the present day." John was an early member of the Eclectic Society.

William Goode (snr.) 1762-1816
Romaine's curate, succeeding him as rector of St. Andrew by the Wardrobe and St. Anne's Blackfriars. He was President of Sion College and an early member of the Eclectic Society and the CMS. The CMS committee met in his study. He lectured at St. Lawrence Jewry and St. John's, Wapping. His *Essays on all the Scriptural Names and Titles of Christ* was published posthumously by his son, William jnr.[1801-1868], who became Dean of Ripon and editor of the *Christian Observer* (he also wrote his father's *Life*).

Charles Grant (jnr.) 1778-1866
Eldest son of Charles Grant (snr.) [1746-1823]; converted while in India, his position as a Director of the East India Company and his association with the Clapham Sect led to the abolition of the company's temple tax revenue and the appointment of a bishop at Bombay and at Madvor. He was one of the first Directors of the Sierra Leone Company and a founder member of the Bible Society (one of the first Vice-Presidents). In 1831 he was created Baron Glenelg.

Sir Robert Grant 1779-1883
Brother of Charles and Governor of Bombay. One of the Clapham Sect. Wrote the hymn, *O worship the King all glorious above*.

Samuel Greatheed d. 1823
One of Bull's pupils, pastor of the independent church which Bull had started at Woburn. A founder member and a director of the LMS and the first editor of the *Eclectic Review*. He preached Cowper's funeral sermon in Olney. Cowper previously wrote of him, "a well-bred gentleman, a man of letters and of taste, meek and learned as Moses." Greatheed encouraged fellowship across denominations. He was instrumental in forming the Bedford Union of Christians. When he later moved to Bishops Hull, Somerset, he established a Bible Society there, of which he became secretary.

Dr. John Green 1706?-1779
Bishop of Lincoln. Lord Dartmouth prevailed on him to ordain Newton.

William Grimshaw 1708-1763
Vicar of Haworth, Yorkshire. Newton gained much from him spiritually; he wrote his Memoirs, describing how Grimshaw had changed from being preoccupied with the terrors of the Lord to learning, from his own experience, "to invite the weary and heavy laden to apply to Jesus, that they might find rest to their souls."

Grimshaw raised money for a meeting place for the local methodists; a plaque on the Methodist Chapel in Haworth states that it was "Erected by the Revd William Grimshaw, A.B. Minister of the Haworth Church. A.D. 1758." The Trustees of the Chapel included Grimshaw and John and Charles Wesley. When Charles preached in Grimshaw's Church in 1751 he was obliged to repeat the sermon from a tombstone in the churchyard to the three or four thousand who hadn't heard him from the pulpit.

John Fawcett's biographer says, "The erection of a [Baptist] place of worship at Wainsgate must be imputed to the Rev. Mr. Grimshaw of Haworth.... Mr. Richard Smith, who was its first pastor, attended Mr. Grimshaw's ministry, and derived great advantage from it."

Once Whitefield was preaching to Grimshaw's congregation about the damage done by some Christians' conduct and assured them that he knew that wouldn't be the case with them. Grimshaw stood up and interrupted him, "Oh, sir, for God's sake do not speak so; I pray you do not flatter them: I fear the greater part of them are going to hell with their eyes open."

William Alphonsus Gunn 1760-1806
Newton's curate at St. Mary Woolnoth from 1797 to his death in 1806. Newton wrote to the Rev. Coffin, "Mr. Gunn is highly acceptable in my pulpit, and the church is crowded to the steps in the street. I have reason to thank the Lord for such an assistant. I must decrease, but I trust he will increase." Sending some cash to his curate, Newton wrote on the outside of the parcel, "Ammunition for my Gun."

As a child Gunn attended Stepney Meeting under Samuel Brewer. Hervey's *Meditations* had him in tears at the age of eleven. He longed to minister, sometimes standing in the pulpit when the chapel was empty. But when he had the opportunity to study at Oxford and was called upon to read the lesson in chapel, he was so nervous and frozen with fear that the College Head intervened with, "Sir, if you cannot read better than that, do not read at all." The first time he preached he left home at 5 a.m. to make sure he wouldn't be late. Driven out from Farnham as a Methodist, he arrived in London where he preached at St Mary Somerset, Thames Street, later taking on the curacy at St Mary Woolnoth and the evening lectureship at St Margaret, Lothbury. He was a founder member of the CMS. Newton wrote to him in a holiday mood from the Taylors' at Southampton, suggesting that as partners they should share a common firm. "I think I have found one that will suit us both. I deal much in smoke, and you in snuff; suppose, therefore, we assume the firm of DUST AND ASHES!"

John Guyse 1680-1761
Independent minister at Hertford and in New Broad Street. Samuel Brewer was converted through his preaching.

Robert Hall (snr.) 1728-1791
Baptist minister of Arnesby. He was one of those who attended the Baptist Association Meetings in Olney. Newton's concern for Hall prompted him to send a gift of £10 for the family of 14 children.

Hardy
Mate on the *Greyhound* and Captain of the *Brownlow* when Newton was mate of this ship in 1748.

Selina Hastings, Countess of Huntingdon 1707-1791
Wife of Theophilus, 9th Earl of Huntingdon, daughter of Washington Shirley. Converted through her sister-in-law Lady Margaret Huntingdon, Selina became a tireless and generous worker, the founder of Lady Huntingdon's Connexion. She was a member of the first methodist society in Fetter Lane in 1739. Horace Walpole nicknamed her St. Teresa of the Methodists. When evangelical preachers were denied access to the Established Church she invited them to her chapels and drawing rooms. George Whitefield preached often for her. She supported itinerant preachers, establishing Trevecca

College for their training. Haweis was her chaplain. He described her as "one of the poor who lived on her own bounty."

Thomas Haweis 1734-1820
Curate to Martin Madan at the Lock, he was offered the curacy of Olney but suggested Newton instead. He was converted through Walker of Truro. He read Newton's biographical letters to John Fawcett and asked him to write more fully to him on the same topic. These letters became Newton's *Narrative*, edited by Haweis. When Haweis became rector of Aldwinkle in 1764 Newton wrote to Clunie, "His preaching, like the report of a cannon, has already sounded through the whole country adjacent. May the Lord make him abundantly useful." Jay considered him to be the first man in the South Sea Mission. He had tried to prepare and send out two young missionaries to Otaheite, based on accounts published by Captain Bligh and other navigators. He was let down by them, but became a director and staunch supporter of the London Missionary Society. On the day he died, one of the first missionaries sent to Otaheite was expected in Bath. Haweis sent repeatedly to Jay, begging that if the missionary arrived he would bring him immediately. He came just in time, leaving Dr. Haweis "like the expiring Simeon, saying, with tears, 'Now, Lord, lettest thou thy servant depart in peace.'"

William Hayley 1745-1820
Hayley had been preparing his *Life of Milton* when he discovered that Cowper was translating and editing Milton's Poetical Works. Shocked at hearing that he had been called "an antagonist of Cowper" in a newspaper article, he immediately wrote to Cowper offering his assistance and enclosing a complimentary sonnet. Cowper was delighted by the gesture, regarding himself as merely "an unknown author", and a firm friendship developed between them. Hayley subsequently became Cowper's biographer.

Samuel Hayward 1718-1757
Pastor of Potter's Pury, Northants, in 1740. By 1752 he was at Silver Street, London. Newton went to his casuistical lectures on cases of conscience at Little St Helen's on Clunie's recommendation. Hayward was Congregational minister of Silver Street. Subscribers to his *17 Sermons on Various Important Subjects* included Brewer, Jones, Jennings, and Whitefield.

He met with Presbyterians, Baptists and Congregationalists in the Body of Protestant Dissenting Ministers of the Three Denominations in and about the City of London and Westminster (from 1736 they were able to meet in the attic room of Dr Williams's Library). This group approached Pitt in their concern for keeping the Sabbath. Although Pitt personally disagreed with them, they were responsible for his changing a clause in the Militia Bill from "Sunday" to "possibly Sunday", which resulted in the exercises being conducted on a Monday instead. The group was renamed one common denomination of Protestant Dissenting Ministers in 1761.

(The minute book, in three volumes, gives a detailed list of ministers, churches and addresses for the period 1727 to 1827 and would be a most interesting record to have transcribed. Many of the names are of people mentioned in Newton's letters or his wife's letters.)

George Herbert 1593-1633
A favourite poet of Newton's. His chief work, *The Temple*, was read by Charles I in prison. Hymns of his still commonly used are *Teach me my God and King*, *The God of love my Shepherd is*, *Let all the world in every corner sing* and *King of glory, King of peace, I will praise Thee*.

William Herbert 1772-1851
Born in Worship Street, Shoreditch. His mother took him to see the execution of those responsible for pulling down the chapel in Ropemaker's Alley in 1780 [the year of the Gordon Riots], to show him the "consequences of joining mobs of wicked persons". His father, John Wilderspin, was a member of Whitefield's Tabernacle. A clockmaker, John was working as a Smith and Bell Hanger in Long Alley when he met with a fatal accident. Although many from the Tabernacle came to visit his dying father, the one who kept an eye on William and his mother after his death was "one John Newton of Charles Square". With the money he earned from running errands for the Newtons and others he gradually bought himself a "boys' library", groundwork for his later career as first Librarian of the Guildhall (1828-45). Newton helped provide him with employment several times throughout his youth, which Herbert gratefully acknowledged to be the source of his later success in life. His widowed mother had the use of a small house with an outside shop owned by

a strict Whitefieldite, Woodderoffe, the shoemaker, who repaired the shoes of the boys of the Haberdasher's School. She later kept the *Bell Inn*, which Fielding mentions in *Tom Jones*. Herbert's biography was recently written by one of his Guildhall Librarian successors Donovan Dawe, completed on his death by Deputy Librarian Tim Padwick.

James Hervey 1714 -1758
Rector of Weston Favell and Collingtree. He was with Whitefield, Ingham and the Wesleys in Oxford where he joined their methodistic way of life, though with little understanding of gospel truths. John Wesley was his tutor. Early in his ministry he had a discussion with a ploughman which deeply affected him. Hervey suggested to him that the hardest thing in life was to deny *sinful* self. The ploughman, who attended Philip Doddridge's church, replied that the hardest thing was to deny *righteous* self, "I mean, to renounce my own strength and righteousness, and not to lean on that for holiness or rely on this for justification." Hervey thought him an old fool, but was later to admit, "I have since seen clearly who was the fool; not the wise old ploughman, but the proud James Hervey." He became best known for his clear teaching on justification by faith in the imputed righteousness of Christ, communicated particularly well in *Theron and Aspasio*, dialogues and letters between two fictitious characters. His *Meditations and Contemplations* was also very popular. *Meditations among the Tombs* was inspired by a ride to Kilkhampton in Cornwall.

Richard Cecil described him as considerate, gentle, earnest, heavenly and an enlightened teacher who drew people's attention to the truth. Cowper thought him one of the most scriptural writers in the world.

In his funeral sermon for Hervey, William Romaine spoke much of Hervey's heart-love for God, which made him speak often of his Saviour and take great care in pastoring his flock both spiritually and practically. "Drinking tea with him was like being at an ordinance: for it was sanctified by the word of God and by prayer.

"Mr. Hervey walked very close after Christ. I never saw one who came up so near to the scripture character of a Christian. God had enriched him with great gifts, and with great graces, and had made him humble: for he was humbled by the power of grace. He had some very sharp trials of his faith and patience both from God and from men, and he learned obedience by the things which he suffered."

Lady Harriet Hesketh (née Cowper) 1733-1807

Cowper's cousin, sister of Theodora Cowper. She married Sir Thomas Hesketh, who died in 1778. She visited Cowper often in Olney and at Weston Underwood. When Cowper's friend and biographer William Hayley was due to visit him at Weston, she sent him a warning note, "You must be very guarded in what you say." Cowper was upset that Hayley was only coming for 3 or 4 days. "Did he intend to do me good, would he have named so short a time? What good can he do me in 3 or 4 days? Had he said 3 or 4 weeks I might have believed he meant me well.... Could a friend who loved me think 14 days a long period for my life?" After Cowper's death, she was distressed that some of her correspondence might be published by Hayley, not wanting the public to know details of her cousin's state of mind. Hayley wrote in his personal notes [Cowper and Newton Museum], "Send down good Heaven a double portion of patience to those disquieted biographers who in the course of their work are embarrassed with unreasonable requests, especially when post after post produces for them a variety of unexpected vexation.... Surely my dear Lady you must have misinterpreted what I said to you on the latter collections of letters with which you favoured me."

Samuel Greatheed asked her permission to print his funeral sermon for Cowper, offering to inscribe it to her. Having agreed, she later relented, writing to Newton in great distress. His own sermon on Cowper was never published.

Her opinion on Cowper's declining health was that "eternal praying and preaching were too much" for him and that "they might have made a better use of a fine summer's evening than by shutting themselves up to make long prayers."

Benjamin Ingham 1712-1772

Ingham was at Oxford with the Wesleys, Whitefield and Hervey, and accompanied the Wesleys to Georgia. He later joined the Moravians. In 1741 he married Lady Margaret Hastings (through whom Countess Selina Hastings was converted). He was based at the Moravian settlement at Fulneck and was greatly used in spreading the gospel in Yorkshire. Newton preached for him. Ingham later separated from the Moravians, through the Countess of Huntingdon's influence, who considered him a "bishop". Newton made some interesting comments on the Moravians, in a letter to Campbell: 'I am glad you have at last seen a Moravian brother. They are in general so much alike, that one may be taken as a specimen of many. They have a few peculiarities, resulting from their church constitution; but, as a body, I consider them as the most exemplary, peaceful, and spiritual society of all that bear the Christian name. Their grand object, and in which their excellence is most signally displayed, is the conversion of the heathen. In this branch, without noise of notice, they have done more in promoting the knowledge of the true gospel, in about fifty years, than has been done by all Christendom in fifteen hundred years before them. God has given them the true missionary spirit, and I think, excepting Mr. Brainerd, and two or three more in North America, they have hitherto had a monopoly of it, though Mr. Carey, the Baptist missionary in Bengal, is, I hope, treading in their steps. Their patience, fortitude, self-denial, perseverance, courage, holy wisdom and their success, would be astonishing, did we not know whose they are, and whom they serve."

James Janeway d. 1674
Independent Minister at Rotherhithe, London. He was the son of Alexander, a Scotsman, whose two books caused him much suffering. *Zion's Plea, or an Appeal to Parliament*, drew the wrath of Bishop Laud. Alexander was condemned in the Star-chamber to have his ears cut and his nose slit, and was imprisoned for eleven years. James also suffered persecution for his faith. His church in Rotherhithe was attacked and he was shot at by soldiers. Bennett's *Christian Oratory* arose from shared devotions with Janeway. Janeway's *Token for Children* was very popular – Newton sent for copies when he began his children's meetings in Olney.

William Jay 1769-1853
Pastor of Argyle Independent Chapel, Bath, from 1791. John Thornton contributed to his academic fees at Marlborough Academy. He began preaching soon after the age of sixteen, invited by Rowland Hill to preach at Surrey Chapel in 1788 for a season, returning annually. In London John Ryland senior became a friend, as did John Newton. He moved elsewhere, but writes, "I never felt that I was where I *ought* to be, or was likely to remain, till I became, as a preacher, an

inhabitant of Bath; but from that time I said, 'This is my destination, whatever be its duties or trials.'" He remained there for sixty-two years, preaching up to the age of 84. The whole period of his ministry stretched from Wesley through to Spurgeon.

Of Newton, he says, "There was nothing about him dull, or gloomy, or puritanical, according to the common meaning of the term. As he had much good-nature, so he had much pleasantry, and frequently emitted sparks of lively wit, or rather humour; yet they never affected the comfort or reputation of anyone, but were perfectly innocent and harmless. Sometimes he had the strangest fetches of drollery.... When I asked him how he slept, he instantly replied, 'I'm like a beef-steak – once turned, and I'm done.'

"I recollect a little sailor-boy calling upon him, with his father. Mr. Newton soon noticed him, and, taking him between his knees, he told him he had been much at sea himself, and then sang part of a naval song."

Jay would sometimes visit the church in Olney and study his sermon in the pew where Cowper heard [now in the Cowper and Newton Museum], and in sight of the pulpit where Newton preached [kept in St. Peter and St. Paul's Church, Olney]. "'Superstition!' say some. But I found it good to be there. And how I was struck, when at the parsonage house I went up into the attic, which was the study of this man of God, and saw, over his desk, on the wall, in very large letters, *Remember that thou wast a bondman in the land of Egypt, and the Lord thy God redeemed thee*; and *Since thou hast been precious in my sight thou hast been honourable, and I have loved thee*; and – *Unus Pro omnibus!*"

Jay found great refreshment and benefit at the end of each Sunday to have one of Newton's letters [from *Cardiphonia*] read to him.

David Jennings 1691-1762

Pastor of the Independent Meeting at Old Gravel Lane, Wapping New Stairs. He was particularly noted for his ability to communicate clearly and simply. Newton's mother, Elizabeth, was a member of his church and John was baptised there. Jennings was a close friend of fellow pastors Isaac Watts and Samuel Brewer. His brother John, [d. 1723] started a nonconformist academy where one of his first pupils was Philip Doddridge, who also became a close friend of David's. Newton regarded Jennings as a spiritual father and corresponded with him regularly after his conversion. An anonymous picture of "Dr. Jennings's Meeting House", about 1796, can be seen in the Guildhall Art Gallery's Collage at www.cityoflondon.gov.uk (as Record: 23497).

John Johnson 1706-1791

Called to pastor the Baptist Church in Byrom Street, Liverpool, in 1741, moving on to Stanley Street after a split in 1750. Newton attended this church on his arrival in 1755 as Tide Surveyor. Whitefield tactfully suggested Newton might benefit from hearing another Baptist, John Oulton. Haykin, quoting from *Our Heritage*, says, "Johnson has recently been described as 'basically a prickly hyper-Calvinist with a taste for travel, theological hair-splitting and provoking strife'; everything which he touched was 'soon seething with controversy'." His followers were known as Johnsonian Baptists.

Johnny Johnson d. 1833

William Cowper's cousin, Rector in the parish of East Dereham, Norfolk. Cowper and Mary Unwin spent their final days under his care.

Joseph Johnson 1738-1809

William Cowper's publisher and bookseller. Cautioning Newton in his "obstetrical assistance" in delivering some copy to Johnson, Cowper explained that, while he was unaware whether Johnson deserved his suspicion, he had previously had experience of another printer who had taken the liberty of mingling with Cowper's lines some of his own, being "at the same time as illiterate a blockhead as ever presumed to tread upon a poor poet's toe". Johnson fared better, for in 1793 Cowper wrote to a friend, "I am now satisfied with my bookseller, as I have substantial cause to be, and account myself in good hands."

Richard Johnson 1753-1827

Served his second curacy as the assistant of Henry Foster. He was appointed Chaplain to Botany Bay (or, as Newton regarded him, Bishop of New Holland), accompanying the first settlement of convicts to New South Wales in 1786. His appointment was achieved through the efforts of Wilberforce and John Thornton, who approached Pitt as the first fleet was on the point of sailing. His departure prompted Newton to write these lines to William Bull:

Go, bear the Saviour's name to lands unknown,
Tell to the southern world His wondrous grace;
An energy divine thy words shall own,
And draw their untaught hearts to seek His face.

Many in quest of gold and empty fame
Would compass earth, or venture near the poles;
But how much nobler thy reward and aim
To spread His praise and win immortal souls.

Sally Johnson

One of Newton's servants. Letters to her, filled with encouragement, advice and cautions, were published in *Cardiphonia*. "How often have I longed to be an instrument of establishing you in the peace and hope of the Gospel!" he wrote, "and I have but one way of attempting it, by telling you over and over of the power and grace of Jesus.... Put your trust in Him; believe (as we say) through thick and thin, in defiance of all objections from within and without." She generally accompanied Mary to Chatham.

Samuel Johnson 1709-1784

Dr. Johnson, who compiled the English Dictionary of 1755, and whose writings included the *Rambler* and the *Idler*; his friend Boswell wrote his *Life*. Johnson feared death. In his last years he spoke especially with the Moravian, Benjamin La Trobe [1728-1786] of Fetter Lane about eternity. Before he died he professed faith in Christ. Cowper and Newton each wrote an epitaph for him:

Henceforth I shall *Ramble* and *Idle* no more,
My versing and prosing and printing are o'er;
With joy I have quitted my critical throne
For a bed in the dust and a burial stone;
My studies are ended, the last was the best
That taught me a Saviour, and sent me to rest.   [*Cowper*]

The scholar, genius, author, here
Finished his long adorned career.
But when the man resigned his breath
The Christian triumphed over death.
What once he was his writings show,
What now he is, immortals know.   [*Newton*]

Thomas Jones   1729-1762
Converted through Madan and Romaine in 1754. Rector of St.
Saviour's, Southwark. For several years he was the only beneficed
evangelical clergyman in the entire London area. He preached in the
Countess of Huntingdon's Park Street residence. She wrote of him,
"Dear Mr. Jones lived happily and died rejoicing. He was long the
subject of affliction, and often at death's door; but he was refined in
the furnace of affliction, and his growth in grace and knowledge of
the Saviour great and remarkable." He died at the age of thirty-three.
His death spurred Newton on in his resolution to enter the ministry,
balanced by Polly's prudent restraints. In *The Works of the Rev.
Thomas Jones* there is an account of his life in the preface by William
Romaine.

Thomas Jones   1747?-1817
Jones was a hairdresser. When he decided to enter the ministry
Newton invited him to their home at Olney and gave him tuition in
Greek and Hebrew. He went on from there to Oxford. While there he
wrote urgently to Newton about objections being made to Newton's
sermons and against preaching Christ, receiving a rapid reply from
him, "In the first place, I beg you to be upon your guard against a
reasoning spirit. Search the Scriptures; and where you can find a
plain rule or warrant for any practice, go boldly on; and do not be
discouraged because you may not be clearly able to answer or
reconcile every difficulty that may either occur to your own mind, or
be put in your way by others.... I advise you to keep close to the
Bible and prayer; bring your difficulties to the Lord, and entreat him
to give you, and maintain in you, a simple spirit." Newton directed
him to Owen's exposition of Psalm 130 for further help. But he was
expelled from St. Edmund Hall, as one of the Oxford six, for holding
methodistical tenets. After his expulsion, Lady Huntingdon took up
his cause. He was ordained and became curate of Clifton Reynes, a
short walk alongside the river and over the hill from Olney. He married
Lady Austin's sister, a relative of Cowper's.

John Jowett   1743-1800
John was a friend of Newton's. He frequently walked from Leeds to
Huddersfield to hear Henry Venn preach. When he moved to London
he became a member of the Eclectic Society and a founder member

of the CMS. His daughter Elizabeth married Josiah Pratt. His youngest son William succeeded John Venn at Clapham, later volunteering as a missionary with the CMS. His daughter Hannah was present at Newton's funeral sermon for Cowper and wrote notes of it (now kept by the Cowper and Newton Museum – see Appendix 6).

Benjamin La Trobe 1728-1786

An ardent follower of John Cennick, he entered the Moravian church, taking charge of a settlement at Fulneck in Yorkshire. He was introduced to Newton by Joseph Foster Barham of Bedford. After the Moravian leader Count Zinzendorf's death, La Trobe was appointed leader of the British Moravians. He moved to London where he became pastor of Fetter Lane, where the family lived at number 32. He was a popular preacher, invited to preach, for, amongst others, the Baptists, Methodists and the Bible Society. He was chosen to be a member of the Eclectic Society in 1783. In his dying moments Samuel Johnson sent urgently for him and was said to have been converted through La Trobe's ministry. In his own will, La Trobe asked that "there may be none of the signs of dismal and dark mourning at my burial. Nor let my family go into mourning, but though they may weep for a friend, let them rejoice that that friend is promoted to the highest pitch of honour and happiness."

William Law 1686-1761

Law's *Serious Call* was used to encourage many to a deeper faith, including Whitefield and the Wesleys at Oxford. Newton appreciated his work at first but this changed with Law's increasing mysticism.

Richard Lea d. 1828

A weaver, alderman of Coleman Street Ward, who supplied his carriage to take the elderly Newton to church. Lea was a member of the first committee of the British and Foreign Bible Society. His son-in-law, Warren Stormes Hale, Lord Mayor of London, was the chief founder of the City of London School.

Job Lewis d. 1754

Lewis sailed with Newton as a midshipman on HMS *Harwich*. Newton hoped to do him some good by taking him on board *The African* in 1752. He is entered in the Ship's Muster in Newton's Log

Book as 'Captain Job Lewis, Volunteer & Captain's Commander', but Lewis was such an impediment that Newton eventually bought and supplied a separate ship for him. A few days later, Lewis caught fever and died.

Zachary Macaulay 1768-1838

One of the Clapham Sect, Zachary managed an estate in Jamaica, where he became concerned about the conditions of the slaves. He went to Sierra Leone at the age of twenty-four to oppose free labour. Settling in England as Secretary to the Sierra Leone Company, he lived in High Street, Clapham. He initiated *The Christian Observer*, which brought the issues of slavery to light. He was Secretary to the African Institute and helped to form the Anti-Slavery Society. He was on the first committee of the British and Foreign Bible Society. His son was Lord Macaulay [1800-1859], author of *Macaulay's History* and tireless worker for the public in India. (A great talker from his youth – at the age of four he replied to a lady who offered her condolences when hot coffee was spilt on his leg, "Thank you, madam, the agony is abated.")

McCraig

Newton and McCraig were in charge of Williams's factory at Boom Kittam. It was McCraig who signalled the passing ship which took Newton back to England.

Peter Mackdonald d. 1752

Ordinary seaman on *The African* in 1752. One of the crew who had planned a mutiny, he was taken ill, the delay of the ship leading to the discovery of his plot. He died of this illness two days later.

Judith Madan (née Cowper) 1702-1781

Daughter of Judge Spencer Cowper, she was William Cowper's aunt and the mother of Martin. Wesley responded to her urgent request to visit her seriously ill husband, setting out in the frost and snow to meet the need. Major Cowper was led from deism to faith. He died four years later in 1756. There is a review of Judith Madan's devotional poems in the *Evangelical Magazine*, vol. 1, p.84, and some of them are in *Poems of Eminent Ladies*, 1755. Cowper corresponded with her about their search for somewhere to move from Huntingdon and his gratitude for Newton's interest and practical concern in looking for a house for himself and Mrs. Unwin, "The Lord seems to have filled the hearts of Mr. and Mrs. Newton with Christian tenderness and affection towards us." When they arrived in Olney to spend their first five months at the vicarage until their own accommodation was ready, he added, "Nothing can exceed the kindness and hospitality with which we were received here by His dear servant Newton, and to be brought under the ministry of so wise and faithful a steward of His holy mysteries is a blessing for which I can never be sufficiently thankful." He wrote to tell his aunt about the conversion of his servants and the trauma he went through to start up the custom of family prayers with them.

When Cowper became so ill in 1773, it was to this relation that Newton wrote with his suggestion that medical intervention was needed for his serious condition. She replied, "Nor can I be insensible of what yourself, Mrs. Newton, and Mrs. Unwin must suffer in your attention to him – may every comfort you are enabled to give, be returned in multiplied blessings on your own souls!"

Martin Madan 1726-1790
Cowper's cousin, who had tried to lead him into faith during his state of conflict over his post at the House of Lords. As an unbeliever, Madan was with some of his friends in a coffee-house when they challenged him to go and hear John Wesley preaching nearby, "and then to return and exhibit his *manner* and *discourse* for their entertainment. He went with that intention, and just as he entered the place, Mr. Wesley named his text, 'Prepare to meet thy God!' with a solemnity of accent which struck him, and which inspired a seriousness that increased as the minister proceeded. He returned to the coffee-room, and was asked by his acquaintances, if he had 'taken off the old Methodist.' To which he answered, 'No, gentlemen, but he has taken me off.'"

From a legal background, he became the first chaplain to the Lock Hospital. Newton was very grateful for his hospitality in London while arranging the Olney curacy. He wrote to his wife, "I cannot say enough of Mr. Madan's kindness, nor of the great satisfaction I take in him as a minister and a Christian ... in the midst of affluence, success and esteem, [he] is simple and humble as a child.... The eminent Christian shines in Madan."

Madan wrote several hymns, including having a share in *Hark the Herald Angels sing*, and is also credited with having written the last two verses of *Lo, He comes with clouds descending,* at Charles Wesley's request.

Concerned over the predicament of the prostitutes in the Lock Hospital, Madan decided that a solution would be to advocate polygamy and wrote his arguments for this in a book entitled *Thelyphthora.* It caused great consternation amongst Christians. Many tried to prevent him from going into print. Lady Huntingdon had 3,000 signatures against it and, when that failed, offered to buy up remaining copies if he would print no more. But Madan continued. The book was published and much damage done by it. Newton had tried unsuccessfully to intervene, and was very saddened by the events. He wrote to Bull, "I feel a sort of trembling for its appearance. Much has been attempted to prevent its coming abroad, but in vain." He destroyed his correspondence with Madan over this.

Martin's younger brother, Spencer [1729-1813] was successively Bishop of Bristol and Bishop of Peterborough.

Joseph Manesty d. 1771
Captain John Newton's friend in Liverpool, who assumed a fatherly role over Newton in securing his rescue from Sierra Leone and supplying him with employment at sea for several years. He was a Town Clerk. His company went bankrupt in 1766, which resulted in the loss of all Newton's savings. His daughter was converted in 1772 while staying with Newton in Olney. The Diocese of Liverpool's "Church House" in Hanover Street and Radio Merseyside in Paradise Street both back on to Manesty Lane, where the Manestys lived. Their garden was renowned for its lavender bushes. Newton stayed with the Manestys when he first arrived in Liverpool as Surveyor of Tides (the Albert Dock's Museum of Life is virtually on the site of his office) and would often have visited their home during the years he worked there.

Henry Martyn 1781-1812
Curate to Charles Simeon at Holy Trinity in Cambridge, chaplain in Bengal, translated scriptures into Hindustani, Persian and Judaeo-Persic. When Martyn arrived in Calcutta in 1806, Buchanan and David Brown were away. "With Carey I breakfasted," wrote Martyn in his Journal, "and joined him in worship, which was in Bengali for the

advantage of a few servants." (It was Brown who had the original idea for a Church Mission for Bengal; he draughted a scheme which he sent home to the Revs. N&S – Newton and Simeon – which was the beginning of the CMS.)

John Mason 1646?-1694
Rector of Water Stratford, Buckinghamshire. He was one of the earliest writers of hymns used in congregational worship. Newton used his children's *Catechism* at Olney. Mason developed strong views on the millennium, believing it would start at Water Stratford.

Vice-Admiral Henry Medley d. 1747
Captain Newton unsuccessfully appealed to him for John's release from HMS *Harwich*.

Charles Middleton (Admiral Lord Barham) 1726-1813
Captain Sir Charles was an ardent supporter of the Moravian missions. He worked closely with Wilberforce in the abolition of the slave trade, encouraging him to take up the cause in the Commons. They also promoted missionary causes together. Pitt appointed Sir Charles First Lord of the Admiralty, Lord Barham, in 1805. Middleton asked Wilberforce for prayer support. The very next day the French entered the Atlantic. Middleton's quick responses earned him recognition as the architect of Lord Nelson's victories.

Isaac Milner 1750-1820
Brother of Joseph Milner, President of Queen's College, Cambridge, Dean of Carlisle. William Wilberforce travelled with him to Europe and was converted through their reading together Doddridge's *Rise and Progress*.

Joseph Milner 1744-1797
Brother of Isaac Milner, headmaster at Hull Grammar School, vicar of North Ferriby. He and Isaac visited Newton at Olney in July 1773. The preface to his *Church History* states, "The volume of Mr. Newton is well known [his *Review*], and its merit has been acknowledged by men of piety and judgement. I once thought of beginning only where he ended. But as there is an unity of manner and style which belongs to every author who plans and executes for himself; and, as in some

points I really found myself to differ in sentiment from this very respectable writer, I altered my opinion, contented in this place to acknowledge, that, so far as I can recollect, the perusal of his instructive volume of *Ecclesiastical History* first suggested to me the idea of this work."

James Moody 1756-1806
Pastor of Brook Street (originally called Cow Lane) Independent Church, Warwick, where Newton began his ministry. Moody's mother had taken him to hear Romaine and he was also helped by Alleine's *Alarm to the Unconverted*. He had the offer of two churches, but embarrassingly lost his sermon notes when members of the larger church in the North came to hear him preach, so they took back a bad report. His congregation in Brook Street grew from about 20 members in 1781 to 5 or 6,000 hearers in 1798. Warwickshire County Records Office has two documents by James Moody: one lists the Scripture Doctrine headings he delivered at Brook Street on 16th April 1788; the other is signed by himself and all the members "of the Church of Christ called Independents meeting together in Cow Lane, Warwick" in 1790, renewing their covenant to resign themselves wholly to Christ. A plaque in his memory was placed on the wall next to the pulpit, commending his zeal, simplicity, faithfulness and diligence both in public and private life. The tablet was presented by his friend John Bacon, the sculptor. The first meeting connected with the LMS took place in his home.

Hannah More 1745-1833
Referred to as both Mrs. More and Miss More. A writer, she associated with celebrities such as the actor Garrick and Dr. Johnson. Her spiritual growth was gradual. She was particularly concerned for the poor and started Sunday Schools in Cheddar. The popularity of a tract of hers, as "a substitute for the poor, licentious, and injurious trash found on stalls", inspired a series, *Cheap Repository Tracts*, which led in turn to the formation of The Religious Tract Society.

She was very impressed with Newton's *Cardiphonia*, and began a correspondence with him. They met at the home of Sir Charles Middleton. He visited her in Cowslip Green and preached to the children in her Sunday School. She wrote to him afterwards, "Your pipe still maintains its station in the blackcurrant tree, and that hand would be deemed very presumptuous and disrespectful which should presume to displace it.... And even the little sick maid Lizzy, who gratefully remembers the spiritual comfort you administered to her, often cries out, 'Oh dear! I hope nobody will break Mr. Newton's pipe!'"

After commenting on his own age and health, one of Newton's letters continued to her, "If Miss Patty [her sister] and you had sinews of brass and nerves of steel, the exertions the Lord enables you to make in his service would be less wonderful. But that he should enable two such delicate frames to traverse mountains and valleys affords a more striking proof that the work and the power are his own."

He assured her of his prayers, "I frequently look for you on a Sunday morning somewhere about Mendip or Shipham."

Jay says, "She was perfectly free from all direct and indirect attempts at display, so that no-one in the company was terrified into silence by a profusion of talent, but each was rather encouraged to speak." She spent her winters in Bath where she broke with her Episcopalian views to attend Argyle Chapel to receive William Jay's teaching. One Sunday morning she actually stayed on for communion with the dissenters, but years later applied to Jay for "a kind of certificate that she had only received the communion in Argyle Chapel *once*", hastening to add that it was to establish the truth of her statements to others that it had been a *single* event, whereas some charged her with the thing as *common* practice.

Of her books, one of her classics is *The Spirit of Prayer*. Although she was dying, she found a way to edit it by getting her friends to read extracts of all her works to her, from which she made selections of portions on prayer for this collection.

Cardinal John Henry Newman 1801-1890
When he was at Oxford, training for the Anglican ministry, Newman found Thomas Scott's essays so enlightening that he felt he owed his soul to him. His later conflict on leaving the Established Church for Rome prompted from him the hymn, *Lead kindly light*, which he wrote in a fever on board an orange-boat in the Mediterranean. In 1845 he was received into the Roman Catholic Church, in which he was created a Cardinal in 1879. It was as a Catholic that he wrote so highly of Scott's views of Scripture in his *Apologia*, published in 1864.

Ann Newton (née Manby) 1740-1812

Ann's family lived in Hayton, Yorkshire, where she and Harry were married in 1765. Harry and Ann (Nancy) stayed a while with John and Mary in 1782 when they were in Charles Square. This was the first time that Newton had met his sister-in-law, though from her letters he judged that she had "some spiritual desires". In her Will Ann left the four acres of land in Shipton, near Market Weighton, to her great niece Ann Newton Foster, daughter of James the butcher.

Elizabeth Newton (née Seatliffe) 1705-1732

Wife of Captain John Newton and mother of John. She was born in Chatham, baptised at St. Mary's. Related to Elizabeth (née Churchill) Catlett, whose daughter Mary (Polly) John married. Elizabeth taught John to read and write. She attended David Jennings's Independent church in Old Gravel Lane and prayed much for her son. She died when he was six, but her prayers for him were answered above all that she could have known or asked for at the time.

It seems probable from church records that Elizabeth's maiden name was Seatliffe. St. Mary-le-bow Church records have the entry of the marriage between a John Newton and an Elizabeth Seatliffe, both of Stepney, on 24 September 1724, the year before John was born. At the time this was the Parish Church for Stepney, which included Wapping (St. John's Wapping was still a chapel). Elizabeth's friends from Chatham, the Catletts, were also married in this London Church, a few years later (Elizabeth died in the Catletts' home and was buried at St. Mary's, Chatham).

Land Tax records for Wapping show a Daniel Seatliffe, mathematical instrument maker, living in Green Bank, between Meeting House Alley and Queen's Head Alley, round the corner from John Newton, mariner, Red Lyon Street, in 1730 and 1731, but not in 1732, which was the year of Elizabeth's death while the Captain was at sea. This Daniel had a son, also named Daniel, in 1727. From another branch of the Wapping Seatliff[e] family, Samuel, spectacle maker, had a daughter Hannah in 1734. All were members of David Jenning's church, to which Elizabeth belonged. Newton mentioned both Daniel and Hannah in his letters, referring to Daniel as his friend (and maker of a particular instrument he needed). His reference to Hannah Seatliffe has been misprinted in his *Works* as Scutliff and in Martin as Scatliff (MSS 2936, Lambeth Palace Library).

Perhaps someone researching the Newtons or Wapping families might find the connection between this family and the Churchills.

Harry [Henry] Newton 1740-1797
Newton's half-brother Harry, who served three years with the Royal Navy as 1st Lieutenant on HMS *Lizard* in Boston. He returned home in December 1773, having unsuccessfully attempted to make a seaman out of a young lad whom Thornton had put in his care. Now on half-pay, Harry put John under some pressure to get him employment through his contacts. Newton appealed to Thornton, who introduced him to Lord Dartmouth. Little seemed to come of this, for a couple of years later John had another request to trouble Thornton "upon the subject of his living an idle life upon scanty half-pay". Newton begged Thornton to write to Harry, supposing this would be more convincing "than a seeming put-off from me". He added that he was not unduly worried about Harry's disappointments in life, if only they would make him seek the Lord. "I tell him that if he would begin at the right end, and seek the kingdom of God and his righteousness in the first place, he would certainly be either made easy in his present situation, or provided with better. But he looks upon such advice to be but cold comfort... I had rather he should be a believer in a workhouse, than an Admiral, to go in the ways of sin." Harry became resident Agent to HM Royal Transports in Leith, Edinburgh.

Sir Isaac Newton 1642-1727
The natural philosopher, mathematical and scientific inventor. No known relation of John's.

Captain John Newton d. 1750
The father of the Rev. John Newton. His first wife was Elizabeth, mother of John. Shortly after Elizabeth's death he married Thomasina, by whom he had two sons, William and Henry, and a daughter, Thomasina. Records also show the birth of James and Thomas, who presumably died prematurely as there seems no further mention of them. He worked for the East India Company in Mediterranean service as Captain of the *Hind* and later for the Royal Africa Company before leaving England to become Governor of York Fort in Hudson Bay. Just a few days before he was due to return he drowned while bathing.

The accident is recorded in the *Dictionary of Canadian Biography*: "On 28 June 1750 Samuel Skrimsher recorded in the York journals: 'the water being Clear and Smooth he [Newton] had a mind to Treat his Selfe with a Swim.' His men soon saw him in distress and rushed to his assistance 'but poor Gentel Man Never apering the Second time Renderd our indeavers on Servesable.'" By this time John had established a warm relationship with his father, but had never seen him again since leaving England in HMS *Harwich*.

John Newton 1725-1807

Son of John and Elizabeth. Born in Wapping, baptised at Old Gravel Lane Independent Church, he spent two years at a private boarding school in Stratford, Essex, before following his father into a career at sea. Initially this was across the Mediterranean in merchant ships, but he was impressed and taken aboard a Man-of-War, eventually transferred to a Guinea ship from which he went into the service of a trader at Sierra Leone. He became a slave himself, living under oppressive conditions. His father arranged for his rescue. On his return voyage a storm at sea made him cry out to God for mercy. He returned home a believer, though it was several years before he found clarity in this. He married his childhood sweetheart Polly (Mary Catlett) and continued a career in the slave trade. When illness necessitated his leaving the sea, he took on work as Surveyor of Tides at Liverpool, where his desire to enter the ministry grew stronger. He patiently awaited an entrance into the Established Church, first at Olney, and then in London at St. Mary Woolnoth's. His deeply spiritual and practical teaching, writing and wise counsel were of great value to Christians of all denominations. A man of great spiritual stature, his humility, warmth and sincerity won him a place in the hearts of many and spurred them on to deeper faith and action. His obituary in *The Times* stated, "His unblemished life, his amiable character, both as a man and as a Minister, and his able writings, are too well known to need any comment."

In his own words, "My history is briefly expressed in Deuteronomy 32:10 and in Isaiah 42:16. He found me in a howling wilderness indeed! He has led me about into a variety of situations, and in them all He watched over me, and kept me as the apple of his eye. When I was blind, He led me in ways which I knew not, and which no mortal could have supposed were likely to bring me where I am. I was once an utter stranger to the paths of truth and righteousness, but in a wonderful manner He drew and guided me into those paths which I had not known; and though my heart is prone to wander, He has kept me with a high hand, so that I have not wholly declined from them. How often has He made darkness light before me, and crooked things straight! These things has He done for me, as I am encouraged to hope He will continue to do them, for His promise is, 'I will not forsake them!'"

Mary (Polly) Newton (née Catlett) 1729-1790

Eldest daughter of George and Elizabeth Catlett. She was married to John at St. Margaret's church in Rochester, Kent, on 12 February 1750. They were devoted to each other. It was difficult for them to be separated so much, both when he was at sea and later when she was sometimes needed at her father's home in Chatham.

She wrote from there, "My dearest dear, Ten weeks, 70 nights, 3 days since I saw you and the pleasantest half hour I have had was in dreaming I was with you the other night.... Your dear letter today gave me great pleasure as indeed every one does. But my heart went pit a pat lest you should go to Yorkshire.... I am so selfish, I like to have as much of your company as I can.... You must not mind if I write peevish. Perhaps I shall be better next time I write but I meet with so many disappointments, that I know not how to behave as I ought. If I could look to the Lord every thing would be well."

She mentioned the preachers she heard in London and the texts they spoke from. Interspersed are practical queries about the home in her absence, "Has Richard taken care of my garden or not? I am afraid my geraniums, auriculas and carnations are rotted with the snow, but it cannot be helped." Then there are prayers for him, "The Lord bless and grant you a good day tomorrow. May your own soul be abundantly watered and may you be enabled to declare the whole counsel of God."

She described to him one of her trips home, "At St. Alban's we got a dish of coffee which refreshed and strengthened us for the trial of a very, very drunken postillion. You would have thought he had served his time at Astley the famous man at London and that he was practising his surprising feats of horsemanship all the way. But to be serious I knew the Lord could take care of us and I did hope He would, though to outward appearance we were in a very dangerous situation. I thought of that text, *but mine eyes are unto Thee*, though cannot say I felt it heartily as I ought. The Lord grant me more heart felt experience of that and every precious text from the word of God. We eat cold round of beef and[at?] Woobourn. Got here without the fright or appearance of danger afterward. How has the Lord always kept me – when shall I learn to trust Him? May the Lord preserve my dear sister, give her strength and spirits for her long journey and may we all meet at the end of our great journey at the right hand of God to part no more. I wish she may have no drunken man to drive her to Scotland."

Dr. Thomas Newton 1704-1782
Mentioned here as the Archbishop of York's Chaplain, who referred Newton's application for ordination in 1758 to the secretary, where it was not accepted by Archbishop Gilbert. He held the position of a prebendary of Westminster when Newton met him and was about to be made precentor at York. He later became Bishop of Bristol.

Thomasina Newton d. 1776
Newton's step mother from Aveley, probably since about 1733. Her father was "a substantial grazier" on Moor Hall Farm on the Belhus Estate but their surname has not been established. She remarried after Captain Newton's death, but John disapproved of her husband, of whom he wrote to Polly, "Methinks it was somehow prophetical that we used to call him father, but believe he has forfeited that title with me for the future." (from St. Kitts 23 June 1753)

Thomasina's children by John Newton were William, Henry and Thomasina. Newton wrote to Thornton on 16 July 1776, "Their mother lived many years, without the least thought of religion, never going so much as to a place of worship, except for the birth of a child. Yet the Lord was pleased to call her in his good time, and she died comfortably about 6 weeks ago."

Thomasina Newton (later Nind) 1746 -1814
Newton's half-sister. In his will, Newton refers to "my dear sister Thomasina the wife of Benjamin Nind... my nephew Benjamin Nind... my nephew Henry Nind..." He described her to Thornton as a "truly gracious woman, happily married to an industrious Christian". When conflict with America affected employment in Britain, Newton sought

help for his brother-in-law from Thornton, who replied, "What can be done for Mr. Nind I see not unless he could get employment in the paper way.... Probably Lord Dartmouth could get Mr Nind's son into the Charter House or Blue Coat Hospital." [January 1778]

Thomasina and Benjamin were married at St. Olave's, Old Jewry, London, in 1768. They owned a house in Rye Lane, Peckham. Benjamin came from Overbury, Gloucestershire (now in Worcestershire). They had two sons, Benjamin and Henry Newton, in 1773 and 1776 respectively. Henry Newton Nind married Miss Andrews and had a family in Billericay, Essex. He died leaving five young children. His father passed on "6 volumes of Mr. Newton's *Works*" and "Mr. Scott's *Bible* in 5 volumes" to two of the grandchildren. Benjamin jnr. married Sarah Gardiner and had a son in Peckham, Surrey. Both nephews continued the name of Newton in their families.

Tower Hamlets has documents signed by a Benjamin Nind (of Great Prescott Street) in 1799 and (of 32 Throgmorton Street) in 1821. Benjamin snr. retired to Oldiham, Hampshire.

William Newton b. 1736
Newton's step-brother, born in Aveley the year after John completed his two years' schooling. Newton wrote to John Thornton in 1776 that his brother, "who died a few years ago, I hope died in the faith, though he had been a debauchee and an infidel."

John Oulton 1738-1780
Particular Baptist minister in Liverpool. Newton attended his services at Byrom Street and took part in his mid-week meetings.

John Owen 1616-1683
A leading Puritan non-conformist theologian and pastor, Cromwell's chaplain, Vice-Chancellor of Oxford until ejected, preached at Leadenhall Street – one of his successors in this church was Isaac Watts.

John Owen 1766-1822
One of the first secretaries of the British and Foreign Bible Society. Curate of Fulham, rector of Paglesham, minister of Park Chapel, Chelsea. His daughter married Wilberforce's son William.

Samuel Palmer 1741-1813

Pastor of the Independent Church at Mare Street, Hackney. Palmer
was a member of Bunyan Meeting in Bedford at the same time as
William Bull. He wrote a *Catechism* for Dissenters. Newton's
Apologia was addressed to him. When Palmer dreamt of preaching
in Newton's church, Newton replied that it wouldn't be possible,
adding however, "Were it not for the sake of expediency and
consistency, I would very gladly preach either in your meeting-house,
or under your pear tree, if you asked me; for I believe whenever two
or three meet together in the Saviour's name, to adore Him, and to
praise Him for His great love to sinners, the spot whereon they stand
is, for the time, *Holy Ground.*" In a Funeral Sermon for Newton on 3
January 1808 Palmer gave this testimony of him, "Though he kept
close to the *Rubric* of the Church, and read the Liturgy without
variation or omission (in which his consistency was to be commended)
yet he used extempore prayer before and after his sermons: as also in
his own family, and in the private houses of his friends. – And I can
testify, from a personal knowledge, that herein he discovered both
the gift and the grace of prayer, in a considerable degree; so as to
obviate that common objection against a Liturgy, 'that the use of it
disables a person for praying without it.' I believe few Dissenting
Ministers pray more pertinently or more devoutly than Mr. Newton
did."

George Pattrick 1746-1800

Rector of Aveley 1772-87. A fox-hunting parson, one of his
parishioners told him of Newton, Foster and Cecil. He decided to go
and hear them and found personal faith. He is described as having
had a large congregation and a large opposition. In 1790 he was
dismissed from Morden College, Blackheath for his evangelical
views. He was curate to William Rose, then to Foster. From 1796 he
held the afternoon lectureship of St. Leonard's, Shoreditch, and the
curacy of St. Brides on Sunday evenings. His congregations averaged
1,500 – larger than for any other London church. He was a member
of the Eclectic Society. He lived in Wilderness Row, Clerkenwell.

Guy James Penrose d. 1745

Captain of the Guinea Snow, *Pegasus*. Newton asked to be exchanged
from HMS *Harwich* to the *Pegasus* at Madeira in May 1745,
discovering afterwards that Penrose knew his father. The Captain

treated him kindly but this did not prevent Newton from becoming
more corrupt than he had been on the *Harwich*. He was the humiliated
target of what was Newton's first recorded attempt at composing a
song. It was Penrose's death which prompted Newton to opt for
employment with the trader Clow at Sierra Leone, rather than risk
retribution for his behaviour from the mate, who was assuming
command of the ship.

PI
Mistress of Newton's master Clow in the Plantanes. She disliked
Newton. It was under her heartless treatment that he became a servant
of slaves.

William Pitt [the younger] 1759-1806
Prime Minister, 1st Earl of Chatham. Pitt personally introduced
Newton before the Privy Council when he was called to give evidence
on the slave trade in 1788.

Sir George Pocock 1706-1792
Commodore of HMS *Sutherland*, flagship of the fleet which included
Newton as midshipman on HMS *Harwich*. He was promoted to
Admiral in 1761.

Alexander Pope 1688-1744
Poet. His father [1641-1717] was a linen merchant, living at No. 1
Plough Court, Lombard Street, in Newton's parish of St. Mary
Woolnoth, though before his time.

Josiah Pratt 1768-1844
A member of the Eclectic Society, secretary of the CMS, founder
member of the BFBS. When he began his curacy for Cecil as a shy,
downcast young man, Cecil's advice to him was, "Never mind, Pratt;
make yourself useful, and the time will come when you will be
wanted." He became Newton's curate, then vicar of St. Stephens,
Coleman Street. In reporting the death of Newton, *The Times* of 23
December 1807 dismissed his demise in a single sentence, "His
unblemished life, his amiable character, both as a man and as a
Minister, and his able writings, are too well known to need any
comment." It went on to add, "We understand it to be the almost

unanimous request of the parishioners, that the present Curate and Lecturer, the Rev. Josiah Pratt, should succeed to the living." *The Times* later printed an apology for its "indelicate and obtrusive" hints.

Thomas Ring 1760?-1840
Newton's medical friend in Reading, whom he met through their mutual friend Ambrose Serle. Ring was converted through the ministry of Cadogan. It was largely due to his efforts that St. Mary's chapel and the Royal Berkshire Hospital were founded. It was Ring who provided a country refuge for Eliza Cunningham in the final stages of her illness.

John Rippon 1750-1836
Pastor of the Baptist church at Carter Lane, London and editor of the *Baptist Annual Register*. He chaired the inaugural meeting of the Baptist Union in 1813. Rippon had been a student with Sutcliff in Bristol.

Ralph Robinson 1614-1655
One of Newton's predecessors at St. Mary Woolnoth, he was the author of, *"Christ is All in All* or Several significant similitudes by which the Lord Jesus Christ is described in the holy Scriptures. Being the substance of many sermons preached by that faithful and useful servant of Christ, Ralph Robinson, late pastor of Mary Woolnoth, London, which were appointed by the Reverend Author on his deathbed (if his Brethren should think fit to be published), 1660, the second edition corrected and enlarged." It contains thirty-seven sermons, the first on *Christ is All in All*, others on *The dew of heaven* and other scriptural references to Christ. Robinson was imprisoned for conspiracy but later pardoned.

Thomas Robinson 1749-1813
Vicar of St. Mary's, Leicester. He raised a charity school for boys where he gave instruction. Henry Venn says of him, "For learning, wisdom, grace and humility, he resembles Daniel." William Carey was Baptist pastor in Leicester and it was Robinson who wrote a letter of introduction to Newton for him when Carey needed help in getting to India.

William Romaine 1714-1795

Rector of Blackfriars. For some time the only evangelical preacher in the Established Church. Lecturer of St Botolph's, Billingsgate, St Dunstan's in the West (where the vicar refused him entry into the pulpit and his congregation was obliged to queue in Fleet Street until the exact starting time. Frequently the only light in the building was Romaine's candle – until the Bishop intervened), assistant morning preacher at St. George's, Hanover Square (where he was asked by the vicar to leave after five years, because the regular parishioners were inconvenienced by the crowds), Professor of Astronomy at Gresham College, briefly. He opposed the Bill for removing Jewish disabilities. He was banned from preaching at Oxford University after giving a sermon there on *The Lord our Righteousness*. He became one of Lady Huntingdon's domestic chaplains. Romaine occupied several posts until he was finally chosen rector of St. Anne's, Blackfriars in 1764. He began at St. Anne's with considerable apprehension, "I am frightened to think of watching over two or three thousands, when it is work enough to watch over one." J. C. Ryle considers Romaine's letters to be similar to Newton's – Christ and the Bible being the two common threads. He published an invitation to prayer which Ryle believed led to many such meetings down through the years. When he published this in 1757 he knew only a dozen clergy in the whole of England who were willing to unite with him. When he died, there were at least three hundred, some say more than five hundred. Towards the end of his life, Newton wrote to John Campbell, "I believe the Lord's old and faithful servant, Mr. Romaine, is going home. He is nearly 82 years of age; has been 58 years in the ministry, and was never laid by a single Sabbath till very lately. I have known him as a preacher of the gospel since about the year 1750, and I believe he began sooner. He has been an honourable and useful man, a burning and a shining light – inflexible as an iron pillar in publishing the truth, and unmarked either by the smiles or the frowns of the world. He is the most popular man we have had since Mr. Whitefield; and few now living will be more missed."

Thomas Ruffin

1st Lieutenant Ruffin recorded Saturday 25 February 1743 in his log as a day of uncertain weather developing into rain and strong gales. At 4pm the *Betsy Tender* anchored alongside HMS *Harwich* with "the Men that went a pressing and 8 Imprest Men". It was Newton's introduction to life in the Royal Navy.

Sir William Russel 1735?-1757
Cowper's friend at Westminster, only son of Sir Francis and Ann, whose family home was at Chequers (now the country home of the Prime Minister). William entered Westminster at the age of seven in February 1742/3, leaving in 1747. He was Ensign in the 1st Foot Guards, promoted to Captain in 1755. He died in 1757 while bathing in the Thames. His death affected Cowper deeply.

John Russell 1745-1806
Portrait painter to George III, exhibitor at the Royal Academy, he painted Newton's portrait. It is now held by the Church Mission Society. Russell was a member of Whitfield's Tabernacle.

John Collett Ryland (snr.) 1723-1792
His grandfather, John Ryland, was a member of Hook Norton Baptist Church in Oxfordshire. His father, John Ryland, married Freelove Collett and became a member of the Baptist Church in Bourton on the Water, in the Cotswolds. John Collett Ryland was converted through the pastor, Beddome. He studied at Bristol and was pastor at Warwick Baptist until 1759. The Rylands ministered at College Lane, Northampton and got to know Newton well while he was at Olney.

Jay says, "His apprehension, imagination, and memory, to use an expression of his own, rendered his brains like fish hooks, which seized and retained everything within their reach. His preaching was probably unique, occasionally overstepping the proprieties of the pulpit, but grappling much with conscience, and dealing out the most tremendous blows at error, sin, and the mere form of godliness."

He was somewhat eccentric. Jay was at the house of a wholesale linen draper in Cheapside when Mr. Ryland called. His host asked him to go into the parlour to meet Jay, who writes, "At this moment I did not personally know him. He was singular in his appearance: his shoes were square toed; his wig was five-storied behind; the sleeves of his coat were profusely large and open; and the flaps of his waistcoat encroaching upon his knees. I was struck and awed with his figure; but what could I think when, walking towards me, he laid hold of me by the collar, and, shaking his fist in my face, he roared out, 'Young man, if you let the people of Surrey Chapel make you proud, I'll smite you to the ground!' But then, instantly dropping his voice, and taking me by the hand, he made me sit down by his side, and said, – 'Sir, nothing can equal the folly of some hearers; they are like apes that hug their young ones to death.'"

Ryland moved into Jay's chapel house because the quietness appealed to him. Rising early, as Jay also did, Ryland would "put him to account" by dictating work for publishing. So it was that Jay wrote down Ryland's *Qualifications of an able Expositor* for Scott's Bible.

John Ryland (jnr.) 1753-1825

Son of John Ryland snr., he served as co-pastor with his father at College Lane Baptist Church, Northampton, then as pastor. As a pupil at his father's school, John formed a little society of boys who were serious followers of the Lord Jesus Christ. His handwritten *Account of the Rise and Progress of the Two Societies at Mr. Ryland's and at Mrs. Trinder's Boarding School in Northampton* is kept at Regent's Park College, Oxford. In this, he states that Thomas Brewer (son of Samuel) "began to seek the Lord soon after Whitsuntide 1766" and that Benjamin Flower "was first impressed at Whitsuntide by his father's and sister's talking with him, and his concern about his salvation was increased by Mr. Ryland's lecture to the boys on Saturday night." At the beginning of 1769 there were just three of them left and in June "Master Flower leaves us so we are brought to the last gasp, but two of us."

Newton invited him to Olney at the age of fifteen and they began a warm correspondence. Replying to a "sorrowful epistle" from Ryland, Newton encouraged him, "If your anxiety makes you pray, and my composure makes me careless, you have certainly the best of it. However, the ark is fixed upon an immovable foundation; and if we think we see it totter, it is owing to a swimming in our heads." Ryland had a strong friendship with Sutcliff, Fuller and Carey, whom he baptised in 1783.

Ryland consulted Newton over major decisions such as proposing to his future wife and assisting his father with his debts (Newton wisely urged him to make sure his wife agreed to any of the latter arrangements).

He sought Newton's advice (which was to stay put!) when called to Broadmead Baptist in Bristol, where he later became President of the Bristol Baptist College. Twenty-six of his students became missionaries with the BMS.

Thomas Brereton Salusbury d. 1756
Member of Parliament for Liverpool at the time that Newton became Surveyor of Tides. As Thomas Brereton, he changed his surname to Salusbury in 1749, the condition for inheriting the estates of Salusbury Lloyd of Leadbrook, father of Brereton's second wife, Catherine. Owen Salusbury Brereton [1715-1798], his son by his first wife, Mary Trelawny, was recorder of Liverpool for fifty-two years.

James Scott 1710-1783
An Independent at Heckmondwike and a tutor at the academy. He made a significant contribution to the supply of evangelical ministers in Northern England.

Thomas Scott 1747-1821
Converted through Newton's patient and uncontroversial friendship. As with Newton and Wilberforce, it was from Luke 11:13 that he gained encouragement to pray for personal faith. "Despising to be taught by men," he had spent three years "hammering out for myself, with no small labour and anxiety," the doctrines which he then found, to his surprise, were to be found "ready made in every book I opened." The prayers for Scott in Newton's diary show how he grew in faith between 1776 and 1779: "Though he does not see things clearly, I have reason to hope the Lord has begin a good work in his heart. Lord, confirm my hopes, and reach him, that he may be a blessed instrument of reaching others.... O my Lord, I thank Thee for Thy goodness to him; I think he goes forward into the light of Thy truth.... Was rejoiced to see how Thy goodness has confirmed the hopes I conceived two years ago when we corresponded for some months. Though his views were then very dark, and he objected to almost every point proposed, yet I could perceive Thou hadst given him a sincerity, which I looked upon as a token of Thy further favour. And now he seems enlightened and established in the most important parts of the gospel, and will I trust prove an instrument of usefulness in Thy hand.....The Lord has answered my desire, and exceeded my expectation in him. How gradually and yet how clearly has he been taught of God the truth of the gospel, and favoured with a single eye

to seek that truth above all. I hope to see him (if my life is spared) eminent in knowledge, power and usefulness. What an honour and a mercy should I esteem it to be any way instrumental in this good work! All the praise be to God! ... O my Lord what a Teacher art Thou! How soon, clearly and solidly is he established in the knowledge and experience of Thy gospel, who but lately was a disputer against every point! I praise Thee for him. Often in my faint manner have I prayed to see some of my neighbours of the clergy awakened. Thou hast answered prayer. Oh may it please Thee yet to add to the number.... I think I can see he has got before me already. Lord, if I have been useful to him, do Thou, I beseech Thee, make him now useful to me." Shortly after Newton left Olney, Scott was called to minister there. His autobiographical *Force of Truth* was revised and improved by Cowper before it went to the press, on account of Newton's thinking it had a very good introduction but was "capable of amendments." Moving to London he preached at the Lock and took the afternoon lecture at St. Mildred's, Bread Street. He also had the morning lectureship at St. Margaret's, Lothbury and sometimes the evening at Long Acre chapel. His excellent Bible commentary began as a regular contribution to a magazine, with many years spent in revising and improving it. He was instrumental in the founding of the British and Foreign Bible Society and was a founder member of the Eclectic Society and the CMS. Wilberforce constantly sought his teaching. Simeon was a great comfort to Scott in his last years, assisting him in the undeserved debts he encountered through his publishers. Scott's sons, John, Thomas and Benjamin, were all ministers.

Lord (Anthony Ashley Cooper) Shaftesbury 1671-1713
3rd Earl of Shaftesbury, a deist. His *Characteristiks* destroyed Newton's interest in religion as a young sailor. Not to be confused with the 7th Earl of Shaftesbury.

Lord (Anthony Ashley Cooper) Shaftesbury 1801-1885
7th Earl of Shaftesbury, an evangelical social reformer.

John Shoolbred 1740? -1802
Merchant, 60 Mark Lane, behind Mincing Lane, to whom Mrs. Newton sent young William Herbert on an errand. In his sermon

notes on Zechariah 3:1-2 Newton wrote, "For Mrs. Shoolbred, 7
March 84. When I told you lately I had lost a dear and valuable
friend, I did not expect to recall your thoughts to the subject. All that
is personal may be soon dispatched. Would you know her character?
She has frequently given it herself in these words – A brand plucked
out of the fire. She would give herself no higher title than a brand –
but she knew she was a brand, plucked out of the fire by the arm of
Almighty Grace. Let this suffice. My business now is with the living."

Josiah Shute 1588-1643
Rector St. Mary Woolnoth, Archdeacon Colchester, son of a
Yorkshire minister and one of five famous brother preachers, called
the Chrysostome of his time. He was said to be a talented orator who
"instantly caught and immovably fixed the attention of his auditors."
The article in the *Christian Observer* says, "He preached Jesus." Some
of his sermons were published as: *Sarah and Hagar* (19 sermons on
Genesis 16) and *Divine Cordials delivered in Ten Sermons upon the
ninth and tenth Chapters of Ezra, in a time of Visitation* (the front
piece has on it Hab. 3:17-18, the text Newton had reserved for his
wife's funeral sermon).

Charles Simeon 1759-1836
Appointed to Holy Trinity, Cambridge, Simeon was a great
evangelical leader whose steady expositions and regular prayer
meetings stirred up many students to faith and had a strong influence
on many of them to enter the mission field. Henry Martyn was one of
his curates. Simeon was a country member of the Eclectic Society,
encouraging the formation of the Society for Mission to Africa and
the East, which became the CMS. He was also involved in the Bible
Society and the LSPCJ (CMJ). One of Newton's breakfast guests,
they preached in each other's churches. Henry Venn writes of him,
"They are the truly excellent of the earth, its salt, who, wherever
they go, reach the heart and conscience, and excite the devout wish,
'Oh, that I may follow Christ, like these true-hearted disciples!'"
Simeon purchased twenty-one livings in order to fill them with
evangelicals. *The History of Christianity* states, "By 1820, one in
twenty of the Anglican clergy were evangelical; by 1830 it was one
in eight."

Joseph Smith 1766?-1825

Joseph married Elizabeth (Betsy) Catlett, Newton's adopted niece, at St. Mary Woolnoth's on 2nd May 1805. Newton's shaky signature (he was almost 80) appears on the entry in the marriage registry. Smith was an optician who had a shop at the North Gate of the Royal Exchange, with another in the mid 1820s in Tottenham Court Road, and later in the New Road (Euston Road). The couple lived with Newton at Coleman Street Buildings. Joseph's name appears in the Annual Reports of the British and Foreign Bible Society as a subscriber from 1809. He bequeathed Newton's portrait to the CMS.

Josiah/Joseph Smith 1704-1781

Joseph Smith, an Independent Minister in Charleston, South Carolina, whom Newton heard preach there. He was a graduate of Harvard. Smith previously defended Whitefield from attacks from within the church (Whitefield was refused communion by the local minister, Alexander Garden, the Commissary of the Church of England, for failing to use the form of prayers prescribed in the Communion Book when preaching at Independent and Baptist meeting houses. Garden spent over a year attempting to have him banned from preaching). In his sermon, *The Character, Preaching, etc., of the Rev. Mr. Whitefield, Impartially Represented and Supported*, Smith spoke of the awe and silence and attention on the faces of Whitefield's audiences, "So charmed were the people with the manner of his address, that they shut up their shops and forgot their secular business ... yet he was no flatterer, and did not prophesy smooth things."

Smith himself had a stroke in 1749, never fully recovering his speech, but continuing to write and publish. He became a prisoner of war in 1780 and died the following year.

In his *Narrative*, Newton accounts for his own lack of understanding of Smith's gospel preaching: "The best words that men can speak are ineffectual till explained and applied by the Spirit of God, who alone can open the heart."

John Sutcliff 1752-1814

Baptist pastor at Olney from 1775. He was converted at seventeen through the ministry of John Fawcett of Wainsgate (whose letters from Newton resulted in the *Narrative*, the basis of this book) and baptised by him. When he went to train at Bristol Baptist College he

walked from Yorkshire to save money for books. He began his
ministry in Olney at the same time that Thomas Scott came to
Ravenstone. Newton attended Sutcliff's ordination (he thought the
charge, preached from Heb. 13:17 by Sutcliff's former tutor at Bristol,
Caleb Evans, "sensible and solid") and began a friendship with him
which was to temper his high-Calvinism. It was Sutcliff who put
forward the appeal to set apart an hour once a month praying for the
success of the gospel, which later gave rise to the Baptist Missionary
Society, soon to be followed by many other missionary societies.
William Carey was under his ministry at Olney for a couple of years.
Sutcliff stayed in the home of Mary Andrews whose sister Hannah
married William Bull.

Richard Swain
Midshipman on the *African*. He solicited the crew to sign a round
robin, intending mutiny. He was put in double irons and transferred
to the *Earl of Halifax* "to be put on board the first Man of War for his
misdemeanour".

Swanwick
Captain of the *Greyhound*, who rescued Newton from Africa at
Manesty's request.

Josiah Symonds 1739-1788
Pastor of Bunyan Meeting, Bedford. He visited Newton as often as
he could, staying at the vicarage during the Baptist Association
Meetings in Olney. Newton kept up a correspondence with him over
many years. Symonds took offence once at something Newton had
intended should have made him smile, prompting the reply from
Newton, "An enemy of yours and mine, I believe, whispered in my
ear, to take notice of an expression or two, which I dare say he would
have been glad I should have expatiated largely upon in my answer.
But through grace he shall be disappointed this time. After we have
been long and tried friends, he would be mighty glad to see us enter
deeply into the important subject of Self-vindication – and by degrees
to make us either as hot as two salamanders, or as cold as two
cucumbers – But let us watch and pray against him, as we are not
altogether ignorant of his devices." The friendship was preserved.

William Talbot 1717-1774

Vicar of Kineton, Warwickshire, until 1767. He preached also in
Lady Huntingdon's chapels. Newton developed a strong friendship
with him and his wife Sarah, sometimes staying with them at the
vicarage (which still has its original flagstone floor and low-beam
study). Talbot moved to the living of St. Giles, Reading. While visiting
Lord Dartmouth in London, he succumbed to a fever, probably caught
during a home visit in Reading. He died in the house of Hannah
Wilberforce. Sarah's patient and prayerful witness resulted in the
conversion of Talbot's successor, Cadogan.

John Taylor 1694-1761

At first Newton was impressed with Taylor, founder of the dissenting
Octagon Chapel in Norwich. However he later found he could not
agree with his views of scripture. Taylor's *Scripture Doctrine of
Original Sin* prompted this response from John Wesley:

> Hartlepool,
> July 3, 1759

"Rev. Sir,

"I esteem you as a person of uncommon sense and learning, but your
doctrine I cannot esteem: and some time since I believed it my duty
to speak my sentiments at large concerning your doctrine of Original
Sin. When Mr. Newton of Liverpool mentioned this, and asked,
whether you designed to answer, you said, 'You thought not; for it
would only be a personal controversy between Jo. W_y and Jo. T_r.'
How gladly, if I durst, would I accept of this discharge from so unequal
a contest! for I am thoroughly sensible, humanly speaking, it is
formica contra leonem [an ant against a lion].

"How gladly were it indeed no other than a personal controversy!
But certainly it is not; it is a controversy *de re*, if ever there was one
in the world. Indeed, concerning a thing of the highest importance;
nay, all the things that concern our eternal peace. It is Christianity or
Heathenism! for take away the doctrine of redemption or justification,
and that of the new birth, the beginning of sanctification, or which
amounts to the same, explain them as you do, suitably to your doctrine
of Original Sin, and what is Christianity better than Heathenism?
Wherein (save in rectifying some of our notions) has the religion of
St. Paul any pre-eminence over that of Socrates or Epictetus?

"This is, therefore, to my apprehension, the least a personal controversy of any in the world: your person and mine are out of the question: the point is, Are those things, that have been believed for many ages throughout the Christian world, real, solid truths, or monkish dreams and vain imaginations?

"But farther, it is certain, between you and me there need be no personal controversy at all: for we may agree to leave each other's person and character absolutely untouched, while we sum up and answer the several arguments advanced, as plainly and as closely as we can.

"Either I or you mistake the whole of Christianity from the beginning to the end! Either my scheme or yours is as contrary to the Scriptural as the Koran is. Is it mine or yours? Yours has gone through all England, and made numerous converts; I attack it from end to end. Let all England judge, whether it can be defended or not!

"Earnestly praying that God may give you and me a right understanding in all things,

"I am, Rev. Sir,

"Your servant, for Christ's sake,

"J.W."

David Jennings published a response to Taylor's views, *A Vindication of the Scripture Doctrine of Original Sin from Mr. Taylor's free and candid Examination of it.*

Walter Taylor 1791-1803

Walter Taylor, an engineer whose skill and inventions on behalf of the Navy drew national recognition and appreciation, lived at Portswood House, Portswood Green, near Southampton. His father was a close friend of Isaac Watts – they had attended Above Bar (Congregational) together. Walter himself was a deacon at Above Bar from 1791 to 1803. When staying with Taylor in Portswood, Newton would attend Above Bar in the morning and in the evenings he preached in Taylor's laundry to his family, workmen and neighbouring villagers. Later a chapel was added to his house, used by preachers of all denominations – for there was a lack of gospel preachers in neighbouring villages where the people were keen to hear. "Alas!" said Newton, "the hungry sheep look up and are not fed." Eliza Cunningham was brought to the Taylors to bathe in the sea. Newton encouraged his wife to take communion at Above Bar.

The Bodleian Library has a copy of Newton's Small Tracts with the inscription "A token of affection and gratitude to his dear friend Mrs. Taylor of Portswood Green; from the Author. 29 July 1798."

Lord (John Shore) Teignmouth 1751-1834
Governor General of India, he returned to England with Warren Hastings and became Privy Councillor. He lived in Clapham, was one of the Clapham Sect and the first President of the British and Foreign Bible Society.

John Thomas 1757-1800
A surgeon in the East India Company, Thomas preceded Carey in undertaking evangelistic work in Bengal. When Carey left England Thomas was with him, and translated the book of Genesis into Bengali on their voyage out to India, helped by Carey's knowledge of Hebrew, Latin and Greek.

Henry Thornton 1760-1815
MP for Southwark, son of John, Governor of the Bank of England, one of the Clapham Sect, he continued his father's generosity to many in need, including Claudius Buchanan, Patrick Brontë, the Dissenting Academy at Newport Pagnell and Hannah More's schools. Until his marriage to Marianne Sykes in 1796 he gave away six-sevenths of his income, later reducing this to one-third. He was the first treasurer of the CMS and the British and Foreign Bible Society. For several years William Wilberforce lived with him at Battersea Rise. Henry died at Wilberforce's house after a year of ill health.

Thornton once spoke to Jay about Newton's curate, Mr. Gunn, "I went to hear him, and was much dissatisfied with the lowness of his address, and the manner in which he spiritualized his subject, which was, 'I will make you fishers of men;' in the discussion of which everything, with regard to fishing and fish, was quaintly and facetiously explained and applied. Deeming it very objectionable, and likely to cause reproach, I wrote my complaint to Mr. Newton; in reply to which here is his answer: 'My dear Sir, – I fear you did not go to hear my good man with a spiritual appetite, or you would have found food, as well as the many who hung on his lips.'" Jay adds that Thornton was not offended, but rather admired his rebuker.

John Thornton 1720-1790
Converted through Whitefield, he was a friend of Lord Dartmouth.
Hannah Wilberforce was his sister. He was a Director of the Bank of
England, as had been his father, Robert, and also a Director of the
Russia Company. His "counting-house" was in Kings-Arms Yard,
close to Coleman Street Buildings. He was the first Treasurer of the
Royal Marine Society. Gainsborough painted his portrait for the
Society. Thornton's wife, Lucy, had been greatly influenced by Isaac
Watts. John and Lucy had four children: Samuel, Robert, Jane and
Henry. Thornton contributed liberally for the cause of the gospel,
freeing many, such as Newton, to exercise their own gifts of ministry.
One of the many causes dependent on his generosity was the Countess
of Huntingdon's College at Trevecca. He also undertook to finance
William Bull's Academy at Newport-Pagnell during his lifetime. On
his death Newton commented, "I think it probable that no one man
in Europe, in private life, will be so much missed."
  Cowper composed this tribute to him:

> Such was thy charity: no sudden start,
> After long sleep, of passion in the heart,
> But steadfast principle, and, in its kind,
> Of close relation to the Eternal Mind,
> Traced easily to its true source above,
> To him whose works bespeak his nature, Love.
> Thy bounties all were Christian, and I make
> This record of thee for the Gospel's sake;
> That the incredulous themselves may see
> Its use and power exemplified in thee.

Samuel Thornton 1755-1838
MP, son of John, he became a Director of the Bank of England at the
age of twenty-five. He sold his home in Clapham to Lord Teignmouth.
He was Governor of Greenwich and President of Guy's Hospital. His
son John [1783-1861] was on the first committee of the British and
Foreign Bible Society.

Martha Trinder (née Smith) 1736-1790
A member of the Rylands' Baptist church in College Lane,
Northampton. She was Governess of the Boarding School which
Elizabeth Catlett, Newton's niece, attended. Newton sometimes

preached there. She married Thomas Trinder in 1768. They lived in a large house in Horsemarket, St. Mary's Street.

Thomas Trinder 1740-1794

Thomas, Martha's husband, was a deacon in John Ryland's Baptist Church at Northampton. He had been converted as a schoolboy at Samuel Well's seminary in Cheltenham while listening to Martin Madan preach from John 3:9 on the conversation between Nicodemus and our Lord Jesus Christ. "When the service was over I came home with my master and schoolfellows, but I think it was with great difficulty that I could refrain from tears in going along the streets. When at home I retired into my chamber, upon my knees, there to give vent to my tears, and prayed, if I could pray, that I might be born again.... I, with some others who were most affected, were ready to break through the rules of decency and good manners to hear but a single word concerning salvation. I well remember that whenever Mr. Madan came to Mr. Well's, as he commonly did two or three times a week, if we could obtain the knowledge of it, we should immediately run down from school; and happiest was he who could obtain the key-hole to hear the conversation." Thomas contributed (financially) to the formation of the Baptist Missionary Fund and was the first to leave a legacy to them.

Harry Tucker

"My friend Harry ... Henry Tucker, a Mulatto, at Shebar, was the man with whom I had the largest connexion in business, and by whom I was never deceived", wrote Newton in his *Letters to a Wife*. Tucker is mentioned several times in Newton's Log Book. Another slave dealer living near Tucker in 1757 described him as "a fat man and fair spoken". Tucker spoke English well, having travelled to England, Spain and Portugal. He had 6 or 7 wives and numerous offspring. His contemporary wrote, "This man has the character of a fair trader among the Europeans, but the contrary among the Blacks." His riches and strength in number of family around him gave him a power over his neighbours. His eldest brother, Peter, resented being financially dependant on him and in his jealousy plotted to kill him in 1754. He was unsuccessful in this, but managed to persuade some of the kings to cease trading with him and to seize whatever of his goods they could as "customs duty".

Mary Unwin (née Cawthorne) 1724-1796

She married Morley Unwin in 1744. They lived in Huntingdon, where Cowper sought a quiet country residence on his discharge from St. Alban's Asylum. He struck up a friendship with her son, William. This led to his being accepted into the family as a boarder. Not long after, Morley died after a fall from his horse. Cowper continued to stay with Mary Unwin. They came to Olney in 1767, moving on to Weston Underwood in 1786. Newton was asked by family to intervene in Cowper's later years by writing to her. His requests went unheeded, but he faithfully defended her character in a letter to Mrs. Cowper of 28 Devonshire Place, Bloomsbury, 8 August 1794, "Perhaps her repeated [strokes] of the Palsy and other infirmities of advancing age may have had some effect upon her mind. In this point she is certainly wrong. But their lives seem wrapped up in each other. And I am afraid that a forced and violent separation, would hasten the death of them both. *Her* situation demands compassion likewise, and notwithstanding the uneasiness she now gives us, I am persuaded if you knew her as well as I, you would suppress the epithet *detestable*. Excuse me, Madam, Mrs. Unwin is an old and dear friend of mine, with whom I have had much communion in the ways of God, and I would willingly make the best apology that I can for her present conduct. I believe for about 14 years we never passed the whole day asunder, excepting when I was from home. And my long acquaintance did not abate the high opinion, I at first formed of her as a servant of the Lord; though her great attachment to dear Mr. Cowper, has certainly misled her upon some occasions, as it does now."

William Cawthorne Unwin 1745?-1786

Son of Morley and Mary, rector of Stock, Essex, and a great friend of Cowper's, who corresponded frequently with him.

Helperus Ritzema van Lier 1764-1793

The Rev. Van Lier was a Dutch minister of the Reformed Church who later became Chaplain at the Cape of Good Hope. Newton says, "He was a clever youth while at the University, and his reason and abilities were leading apace to scepticism and infidelity." In the process of his conversion he was helped by reading Newton's *Cardiphonia*. Van Lier, then twenty-three, wrote an account of his conversion in Latin, addressed to Newton. Newton sent Cowper his own translation of part of the manuscript, which Cowper returned with this comment: "I have made here and there an alteration, which appeared to me for the better; but, on the whole, I cannot but wonder at your adroitness in a business to which you have been probably at no time much accustomed, and which, for many years, you have not at all practised. If, when you shall have written the whole, you shall wish for a corrector of the rest, so far as my own skill in the matter goes, it is entirely at your service." December 9, 1788.

And again on October 15, 1790, "I have no objection at all to being known as the translator of Van Lier's Letters, when they shall be published. Rather, I am ambitious of it as an honour. It will serve to prove, that, if I have spent much time to little purpose in the translation of Homer, some small portion of my time has, however, been well disposed of."

Henry Venn 1725-1797
Curate at Clapham in 1754, vicar of Huddersfield in 1759, where in three years he saw nine hundred converted, and rector of Yelling from 1771 to his death. He was one of Newton's earliest Christian clergy friends. He visited him and preached for him in Olney, where he was careful to preach for only forty-four minutes, and also in London. Venn's letters were published by his grandson Henry with a memoir by his son John. A few of them have reference to Newton, "who made me quite ashamed by my little scrawl to him upon his wife's death, by writing, in return, a very long, excellent, and most affectionate letter to me."

John Venn 1759-1813
Son of Henry and vicar of Clapham, a friend of William Wilberforce and one of The Clapham Sect. He drew up the rules for the CMS, of which he was a founder member. His preaching was much appreciated, though he was very apprehensive of his responsibility from the start. His father wrote to remind him, "You are no otherwise afflicted with a sense of your own deficiency, than the very excellent of God's servants were in their trials", citing Isaiah, Jeremiah, Ezekiel and Paul. Henry Venn reflected on the Providence which sent him *"from Clapham*, that at Huddersfield I might be taught the plagues of my own heart ... *To Clapham* you are led, in order to be experimentally taught what is in your heart."

Samuel Walker 1714-1761

'Walker of Truro'. He began his ministry at Truro as a dancing, card-playing, party-going clergyman, but was led to faith by the Grammar School master, Conon. His new style of preaching both intrigued and convicted his parishioners. J. C. Ryle records that "such crowds attended his ministry that the thoroughfares of the town seemed to be deserted during the hours of service, so that it was said you might fire a canon down every street of Truro in church time, without a chance of killing a single human being." The theatre and cockpit closed down. When a regiment of soldiers stayed in Truro 250 of them were converted. His week was filled with pastoral care and teaching, starting his sermon preparation on Fridays, with Saturdays set aside "in the morning for humiliation and solemn prayers, as a preparative for composing a sermon in the afternoon and at night."

Caleb Warhurst 1723-1765

Independent minister in Manchester with whom Newton shared his despair of entering the Established Church.

Joseph Warner 1717-1801

A surgeon at Guy's Hospital who successfully operated on a tumour on Newton's thigh. The previous year Warner had become the first surgeon to tie the common carotid artery. His reputation had been established after publishing, in 1754, his book on the *Preparation and effects of the Agaric of the Oak in Stopping of Bleedings &c.* Polly went to him about her cancer, but there was nothing he could do for her.

Phoebe Warner 1735?-1799

One of Newton's servants. In a letter to the Coffins in 1799, in which Newton wrote, "Phoebe is drooping, and I think will not hold out long", a postscript was added, "Phoebe went home quietly yesterday, rather more suddenly than we expected, aged sixty-four. She lived sixteen years with us in London, and though she was not a hired servant, nor slept often in the house, she was as one of our family fourteen years at Olney. She was ignorant, and could not read; but she knew she was a sinner, and I trust she knew the Saviour, and is now with Him. She never could say very much about herself. She was an honest, faithful, careful, and affectionate friend; but for her own sake, I am glad she is gone. She was a great sufferer."

Isaac Watts 1674-1748

The well known hymn writer, friend of David Jennings (pastor of John Newton's mother). Watts was brought up in a dissenting family, attending an Independent Meeting in Southampton later known as Above Bar, where his father was a deacon. He was pastor of John Owen's church, Mark Lane Independent Meeting (which later moved to Pinner's Hall, then to White Horse Yard, Duke's Place, St. Mary Axe), family chaplain of Sir Thomas Abney (Lord Mayor of London) and tutor to his daughters. Newton's links were therefore with him from his birth to old age, where he also attended Above Bar. Watt's hymns were the foundation for many of Newton's. Whitefield visited Watts half an hour before he died, helping to raise him to take some medicine. Jennings preached the Funeral Sermon for Watts in his church, from Hebrews 11:4, *By it he being dead yet speaketh.*

Charles and John Wesley 1707-1788 and 1703-1791

The Wesleys were at Oxford with Whitefield, Ingham and Hervey. After a voyage to Georgia and contact with the Moravians both of them experienced a personal conversion. They travelled throughout the country, preaching outdoors where no pulpit was offered, gaining the name of methodists. Charles settled in Bristol for twenty years, later moving to London. Several thousand hymns of scriptural content were attributed to him. John continued travelling, preaching and writing. Newton enjoyed John's visits to Liverpool when he was Surveyor of Tides. When Newton preached at Grimshaw's he wrote eagerly to tell Wesley that he had preached in the methodist way. John read Newton's *Narrative* more than once, writing in his Journal that there was "something very extraordinary therein," adding, "but one may account for it without a jot of Predestination." Newton was one of the pallbearers at Charles's funeral, honouring his friend's wish, though he was not well himself at the time and it was "a walking funeral" in icy winds and falling snow.

George Whitefield 1714-1770

Whitefield joined the Wesleys at Oxford and followed them to Georgia. Newton first met him in London. The first time he attended one of his services he came away echoing the words of the Queen of Sheba's first meeting with Solomon, *Behold the half was not told me.* "Many were the winter mornings I got up at four, to attend his

Tabernacle discourses at five; and I have seen Moorfields as full of lanthorns at these times as, I suppose, the Haymarket is full of flambeaux on an open night." He was very encouraged by Whitefield's visits to Liverpool, writing to his wife, "He warms my heart, makes me more indifferent to cares and crosses, and strengthens my faith." He followed him so eagerly that he became known as "the young Whitefield".

There were some in Newton's church at Olney who were the spiritual fruit of Whitefield's visit to the town in 1739. In the funeral sermon Newton preached at Olney for Whitefield he said, "I have had some opportunities of looking over the history of the Church in past ages [through writing his *Ecclesiastical Review*], and am not backward to say, that I have not read or heard of any person, since the days of the apostles, of whom it may more emphatically be said, *He was a bright and shining light*, than of the late Mr. Whitefield. The Lord gave him a manner of preaching peculiarly his own. He copied from none and I never met any one who could imitate him with success. Other ministers, perhaps, could preach the gospel as clearly, and in general say the same things; but, I believe, no man living could say them in his way."

Certainly the great Shakespearean actor of the day, David Garrick, echoed this tribute to Whitefield's gift of oratory. He longed "to be able to say, 'Oh!' like Mr. Whitefield!" He thought Whitefield could have made people laugh or cry simply by the way he pronounced a single word, even were it "Mesopotamia".

Whitefield was persuasive in collecting for the needs of others. When an area of Brandenburg suffered plunder, torture and abuse by Cossacks and Russian troops, Whitefield's heart went out to those involved and he immediately raised £400 for them. Tyerman quotes Newton as relating that after his sermon that day Whitefield had said, "We shall sing a hymn, during which those who do not choose to give their mite may sneak off." None of the congregation stirred. Whitefield ordered all the doors to be shut but one; at which he himself held the plate. The amount raised was reported in *Lloyds Evening Post*.

Brewer preached Whitefield's funeral sermon at Spitalfields from Psalm 37:37, *Mark the perfect man, and behold the upright: for the end of that man is peace.*

John Whitford d. 1782

A Methodist minister in Liverpool while Newton was there, he became pastor of the Independent Church at Olney after Drake's death in 1775.

Newton's advice to him when he must have been deliberating on doctrines in Liverpool was, "When our dear Lord questioned Peter, after his fall and recovery, he said not, Art thou wise, learned, and eloquent? nay, he said not, Art thou clear and sound and orthodox? But this only, 'Lovest thou me?' An answer to this was sufficient then, why not now? Any other answer, we may believe, would have been insufficient then. If Peter had made the most pompous confession of his faith and sentiments, still the first question would have recurred, 'Lovest thou me?' This is a scripture precedent."

He commented in his diary after one of their shared New Year's Eve services for the youth in Olney, "In the evening heard Mr. Whitford's sermon to the young people. He was very faithful and earnest. May Thy blessing crown this threefold service."

Hannah Wilberforce (née Thornton) d. 1788

John Thornton's (half) sister, wife of William (the uncle of William the MP). She cared for her young nephew William for a few years, which was when he first met Newton. In one of his many letters to her, Newton wrote, "It is now Saturday evening, and growing late. I am just returned from a serious walk, which is my usual manner of closing the week when the weather is fine. I endeavour to join in heart with the Lord's minister's and people, who are seeking a blessing on tomorrow's ordinances. At such times I especially remember those friends with whom I have gone to the house of the Lord in company, consequently you are not forgotten. I can venture to assure you that if you have a value for our prayers you have a frequent share in them." When in London, Newton preached in their home in John Street, Bedford Row, where he also gave a series of lectures on the *Pilgrim's Progress*. Hannah stayed with the Newtons in Olney after her husband's death, meeting William Bull who became a firm friend.

William Wilberforce 1759-1833

Nephew of Hannah Wilberforce, he was brought up in her home for a few years. As a young boy having recently lost his father, it was at this time that he met and reverenced Newton as a parent. Later as an

MP he sought his wise counsel after reading Doddridge's *Rise and Progress* and becoming a Christian.

Newton persuaded him to remain in politics and directed him to the teaching of Thomas Scott at the Lock Hospital chapel. An early test of his new priorities came in the form of an invitation to dine with the Speaker of the House of Commons one Sunday. Wilberforce wrote him an apology "that he kept with his family that day".

Newton constantly encouraged Wilberforce in his parliamentary work and in missionary projects. He was invited to become the first President of the CMS, but declined, becoming instead one of the seven Vice-Presidents. He was one of the first Vice-Presidents of the British and Foreign Bible Society. He also supported the BMS and the LMS.

Wilberforce was a firm friend of Henry Thornton. Together with a group of influential friends they became known as The Clapham Sect, working tirelessly for the improvement of social conditions and the spread of the gospel. The first Bill he introduced in Parliament on the slave trade was in 1789. When success finally came in 1807 with the passing of the second reading of his Abolition Bill (Newton was still alive), he is reported to have said to Thornton on the way out, "Well, Henry, what shall we abolish next?" To which Thornton replied, "The Lottery, I think".

Although he had not been expected to live beyond the age of 29 (the eminent physician Dr. Warren pronounced in 1788 that he had "not enough stamina to last a fortnight"), Wilberforce saw the abolition of the slave trade before he died (a few days before his 74th birthday). The Bill passed its third reading in Parliament on Friday 26 July. He died in the early hours of the following Monday morning. Married to Elizabeth Bird, Wilberforce had two daughters and four sons, three of whom entered the ministry. His sons Robert and Samuel wrote his *Life*.

Inscribed in Newton's own copy of Wilberforce's *Practical View* was this message, "My regards for the author, who gave me this book, will not permit me to part with my property in it, and I therefore can only *lend* it to my dear Eliza [Catlett] during my life. If she survives me, it will be her own. I commend it to her as one of the best books (in my judgment) extant, and I hope she will find much pleasure and much profit from a frequent perusal of it. The Lord accompany her reading with His especial blessing." This was in May 1797. In

October Newton made a note in the book that he had just finished his 4th reading of it.

Williams
Newton's second employer on the west coast of Africa, who owned several "factories", or trading depôts, where goods were stored for sale or purchase.

Daniel Wilson 1778-1858
In a visit to Newton's home in 1796 Daniel was told, "Unbelief is a great sin. If the Devil were to tempt you to some open notorious crime, you should be startled at it; but when he tempts you to disbelieve the promises of God, you hug it as your infirmity, whereas you should consider it as a great sin and must pray against it." Daniel wrote to his mother, "The words of Mr. Newton that unbelief is a great sin and should be prayed against as such, continually recur to my mind – alas! my heart is unbelieving and hard, but I hope I endeavour to pray to the great Redeemer to give me a believing heart." He studied under Thomas Scott for the next couple of years, spending time with Josiah Pratt, whom he regarded as his brother, then studied at St. Edmund in Oxford. His ministry in North Oxfordshire was especially well received and remembered for years afterwards. He became Cecil's curate at Chobham. Simeon said he had the congregation at his feet. When Thomas Scott died, he preached his Funeral Sermon. In 1824 he became vicar of St. Mary's Islington and in 1832, Bishop of Calcutta.

Basil Woodd 1760-1831
An early member of the Eclectic Society and the CMS, who called himself a Baxterian. He was lecturer at St. Peter's, Cornhill, London. In 1785 he became the minister at the Bentinck Chapel, Marylebone, where he remained until his death. He undertook the first CMS deputation in 1813 and was also active in the BFBS and Society for Promoting Christian Knowledge. Bishop David Wilson said of him, "He was of the old school – he preached JESUS CHRIST, and Him crucified." The hymn, *Hail Thou Source of every Blessing*, was written by Woodd.

Edward Young 1683-1765

Young was a Doctor of Law, once a candidate for parliament, the author of poetry, prose, tragedies and satire and chaplain to George II in 1728. Some of his works were performed at Drury Lane. He was considered a genius, witty and vivacious, imaginative, strong and rich. A memoir of him (written by Herbert Croft) is in Johnson's *Lives of the Poets*. His work was very popular in his day – a number of his expressions became common use, such as " procrastination is the thief of time". He entered the ministry when he was almost fifty and became Rector of Welwyn. He was the author of *Night Thoughts*, a meditation reflecting the grief caused by the loss of his wife, her daughter and son-in-law within a short time of each other. The characters of the meditation are assumed to be his family.

Great-Aunt Henrietta

[Regrettably unable to identify]

APPENDICES

Contents

APPENDIX 1

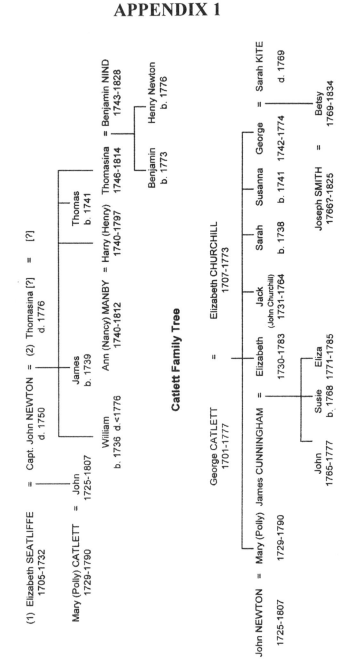

APPENDIX 2

MS Eng Poet c.51, pp.253-6,Mary Madan's Scrapbook, Bodleian Library, University of Oxford [spelling modernised]

The Revd. John Newton was requested by a Friend to compose two hymns, each last line ending "remember me".

1st hymn

> Jesus the Truth, the Life, the Way,
> Unworthy though I be,
> I trust since thou hast bid me pray
> Thou wilt remember me.
>
> Thou who didst bleed, and groan, and die,
> From guilt to set me free,
> In glory now, enthroned on high,
> Will still remember me.
>
> When tempest tossed with care, my breast
> Is like the troubled sea,
> Sweet peace shall hush the storm to rest
> If Thou remember me.
>
> My former friends regard me not
> Since I have followed Thee,
> But let me be by them forgot,
> So Thou remember me.
>
> When I was bound and chained in sin
> Thy mercy set me free.
> And each day since, a proof has been
> Thou dost remember me.
>
> I hope though now my time of death
> Unable to foresee,
> To say, when yielding up my breath,
> Now Lord, remember me.

2nd hymn

The thief who near the Saviour hung
(In death, how happy he!)
Was answered when his dying tongue
Said, "Lord remember me."

My sins are not less black than those
Which brought him to the tree:
No thought can give my heart repose,
But Lord remember me.

When Jesus died, death lost its sting,
Like the enraged bee.
And I may now address the King
With, Lord remember me.

I take my pattern from the thief,
I have no other plea;
For I of sinners am the chief,
Then Lord remember me.

The Lamb upon his glorious throne
As newly slain I see,
And trust he will not those disown
Who plead, remember me.

And when before him face to face
I bow my thankful knee,
In joyful strains I'll praise his grace
Who now remembers me.

APPENDIX 3

Newton was asked by Samuel Palmer, Dissenting Minister at Mare Street, Hackney, to write a preface to a book for seamen which he wished to republish. Newton did so, but added, as he had done many years earlier to David Jennings, "You must excuse me from writing a prayer. This I think the most difficult composition of all."*

Palmer says, "Several Prayers were subjoined, chiefly from Jenks's *Devotions* and a Hymn was added to each Sermon, mostly from Newton's *Olney Hymn-Book*." Newton's preface follows.

The Seaman's Preacher, 9 short discourses on Jonah's voyage, addressed to Sailors, by John Ryther, an ejected minister in Wapping, 1675, reprinted 1802

RECOMMENDATORY PREFACE

Addressed to Seamen

My reverend and respected friend, the Editor, applied to me as a proper person to recommend this Book (which his benevolence led him to republish) to the serious attention of Mariners; as he thought, from my former acquaintance with Sea-affairs, I must have some feeling of the situation of Mariners myself. In this, I trust, he was not mistaken.

I was first on Ship-board the day I was eleven years of age, in the station of a Cabin-boy. I was afterwards in the Navy. I then passed through the usual graduations in the merchants' service; and was Master of a merchant ship in my last three voyages. Thus I traversed the Ocean, in a great variety of situations and circumstances, near twenty years.

But long, too long, I was a careless inattentive spectator of the wonders of the Lord in the great deep. My heart was hard, my language profane, my conduct most profligate and licentious.

---

*John Newton, *Correspondence of the late Rev. John Newton, with a dissenting minister [Samuel Palmer], on various subjects and occasions. With a brief sketch of his character, and a ministerial charge (The necessity of keeping our own vineyards) by him revised*, 1809.

Thus I know, not only from observation, but from sorrowful experience, the disadvantages Seamen are in general under, with respect to the concernments of their precious souls. They usually pass the greatest part of their lives upon the Sea, and therefore can derive little benefit either from instruction or example. Rather they too frequently strengthen and confirm each other in habits of wickedness. The frequency of their deliverances from the dangers to which they are exposed, often harden them into a fearless insensibility. Thus they go from bad to worse, strangers to God, and thoughtless of Eternity.

May the perusal of this Book, now put into your hands, my brother Sailor, be accompanied by a divine blessing to your heart: it is well calculated to instruct you if ignorant; to rouse you if careless; to encourage you if you have a desire to seek God, and to comfort you if your mind is distressed. May the Holy Spirit enlighten your understanding, that you may discern the things pertaining to your everlasting peace, before they are hidden from your eyes!

Death, Judgment, Heaven and Hell, are words of awful importance. But the Son of God veiled his glory, united the human nature to himself, that he might redeem us to God by his blood; and now Pardon, Peace, and eternal Life are truly promised, without money or price, to all who put their trust in him. In the perusal of this Book, I commend you to his blessing: I am, for his sake, your willing servant in the Gospel,

John Newton
Minister of St. Mary Woolnoth
London

APPENDIX 4

John Newton's Preface to
The Pilgrim's Progress by John Bunyan
[1776 edition, BL 1076.e.30]

The writings of Mr. BUNYAN need no recommendatory Preface. The various editions they have passed through, and the different languages into which many of them have been translated, sufficiently prove that the gifts of GOD which were in him, have, by the divine blessing, been made very acceptable and useful to the Churches. Though he was called to the knowledge and ministry of the Gospel from a low state of life, as well as from a vicious course of conversation, and was unfurnished with human literature, the LORD, the *great*, the *effectual*, the *only effectual* teacher, made him, in an eminent degree, an able and successful minister of the New Testament. It is probable that only the people to whom he personally preached would have been benefited by his zeal and experience, had not the LORD permitted the rage of his enemies to prevail against him for a season. He lived in more trying days than those in which our lot is fallen. For preaching the Word of Life to sinners, he was *sentenced* to perpetual banishment, but what he *actually suffered* was imprisonment for more than twelve years. But his spirit was not bound. Though secluded from his public work, he could not be idle. He applied himself to writing books, and most of the Treatises, by which being dead he still speaketh; (in number about threescore) were composed during his confinement in *Bedford Gaol*. Thus his adversaries themselves contributed to extend his usefulness by the very methods they took to prevent it. And (as in the Apostle's case) the things that happened to him, proved rather to the furtherance than the hindrance of the Gospel.

His Books, though devoid of that art and those ornaments, on which writers who seek the praise of men lay so great a stress, have been, and still are highly esteemed by those who have a taste for divine truth; and greatly instrumental, in the hands of the holy Spirit, to the awakening of the careless, and the encouragement of those who are seeking salvation. And we doubt not that they will be farther owned of GOD for these purposes, to many who are yet unborn. But as among the stars one excelleth another in glory, so of all our Author's

Writings, there is no one perhaps so universally and deservedly admired as his PILGRIM'S PROGRESS, in which he gives a delineation of the Christian life under the idea of a journey or a pilgrimage, from the City of *Destruction* to the heavenly *Jerusalem*. In this Treatise he appears not only as a writer well instructed in the mysteries of the kingdom, but a man of real genius. Though he had not a learned education, GOD had given him considerable natural abilities, a lively invention, a penetrating spirit, a strong judgement, and his style, though plain and simple, is remarkably clear, animated, and engaging. By the exercises through which the LORD led him, and a close study of the Word of GOD, he acquired a singular knowledge of the human heart, and its various workings, both in a state of nature and grace, and of the various snares and dangers to which a Believer is exposed from the men and the things of the world, and the subtilty of Satan. These fruits of his experience and observation he has exhibited in a very pleasing and instructive manner in his PILGRIM, which may be considered as a map of the Christian profession in its present mixed state, while the wheat and the tares are growing in the same field. A map, so exactly drawn, that we can hardly meet with a case or character, amidst the vast variety of persons and incidents, that daily occur to our observation, to which we cannot easily point out a counterpart in the PILGRIM. And he is peculiarly happy in fixing the attention of his readers: many have read this Book with a kind of rapturous pleasure, though they have not understood the Author's design, (which only they who have the eyes of their minds enlightened by the Spirit of GOD can fully enter into) and they who understand it best, and who have read it often, usually find fresh pleasure and instruction upon every perusal.

As many persons who read this Allegory, though they find benefit from the whole, are at a loss to determine the Author's meaning in some particular parts of his representation, an Edition containing some brief Notes to illustrate the more difficult passages, has been long desired. An attempt of this kind is now submitted to the Public. The Annotator does not pretend to be positive that he has always precisely taken up the thought the Author had upon his mind at the time of writing, though he thinks there are but few places in which he is in danger of greatly missing it. He hopes however that he has proposed no illustration but what will be found agreeable to the analogy of Faith and the experience of Believers.

The unusual demand for the PILGRIM'S PROGRESS upon its first appearance, induced the Author some time after to send forth a Second Part. In which there are many beautiful passages that sufficiently demonstrate it to be the work of the same masterly hand. But the plan of that which is now called the First Part, was so comprehensive, and so well executed, that the subject was too much exhausted to admit of a Second Part, capable of standing in competition with the former. It is upon the whole greatly inferior to it, though a few pages here and there might be selected, which, for their beauty, propriety, and energy, almost deserve the epithet of *Inimitable*.* The First Part therefore is only published with Notes, which it is hoped may afford a sufficient key to the Second.

There is a small book in print which bears the title of the Third Part of the PILGRIM'S PROGRESS. It can hardly be necessary to inform any but those who have not read it, that this pretended Third Part, with Mr. BUNYAN'S name is a gross imposition upon the Public, and that the Title is almost the only part of it in which it bears any resemblance to BUNYAN'S PILGRIM, excepting when the Writer has borrowed the same names. But BUNYAN'S spirit and manner he could not borrow, and his principles he openly contradicts. A common hedge-stake deserves as much to be compared with AARON'S rod, which yielded blossoms and almonds, as this poor performance to be obtruded upon the world under the Title of the Third Part of the PILGRIM'S PROGRESS.

Thus much concerning our Book: Let the Preface close with a word for the Reader's heart. If you are not convinced of sin, and led by the Spirit to seek JESUS, notwithstanding the Notes, the PILGRIM will still be a riddle to you. A well-wisher to your soul assures you, that whether you know these things or not, they are important realities. The PILGRIM is a parable, but it has an interpretation in which you are nearly concerned. If you are living in sin, you are in the City of *Destruction*. O hear the warning voice! *Flee from the wrath to come*. Pray that the eyes of your mind may be opened, then you will see your danger, and gladly follow the shining light of the Word, till you enter by CHRIST, the strait gate, into the way of salvation. If death surprise you before you get into this road, you are lost for ever.

If you are indeed asking the way to *Zion* with your face

* See the Character of Mr. Fearing, and Standfast's discourse when in the River.

thitherward, I bid you good speed. Behold an open door is set before you, which none can shut. Yet prepare to endure hardship, for the way lies through many tribulations. There are hills and valleys to be passed, lions and dragons to be met with, but the LORD of the Hill will guide and guard his people. *Put on the whole armour of God, fight the good fight of faith.* Beware of the Flatterer, beware of the Enchanted Ground. See the Land of *Beulah*, yea, the City of *Jerusalem* itself is before you:

> Then JESUS the Forerunner waits
> To welcome travellers home.

Some of Newton's comments on Bunyan's text

p. 1
Bunyan: As I walked through the wilderness of this world, I lighted on a certain place, where was a den (a) [the jail], and laid me down in that place to sleep: and as I slept, I dreamed a dream.

Newton's Notes:
(a) Mr. BUNYAN was put into *Bedford* jail for preaching the Gospel. We live in happier times, when none are permitted to interrupt us; may we prize and improve our liberty, and be thankful for it. While he was in prison he wrote this book, and many other valuable treatises, which have, by the LORD'S blessing, administered edification and comfort to many who were then unborn, and will doubtless be serviceable to many who shall live after us. Thus by his confinement he became more extensively useful. The LORD will always so restrain and manage the wrath of men, that the methods by which they attempt to hinder the success of the Gospel, shall in the event promote it.

p. 6
Bunyan: 'Then said EVANGELIST, pointing with his finger over a very wide field, Do you see yonder *Wicket-Gate*? The man said, No: then, said the other, Do you see yonder *Shining Light* (g)? He said, I think I do. Then said EVANGELIST, Keep that light in your eye, and go directly thereto, so shalt thou see the gate; at which, when thou knockest, it shall be told thee what thou shalt do.'
   [Matt. 7:13,14; Psalm 119:105; 2 Pet. 1:19
   CHRIST and the way to him, cannot be found without the word.]

Newton's Notes:

(g) A convinced sinner must sink into despair, but for the reports of the Gospel. He hears there is a Saviour, but his thoughts of him are very confused. He cannot yet be said *to see the Son*, but he embraces the word of GOD as true; he renounces all hope in himself, and follows the *shining light*; waiting in the use of means, not to qualify himself for mercy, but that CHRIST may be revealed unto his soul.

[Newton then added this hymn]

THE SHINING LIGHT!

My former hopes are fled,
My terror now begins;
I feel, alas! That I am dead
In trespasses and sins.

Ah! whither shall I fly?
I hear the thunder roar:
The Law proclaims destruction nigh,
And vengeance at the door.

When I review my ways,
I dread impending doom;
But sure, a friendly whisper says,
"Flee from the wrath to come."

I see, or think I see
A glimm'ring from afar,
A beam of day that shines for me,
To save me from despair.

Forerunner of the Sun,
It marks the Pilgrim's way;
I'll gaze upon it while I run,
And watch the rising day.

[*Olney Hymns*, Book 3, Hymn 8, written by William Cowper, probably for one of their Tuesday evening prayer meetings where Newton read from *Pilgrim's Progress*]

APPENDIX 5

John Newton, *A dialogue* [on Matt. 11:28], c. 1785, Bodleian Library, Oxford, *Small Tracts, and Occasional Sermons, collected and republished*, 1798 [141m.288]

Lambeth Palace Library also has a copy of this tract entitled *Consolation under Convictions. A Dialogue Between a penitent* [Mary (B below)] *and her Christian friend* [Barnabus (A below)] [96 Tracts H5013.R35 1 No. 26]

A DIALOGUE

A   What! Are you in tears again?

B   Oh! Tears are become my food.

A   What is the cause of your constant grief?

B   Alas! I am a sinner.

A   Then I cannot blame your tears: for sin and sorrow are very well suited; but who told you, that you are a sinner?

B   The Lord has set my sins in order before mine eyes.

A   How long have you been a sinner?

B   Alas! I was born in sin and have lived in sin to this very hour; I am a great sinner indeed.

A   And what do you intend to do?

B   I really know not what to do.

A   Have you thought what will become of you?

B   I fear I am lost forever.

A   How forever? What! Cannot you repent?

B   No, my heart is as hard as a stone.

A   Cannot you amend?

B   *Who can bring a clean thing out of an unclean? Not one.*

A   Cannot you believe?

B   I cannot believe. Unbelief is the worst of all my sins and gives me the greatest uneasiness.

A   All this is very well.

B   How well: what do you mean Sir? I tell you that I am a sinner and that I can neither repent, amend, or believe and then you answer, "It is very well". Do you herein show the friendship which you have always professed for me?

A   I am indeed your friend and I have many dear friends in the world, whom I should rejoice to see in your case. Do you not pray sometimes?

B   I can neither pray, nor live without prayer. I kneel down and weep and utter some broken words, but I am afraid I know not what it is to pray.

A   You read the Scripture, I suppose.

B   I do. But I find it a sealed book: I have little light into it and get little comfort from it.

A   Have you ever read Matt. 11:28?

B   Yes, very often.

A   Can you repeat the words?

B   *Come unto Me all you that are weary and heavy laden, and I will give you rest.*

A   Was you never able to find comfort in these words?

B   Very little.

A   Have you considered whose words they are?

B   Yes, they are the words of Jesus Christ.

A   And do you think He meant what He said when He used these words?

B   That's a strange question! I know He is the faithful witness and all His words are truth.

A   Do you think He is able to make them good?

B   Yes: for all heaven and earth.

A   Do you think that *rest*, which Jesus has promised to give us is desirable?

B   Happy indeed are they who find it.

A   And who are the weary and heavy laden then, the persons invited to receive it?

B   I should be glad to hear your opinion. Wherein do these words differ?

A   They are different parts of the same character; *weary* implies the sense and feeling of the trouble, *heavy laden* specifies its cause and continuance.

B   Cannot you express you meaning more clearly?

A   A man who is weary with work can rest when his work is finished and rise with new strength to repeat his labour; but a man wearied with an heavy burden cannot rest till his burden be removed. If you put him on a down bed, he can find no refreshment. He still feels the weight of his load and becomes weaker and weaker. He can take little pleasure in his food or his friends; he has no strength for business, nor spirits for amusement. Whether sitting, standing, or walking his burden weighs him down, till his very life becomes a burden too. If you could see a person in such a case, you would have a lively illustration of the words *weary and heavy laden*.

B   Surely I have more than seen such an one. I am myself the very person you describe. My sins are a heavy burden, bowing me down continually; they fill my thoughts by day and hurry my dreams by night. In the morning I say, When will it be evening? And in the evening, When will it be morning? My friends, my books, my business, every- thing is tedious. I am weary of living and afraid of dying.

A   You see *now*, what made me say, *all this is very well.* You acknowledge yourself such an person as our Lord invites to come to Him, that they may have rest; you think the rest which He promises most desirable in itself and suitable to your case and you could not bear I should seem to question either His power or inclination to make good His own word. Put those things together and then see whether you have not reason to wipe away your tears and to be no more faithless but believing.

B   Our Saviour says, *Come unto Me*, but I find I cannot come; guilt and unbelief keep me back.

A   How then do you understand the expression, *Come unto Me*?

B   I have told you that I have little understanding.

A   After our Saviour was risen from the dead He names a certain mountain in Galilee to His disciples, where He appointed to meet them. If you had been present when He named it and acquainted with the country, do you think you should have understood Him?

B   Certainly I should.

A   Suppose the disciples had refused, or neglected to go to the place?

B   They could not – they loved their Saviour and could not bear either to neglect His command or miss an opportunity of seeing Him.

A   Suppose they had come to the place first and refused to wait for Him?

B   They could not do so. They would remember He had promised, they knew He was faithful to His word and they would think His company very well worth waiting for.

A   Our Saviour is now withdrawn from the earth; yet He still says as of old, *Come unto Me*. He does not mean that we should climb the clouds, but come to meet Him in the ways of His own appointment.

B   Which are they?

A   Chiefly these, His word, His mercy-seat and His assemblies: He converses with His people in His word, He draws near to them in prayer and when two or three of them are met together in His name He is present in the midst of them.

B   True, He meets His *people*, but not *me*. I have sought Him in these ways many times. I sought Him but I found Him not. I am weary and ready to faint. I think I shall give all up. He will not look upon me at all: So far from it, that is never worse with me, than sometimes when I am seeking Him in the manner you speak of.

A   I need only refer you to your own words. He has promised to meet you, He is faithful to His engagements and His company is worth waiting for. Why cannot you judge for yourself, as you did for the disciples just now?

B   If I was sure He would come at last, I should be willing to wait, but I am afraid He will never meet me, never accept me, no never.

A   He has not met with you, therefore He never will. – This is no good argument unless you can prove that Christ promised to meet you the first time, or at least within such a number of days, weeks or months. Have you found any text in the Bible to prove this?

B   Indeed He has not fixed any time.

A   How inconsistent is your unbelief! You will not believe what the Lord has promised and yet you expect what He has given you no grounds to hope for. Has He not rather told you before, that you will have need of patience? And has He not left a gracious parable to encourage you not to faint?

B   It is very true.

A   You forget that passage, I suppose, when you think of giving it all up.

B   I confess I have been too impatient.

A   Besides – are you positive the Lord has never met you according to this promise? Has He not in a measure enlightened you to understand scripture and have you not tasted of the good word of God? Have you not sometimes found your affections drawn faith towards Jesus in prayer? Have you never received any instruction or comfort, when you was hearing his ministers preach the salvation of Jesus, or when you conversed with His people of the love of Jesus?

B   I cannot say I never had a taste of these things, but it has been so little.

A   So little – what then, you would limit the Lord, would you, not only as to the time of His coming, but also to the degree of His comforts? He says, that he does not despise the day of small things, and surely you should not? Should not you be thankful for that you call *little*? Ought you not to take all fit opportunities of acknowledging His goodness for the *little* He has done for you? Oh smother not His mercies in unthankful silence, but call upon your friends to help you to praise Him.

B   Indeed I have been ungrateful. I see it now, and I deserve nothing, nothing but wrath. It is an unspeakable mercy, that I am out of hell. But what would you have me to do?

A   Believe.

B   Lord increase my faith.

A   It is a good prayer, and where it expresses the desire of the heart, it is never used in vain.

B   But what are the best means?

A   The Cross of Christ.

B   Pray explain yourself.

A   Suppose that knowing all you know at present, the evil of
         sin, your own guilt and misery, and suppose that there was
         no Saviour but Jesus, I say, suppose that knowing all this
         you had lived at the time when He conversed with men in
         the form of a servant. And being in a dull and desponding
         frame, as you are now, you had come, without any appre-
         hension of what was transacting, to Mount Calvary, just
         time enough to see Jesus nailed to the Cross, and to see
         His hands and His feet pierced with spikes, to see Him
         raised on high, the mark of contempt and cruelty, covered
         with blood and full of wounds: And suppose while you
         beheld Him thus dying a thousand deaths as one for the
         sins of His very murderers, you had heard the prayer for
         them, and His gracious answer to the dying thief. Would
         not such a sight and such words have sweetly suited the
         state of your mind? If I mistake not, you think you should
         almost have interrupted the solemn scene, you would have
         been ready to run up to Him, and say, Lord pray *for me
         too*, Lord remember *me likewise*, when Thou art in Thy
         kingdom.

B   Indeed you have read my heart.

A   I dare say you are as firmly persuaded in your mind that
         these things did once happen, as if you had been present
         and seen them with your own eyes.

B   I have not the least doubt concerning them.

A   Well then, here is the cure of unbelief. Look unto the divine
         Saviour, as becoming obedient unto death, even the death
         of the Cross for sinners, yea glorious truth: for the chief of
         sinners. He loved them and gave Himself for them. And
         why? That they might believe on Him, as their perfect and
         eternal Saviour, and love Him as their Lord and their God,
         and be happy. Look upon Him in this light, and His
         promised rest shall be yours. View Him as living and dying
         that He might be able to save to the uttermost, and that
         whosoever cometh to Him, might in no wise be cast out,

and then you will find matter of comfort to your afflicted conscience. This sight rightly applied is the source of peace, and the fountain of joy. Thus have I explained to you, how the Cross of Christ is the best means.

B   Oh that I could but look up to Him, and be saved. Still something hinders me. My natural wretchedness, and my spiritual weakness fill me with fears.

A   Be not discouraged by the one, nor despair for the other. Jesus is the antidote against the former. His Spirit is the cure of the latter. It is His office to glorify Jesus by taking the things that are His, and showing them to His people, whereby they see the infinite dignity of His person, and the infinite sufficiency of His undertakings, and have faith to receive and apply Jesus to their souls for salvation. It is this good Spirit, who fills their minds with joy and peace in believing, and produces all the fruits of righteousness in their lives. May He witness with your spirit, that you are a child of God, a member of Christ and an heir of glory. So shall you possess present peace, and receive future happiness. To the love of the Lord God I commend you. Remember once more, that Jesus died for sinners.

B   And I hope He will not cast me out, though I come as a great sinner to Him.

A   You have His word that He will not, His word that cannot be broken.

B   To that then will I trust, the Lord being my helper, "I come unto Thee, Lord Jesus, because Thou hast promised not to cast me out, and on Thee will wait. Let it be done unto me according to Thy word." Amen.

APPENDIX 6

Notes taken by Hannah Jowett [whose father, John, was a friend of Newton's], MSS, Cowper & Newton Museum, Olney

Mr. Newton's Account of Mr. Cowper in a Funeral Sermon
Preached in St. Mary Woolnoth, Lombard Street
May 1800

Exodus Chapter 3 verses 2, 3:
And the angel of the Lord appeared unto him in a flame of fire out of the midst of a bush: and he looked, and behold, the bush burned with fire and the bush was not consumed. And Moses said, I will now turn aside, and see this great sight, why the bush is not burnt.

The Lord has given me many friends but with none have I had so great an intimacy, as with my friend Mr. Cowper. But he is gone. I was glad when I heard it. I know of no text in the whole book of God's word more suited to the case of my dear friend than that I have read. He was indeed a bush in flames for 27 years but he was not consumed. And why? Because the Lord was there. I think it probable there is hardly a person in the church who ever saw him yet there is few but know him in his writings. I can think of no motto more suitable than that of the apostle *as unknown yet well known*[1] particularly in his poems, 2nd volume, called *The Task* by which *he being dead yet speaketh*[2] – speaks to the glory of God and the good of mankind and which I think will not be forgotten as long as the English language is current.

Mr. Cowper was afflicted with what is called a nervous complaint to such a degree as might justly be called insanity. He had an attack very early in life which did not continue long. He was afterward at the Temple, being designed for the Law. He became acquainted with Mr. Coleman and a Mr. & Lord Thurlow. He assisted them in writing a book [periodical] called the *Connoisseur*. Those four men were very gay and men of great abilities but the Lord had designs of mercy towards my friend. One night he had a remarkable dream or vision.

1. 2 Corinthians 6:9
2. Hebrews 11:4

He thought a child, a very beautiful little boy, came and looked on him while he was asleep. When he awoke he felt his mind much affected by his dream, but as he was sitting at his breakfast the Lord shone in upon his soul and so enlightened his understanding and gave such a clear view of the gospel and his interest in it without his ever reading it or hearing a gospel sermon that for seven years afterwards I never in all my life saw a man walk – I want to say so honourably – but so closely with God and always set the Lord before him in all he did. I believe during that time we were not seven hours without being together.

The last sermon he ever heard preached was on New Year's Day 1773. He drank tea with me in the afternoon. The next morning a violent storm overtook him which caused a very great shyness. I used to visit him often but no argument could prevail with him to come to see me. He used to point with his finger to the church and say: you know the comfort I have had there and how I have seen the glory of the Lord in his house and until I can go there I'll not go anywhere else. But after some time this shyness wore off. I remember one time we were walking together in a very deep snow. The weather was remarkably severe. He desired me to stop. I observed the sweat drop from his face occasioned by the agony of his mind. He said he knew the Lord was a Sovereign and had a right to do with and lay upon him what he pleased and if he [it?] was that by holding out a finger he could remove what he then felt, he would not do it unless he knew it were the will of God. He has often said he thought the Lord had not a child who loved him with a more simple heart than he did.

The first temptation the enemy assaulted him with was to offer up himself as Abraham his son. He verily thought he ought to do it. We were obliged to watch with him night and day. I, my dear wife and Mrs. U[nwin] with whom he lived left him not an hour for seven years. He was also tempted to think butcher's meat was human flesh, therefore he would not take it. We found it very difficult to provide any sustenance he would take. He had various temptations which would be very improper for me to mention in this place. I was at that time obliged to leave Olney but the Lord did not leave him without friends but provided for him persons of abilities and respect who did that for love which no money could have procured.

I don't know a person upon earth I consult upon a text of Scripture or any point of conscience so much to my satisfaction as Mr. Cowper. He could give comfort though he could not receive any himself. He was not only a comfort to me but a blessing to the affectionate poor people among whom I then lived. He used frequently to visit them and pray with them. I had the honour to be rector[?] over a set of poor plain people chiefly lace makers. Their great confinement caused in them great depression of spirits. They used to say, O Sir if I was right, sure I should not feel so. But they well knew Mr. Cowper: they knew he was right, and from him they could take comfort.

I have had hopes the Lord would remove his malady a little time before his death but it continued. The last twelve hours of his life he did not speak nor seem to take notice of anything but lay in a state of apparent insensibility. But I seem to think that while the curtains were taking down in the tabernacle removing, glory broke in upon his soul. The Lord had set his seal upon him and though he had not seen him he had grace to love him. He was one of those who came out of great tribulation. He suffered much here for twenty-seven years, but eternity is long enough to make amends for all. For what is all he endured in this life, when compared with that rest which remaineth for the children of God?

APPENDIX 7

Newton's hymn *Amazing Grace* seems to have been specially written to accompany this sermon [these are his own notes, which he would presumably have illustrated with anecdotes on the day]. The hymn has the same Scripture references above it in the *Olney Hymns*.

New Year's Morning

1 Chronicles 17:16,17

Then David went in and sat before the LORD, and he said, Who am I, O LORD God, that you have brought me this far? And as if this were not enough in your sight, O God, you have spoken about the future of the house of your servant. You have looked on me as though I were the most exalted of men, O LORD God.

The Lord bestows many blessings upon his people, but unless he likewise gives them a thankful heart, they lose much of the comfort they might have in them. And this is not only a blessing in itself but an earnest of more. When David was peacefully settled in the kingdom, he purposed to express his gratitude by building a place for the Ark. This honour the Lord had appointed for his son Solomon, but he graciously accepted David's intention, for he not only notices the poor services of his people, but even their desires to serve him, when they spring from a principle of simple love, though opportunity should be wanting. He sent him a message by Nathan assuring him that his son should build the house and that he himself would build David's house and establish his kingdom. This filled his heart with praise. My text is part of his acknowledgement. Omitting David's personal concerns, I would accommodate them to our own use as a proper subject for our meditations on the entrance of a new year. They lead us to a consideration of past mercies and future hopes and intimate the frame of mind which becomes us when we contemplate what the Lord has done for us.

1.   The frame of mind: Humility and admiration

Who am I, etc. This question should be always upon our minds. Who am I? What was I when the Lord began to manifest his purposes of love? This was often inculcated upon Israel, Thou shalt remember – Look unto the pit from which we were taken. Lord, what is man! At that time we were:

1.1   Miserable

Shut up under the law and unbelief. What must have been the event had the Lord left us there? After a few years spent in vanity, we must have sunk to rise no more.

1.2   Rebellious

Blinded by the god of this world. We had not so much a desire of deliverance. Instead of desiring the Lord's help, we breathed a spirit of defiance against him. His mercy came to us not only undeserved but undesired. Yea few [of] us [?] but resisted his calls, and when he knocked at the door of our hearts endeavoured to shut him out till he overcame us by the power of his grace. See our proper characteristics (Titus 3:3).

1.3   [*Undeserving*]

It was the Lord against whom we sinned and who showed us mercy. He needed not. What just cause of admiration, that he should appoint such salvation, in such a way, in favour of such helpless, worthless creatures.

2.   That thou hast brought me hitherto

Here let us look back.

2.1   Before conversion

His providential care preserving us from a thousand seen, millions of unseen dangers, when we knew him not. His secret guidance, leading us by a way which we knew not, till his time of love came.

2.2   At conversion

The means by which he wrought upon us, supports in the time of conviction, and the never to be forgotten hour when he enabled us to hope in his mercy.

2.3   Since we first were enabled to give up our names to him
Mercy and goodness have followed us. In temporals, he has led and fed us. Many have fallen when we have been preserved, or if afflicted, we have found him a present help in trouble. Some may say, *with my staff I passed over this Jordan* [Gen. 32:10]. In spirituals, preserving us from wasting sins, from gross errors, or restoring and healing, maintaining his hold in our hearts, notwithstanding so much opposition, so many temptations and provocations. The comforts we have had in secret and public worship, the seasonable and undoubted answers to prayer. Grace to any dear to us, peace in our families, his blessing with us a church and a people.

3.   Are these small things?
Yes, compared to what follows – He has spoken for a great while to come, even to Eternity. Present mercies are but earnests of his love, present comforts but foretastes of the joy to which we are hastening. O that crown, that kingdom, that eternal weight of glory! We are travelling home to God. We shall soon see Jesus, and never complain of sin, sorrow, temptation or desertion any more.

He has dealt with us according to the estate of a man of high degree. He found us upon the dunghill and has made us companions of princes – in a wilderness and has led us to the City of God.

From hence infer:

1.   Love, gratitude, obedience
Romans 12:1 *[I beseech you therefore, brethren, by the mercies of God, that ye present your bodies a living sacrifice, holy, acceptable unto God, which is your reasonable service].*

2.   Trust and confidence
We have good reason to cast our cares upon him, and to be satisfied with his appointments. Hitherto *he has done all things well* [Mark 7:37].

3.   Patience
Yet a little while and we shall be at home. Romans 13:11 *[And that, knowing the time, that now it is high time to awake out of sleep: for now is our salvation nearer than when we believed].*

We are spared thus far – But some, I fear, are strangers to the promises.
You are entered upon a New Year. It may be your last. You are at
present barren trees in the vineyard. O fear lest the sentence should
go forth – *Cut it down* [Luke 13:7].

Sermon notebook, Lambeth Palace Library, MS 2940.

1 Chronicles 17:16,17
Faith's review and expectation

Amazing grace! (how sweet the sound)
That saved a wretch like me!
I once was lost, but now am found,
Was blind, but now I see.

'Twas grace that taught my heart to fear,
And grace those fears relieved;
How precious did that grace appear,
The hour I first believed!

Through many dangers, toils and snares,
I have already come;
'Tis grace has brought me safe thus far,
And grace will lead me home.

The LORD has promised good to me,
His word my hope secures;
He will my shield and portion be,
As long as life endures.

Yes, when this flesh and heart shall fail,
And mortal life shall cease;
I shall possess, within the veil,
A life of joy and peace.

The earth shall soon dissolve like snow,
The sun forebear to shine;
But GOD, who called me here below,
Will be forever mine.

John Newton, *Olney Hymns*, 1779, Book 1, Hymn 41

APPENDIX 8

Newton's hymn, *How Sweet the Name of Jesus sounds*, seems to have been specially written to accompany this sermon [these are his own notes, which he would presumably have illustrated with anecdotes on the day]. The hymn has the same Scripture reference above it in *Olney Hymns*.

Sermon on SONG OF SOLOMON 1:3

Because of the savour of thy good ointments
thy name is as ointment poured forth...

A chief part of this little book is an attempt to answer that question: What is thy beloved more than another beloved? The unbelieving world discover much of the enormity and ignorance of their hearts in this: that one of the greatest quarrels they have with the people of God, is for their having such high thoughts and so much to say about the L.J.C. [Lord Jesus Christ]. They are ready to say, Can you not be content with fearing God and keeping his commandments, without so much talk of Christ? This makes the believer sigh, Alas that you did but know him too. If you did surely you would think you could not speak enough of him.

I knew nothing about the fear of God. I never had a hearty desire to keep his commandments, till I began to know a little of Christ. I was starving and he fed me, I was sick and he visited me, I was naked, destitute of all good, and he clothed me with his own righteousness; I was shut up in the prison of sin and he came and burst open the doors and set me at liberty. How great is his goodness; how great is His beauty. In comparison of this tree of life, all the tallest of the sons of men are empty and barren. He is the chief among ten thousands and altogether lovely. The soul ranges as it were through the whole creation to find some worthy similitudes of her Lord but all are scanty and insufficient. Let us present consider this in my text. It may lead our thoughts to not only the excellency that is in Christ, but to his suitableness to us, and afford a glass in which you may see yourselves and be able to judge by the light of the Holy Spirit whether you are indeed worthy the name of Christians.

We shall enquire:
1. What is meant by his name
2. Why compared to ointment
3. How this ointment is poured forth

1.   Thy name

This in general means his person (as Rev. 3:4) or rather the manifestation of his person, that by which he is known. The name of Christ includes the whole revelation concerning him, who he is, what he has done – all that we read of his love, his power and his offices make a part of his great and glorious name. The soul that is taught by the Word and Spirit of God to understand a little of these things receives such a sense of love and joy that the very sound of his name is sweeter than music to the ears, sweeter than honey to the taste.

He is named:

1.1   A Saviour

to save from guilt, sin and hell, this implies:
      (i)   his sufferings
      (ii)   his victory

1.2   A Mediator

There is an important concern between us and God – but how shall we approach? – who shall interpose? This name affords a comfortable answer.

1.3   A Husband

Our wants, debts and fears are many. But he is made known by this name (Isaiah 54) and he is rich enough to supply all.

2.   This name compared to ointment

These were more frequent in use and many of more costly composition than common amongst us.

2.1   Some were healing

Applied to wounds and bruises and putrefying sores. Now the sinner when he is awakened and comes to himself, finds himself like the man (Luke 10) stripped and wounded and half dead. Jesus like the good Samaritan comes with an eye of pity, to pour in the ointment of his name. This is a certain and the only cure for the wounds of sin.

Many can witness to this. How when they began to feel their misery and see their danger, they made use of many means but found them all physicians of no value. Like the woman in the gospel when they had spent all their time and strength in this way they were no better but rather grew worse. But this ointment made them whole.

2.2 Some were cordial and reviving
The believing soul is subject to fainting – it has but little strength and meets many discouragements – but is relieved from time to time by the good savour of this ointment. The name of Christ refreshes it with new strength under the

(i)   remains of sin
(ii)   assaults of Satan
(iii) troubles of life

2.3 Ointments were used in feasts
(Luke 7:46. Hence Psalm 23:5) And the name of Jesus is a precious banquet to the believing soul. This fills him as with marrow and fatness – this puts an honour and a beauty upon him – therefore (verse 4) more than wine.

2.4 [The savour]
Precious ointments have a savour, a perfumed smell, which distinguishes the person that bears them. So this ointment of the name of Jesus, when poured into a believer's heart, it makes him smell as a field which the Lord has blessed. It is this communication of grace and holiness which they have received from their beloved which makes them known to each other and distinguishes them from the world.

3. How poured forth
We read (Mark 14) that the woman brought precious ointment in a box – and when she broke the box then, and not before, the whole house was filled with its fragrance. Thus the grace and virtue of this name was confined and known but to few while our Lord conversed upon earth – but afterwards it was poured forth:

3.1 When he suffered
The precious vessel that contained this precious ointment was broken upon the Cross – the savour of his name, his love, his blood, poured

out from every wound [in] his sacred body. See from his head, his hands, his feet, sorrow and love flow mingling down. From that hour it was quickly spread and diffused far and near. And here we are still to look for it. When we desire a new savour of this ointment, let us turn our eyes, our thoughts, to Golgotha. To behold him by faith as he hung bleeding and dying, with outstretched arms inviting our regards and saying, See if any sorrow was like to my sorrow.

This is:

(i)   a sovereign balm for every wound
(ii)   a cordial for our care

3.2   *In the preached gospel*

It was appointed for this end. And everything that bears the name of preaching – if it does not diffuse the knowledge of this good ointment – is dry and tedious, unsavoury and unprofitable. But by this foolishness of preaching it is spread abroad. The scene of our Lord's life was confined to a few places and it was a long while ago – but the ointment thus poured out has reached to distant lands and ages. Countless thousands have experienced its efficacy, and blessed be God, it is still fresh and still flowing. It is poured out amongst us at this day. Farther the expression poured forth may signify:

(i)   *Abundance*
       There is enough to spare.
(ii)   *Freeness*
       It is not enclosed but open and common to all who know its value, as the light or water.

3.3   *[At times of refreshment]*

The Lord has likewise peculiar seasons of pouring it into the hearts of his people. These are called times of refreshment (Acts 3:19).

(i)   Usually at the time of their first conversion.
(ii)   Often in an hour of distress and trouble.
(iii) They may expect it likewise at the hour of death.
(iv)   He often meets them with it in the ordinances – particularly when they approach his table. At this feast he revives them with the savour of his ointment and pours it upon their heads. He anoints them with this oil of joy and gladness above their fellows.

Learn hence:

1.   The happiness of the believer, above those who have their portion in this world. They have a medicine, a cordial always at hand.

2.   You that have your hearts set upon sin – see how poor you are. Which of your vain pleasures and pursuits is it that you can say of it, Thy name is as ointment poured forth? Quite the contrary. Are they not briars and thorns? Is there not poison in your cup? Take heed lest that which is a savour of life unto life to many should be a savour of death unto death to you.

3.   Who have a right to the bread and wine – even all those who see the value and long to know more of the virtue of this ointment. Fear not ye who seek Jesus, but come. Are you wounded? are you fainting? – let not this keep you away, but rather constrain you. You cannot do without it.

But as to those who live in sin, or who seek a righteousness of [your] own, from your attendance on outward ordinances, you have no right to the children's bread. I beg you, may I charge you, not to profane his institutions. If you will, you must, but remember the king will be there to view the guests. Take care lest he frown upon you. Such only would I keep away, but all that are awakened, that groan being burdened, that think yourselves unworthy of the smallest mercies, in his name I bid you heartily welcome, and I have his warrant for it (Isa. 55:1; 66:2).

Sermon notebook, Cowper and Newton Museum, Olney

The hymn to accompany this sermon follows on the next page.

Solomon's Song 1:3

The name of JESUS
[note the inclusion of the original middle verse below]

How sweet the name of JESUS sounds
In a believer's ear?
It soothes his sorrows, heals his wounds
And drives away his fear.

It makes the wounded spirit whole
And calms the troubled breast;
'Tis manna to the hungry soul
And to the weary rest.

Dear name! the rock on which I build,
My shield and hiding place;
My never-failing treasury filled
With boundless stores of grace.

By Thee my prayers acceptance gain
Altho' with sin defiled;
Satan accuses me in vain
And I am owned a child.

JESUS! my Shepherd, Husband, Friend,
My Prophet, Priest and King;
My LORD, my Life, my Way, my End,
Accept the praise I bring.

Weak is the effort of my heart
And cold my warmest thought;
But when I see Thee as Thou art
I'll praise Thee as I ought.

'Till then I would Thy love proclaim
With every fleeting breath;
And may the music of Thy name
Refresh my soul in death.

Olney Hymns, Book 1, Hymn 57

APPENDIX 9

THE CHARACTER AND COMMENDATION OF A
FAITHFUL MINISTER

A SERMON

PREACHED, JANUARY 8, 1808

AT THE CHURCH OF THE UNITED PARISHES OF

ST. MARY WOOLNOTH AND ST. MARY WOOLCHURCH HAW,
LOMBARD STREET

On the death of their late Rector

THE REV. JOHN NEWTON

WHO DEPARTED DECEMBER 21,

IN THE EIGHTY-THIRD YEAR OF HIS AGE

*THE Author of this Discourse has endeavoured to meet the request of the
Executors and Friends of the Deceased, by publishing all that his notes and
recollection will supply. He hopes that his having Memoirs of the late Rev.
Mr. Newton now in the press, will account for so little having been said in
the Sermon respecting the circumstances of the life and death of that eminent
character. He has often had occasion to remark how spiritless a sermon
appears when printed, which, in a more free delivery of it, is felt impressive;
but, in both instances, he trusts it will suffice, that, under great bodily pain
and infirmity,* "he hath done what he could."

A SERMON

LUKE 12:42,43

And the Lord said, Who then is that faithful and wise steward, whom his Lord shall make ruler over his household, to give them their portion of meat in due season? Blessed is that servant, whom his Lord, when he cometh, shall find so doing.

I should not have ventured to appear this day in this place, and on this solemn occasion, but at the express desire of your departed minister: nor can I think of any scripture which more suitably applies to his past character and present state, than the passage before us. May a divine blessing accompany our meditations on it; that we may not only *mark the perfect man, and behold the upright*, but that our end also, like his, may be peace!

Our Lord had said, v. 35, *Let your loins be girded about, and your lights burning; and ye yourselves like unto men that wait for their Lord, when he will return from the wedding: that when he cometh and knocketh, they may open to him immediately. Blessed are those servants, whom the Lord, when he cometh, shall find watching. Be ye therefore ready also: for the Son of Man cometh at an hour when ye think not.*

Then Peter said unto him, Lord, speakest thou this parable unto us, or even to all?

And the Lord said, Who then is that faithful and wise steward, whom his Lord shall make ruler over his household to give them their portion of meat in due season? Blessed is that servant, whom his Lord, when he cometh, shall find so doing.

As if Jesus had said, "Though all have a general concern in the words which I have spoken you, my disciples and ministers, have a special interest in them, and a particular obligation laid upon you by them. You are not only *servants* in general; but servants also of a particular description: you are placed as *stewards* over my household; having a peculiar and specific charge to execute. And blessed are you, if your Lord, when he cometh, shall find you executing it faithfully and wisely."

In the words of the text, taken in connection with those which lead to it, we have our Lord's view of the CHARACTER AND COMMENDATION of a faithful minister. He is represented in the text both as a steward and a servant: as a SERVANT he is before described as vigilant and prepared; as a STEWARD, he is faithful and wise. Let us attend to both descriptions in this account of:

1. HIS CHARACTER
The faithful minister's character resembles that of a trusty *servant* watching the coming of his Lord. For, even among men, such a servant will not only consider his wages, but also the obligations which he is under. If his Master

be from home, especially at a late hour, he will stand prepared to receive him on his return. If (as in the east) long garments are in use, he will have them *girded about*, that no impediment may prevent his activity. If the night requires a lamp or torch, it will be kept *burning*. He even watches his master's tread: he knows his knock: he springs to open the door: his very face welcomes him; and, whether his master comes at the second or third watch, such a servant complains not, he sleeps not, but steadily remains on his post. "I know not," says he, "at what hour my Lord may come; but I well know in what position he ought to find me." It is nothing to him, that other servants in the same house may be off *their* watch. Some may be absent, some gaming, some wasting their master's substance, some stealing his property, some abusing his character, and some quarrelling and fighting. But what is all this to him? His thoughts are on his Lord.

Thus the vigilant and prepared servant, who is now called off his post, saw indeed and lamented the state of the household in which he had long kept watch; and faithfully protested against the neglect, carnality, and contention which he observed therein: but while he thus warned the unruly, his own heart was continually fixed on the coming of his Master. His own heart spake its real feelings, when he wrote that hymn which you have often sung:

"Fix my heart and eyes on thine,
What are other objects worth?
But to see thy glories shine
Is a heav'n begun on earth."

Thus, I say, with his *loins girded*, with his *lights burning*, and looking for the coming of his Lord, departed JOHN NEWTON, servant of the Most High God.

But this servant is also described as a faithful and wise STEWARD; one set over the household of God, and expressly appointed to his office of administering therein. *Let a man*, saith the apostle, *so account of us, as of the ministers of Christ, and stewards of the mysteries of God. Moreover it is required in stewards that a man be found faithful.* But the steward is not faithful, if he does not give the due portion to each: not putting them off with half a meal. He is not faithful, if he regards the *quantity*, but pays no attention to the *quality*: it must be their portion of MEAT: it must be that which will support and *nourish* them. A steward needs also to be not only faithful, but *wise*, that he may be able to discern both the portion of meat and the due *season* for delivering it. He must be *wise*, to mark the wants, complaints, and infirmities of the household: and he must be *wise*, to discriminate and patiently to bear the false charges and unkind remarks which he often hears while he thus acts faithfully and wisely. A minister is sometimes called to exercise a solitary faith and an invincible patience, in order steadily to proceed for the good of his Master's household, in the midst of the various cabals and impositions which he sees continually forming in it.

Thus acted your late minister, *as a good steward of the manifold grace of God.* He faithfully, as well as *rightly divided the word of truth* among you; giving *their portion to each in due season.* He dispensed the word of God, and that only. He employed it as *profitable for doctrine, for reproof, for correction, and for instruction in righteousness.* Whatever men may plead for elaborate discourses on moral goodness and the rewards of virtue, he determined to advance the doctrine of a crucified Saviour, as the only hope and strength of fallen man; whose *flesh is meat indeed,* and whose *blood is drink indeed.* And he dispensed this, as one that had felt the power of it in his own soul, and tasted the savour of the *meat* which he delivered to others. A few of his hearers might, at times, come rather to find fault than to be fed; but he regarded not the person of men: he went on with his work, seeming to say with holy Herbert,

"Thou shalt answer, Lord, for me."

I think I may assert, without fear of contradiction from such as knew the character of your late minister, that no man ever executed his office with a more *single eye,* or a more *disinterested heart.* Unlike that unjust steward in the parable, who, throughout all his management, merely considered how to keep himself from sinking under his delinquency, your late minister considered simply the interest of his Master and his household. He might truly say, "*God is witness, that, instead of being burdensome, we were gentle among you, even as a nurse cherisheth her children: so, being affectionately desirous of you, we were willing to have imparted unto you not the Gospel of God only, but also our own souls, because ye were dear unto us. Ye are witnesses, and God also, how holily, and justly, and unblameably we behaved ourselves among you that believe. As ye know how we exhorted, and comforted, and charged every one of you, as a father doth his children, that ye would walk worthy of God, who hath called you unto his kingdom and glory.*"

Ill nature, indeed, might term this statement *a flattery of the dead.* But I confidently reply, No; in no wise. It is too late now to question the fact. Most of your know that I have stated but the simple truth, and that the truth itself demands this of me. This thing was not done in a corner, or in the presence of two or three interested witnesses; but it was done in the centre of the largest city in the world, amidst a multitude of disaffected witnesses, and before the eyes of the Church of God, to the members of which he might justly have appealed, *Ye know, from the first day that I came among you, after what manner I have been with you at all seasons: serving the Lord with all humility of mind and with many tears and temptations: and how I kept back nothing that was profitable unto you, but have showed you, and have taught you publicly and from house to house, testifying repentance towards God and faith towards our Lord Jesus Christ. Wherefore I take you to record this day, that I am pure from the blood of all men; for I have not shunned to declare unto you all the counsel of God.*

But the *character* and *commendation* of your late faithful and wise steward must be referred to a higher bar of decision than yours or mine. The Judge of the world, who describes his character, pronounces what we proceed to consider –

2. HIS COMMENDATION

Blessed is that servant, whom his Lord when he cometh shall find so doing.

BLESSED, indeed, if he received no other commendation than the APPROBATION OF HIS LORD.

He, when he cometh, shall bring to light the hidden things of darkness, and then shall every man, thus found faithful, *have praise of God.* Sin has made such a bedlam of this world, that it is full of false associations. *Precious sons of Zion, comparable to fine gold, how are they esteemed as earthen pitchers, the work of the hands of the potter!* But, when the Master comes, he will say (and it is enough if he says it), *Well done, thou good and faithful servant! Thou hast been faithful over a few things, I will make thee ruler over many things: enter thou into the joy of thy Lord.* To set forth the special honour which Christ will put upon those servants who wait for his second coming, he employs, in the 37th and 44th verses, allusions to those ancient customs, where the master, at certain festivals, attended upon the servants, and afforded peculiar tokens of his respect and confidence to the faithful individuals among them. It is as if he had said, in other words, *Blessed are they which are called to the marriage-supper of the Lamb. Where there shall be no more curse; but the throne of God and of the Lamb shall be in it, and his servants shall serve him: they shall see his face, and his name shall be in their foreheads. There shall be no night there, and they shall need no candle, neither the light of the sun; for the Lord God giveth them light, and they shall reign for ever and ever.*

BLESSED is such a servant, also, in THE TESTIMONY OF THE HOUSEHOLD, over which his Lord had placed him as a steward.

Speak, ye, who have been the seals of his ministry – *begotten again to a lively hope through the resurrection of Jesus Christ from the dead!* Can ye refrain from pronouncing him *blessed*, who was the happy instrument of making you feel your ruin and your *relief*? Will not many of you, who have been warned, instructed, encouraged, and tenderly conducted as by a nursing father – meet him in the great day with heart-felt gratitude? You feel what you owe to his labours; and what peculiar act of grace it was that placed you where the bread of life was dispensed in season, with integrity, wisdom, and affection. It maters not what others thought of your privileges; but it is impossible for *you* to think of them, and not to say, *Blessed is that servant.*

BLESSED is that servant, likewise, in THE TESTIMONY OF HIS OWN CONSCIENCE.

I remember, on hearing a pious minister, under depression, express some doubts of his own conversion, Mr. Newton replied, "Whatever I may doubt on other points, I cannot doubt whether there has been a certain gracious transaction between God and *my* soul. I cannot doubt whenever I look at my former and present objects, whether I ought not to cry, *What hath God wrought!*" It was not the peculiar privilege of Paul to say, *I have fought the good fight: I have finished my course: I have kept the faith: henceforth there is laid up for me a crown of righteousness, which the Lord, the Righteous Judge, shall give me at that day*: for, observe the words following, where he adds, *not to me* ONLY, *but unto all them that love his appearing.* Such a witness will not detract from the glory of God: he rather magnifies the power of his grace: he stands, like Legion, as a monument of it: and he will cry, after his boldest efforts to display it, *Yet not I, but the grace of God which was with me.* In the testimony of his own conscience, therefore, *Blessed is that servant.*

One cannot help here contrasting the real state of such a servant with his reception among men. A real Christian, and much more a Christian minister, is a character utterly unknown in the world. He reminds us of that scripture, *He, that is spiritual, judgeth* (ανακρινει, discerneth) *all things, yet he himself is judged* (or discerned) *of no man*: that is, he knows *them*, but they do not know *him.* It is, therefore, no matter of surprise, with the real servant of God, if he be scouted as a fanatic, by the profane; if he be scorned, by the proud; if his character be misunderstood, by the ignorant; or if his doctrine be wilfully misrepresented, by the malicious. All this he is taught to expect; and all this, and much more than this, he is willing patiently to bear. For, as that *faithful witness in heaven*, the moon, appears steadily to pursue its course among opposing clouds, cheering the pilgrim through the horrors of the night, while owls hoot and dogs bark at its splendour; so the faithful witness on earth above mentioned; while he illuminates his particular station, – hailed by the children of light, but neglected, if not hated, by others, – will recollect how his master was received, and that he testified, *This is the condemnation, that light is come into the world, and men love darkness rather than light, because their deeds are evil.*

Consider such a minister coming to bring men from their state of apostacy back to God. If we regard the standard of truth on this point, and see the end of men, we shall learn, that *many of them that sleep in the dust shall awake, some to everlasting life, and some to shame and everlasting contempt.* But, where are their instructors? And what is said of them? It is added, *and they that be wise* (or instructors, as the word signifies) *shall shine as the brightness of the firmament; and they, that turn many to righteousness, as the stars for ever and ever.*

One cannot help viewing with grief the reception which such an instructor meets with, when placed in the centre of a great city. In such a station he may present (as your late instructor did) the inestimable treasure of the gospel, not only on the Sunday, but in the course of the week. What then did you see? The merchant rushes to the exchange, heedless of his privilege: some friend points to the church as he passes, but he replies, "I have no time now: *I pray thee have me excused.*" The banker, engrossed with the *gold that perisheth*, forgets that *gold tried in the fire* which would make him really rich; and he also *prays to be excused.* The stock-broker hastens to his one object, and enquires of the first man he meets, "How are things now?" Would to God he knew! Would to God he had asked your late minister as to the real state of things! Things that infinitely more belong to his peace, than those which he seeks. The lady drives hastily by the church to purchase a toy, totally unmindful of that *pearl of great price* now offered to her without money. In the mean time we are deafened with the clamour. Commerce, with its ten thousand voices, seems to cry aloud, "Money is the *one thing needful.*" Crowds passing to the *temple of Mammon*, are ready to trample you under foot, as you endeavour to approach the *temple of God.*

Besotted men! To pursue business, is your duty; but to pursue that ONLY, is your crime. What! Has wisdom so long cried aloud among you for this? Has she uttered her voice *in the chief place of concourse, that scorners should still delight in their scorning, and fools hate knowledge? – What shall it profit you*, cries her preacher, *if ye gain the whole world, and at length lose your own soul? Or what shall a man give in exchange for his soul?* Some, with a death-like apathy, pass the church, and say, *He seems a good man*: others say, *Nay, but he deceiveth the people; when will he die and his name perish?* We reply, NEVER. For, at length, the JUDGE HIMSELF rises up, and pronounces, *Blessed is that servant – yea, blessed are those servants, whom the Lord when he cometh shall find watching!*

The righteous perisheth, and no man layeth it to heart; and merciful men are taken away, none considering that the righteous is taken away from the evil to come. HE SHALL ENTER INTO PEACE. The change of your late minister is but a change of preferment: it is but the call of his Master to *come up higher* – to take his harp, his palm, his crown, and bid eternal farewell to all his cares and sorrows. Blessed are those servants: *for God shall wipe all tears from their eyes; and there shall be no more death, neither sorrow nor crying, neither shall there be any more pain, for the former things are passed away.*

Having attempted to drop a few general hints on the CHARACTER and COMMENDATION of a faithful minister, and having shown their application to your late pastor, permit me to address a word,

1. To his stated CONGREGATION

Your vigilant and prepared servant is now called off his post: your faithful and wise steward is gone to deliver his account. He doubtless will do it with joy, having made it the grand object of his life. But let us consider, my dear hearers, the account which *we* also have to give. If special benefits involve special obligations, where are the people that have enjoyed your privileges? Some of you are his spiritual children, born and brought up in this house of prayer. Many of you have been *nourished up in the words of faith and of good doctrine*, as by a nursing-father. Others have been warned to *flee from the wrath to come*, as by a faithful monitor; and others cautioned by a guide who seemed in his experience to have explored the very *depths of Satan*. The afflicted have been comforted: the doubtful have been relieved; and ministers (among whom I stand as a witness) have been enlarged and confirmed, as by a father in Christ.

Let us admire and adore the grace, which *plucked such a brand from the burning*, and marvellously formed him afterwards to be that *vessel of honour* which he became. Let us recollect to WHOM we are indebted for such a Steward; who, with wisdom and faithfulness, apportioned our meat in due season. And, if the remark of one of our divine be just, that "a faithful minister being taken away before the age of threescore is taken in judgment", let us stand encouraged that the departed lived far beyond the age of man before he was removed; and let us earnestly pray to the Lord of the harvest, that this church, which has been favoured with eminent pastors long before the coming of your late minister, may enjoy a continuance of them till shall be no more.

But infallible authority lays a ground for the comfort of every mourner in Zion when it enjoins, *Remember them which have the rule over you, who have spoken unto you the word of* GOD; *whose faith follow, considering the end of their conversation,* [1] or as the word is, the blessed *departure* which they made; and more especially considering that *Jesus Christ is the same yesterday, and today, and for ever.* He ever lives! He, the great *Shepherd and Bishop of souls*, will still provide for his flock; that *where he is they may be also.*

Mr. Newton gradually sunk as the setting sun, shedding to the last those declining rays, which gilded and gladdened the dark valley. In the latter conversations which I had with him, he expressed an unshaken faith in eternal realities; and, when he could scarcely utter words, he remained a firm witness to the truths which he has preached. In so very gradual a declension, interesting particulars can scarcely be expected: should any be gathered,

---

1. The word εκβασι, here rendered, *the end of their conversation*, is used but once more in the New Testament, 1 Corinthians 3:10, where it is justly rendered *escape*.

they will appear in the Memoirs of his Life, which I have collected under his direction; and which will further tend to prove the force of truth, the blessedness of its great service, and the greatness of its present as well as future reward.

My honoured brethren in the ministry – *Servants, Stewards, Watchmen!* How much have WE to learn on this occasion! What need to cry, *My father, my father, the chariots of Israel and the horsemen thereof! Let a double portion of thy spirit rest upon us!* For *our* hour is also hastening: *our* account is soon to be given in: *our* Master is coming: *our* character will be proclaimed: *our* state will be fixed! Think on these momentous things. Think of your Lord's words, *Be ye ready also; for the Son of Man cometh at an hour when ye think not.*

2. To his PARISHONERS, also, I would address the feelings of my heart.

I speak more especially to such as have not duly appreciated the ministry of their late worthy pastor. The worn-out body of him who long entreated you to be mindful of the day of your visitation, now is a mass of inanimate clay under that communion table – his lamp broken – his tongue silent –

Disarm'd, disabled, like a wretch that's gagg'd,
And cannot tell his ills to passers by.

While he borrows my tongue to address you on the occasion.

And what can I say to you that he has not said a thousand times? I can only say, Lay the day of your visitation to heart, for God has spoken to you again and again by the mouth of his servant. If he were to return from the dead, he could only repeat the same message; and then sigh and say with one of old, *Oh, that they were wise! That they understood this! That they would consider their latter end!*

Some of his parishioners have, I hope, felt the truth of his character; and are now convinced that he was that very man who kept his eye on his sacred rule, inquiring what sort of man the minister of a parish ought to be. Since his death, perhaps, you have been ready to say, *Let me die the death of the righteous, and let my last end be like his*: for the true minister is seldom fully known till he is gone. But let us allow something to imagination – Let us suppose your late minister to rise like SAMUEL from the dead. Suppose him to learn that some of you, his parishioners, had begun to recollect yourselves; had resolved to pray, to turn to God, to embrace his Son, and to obey the gospel; – nay, that some of you were supposing that you even *do* serve God, because you begin to pay a formal attention to the externals of religion, and admit the general truths which he preached.

I ask, would he not say to such, like SAMUEL, on another occasion, "Ye serve God! *What meaneth then this bleating of the sheep in mine ears, and this lowing of the oxen that I hear?*" What meaneth this frequent breaking of the sabbath, by business or pleasure? What meaneth this chosen friendship with the enemies of truth? This idolatry of the world? This strangeness to the active servants of your Lord's house? This slighting of his children? This neglect of his only begotten Son? Ye serve God! How is it possible to serve God through such days of vanity and nights of carnal amusement? Can this be the service of God, who loathes a mere lip service? Who cries, *My son, give me thy heart? Oh that thou, even thou, at least in this thy day,* knewest the things *that belong to thy peace!*"

But I should apologise for the bare supposition of such a return from the grave; for *there the weary are at rest*: as it is said in the book of wisdom, "The souls of the righteous are in the hand of God. In the sight if the unwise they seemed to die, but they are in peace. Then shall the righteous stand in great boldness before the face of such as have afflicted him, and made no account of his labours. When they see it, they shall be troubled with great fear; and shall be amazed at the strangeness of his salvation; so far beyond all that they looked for; and, in anguish of spirit shall say, This was he whom we had sometimes in derision, and a proverb of reproach. We fools accounted his life madness, and his end to be without honour; how is he numbered among the children of God, and his lot is among the saints.

Such a recall, therefore, of your late minister to future labour on earth, is purely imaginary. But, away with the phantoms of imagination, while certain realities demand our attention! I am bound to enounce a truth firmer than heaven or earth: I am bound to assert, that your late minister SHALL return from the dust: not as a preacher, but as a *witness*: not as a warning voice, but as an unquestionable *evidence*. For *the day cometh that shall burn as an oven, when all the proud and all that do wickedly shall be as stubble –* When these massy pillars shall give way! When this temple shall be crushed in dust! When these tombs shall be opened! When these dead shall awake! *Marvel not at this, for the hour is coming, in which all that are in the graves shall hear the voice of the Son of God, and come forth: they that have done good, unto the resurrection of life; and they that have done evil, unto the resurrection of damnation.*

Then will your late faithful minister present his testimony to his Lord and judge, respecting the impenitent of his charge. He will declare, 'Near thirty years I stood on my appointed watch in the parish of St Mary Woolnoth. I knew no rule, but thy word, and declared the message which thou gavest me. *I hearkened and heard, but they spake not aright: no man repented of his wickedness, saying, What have I done! Every one turned to his course, as the horse rusheth into the battle.* I called unto them from my *pulpit*; I sent warnings and invitations to their *houses*; I exhorted them as a *friend*; I cried as a *watchman*; I entreated them as a *father, Turn ye, turn ye, for why will ye die?* O my God, thou, that searchest the heart and triest the reins, THOU knowest this!' May his parish also know it before THEY also follow him to the silent grave.

My dear fellow-citizens and fellow-sinners, standing on the brink of an awful precipice; you *must* know, that tomorrow your cares, your sorrows, and your joys will be recollected but as a dream; and that the grand objects long presented to you from this pulpit will be then your only anxious concern. Remember, that the admonition before us respects not ministers only. The conscience of every man before me is also addressed. The happiness or misery of every man is at stake. May God, of his infinite mercy, fix these considerations with a lasting impression on our hearts, for Jesus Christ's sake! To whom, with the father and the Holy Ghost, be all honour and glory, now and for ever. Amen.

ACKNOWLEDGEMENTS

I am grateful to the following for permission to refer to and quote from manuscripts and other archives held by:

Angus Library, Regent's Park College, Oxford; Bodleian Library, University of Oxford; Borthwick Institute of Historical Research, University of York; British Library; Cambridge University Library; British and Foreign Bible Society; Church Mission Society; The Trustees of the Cowper and Newton Museum, Olney, Buckinghamshire; The Trustees of Dr Williams's Library, London; East Riding of Yorkshire Council Archive Office, Beverley; Essex County Record Office, Chelmsford; Evangelical Library, London; Guildhall Library, Corporation of London; Hackney Archives Department; Hudson's Bay Company Archives, Winnipeg, Manitoba; The Archbishop of Canterbury and the Trustees of Lambeth Palace Library, London; Leicester University Library; Lincoln Diocesan Record Office, Lincolnshire Archives; Liverpool Record Office and Local Studies; London Metropolitan Archives; Medway Archives and Local Studies Centre, Strood; Maritime Archives and Library, Merseyside Maritime Museum; The Trustees of the National Maritime Museum, Greenwich; Naval, Military & Air Force Bible Society; Public Record Office, Kew; Shakespeare Birthplace Trust Records Office, Stratford-on-Avon; Tower Hamlets Local History Library & Archives; Warwickshire County Record Office, Warwick; University Library, University of Birmingham.

Information and encouragement was readily supplied by Tony Baker, Brian Edwards, Michael Haykin, Bruce Hindmarsh, Elizabeth Knight, Derek Morris, John Pollock; Gavin Reid; John Reynolds, Robert Watson [William Bull's great-great-great-great grandson] and many others, including friends who generously helped in various ways, transcribing, proof reading, offering advice and periodically restoring the computer to life (and the church youth group, who twice restored the garden). Their help was and is very much appreciated.

Especial thanks to Frank Wallis, who kindly and meticulously supplied the index.

Finally my thanks to Malcolm Maclean, Managing Editor of Christian Focus, for his patient guidance and to William MacKenzie, Managing Director, for the opportunity to augment Cecil's biography.

Angus Library, Regent's Park College, Oxford
An Account of the Rise and Progress of the Two Societies at Mr Ryland's and at Mrs Trinder's Boarding School in Northampton, drawn up by John Ryland jnr, 1768-70

Bodleian Library, University of Oxford
Full details are given in the References.

MS Wilberforce c.3, ff 27-8, 33-4	correspondence of and about William Wilberforce
MS Wilberforce c. 49, ff 1-128	letters from Newton to Wilberforce
MS Wilberforce d.14, ff 152-3	letters mainly to Wilberforce
MS Wilberforce d.15, ff 1-240; 38-9, 198-9	letters to and from Wilberforce
MS Wilberforce d.16, ff 25a-b	letters of Wilberforce
MS Wilberforce d.17, ff 1-333	letters mainly to Wilberforce
MS Autogr. c.24, f 193	autographs, letters and portraits
MS Autogr. d. 21, ff 194-5	Guard-book of letters
MS Eng. poet. c. 51, pp 253-6	Scrapbook of Mary Madan

Borthwick Institute of Historical Research, University of York

BIHR	Wills proved 12 Feb 1798 [Henry Newton] and 31 May 1813 [Ann Newton]
MB/N 1765	Marriage Allegations [Henry Newton and Ann Manby]
pr. Hay/1	Hayton Parish Register [Baptisms]
pr. Hay/2	Hayton Parish Register [Burials]

British Library (BL)

MSS Add 70949/110	Letter from John Newton to John Bacon [jnr] 25 Sept 1801
Eg. MS 3662	Letters from John Newton to William Cowper 1767-81

Cambridge University Library
Thornton Papers:

Add 7674	many items of interest including: Religious Meditations of Lucy Watson Thornton [1722-1785]; Printed discourse on death of John Thornton by Thomas Scott, 1791; correspondence between John Newton and John and Lucy Thornton [quoted letter 16 July 1776: Add 7674/1/A]
Add 7826	correspondence between John Newton and John and Lucy Thornton [quoted letter 18 November 1777: Add 7826/1/A]

British and Foreign Bible Society Archives
Held at Cambridge University Library

Cowper and Newton Museum, Olney, Buckinghamshire
(many C&N manuscripts now kept in the County Museum at Aylesbury)
A Catalogue of the Library of the late William Cowper
A Collection of Material towards a Life of Cowper (Hayley's)
A List of the Children: The meetings for the children at the Great House until Jan 1765 (Newton's)
A Monument to the praise of the Lord's goodness and to the memory of dear Eliza Cunningham (Newton's)
Collections: The Avenell Album, The Drinkwater Album, The Harvey Albums
Correspondence: William Bull, George Catlett, Alexander Clunie, William Cowper, Andrew Fuller, Mrs Gardiner, Richard Hansard, Lady Hesketh, William

Hayley, John Johnson, Josiah Jones, Judith Madan, John Sutcliff, Joshua Symonds, Mary Unwin, William Ward, Hannah Wilberforce and others

Eclectic Notes (Newton's notebook, from 6 July 1789 to 9 February 1795

Epitaph on Dr Johnson (by William Cowper and John Newton)

Interleaved copy of *Letters to a Wife* (Newton's)

Maria Cowper, *Serious Commonplace Book*

Maximilian Grindon's *Daybook* (Surgeon and Apothecary at Olney)

Memoir of the Early Life of William Cowper, Esq., written by himself

Mr Newton's Account of Mr Cowper in a Funeral Sermon, notes taken by Hannah Jowett, daughter of Newton's friend John Jowett, during Newton's Funeral Sermon for William Cowper at St Mary Woolnoth, 1800

Observations critical and explanatory, on all the Greek words of the New Testament (Newton's)

Sermon notebooks (Newton's)

Verse and Prose of Cowper

Dr Williams's Library, London

MS 38.98.46-57   Letters from Newton to David Jennings   1750-60
MS 38.105-7   Minute Books of the Protestant Dissenting Ministers of the Three Denominations in and about the cities of London and Westminster, 3 vols, 1727-1827

East Riding of Yorkshire Council Archive Office, Beverley

Map of Market Weighton, 1847, by William Watson
DDPY/14/26   Extract of Will of Ann Newton of Market Weighton, widow
QDE 1/8/14   Land Tax for Hayton [Ann Newton's relations]

Essex County Records Office, Chelmsford

D/ABR 33/160   Will of Benjamin Nind (snr.)
D/P 157/1/2   Aveley Parish Records, Baptisms and Burials [1718-1801]

Guildhall Library, Corporation of London

GL MS 454   Spencer Cowper, Opinions relating to the Customs of London
GL MS 1001/2   St Mary WoolnothVestry Minutes 1776-1817
GL MS 1556   William Herbert, "Memoir of my own Life"
GL MS 2084   Miscellaneous Items relating to the Revd John Newton
GL MS 3638   letters from Newton to Thomas Mitchell, Kent
GL MS 4402   St Olave, Jewry, Marriages [1754-1812] etc.
GL MS 4998   St Mary-le-bow, Baptisms [1697-1771], Marriages [1697-1754], Burials [1697-1769]
GL MS 6010   Tower Division Precinct of St. Katherine by the Tower, Land Tax, 1732-1822
GL MS 6013/1   St John's Wapping Land Tax Assessments, 1730-1826
GL MS 7639   St Mary Woolnoth, Register of Baptisms and Burials [1744-1806], Marriages [1745-1754]
GL MS 7639A   St Mary Woolnoth, Births [1806-1812], Baptisms [1807-1814], Burials [1807-1812]
GL MS 7640/2   St Mary Woolnoth, Register of Marriages [1754-1813], Banns 1801-1823
GL MS 7643   St. Mary Woolnoth, Burials [1813-1852]
GL MS 9660   St. Katherine by the Tower Parish Register, Baptisms [1727-1769] and Burials [1678-1695; 1727-1794]
GL MS 10091/120   Marriage Allegations [for Benjamin Nind and Thomasina Newton,

| | 29 August 1768] |
| GL MS 16949 | St Mary Woolnoth, 2 letters from John Newton to Thomas Scott |

Hackney Archives Department
HAD P/L/LT 25-32   Shoreditch Land Tax Ledgers, 1778-1787

Lambeth Palace Library, London

MS 2872	Correspondence with Mary Newton, 1745-87
MS 2935	*Letters to* Samuel Brewer, Betsy Catlett, Jack Catlett, J Cunningham, Mrs Eversfield, Thomas Haweis, Mary Newton, John Thornton, Martha Trinder, George Whitefield, Mrs Wilberforce *Letters from*, William Carey, Zacharay Macaulay, M Manesty and others
MS 2936	MSS of *Letters to a Wife*
MS 2937	Miscellaneous Thoughts
MS 2938-40	Lectures and sermon notes
MS 2941-3	Diaries 1767-1803
MS 3095	Correspondence with William Bull 1773-1804, Mary Newton to Betsy Catlett
MS 3096	*Letters to* Betsy Catlett, George Catlett, Jack Catlett, Elizabeth Crabb, Elizabeth Cunningham, J Cunningham, Mary Newton, John Thornton, Martha Trinder
	Letters from John Berridge, Claudius Buchanan, Josiah Bull, Richard Conyers, Lady Hesketh, Martin Madan, Thomas Robinson, Charles Simeon, HR van Lier, Henry Venn
	Letters from Mary Newton to Elizabeth Cunningham, Elizabeth Crabb
MS 3534	Miscellaneous papers including correspondence with Lady Hesketh
MS 3970	Diary 1752-1756 (copy)
MS 3972	1760-1804 letters
MS 3973	1768-1804 letters, (includes Thomas Jones, Judith Madan, Thomas Scott and Newton's will)
MS 3974	Letters to William Bull, 1761-81
MS 3975	Letters to William Bull, 1760-1815

Leicester University

| MSS 16 | Thomas Ford's notebook: journey through England and Wales |
| MSS 33-35 | Thomas Ford's diary of sermons, notebook, sermons |

Lincolnshire Archives, Lincoln
Lincoln Diocesan Record Office: Lincoln Episcopal Register No. 39, fo. 32r/33r

Liverpool Record Office and Local Studies
920 MD 409   Archive on John Newton, including:
                       A Series of Letters from Mr Newton to Dr Jennings 1750-1760
                       (copy: original in DW)
                       Journal of John Newton (copy: original in NMM)

London Metropolitan Archives
P73/GIS/049   Parish Register, St. Giles, Camberwell

Medway Archives and Local Studies Centre, Strood, Kent
microfilm P 85   Parish Register, St Mary's, Chatham

Maritime Archives and Library, Merseyside Maritime Museum
C/EX/L/3/1   The Liverpool Statutary Registers of British Merchant Ships
                              (Plantation Registers: Owners' Declarations)

National Maritime Museum, Greenwich
LOG/M/46   Log of John Newton while Master of the Duke of Argyle and
                              African on voyages to Africa and the WestIndies between 1750
                              and 1754
ADM/L/H/67   Lieutenants' Logbook of HMS *Harwich*, Jan 1743- Jun 1744 [Lieut.
                              Thomas Ruffin]
ADM/L/L/179   Lieutenants' Logbook of HMS *Lizard*, Jan 1772- Dec 1773 [Lieut.
                              Henry Newton]

Naval, Military and Air Force Bible Society
                              Archives

Public Record Office
Manuscripts held at Kew:
ADM 8/24   List Book
ADM 36/1444   Muster Roll of HMS *Harwich* Jan 1774- Jul 1745
ADM 36/1449   Muster Roll of HMS *Harwich* Jan 1744- Dec 1745
ADM 36/7635   Muster Roll of HMS Lizard Oct 1770–Dec 1773
ADM 51/3858   Captain's log HMS Harwich, 1743 Dec 26–1748 July 18
ADM 51/550   Captain's log of HMS Lizard Oct 1770–Dec 1773

PRO manuscripts held at Family Record Office, London
RG4/4304   Independent Church Meeting Book, Old Gravel Lane, Wapping
PROB. 11/1474   Probate of Newton's Will, 1803; codicil, 1804
PROB 11/1709   Probate of Joseph Smith's Will, 1825; codicil, 1825
PROB 11/1840   Probate of Elizabeth (Betsy) Smith's Will, 1828

Tower Hamlets Local History Library & Archives
L 2650   Material towards a History of Stepney, 1843-44, collected by MA
                              Gliddon, [1844]
TH/8337/1   Stepney Meeting Church Book, 1644-1894
TH/8337/36   Memorials of Stepney Meeting House, William John Living stone
TH/8337/37/1-2   Watercolours of Old Stepney Meeting by Stoneham Chatterton
TH 8342   Stepney Meeting House Burials Register 1790-1853, indexed in
                              LP. 7838 (pamphlet, class 120.1)

University Library, University of Birmingham Special Collections
Manuscripts of the Church Mission Society:
CMS Acc. 81 [MSS Venn]:
    c.65   letters from Mary Newton to John
    c.66   mainly letters from Newton to the Venn family
    c.67   letter from Mary Newton to Mary Unwin; Newton's sermon notes

Warwickshire County Record Office
CR 895/101   Map of Grove Park, Lord Dacre's Estate near Warwick (Newton's
                              favourite walk)
CR 1054/3   Signed covenant, James Moody and members of Cow Lane
                              Independent, Warwick, 1790

BIBLIOGRAPHY

Adair, James Makittrick, *Unanswerable Arguments*, 1790.

Addington, Stephen, *A Sermon occasioned by the death of Mrs Elizabeth Ford who departed this life May 31 1781 in the fifty-first year of her Age. Preached at Miles-Lane, London, June 10 by William Ford. She being dead yet speaketh. Psalm 73:24.*, 1781
    Peace the End of the perfect and upright Man. A sermon occasioned by the death of the Revd Mr William Ford who departed this life January 26 1783 in the forty-seventh year of his age. Preached at Miles-Lane, February 2, 1783 by Stephen Addington. To which is added the Oration at his interment by Joseph B[othe]. [from Psalm 37:37], 1783

Alldridge, Thomas Joshua, *The Sherbro and its Hinterland*, 1901

Alleine, Joseph, *An Alarme to Unconverted Sinners*, 1671

[Allestree, Richard], *The Whole Duty of Man. With private devotions*, 1657

Andrews, John Richard, *George Whitefield; a light rising in obscurity*, 1864

Atkins, John, *A Voyage to Guinea, Brasil and the West Indies*, 1735

Aveling, Thomas William B, *Memorials of the Clayton Family, with unpublished correspondence of the Countess of Huntingdon*, 1867

Baker, Frank, *William Grimshaw 1708-1763*, 1963

Baldwin, Ronald A, *The Gillingham Chronicles*, 1998

Balfour, Clara Lucas, *A Sketch of Mrs Hannah More and her sisters*, 1854

Balleine, George Reginald, *A History of the Evangelical Party in the Church of England*, 1908, new edtn 1951

Barbot, Jean, A description of Sierra Leona, [with plates], 1745

Barnes, Gordon, *Stepney Churches: an historical account*, 1967

Barrow, Isaac, *Euclidis Elementa*, 1655

Bateman, Josiah, *The Life of the Right Rev. Daniel Wilson, late Lord Bishop of Calcutta and Metropolitan, with extracts from his journals and correspondence*, 2 vols, 1860

Bates, Ely, *A Chinese Fragment containing an enquiry into the present state of Religion in England, with notes by the editor*, 1786

Baxter, Andrew, *An Enquiry into the Nature of the Human Soul, wherein the Immateriality of the Soul is Evinced from the Principles of Reason and Philosophy*, 1733

Baxter, Richard, *The Reformed Pastor: showing the nature of the pastoral work (abridged by Thomas Rutherford), To which is added an appendix, containing extracts from various authors on the same subject*, 1656, 1806 edtn
    The Saints' Everlasting Rest; or, A Treatise on the Blessed State of the Saints in their Enjoyment of God in Heaven, 1649

Beavan, Alfred Beaven, *The Aldermen of the City of London. Temp. Henry III - 1908(-1912). With notes on the parliamentary representation of the city, the aldermen, and the livery companies*, 2 vols, 1908, 13

Beawes, Wyndam, *Merchants Directory*, 1761, 2nd edtn

Bennett, Benjamin, *The Christian Oratory: or the Devotion of the Closet Display'd*, 2 vols, 1726-8

Bennett, James, *The History of the Church in Silver Street, London*, 1842

Beveridge, William [bishop of St. Asaph], *Good Friday to be kept by all Christians and the Manner of keeping it. Zech xii.10*, 1709
    Private Thoughts upon Religion, Digested into Twelve Articles with Practical Resolutions Form'd thereupon, 1709
    Sermons on several subjects, 12 vols, 1708-15
    The Works of the Right Reverend Father in God, Dr William Beveridge, Late Lord Bishop of St Asaph, Containing all his sermons, as well as those publish'd by Himself, as those since his death, 1729

Blackader, John, *Select Passages from the Diary and Letters of the late John Blackader Esq, formerly Lieutenant Colonel of the XXVIth ... Regiment of Foot ... Written chiefly during... the war... conducted by John, Duke of Marlborough*. With...notes. To which is prefixed an account of the life and parentage of the writer [by Charles Stuart, of Dunearn]. With a preface by John Newton, 1806

Bloomfield, William Earnest, *The Baptists of Yorkshire*, 1912

Boardman, James, *Liverpool Table Talk A Hundred Years Ago, or a History of Gore's Directory, with Anecdotes Illustrative of the Period of its first publication, in 1766. In a letter to the members of the History Society of Lancashire and Cheshire. To which is added a continuation of the same subject, and a map of the town in 1650*, eds Henry Young and Adam Bouler, 1871

Bogatzky, Carl Heinrich von, *A Golden Treasury for the children of God, whose treasure is in Heaven; consisting of Select Texts of the Bible, with practical Observations in Prose and Verse, for every Day in the Year*, 1775 edtn [edited by John Thornton, with contributions from Newton]

Bogue, David, and Bennett, James, *History of Dissenters* from the revolution in 1688 to the year 1808, 4 vols, 1808-12

Bonwick, James, *Australia's first preacher, the Rev Richard Johnson*, 1898

Booth, Abraham, *The Reign of Grace, from its rise to its consummation*, 7th edtn, 1803
The Works of Abraham Booth, 3 vols, 1813

Booth, T Wilson, *The First 150 years of the Stepney Meeting Independents from 1644 to 1796, Including the Life of the Rev Samuel Brewer*, 1913.

Boswell, James, *The Life of Samuel Johnson, LLD*, 1791

Bradberry, David, *Sermon: Amos 4:12, Prepare to meet thy God, O Israel*, 1766.

Bradbury, Thomas, *Fifty-four sermons preached by... Thomas Bradbury...Many...being preached in critical times, on days of public humiliation or thanksgiving, but chiefly on the fifth of November, in commemoration of the glorious revolution of King William, &c*, 1762
Life and Letters of Thomas Bradbury etc, 1911
The Joy of a Christian in finishing his Course, 1705
The Justification of a Sinner, 1716
The necessity of contending for revealed religion, with a sermon on the fifth of November 1719. To which is prefixed a letter from the Reverend Cotton Mather, DD, on the late disputes about the Ever-Blessed Trinity, collected of his published sermons, by Mr Winter, 1720
The Power of Christ over Plagues and Health, and his Name as the God of Israel, 1724
The quality and work of a glorified Redeemer, 1703

Brayley, Edward Wedlake, [text], Storer, James, and Greig, James, [plates], *Cowper, Illustrated by a series of views, in, or near, The Park of Weston-Underwood, Bucks, Accompanied with Copious Descriptions, and a Brief Sketch of the Poet's Life*, 1810

Brekell, John, *Euroclydon, or the dangers of the sea considered, and improved, in some reflections on St Paul's voyage and shipwreck, Acts 27*, 1744

Brewster, James, *Life of the Rev. John Newton* [i.e. the Narrative and comments], 1813

Britton, John, *Autobiography*, 1848-50

Brooke, Richard, *Liverpool as it was during the Last Quarter of the Eighteenth century. 1775-1800.* [with plates], 1853

Brooks, Thomas, *Pictures of the Past: The History of the Baptist Church in Bourton-on-the-Water*, 1861

Brown, Alexander, *Smith's Stranger's Guide to Liverpool, its Environs and part of Cheshire for 1842*, 1842 [contains a map by Benjamin Smith showing the location of the Tide Surveyor's office, where Newton worked]

Brown, Raymond, *The English Baptists of the 18th century*, 1986

Browne, Moses, *The Works and Rest of the Creation, containing (1) an Essay on the Universe, (2) Sunday Thoughts*, (1) 1750, (2) 1752

Buchanan, George, *Psalmorum Dauidis Paraphrasis Poetica*, 1566

Buck, Charles, *Memoir of the Life and Death of Mr Thomas Atkins, late of New Street, Gough Square, London*, 1812

Bull, Josiah, *John Newton of Olney and St Mary Woolnoth, an autobiography and narrative*, 1868; reprinted as *But Now I See*, Banner of Truth, 1998.
   Letters by the Rev. John Newton of Olney and St Mary Woolnoth ... with biographical sketches and illustrated notes, 1869
   Memorials of the Rev. William Bull, of Newport-Pagnell, 1864

Bull, Thomas Palmer, *A brief narrative of the Rise and Progress of the Independent Church at Newport-Pagnell, now under the pastoral care of the Reverend William Bull and Thomas Palmer Bull*, 1811
   One Hundred and Twenty-Nine Letters from John Newton to the Rev William Bull, from 1773 to 1805, 1847

Bunyan, John, *Grace Abounding to the Chief of Sinners*, 1666, repr 1983

Burder, George, *The Christian's View of Life, and the Prospect of Futurity, A Sermon preached at Warwick December 7 1806, on account of the much lamented death of the Rev James Moody who departed this life November 22 1806 aged 50*, 1806 [2 Timothy 4:7,8]

Butler, Dugald, *The Life and Letters of Robert Leighton, Restoration Bishop of Dunblane and Archbishop of Glasgow*, 1903

Byrom, John, *Private Journals and Literary Remains of John Byrom*, ed. Richard Parkinson, 2 vols. 1854-7

Cadogan, William Bromley, *The Life of the Rev William Romaine*, 1796

Callis, John, *John Newton, sailor, preacher, pastor and poet: Centenary Memorials*, 1908

Campbell, John, *Letters and Conversational Remarks of the Rev John Newton*, 1808
   Travels in South Africa, undertaken at the request of the London Missionary Society, 2 vols, 1822

Carey, Samuel Pearce, *William Carey, DD, Fellow of Linnaean Society*, 1934

Carus, William, *Memoirs of the Life of the Rev. Charles Simeon*, 1847

Castalio, Sebastian, *Biblia Sacra. Accessere in nova hoc ed. eiusdem Delineato*, 1697.

Cecil, Richard, *A Sermon on the Death of the late Rev. John Newton, preached at St. Mary Woolnoth*, 1808
   Memoirs of Mr Bacon, 1801
   Memoirs of Mr Cadogan, 1798
   Memoirs of Mr John Newton, 1808
   Original Thoughts on Various Passages of Scripture, Sermons, ed by Catherine Cecil, 1848
   Works of the Rev. Richard Cecil, with a Memoir of his life, arranged and revised by J. Pratt, 1827, 3rd edtn

Champion, Leonard George, The Letters of John Newton to John Ryland, *Baptist Quarterly*, 27, 157-63, 1977

Chancellor, Edwin Beresford, *The History of the Squares of London, topographical and historical*, 1907

Clayton, John, *The Duty of Christians to magistrates: A Sermon, occasioned by the late Riots at Birmingham, preached at the King's Weigh-House, East-Cheap, on Lord's Day Morning, July 24,1791*, with a Prefix, intended to remove the reproach, lately fallen on protestant dissenters, 1791

Coleridge, Samuel Taylor, and Wordsworth, William, *Lyrical Ballads [including The Ancient Mariner]*, 1798

Collingwood, Jeremy & Margaret, *Hannah More*, 1990

Cornish, James, *Cornish's Guide through Liverpool and its Environs with a neatly engraved map*, 1845, 3rd edtn.

Courtier, Peter L, *The Pulpit; or a biographical and literary account of eminent Popular Preachers; interspersed with Occasional Clerical Criticism, by Onesimus*, 3 vols, 1816

[Cowper, Ashley], *Poems and translations, by the author of The Progress of Physick [signing himself Timothy Scribble]*, 2 vols, 1767 [as *Norfolk Poetical Miscellany*, 1744?]

Cowper, Frances Maria, *Original Poems, on various occasions, by a lady [FM Cowper]*, *Revised by William Cowper*, 1792

Cowper, William, *Memoir of the Early Life of William Cowper, written by himself*, 1816
Poems [preface by John Newton], 2 vols, 1782, 85
Poems, the early productions of William Cowper. Now first published from the originals in the possession of James Croft. With anecdotes of the Poet. Collected from the letters of Lady Heskith, written during her residence at Olney, 1825

Cragg, George C, *Grimshaw of Haworth*, 1947

Creaton, Heather, ed [with the assistance of Tony Trowles], *The Bibliography of printed works on London history to 1939*, 1994
[and Wycherley, Jeremy Sumner], *Lists of Londoners*, 1997

Cropper, Margaret Beatrice, *Sparks among the stubble* [Studies of Robert Nelson, Thomas Bray, William Law, John Newton, Hannah More, William Wilberforce and Robert Walker], 1955

Dallimore, Arnold, *George Whitefield*, 2 vols, 1970

Dalton, Lilian Howard, *Singing Slave, a Biography of Newton*, 1952

Davidson, Noel, *How Sweet the Sound*, 1997

Dawson [née Flower], Jane, *The Life and Writings of Mrs Dawson of Lancaster... with nine unpublished letters from the Rev John Newton*, 1828

Defoe, Daniel, *A Tour Thro' the Whole Island of Great Britain, by a gentleman*, 3 vols., 1724-27
The Family Instructor, 1715

Derby, Madge, *Captain Bligh in Wapping*, 1990 [History of Wapping Trust]

Dews, D. Colin, *A History of Methodism in Haworth from 1744*, 1981

Dibdin, Thomas Frognall, *Reminisces of a Literary Life* , 1836

Dickins, L, and Stanton, M, eds, *An Eighteenth Century Correspondence*, 1910

Doddridge, Philip, *Some Remarkable Passages in the Life of Colonel James Gardiner*, 1747
The Correspondence and Diary of Philip Doddridge, 5 vols, edited by JD Humphreys, John Doddridge, et alia., 1829-31
The Family Expositor: or, a paraphrase and version of the New Testament: with critical notes, ed by J Orton, 6 vols, 1745-56, 1821, 11th edtn, to which is prefixed a life of the author by A Kipps
The Rise and Progress of Religion in the Soul; illustrated in a course of serious and practical addresses, suited to persons of every character and circumstance: each chapter concluding with a devout meditation or prayer, 1745
The Works of Philip Doddridge, edited by Edward Williams and E Parsons, with a Memoir by Job Orton, in 10 vols, 1802-05

Downer, Arthur Cleveland, *Thomas Scott, the commentator, a memoir of his life*, 1909

Dudley-Smith, Timothy, *John Stott: The Making of a Leader*, 2 vols, 1st vol 1999

Edwards, Brian, *Through Many Dangers*, 1975

Enfield, William, *An essay toward the history of Leverpool*, drawn up from papers left by the late G Perry, and from other materials, 2nd edtn, etc, 1774, BL includes MS notes [by JW Roberts]

Ephemerides, *A Companion to the Almanac*, 8th edtn, To which is added, a map of the world, neatly engraved by Thomas Jefferys, 1759

The Evangelical Museum, or Christian's Pocket Book for 1794 with interesting anecdotes, 1793 [with an engraving of Newton at the front – but perhaps the one Newton says somewhere is not his likeness]

Equiano, Olaudah, *The Interesting Narrative of the Life of Olaudah Equiano, or Gustavus Vassa, The African, written by Himself*, 2 vols, 1789; [subscribers include Lord Dartmouth, John Eyre, Henry Foster, Countess of Huntingdon, Rowland Hill, Sir Charles Middelton, Hannah More, Joseph Pratt, Thomas Scott, Henry Thornton, La Trobe, John Wesley and others] ed by Paul Williams as *The Life of Olaudah Equiano*, 1988

Evans, George Eyre, *Vestiges of Protestant Dissenters*, 1897

Extracts from the Diary of the late Rev Dr Ryland, *The Baptist Magazine*, 53, p279, 1861

Fawcett, John [the younger], *Account of the Life, Ministry and Writings of the late John Fawcett*, 1818

Finch, Harold, *The Tower Hamlets Connection*, 1996

Flavel, John, *Mr. John Flavel's remains: being two sermons. the former preached at Dartmouth on the coronation of William and Mary, the latter intended to be preached at Taunton Sept. 2. With a brief account of the author [by J. Galpine]*, 1691
Navigation Spiritualiz'd: or, a New Compass for Seamen, 1682
The whole works of ... John Flavel, 6 vols, 1820, reprinted by Banner of Truth, 1968

Ford, George, *The Good Man, and a faithful Minister, made eminently useful, A Funeral Sermon preached at Stepney meeting June 19 1796, occasioned by the death of the Rev Samuel Brewer, BD*, 1796

Ford, William, *A Sermon preached by the Rev Mr William Ford at the Ordination of Mr William Ford Junior, at Miles-Lane, December 14, 1757. Together with an Introductory Discourse by the Reverend Mr Samuel Morton Savage, Mr Ford's Confession of Faith and a charge delivered by David Jennings, DD*, 1758

Forster, EM, *Marianne Thornton*, 1956

Foster, Henry, *The Bible Preacher; or Closet Companion...Sermons...by the Late Rev Henry Foster, ed. S Piggot*, 1824

[Frank, Walter, minister of Chatham], *Letters and Instruments relating to the Dispute about the Register Book at Chatham*, 1766

Fryer, Peter, *Staying Power*, 1984

Fuller, Andrew, *Memoirs of the Rev Samuel Pearce, with extracts from his letters*, 1800
The Gospel worthy of all acceptance: or, The duty of sinners to believe in Jesus Christ, 1801, 2nd edtn corrected, to which is added an appendix
The Complete Works of the Rev Andrew Fuller, revised by Joseph Belcher, 1845

Fyfe, Christopher, *A History of Sierra Leone*, 1962

Gadsby, John, *Memoirs of the Principal Hymn-Writers and Compilers of the 17th and 18th Centuries*, 1882, 5th edtn

Gibbons, Thomas, *Memoirs of ... Isaac Watts*, 1780

Gillies, John, *Memoirs of the life of George Whitefield, to which is now added an extract from Mr Whitefield's tracts*, 1798

Goldsmith, Oliver, *Deserted Village*, 1770

Godwin, William T, *The Baptists of Warwick 1640-1955*, 1955

Goode jnr, William, *A Memoir of William Goode, rector of St Andrew, Wardrobe. also the late Rev Rector of the United Parishes of St Andrew, Wardrobe and St Ann, Blackfriars, London*, 1828, 2nd edtn, *to which is added an appendix of letters*

Goode snr, William, *Essays on all the Scriptural Names and Titles of Christ, or the economy of the gospel dispensation as exhibited in the person, character and office of the Redeemer*, 6 vols, 1822

Gore, John Francis, *Gore's Liverpool Directory*, 1766

Goss, Charles WF, *London Directories 1677-1855: A Bibliography*, 1932

Granger, James, *A Biographical History of England, Adapted to a Methodical Catalogue of Engraved British Heads*, 1769

Grant, Gordon, The Call of Dr John Ryland Jnr, *The Baptist Quarterly*, 34, 214-17, 1992

Greatheed, Samuel, *A Practical Improvement of the Divine Counsel and Conduct, attempted in a sermon occasioned by the decease of William Cowper Esq, Preached at Olney May 18 1800*
Memoirs of the Life and Writings of William Cowper, Esqr [An enlarged edition of his anonymous *Memoir of William Cowper, Esq*, in the *Evangelical Magazine*, April,May 1803. Followed by a *Brief Review of Mr Cowper's Writings*. With a portrait], 1803; A new edition: revised, corrected and recommended, by the Rev Samuel Greatheed, 1814

Grimshaw, William, *An Answer to a sermon lately published against the Methodists, by the Rev Mr George White, Minister of Colne and Marshden, in Lancs*, 1749

Grimshawe, Thomas Shuttleworth, *The Life and Works of William Cowper*, 1849

Gunn, William Alphonsus, *An address to all parties upon a subject in which all parties are concerned [on salvation through Jesus Christ]*, [1840?]
Sermons and Letters [ed by R.S.], 1807
Sermons on Various Subjects and Letters to an Undergraduate at the University by the late Rev William Alphonsus Gunn, To which are prefixed Memoirs of his Life by Isaac Saunders, AM, 2nd edtn, 1816

Guy, David, *A Complete Index to Dr Watt's Hymns*, 1773

Hanekom, Tobias Nicolaas, *Helperus Ritzema van Lier, Die Lewensbeeld van 'n Kaapse predikant uit die 18de eeu*, 1959

Hardy, Charles, A Register of ships employed in the service of the Hon. the United East India Company, from the year 1760 to 1812..., 1813, revised by his son, Horatio Charles Hardy, 1835

Hart, Joseph, *Hymns etc., Composed on Various Subjects, With a Preface Containing a Brief Summary Account of the Author's Experience and the Great Things that God Hath Done for his Soul*, 1759

Harvey, William, *London scenes and London people, by Aleph*, 1863, reprinted from City Press
The Old City, and its highways and byways, by Aleph, 1865

Hasted, Edward, *History and Topographical Survey of Kent*, 4 vols, 1778-99; 2nd edtn 8 vols, 1797-1801

Haweis, Thomas, *A Scriptural Refutation of the arguments for Polygomy, advanced in a treatise [by M. Madan] entitled: Thelyphthora*, 1781
Evangelical principles and practice, 15 sermons, 1819, 5th edtn
Life of William Romaine, 1797
The Evangelical Exposition: or, A commentary on the holy Bible, 2 vols, 1765/66

Haykin, Michael AG, *One Heart and One Soul: John Sutcliff of Olney, His Friends and His Times*, 1994

Hayley, William, *The Life and posthumous writings of William Cowper*, 1803

Hayward, Samuel, *17 Sermons on Various Important Subjects*, 1758
Growing in the Knowledge of Christ recommended to young persons, in a sermon [on 2 Peter 3:18], etc, 1746

Hennell, Michael, *John Venn and The Clapham Sect*, 1958

Herbert, George, *The Temple, sacred poems and ejaculations*, 1633
The Works of the Rev George Herbert, with remarks on his writings, and a sketch of his life, by William Jerdan, 1853

Hervey, James, *Meditations among the Tombs, Reflections on a Flower-Garden and a Descant on Creation*, 1746
Theron and Aspasio: or, A Series of Dialogues and Letters, upon the Most Important and Interesting Subjects, 3 vols, 1755

Hindmarsh, Bruce, *John Newton and the English Evangelical Tradition*, 1996

History of the Congregational Church at Olney, 1929

Hogarth, William, *The effects of industry and idleness illustrated; in the life, adventures and various fortunes of two fellow - 'prentices of the city of London, an explanation of 12 prints designed by mr Hogarth*, 1748

Hole, Charles, *The Early History of the Church Missionary Society for Africa and the East to the end of AD 1814*, 1896

Holland, Margaret Jean, *Life and Letters of Zachary Macaulay*, 1900

Hooker, Richard, *Of the lawes of Ecclesiasticall Politie, eyght bookes*, 1594

Horne, C Silvester, *The Story of the LMS 1795-1895*, 1895

Houstoun, Dr James, *Some New and Accurate Observations ... Containing a True and Impartial Account of the Coast of Guinea ... so far as relates to the improvement of that trade, for the advantage of Great Britain in general, and the Royal African Company in particular*, 1725

Howard, Kenneth, John Sutcliff of Olney, *Baptist Quarterly*, vol 14, 304-309, 1951-52

Hyde, Ralph, *A to Z of Georgian London*, 1981, London Topographical Society

A to Z of Victorian London, 1987, London Topographical Society

Ingham, Benjamin, *Diary of an Oxford Methodist, Benjamin Ingham, 1733-1734*, ed. Richard P Heitzenrater, 1985

Irwin, Grace, *Servant of Slaves: a biographical novel of John Newton*, 1961

Ivimey, Joseph, *A History of the English Baptists*, 4 vols, 1823

Janeway, James, *A token for children*, 1671

Janeway, James, *Invisible, realities, demonstrated in the holy life and triumphant death of Mr John Janeway [1633-1657], with a preface by the Rev J Venn*, 1885; (preface to 1st edtn by Richard Baxter, 1672)

Jarvis, Rupert C, *Customs Letter-Books of the Port of Liverpool 1711-1813, ed with an introduction by Rupert C Jarvis*, 1954

Jay, William, *The Autobiography of William Jay, edited by George Redford and John Angell James*, 1854, repr. 1974

Jenkins, Bruce, The Wisdom of John Newton, *Triumph through Tribulation*, Westminster Conference Papers, 1998

Jenks, Benjamin, *Prayers and offices of devotion for families, and for particular persons, upon most occasions...* 1697 [new edtn altered by C Simeon, 1851]

Jennings, David, *A sermon occasioned by the death of the late Rev Isaac Watts DD, Dec 11 1748*, 1749

A sermon [on Timothy 1:11,12] preached at the ordination of William Ford, Junior, December 14, 1752. Together with an introductory discourse by ... SM Savage. Mr Ford's confession of faith, and A charge delivered by David Jennings etc, 1758

A Vindication of the Scripture Doctrine of Original Sin from Mr [J.] Taylor's free and candid Examination of it. an anonymous piece, written with great smartness, in vindication of the superior doctrine of original sin, 1740

An Introduction to the Use of the Globes, and the Orrery with an Appendix attempting to explain the Account of the 1st and 4th days' work of Creation in the first chapter of Genesis, 1752

Christian Preaching and Ministerial Service considered in a sermon preached at St Ives in Huntingdonshire at the Ordination of the Reverend Mr John Jennings, August 12, 1742, By David Jennings. To which is added A Charge, Delivered on the same occasion, by Philip Doddridge, 1742

Jewish Antiquities: or, A course of Lectures on the three first books of Godwin's Moses and Aaron to which is annexed, A dissertation on the Hebrew language, ed P Furneaux, 2 vols, 1766

Sermons upon various subjects preached to Young People on New Year's days, 1730

The Beauty and Benefit of early Piety: Represented in several Sermons preached to the Young People on New-Year's Days and Published out of compassion to the rising generation, 1731, 4th edtn [same contents as above]

The Scripture Testimony examined and confirmed by plain Arguments, or An Appeal to Reason and Common Sense for the Truth of the Holy Scriptures. In 2 discourses [on John 21:24], 1755

Two Discourses of Preaching Christ and of Particular and Experimental Preaching, 1744

Johansen, John Henry, The Olney Hymns, *The Papers of the Hymn Society*, 20, 1956

Johnson, John, *The Love of God. A Sermon preached at the Funeral of Mr Samuel Hunter, jnr, Mariner, in Liverpool, who departed this life the 25th day of January 1758, In the 34th year of his age*, 1758

Johnson, Samuel, *Lives of the English Poets, including The Life of the Rev Isaac Watts DD [by Samuel Palmer]*, 1779-81

Jones, AT, *Notes on the early days of Stepney Meeting, 1644 to 1689, with a preface by... J[ohn] Kennedy*, 1887

Jones, Thomas, *The Works of the Rev Thomas Jones MA, Late Chaplain of St Saviour, Southwark, To which is prefaced A Short Account of His Life, in a Recommendatory Preface, By the Rev William Romaine, MA, Lecturer of St Dunstan's in the West*, 1763

Jowett, William, *A Memoir of the Rev WAB [Wilhelm Augustin Bernhard] Johnson, Missionary of the CMS in Regent's Farm, Sierra Leone*, [compiled from his Journals, etc, 1816-23, by RB Seeley, with some prefatory remarks by the Rev W Jowett], 1852

Kaye, Thomas, [publ], *The Stranger in Liverpool [To which is added A Continuation of the same subject and a map of the Town in 1650]*, 9th edtn, 1829

Kemp, Thomas, *A History of Warwick and its People*, 1905

Kevan, Ernest F, *London's Oldest Baptist Church, Wapping 1633 - Walthamstow 1933*, 1933

Kirby, Arthur, *Andrew Fuller*, 1961

Kirkham, E Bruce, *A Concordance to the Olney Hymns of John Newton and William Cowper* compiled and edited by E Bruce Kirkham, 1983

Kup, Alexander Peter, *A History of Sierra Leone, 1400-1787*, 1961

Law, William, *A Serious Call to a Devout and Holy Life, adapted to the State and Condition of all Orders of Christians*, 1728, repr. 1987

Leaver, Robin A, Olney Hymns 1779: 1. The Book and its Origins, *Churchman*, 93/4, 327-9, 1979

Olney Hymns 1779: 2. Hymns and their Use, *Churchman*, 94/1, 58-66, 1980

Olney Hymns: A Documentary Footnote, *Churchman*, 97/3, 244-5, 1983

Lecky, William Edward Hartpole, *History of England in the 18th Century*, 7 vols, 1878-90

Lee, Sidney and Stephen, Leslie, eds, *Dictionary of National Biography*, re-issue, 1921

Leighton, Robert, *A Practical Commentary upon the First Epistle General of St. Peter*, 2 vols, 1701

The Whole Works of the Most Reverend Father in God, Robert Leighton, DD, abp of Glasgow, to which is prefixed, a Life of the Author by the Rev John Norman Pearson, MA, 4 vols, new edtn 1874 with a table of texts of Scripture [with a portrait]

Lewis, Donald M, ed, *The Blackwell Dictionary of Evangelical Biography, 1730-1860*, 2 vols, 1995

Loane, Marcus Lawrence, *Oxford and the Evangelical Succession [Biographical studies of George Whitefield, John Newton, Thomas Scott, Richard Cecil and Daniel Wilson. With portraits]*, 1950

Lyne, S, and Ilive, J, [pubs], *A New and Compleat Survey of London*, 2 vols, by a Citizen and Native of London, 1742

Macaulay, Lord [Thomas Babington], *Warren Hastings*, 1841

Macaulay, Zachary, *The Slave Colonies of Great Britain*, 1825

Macmillan, D, *George Buchanan, A Biography*, 1906, 2nd edtn.

Madan, Judith, *The Progress of Poetry [A Poem]*, 1783

Poems of Emminent ladies, *Evangelical magazine*, vol 1, p 84, 1755, *Evangelical Magazine*, vol 1, p 84

Madan, Martin, *A Funeral Sermon on the much lamented death of the Rev Mr Thomas Jones, MA, who departed this life June 6, 1762 in the thirty-fifth year of his age, etc*, 1762

Thelyphthora; or, A Treatise on female ruin, 2 vols, 1780

Major, Norma, *Chequers, Country Home of the Prime Minister, Its History*, 1996

Makittrick, James (afterward ADAIR, JM), *Unanswerable Arguments against the Slave Trade. With a defence of the proprietors of the British Sugar Colonies against certain charges* ... published by Luffman, Newton, etc. [1790]

Manners, Nicholas, *Some particulars of the Life and Experience of Nicholas Manners*, 1785

Marshman, John Clark, *The Story of Carey, Marshman and Ward*, 1864, originally published as *The Life and Times of Carey*, 1859

Martin, Bernard Davis, *John Newton and the Slave Trade*, 1961

Some Dissenting Friends of John Newton, *The Congregational Quarterly*, 29, 134-44, 236-45, 1951

The Ancient Mariner and the Authentic Narrative, 1949, revised 1960

Martin, Bernard and Spurrell, Mark, *The Journal of a Slave Trader (John Newton): 1750-54*, 1962

Martyn, Henry, *Journals and Letters of the Rev Henry Martyn, BD, edited by the Rev Samuel Wilberforce*, 2 vols, 1837

Mason, John, *A Little Catechism, with Little Verses and Little Sayings, for Little Children*, 1692 [8th edtn 1755]

Matthews, Lieut John, *A Voyage to the River Sierra Leone on the Coast of Africa ..., containing an account of the trade and productions of the country, and of the ... customs and manners of the people; in a series of letters ... With an additional letter on the subject of the African Slave Trade, etc*, 1788, repr 1966

Mayo, Henry, *An Apology and a Shield for Protestant Dissenters, In These Times of Instability and Misrepresentation. Four Letters to the Rev Mr John Newton ... by a Dissenting Minister*, 1784

Meacham, Standish, *Henry Thornton of Clapham* [1760-1815], 1964

Memoir of the late Rev John Ryland, DD, *Baptist Magazine*, 18, 1-9, 1826

Middleton, Erasmus, *Biographia Evangelica; or, An historical account of the lives and deaths of the most eminent and evangelical authors or preachers, both British and foreign, in the several denominations of Protestants, from the beginning of the Reformation to the Present time, etc*, 4 vols, 1779-86; publ as *A Dictionary of Evangelical Biography*, 4 vols, 1807

Milner, Isaac, *An Account of the Life and Character of the Rev Joseph Milner*, 1804, new edtn

Milner, Joseph, *The History of the Church of Christ, edited by Isaac Milner*, 5 vols, 1794-97, 1803-09

Milton, John, *Cowper's Milton* [ed. W. Hayley], 4 vols, 1810

Moody, James, *Pious Remains of the Rev James Moody, late minister of the gospel at Warwick, consisting of Memoirs of his Life, and a selection of his letters, together with a few original hymns*, 1809

More, Hannah, *The Spirit of Prayer, selected and compiled by herself from portions on that subject in her published volumes*, 1825, 2nd edtn
The Works of Hannah More, 8 vols, 1801

Morris Derek, Mile End Old Town Residents and the East India Company, *East of London History Society*, vol 9, 1986, pp 20-7,

Stepney and Trinity House, *East of London History Society*, vol 13, 1990, pp 33-8

Namier, Sir Lewis Bernstein, and Brooke, John, *The House of Commons 1754-1790*, 1985.

Nelson, Robert, *A Companion for the Festivals and Fasts of the Church of England, with Collects and Prayers for each Solemnity*, 1704

Newman, John Henry, *Apologia pro vita sua: being a reply to a pamphlet [by C Kingsley] entitled "What, then, does Dr Newman mean?"*, 1864

Newton, Isaac, *Principia*, 1687

Newton, John, *A few words of advice & consolation to the worshippers at St. Lawrence's, who dearly love, duly prize, and sincerely lament, the removal of their faithful pastor*, [Cadogan] *in three letters ... to Christiana [ed. by the latter]*, 1812
A Monument to the praise of the Lord's goodness, and to the memory of dear Eliza Cunningham, 1785; 3rd edtn, 1811, *To which is now added some account of her brother, John Cunningham, who died January 22, 1777, in his twelfth year of age. Written by his mother*
A plan of academical preparation for the ministry, in a letter [signed Omicron], 1782
A Review of Ecclesiastical History, 1770
A Sermon preached in the Parish Church of St Paul's Deptford, on Sunday 7 May 1786, on the lamented occasion of the Death of Richard Conyers, LLD, Late Rector of that parish, 1786
A token of affection and respect, to the parishioners of St. Mary Woolnoth, and St. Mary Woolchurch, London, from their minister, Acts 26:3, I beseech thee to hear me patiently, 1781

Adelphi, A Sketch of the Character and Account of the Last Illness of the Late Rev. John Cowper, A.M., ... Written by his brother the Late William Cowper, Esq...transcribed by John Newton, 1802

An Address to the Inhabitants of Olney, 1768

An authentic narrative of some remarkable and interesting particulars in the life of [John Newton]. Communicated in a series of letters to the reverend mr. Haweis, and by him now made public. 1764; reprinted as *Out of the Depths,* 1990.

Apologia, four Letters to a minister of an Independent church [Samuel Palmer], by a minister of the Church of England [J. Newton], 1784

Cardiphonia: or, The utterance of the heart; in the course of a real correspondence, by the author of Omicron's letters, 2 vols, 1781

Consolation under Convictions. A Dialogue Between a penitent and her Christian friend [on Matt. xi,28], c. 1785

Correspondence of the late rev. John Newton, with a dissenting minister [Samuel Palmer], on various subjects and occasions. With a brief sketch of his character, and a ministerial charge (The necessity of keeping our own vineyards) by him revised, 1809

Ebenezer: a memorial of the Lord's unchangeable goodness under changing dispensations, written on occasion of the removal of a valuable ... wife, etc., 1800

Forty-One letters on religious subjects, orig. publ. under the signatures Omicron and Vigil, 1807

Letters, 1960

[ed] *Letters of the Rev Mr Helperus Ritzema van Lier: The Power of Grace Illustrated,* 1792

Letters to a Wife, by the author of Cardiphonia, 1793

Letters from the late Rev Mr Newton of St Mary Woolnoth, London, to a Baptist Minister [John Ryland, jnr], *Baptist Magazine,* 8, 321-3, 1816

Memoirs of the Life of the Late Rev William Grimshaw, in Six Letters to the Late Rev Henry Foster, Minister of St James, Clerkenwell, 1799

Memoir of the Late Rev John Newton, *Evangelical Magazine,* 16, 49-60, 97-112, 1808

Messiah: fifty expository discourses, on the series of scriptural passages, which form the subject of the celebrated oratorio of handel, 2 vols, 1786

Motives to humiliation and praise [Hosea 11:8,9], 1798

Olney Hymns, 1779

One Hundred and Twenty-Nine Letters from the Rev. John Newton to the Rev William Bull from 1773 to 1805 [ed. by Thomas Palmer Bull], 1847

[preface to Bunyan's] *Pilgrim's Progress,* 1776

Religious Tract Society. Select Sermons, No.12, Immanuel

Sermon on the Constraining Influence of the Love of Christ, preached before the the Right Honourable Lord Mayor, Aldermen and Sheriffs ... for the Benefit of Langbourn-Ward Charity School [2 Cor 5:13-15], 1800

Sermons preached in the parish-church of Olney, 1767

Six Discourses, as intended for the pulpit, 1760

Sixty-Eight Letters from the Rev. John Newton to a Clergyman [James Coffin] and his Family [1791-1801], 1845

Small Tracts and Occasional Sermons, collected and republished, 1798

The Aged Pilgrim's Triumph over Sin and the Grave... A series of letters by the Rev. John Newton to some of his most intimate friends, ed. Walter Taylor, William Cadogan, et al., 1825 [2nd edtn]

The Best Wisdom [Proverbs 11:30], 1787

The Christian Correspondent; or A series of religious letters, written by the Rev. John Newton to captain Alexr. Clunie, from 1761, to 1770, 1790

The Great Advent [1 Thessalonians 4:16,17], 1789

The guilt and danger of such a nation as this! [Jeremiah 5:29], 1781

The Imminent Danger and only sure Resource of this Nation [Jonah 3:9], 1794

The Kite, or the Fall of Pride, [1820?] [A chap-book]

The Searcher of Hearts... Lectures from Romans 8:18-34, ed. Marylynn Rouse, 1997

The Subject and Temper of the Gospel Ministry, Ephesians 4.15, Speaking the Truth in Love, 1780

The Works of the Rev. John Newton, 6 vols, 1808, reprinted 1985

Thoughts upon the African Slave Trade, 1788

Twenty-five letters, hitherto unpublished, from the years 1757 to 1779 [to Robert and Josiah Jones], 1840

Twenty-one letters written to a near relative at school [Letters to a niece – Betsy Catlett], 1779

Twenty-six letters on religious subjects, by Omicron, 1762

Nightingale, Benjamin, *Lancashire Non-conformity or Sketches, Historical and Descriptive of the Congregational and Old Prebyterian Churches in the County*, 6 vols, 1890-93

Northcott, Cecil, *Glorious Company,: One Hundred and Fifty Years Life and Work of the London Missionary Society 1795-1945*, 1945

Nuttall, Geoffrey F, Baptists and Independents in Olney to the time of John Newton, *The Baptist Quarterly*, 30, 1983-84, 26-37

Ollard, Sidney Leslie, *The Six Students of St Edmund Hall expelled from the University of Oxford in 1768, with a note on the authorities of their story*, 1911

Orton, Job, *Memoirs of the Life, character and writings of Philip of Doddridge*, 1766

Oulton, John, *A Vindication of the Seventeenth Article of the Church of England from the Aspersions cast on it in a sermon lately published by John Wesley*, 1760

Owen, John, *Two Discourses concerning the Holy Spirit and His Work (edited by Nathaniel Mather)*, 1693

The Works of John Owen, DD, ed by T Russell. With memoirs of his life and writings, by W Orme (Funeral Sermon ... by D Clarkson), 28 vols, 1826 [reprinted 1968 in 9 vols by Banner of Truth Trust, ed William H Goold]

Owen, John, *History of the British and Foreign Bible Society*, 3 vols, 1816

Owen, Nicholas, *Journal of a Slave Dealer – A View of Some Remarkable Axcedents in the life of Nicholas Owen on the Coast of Africa and America from the year 1746 to the year 1757*, [1930 edtn with an introduction by Eveline Martin]

Packer, James I, *Among God's Giants: Aspects of Puritan Christianity*, 1991

Palmer, Samuel, *A Brief Sketch of the character of the late Rev John Newton being an extract from a Sermon preached to a Dissenting Congregation, January 3 1808*

The Non-Conformists' Memorial [of Richard Baxter], 1778 2nd edtn

The Protestant Dissenter's Catechism, 1773

Pattrick, George, *Life of the Rev George Pattrick*, LLB, Vicar of Aveley, Essex, [1833]

Sermons, with a help to prayer. To which are prefixed memoirs of the life of the author, 1801

Pearson, Hugh Nicholas, *Memoirs of the Life and Writings of the Rev Dr Claudius Buchanan.* 2 vols, 1817

Philip, Robert, *The Life, Times and Missionary Enterprises of the Rev. John Campbell*, 1841

Phillips, Sir Richard, *Modern London, being the History and Present State of the British Metropolis*, 1804

Picton, Sir James Allanson, *City of Liverpool municpal archives and records*, 1983

Memorials of Liverpool, historical and topographical, including a History of the Dock Estate..., 2 vols, 2nd edtn revised, with additions, 1907

Piety, Thomas, *The goodness and love of God manifested to a sinful world in the Gift of His Son, A Sermon preached at Chatham on Christmas day*, 1737

Pike, Douglas, ed, *Australian Dictionary of Biography*, 1966-

Pike, Samuel, and Hayward, Samuel, *Some Important Cases of Conscience Answered*, vol 1, 1755

Pink, William Duncombe, and Beavan, Alfred Beaven, *The Parliamentary Representation of Lancashire, (County and Borough), 1258-1885, with biographical and genealogical notices of the members, etc.*, 1889

Pinks, William John, *The History of Clerkenwell, with additions and notes by the editor*, ed
    EJ Wood, 1865
Pollock, John, *Amazing Grace*, 1981
    George Whitefield and the Great Awakening, 1973
    Wilberforce, 1977
    John Wesley, 1992
Poole, EF, *The History of Doddridge Memorial Congregational Church, Northampton*, 1947
Pope, Alexander, *An Essay on Man*, 1733
Porritt, Arthur, *John Henry Jowett*, 1924
Postlethwaite. Malachy, *The Universal Dictionary of Trade and Commerce*, vols 1,2, 3rd
    edtn, 1766 [translation from the French of M. Savary]
Povey, Kenneth, The handlist of Manuscripts, Cowper and Newton Museum, Olney, Bucks,
    Transactions of the Cambridge Bibliographical Society, 4, 1965, 107-27
[Powell, E?], *Gleanings from pious authors with a choice collection of letters (some by the
    late Rev John Newton) and Original Poetry, by the author of Miscellaneous Thoughts*,
    1824
Pratt, John Henry, *Eclectic Notes; or notes of discourses on religious topics at the meetings
    of the Eclectic Society, London, during the years 1798-1814*, 1856, reprinted as *The
    Thought of the Evangelical Leaders, Notes of the Discussions of the Eclectic Society,
    London, During the Years 1798 - 1814*, 1978
Pratt, Josiah, *Memoir of the Rev Josiah Pratt, late vicar of St Stephen's, Coleman Street, and
    for twenty years secretary of the CMS, by his sons the Revs Josiah and John Henry Pratt*,
    1849
    *The Works of the Rev Richard Cecil with a Memoir of his Life Arranged and Revised by
    Mrs Cecil*, 1811
Pye-Smith, Arthur, *Memorials of Fetter Lane Congregational Church*, 1900
Ratcliff, Oliver, *The Register of the Parish of Olney*, 1909
Rawlinson, Richard, *Bunhill Fields*, Written in honour and to the memory of the many saints
    of God whose bodies rest in this old London cemetry ... With chart of the ground and
    many illustrations, 2 vols, 1913
Raymond, SA and MJ, *The London Poll Book 1768*, 1966
Reynolds, John Stewart, *The Evangelicals at Oxford*, 1735-1905: a record of unchronicled
    movement, with the record extended to 1905, 1975
Rideout, Eric Hardwick, *The Custom House, Liverpool, 1928, Letter Books from the Hon
    Board to the P Off's at Liverpool ... (1712-1855)*, 352 vols, Bd to Collector and vv,
    diagram by R Lang 1750
Ridge, Tom, *Central Stepney History Walk*, 1998
Rippon, John, *The Baptist Annual Register, including Sketches of the State of Religion, for
    1790 (-1802)* 1790-1802
Roberts, Sir Charles George Douglas, and Tunnell, Arthur L, (eds), *A Standard Dictionary of
    Canadian Biography*, 1934
Robinson, Ralph, *Christ All and in All. Or, several significant similitudes by which the Lord
    Jesus is described in the Holy Scriptures. Being the substance of many sermons. Ed by S
    Ashe, E Calamy and W Taylor*, 1656; new edition edited and corrected by *T Sharp*, 1827
Roffe, R, *Stenographical Accidence. or Byrom's system of Shorthand made easy*, 1833
Rollin, Charles, *Ancient History: containing the history of the Egyptians, Assyrians [etc]
    from Rollin and other authentic sources [Religious Tract Society]*, 1842
Romaine, William, *An Earnest Invitation to the Friends of the Established Church to join
    with several of their brethren, clergy and laity, in London, in setting apart an hour of
    every week for Prayer and Supplication during the present troubled times*, 1757
    *The blessedness of living and dying in the Lord, proved in a sermon upon the death of T.
    Jones*, 1762
    *The Works of the Rev Thomas Jones, to which is prefixed a short account of his life, by
    William Romaine*, 1763

Treatises upon the Life, Walk and Triumph of Faith, 1911

Royal Commission on the Historical Manuscripts, *An Inventory of Nonconformist Chapels and Meeting Houses in Central England*, 1986

Ryland, John, DD, *The work of faith, the labour of love, and the patience of hope illustrated; in the life and death of Andrew Fuller, Chiefly extracted from his own papers*, 1816

Ryle, John Charles [bishop of Liverpool], *Christian Leaders of the Last Century; or, England a hundred years ago*, 1869 repr.1978

Ryther, John, *The Sea-Man's Preacher, being several short discourses [on Jonah 1:5] addressed to Mariners on Jonah's voyage, preached in ... 1672; A Plan for Mariners ... To which is now added, The Day of God's Patience to Seamen improved*, 1675; *a new edition, revised and corrected by Samuel Palmer, with a preface by John Newton*, 1780

Sellers, Ian, ed, *Our Heritage*, The Baptists of Yorkshire, Lancashire, Cheshire, 1987

Sargeant, George Etell, *The White Slave; a life of J. Newton (written for young children)*, 1848

Saunders, Ann (ed), *The Royal Exchange*, 1997, London Topographical Society

Savage, Samuel Morton, *Good men dismiss'd in peace. A sermon [on Luke 2:29,30] occasioned by the death of David Jennings. To which is added, a funeral oration at his interment*, by W Ford, Junior, assistant preacher etc, 1762

Scott, John, *Letters and papers of the Late Rev Thomas Scott, never before published, with occasional observations, by John Scott, AM, Vicar of Northampton*, 1824
The Life of the Rev Thomas Scott, rector of Aston Sandford, Bucks, including a narrative drawn up by himself and copious extracts of his letters, 1822

Scott, Thomas, *A Thanksgiving Sermon [on Psalm 106:43,44] preached July 29, 1784, at the Parish Church of Olney, Bucks*, [1784]
The Force of Truth: An Authentic Narrative, 1779, rep. 1984
The Holy Bible containing the Old and New Testaments, according to the Authorised Version; with Explanatory Notes, Practical Observations, and Copious Marginal References, 4 vols, 1788-92

Scougal, Henry, *The Life of God in the Soul of Man. Or, The nature and excellency of the Christian Religion. And an account of the beginnings and advances of a spiritual life. Two letters*, 1677, repr 1996

Seeley, Mary, *The Later Evangelical Fathers, J. Thornton, J. Newton [and others]*, 1879

Senior, Benjamin, *A Hundred Years at Surrey Chapel by Benjamin Senior, Pastor of the New Surrey Chapel*, 1892

Seymour, *Survey of Kent*, 1776

Seymour, Aaron Crossley Hobart, The *Life and Times of Selina, Countess of Huntingdon*, 2 vols, 1840

Shaftesbury [3rd Earl of], Anthony Ashley Cooper, *Characteristicks of Men, Manners, Opinions, Times*, 3 vols, 1711

Shaw, George Thomas and Isabella, eds, *Liverpool's first directory; a reprint of the names and addresses from Gore's directory for 1766 etc*, 1907

Shoolbred, John, *Report on the progress of vaccine inoculation in Bengal, from its introduction in November 1802, to the end of ... 1803: with an appendix, submitted to the Medical Board at Fort William*, 1804

Shoolbred, Mary, *Ancient History, remodelled from [Charles] Rollin, with notes and extracts from modern authors*, 3 vols, 1843

Shute, Josiah [archdeacon of Colchester], *An elegiacall commemoration of the pious life, and most lamented death, and funerals, of mr Josiah Shute, republished as The pious life and death of mr Iosiah Shute*, 1643
Some Account of the Rev Josias Shute, BD, Archdeacon of Colchester and rector of St Mary Woolnoth, London, departed this life AD 1643 aged 55 years [viator], *Christian Observer*, January 1804
Divine Cordials: delivered in Ten Sermons [edited by W Reynoldes], 1644
Sarah and Hagar: or Genesis the sixteenth Chapter opened, in XIX Sermons. Published

according to his own MSS, examined and transcribed by E. Sparke, 1649

Sibree, John, and Caston, Moses, *Independency in Warwickshire; a history of the congregational churches in that county*, 1855

Sidney, Edwin, *The Life, Ministry and selections from the Remains of the Rev Samuel Walker*, 1835

Smith, John Thomas, *A Book for a Rainy Day, or, Recollections of the events of the last sixty years, 1766-1833*, 1845, repr. 1905

Smith, Josiah, *The Character, Preaching, etc., of the Rev Mr Whitfield, Impartially Represented and Supported*, 1740

Smith, William, Surveyor of the Royal African Company, *A New Voyage to Guinea ...* [BL MS notes], 1744; facsimile edtn 1967

Snelgrave, Capt William, *A New Account of Guinea and the Slave Trade with a new and correct map of the Coast of Guinea*, 1754

Sortain, Joseph, *Memoir of Mrs George Clayton*, c. 1844

Southey, Robert, *The Works of William Cowper, with a life of the author, by the editor R. Southey*, 15 vols, 1835-37

Spavens, William, *A Narrative of William Spavens, a Chatham Pensioner, Written by Himself (The Seaman's Narrative &c.)*, 1796

Stainer, S, *History of the Above Bar Congregational Church, Southampton, from 1662 to 1908*, 1909

Stanhope, George [Dean of Canterbury], *The Christian's Pattern: or, A Treatise of the Imitation of Jesus Christ in four books written originally in Latin by Thomas-a-Kempis, render'd into English. To which are added, Meditations and Prayers for sick persons*, 1698

Stephen, Sir James, *Essays in ecclesiastical biography*, 2 vols, 1849, 1850

Stow, John, *A Survey of London*, 1598; *A survey of the cities of London and Westminster. Now corrected, and brought down to the present Time, by J. Strype. To which is prefixed, the life of the author [&c.]*, 2 vols, 1720, facsimile edtn 1994

Surman, Charles E, *A Bibliography of Congregational Church History, including numerous cognate Presbyterian/Unitarian records and a few Baptist. Prepared for the Congregational Historical Society*, 1947

Sutcliff, John, Character and death of Mrs Andrews, *Evangelical magazine*, 3, pp 291-3, 1795

Taylor, John, (ed), Mr Thomas Trinder, Biographical Notes, *Biographies: Northamptonshire*, 1901

Taylor, John, (ed), Mr Samuel Pearce, Biographical Notes, *Biographies: Northamptonshire*, 1901

Taylor, John, *The Scripture Doctrine of Original Sin proposed to free and candid examination. To which is added, A Supplement, containing some remarks on two books, The Vindication of the Scripture Doctrine of Original Sin, and, The ruin and recovery of mankind*, 1741, 2nd edtn

The Life of the Rev Samuel Brewer, BD, *Evangelical Magazine*, 5, 5-18, January 1797

The Westminster Shorter Catechism, 1647

Themlow, JA, *Liverpool Town Books 1500-1862*, 1965

Thom, David, *Liverpool Churches and Chapels, Their Destruction, Removal or Alteration, with notices of clergymen, ministers, etc.*, 1854

Thompson, William, *The History and Antiquities of the Collegiate Church of St Saviour (St Marie Overie) Southwark*, 1894

Thomson, RW, John Newton and his Baptist Friends, *Baptist Quarterly 9*, 368-71, 1939

Thompson, Thomas, *Memoirs of an English Missionary to the Coast of Guinea...*, 1788

Thornbury, George Walter, *Old & New London, A Narrative of its History, its People and its Places*, 6 vols, 1874, new edtn revised 1880-86

Tibbutt, HG, *The Minutes of The First Independent Church (now Bunyan Meeting) at Bedford 1656 - 1766*, 1976

Timbs, John, *Curiosities of London exhibiting the most rare and remarkable objects of interest in the Metropolis with nearly fifty years of personal recollection*, 1855

Toulmin, Joshua, A Review of the Life and Writings of the Rev.David Jennings D.D., *The Protestant Dissenter's Magazine*, vol 5, March 1798, 81 - 9, April 1798, 121 - 7

Tyerman, Luke, *The Life of the Rev George Whitefield: A Further Account of God's Dealings*, 2 vols, 1876, 77

Tyndale, TG, Mrs, *Selections from the Correspondence of Mrs Ely [Elizabeth Mary] Bates, and incidents of her early life with an Appendix containing illustrations of the subjects and characters alluded to in her letters*, 2 vols, 1872-73

Venn, Henry, snr., *Christ the joy of the Christian's life, and death his Gain: the substance of a Sermon [on Phil. 1:21] preached ... on the death of the Rev. W. Grimshaw ... to which is added a Sketch of his Life and Ministry*, 1763

    The Complete Duty of Man: or A system of doctrinal and practical Christianity. To which are added Forms of Prayer, etc, 1763

    The Life and a Selection from the Letters of the late Rev. Henry Venn, M.A., edited by H. Venn, with a Memoir of his Life by J. Venn, 1835, repr. 1993

Venn, Henry, jnr., *A Sermon [on 1 Pet. 4:10,11] preached ... on occasion of the death of ... J. Pratt.*, 1844

Waddington, John, *Congregational History 1700-1800 in relation to Contemporaneous Events*, 1876

Walker, John, *An Attempt Towards Recovering an Account of the Numbers and Sufferings of the Clergy of the Church of England who were sequestr'd, harass'd, etc.*, 1714

Walker, Samuel Abraham, *The Mission in West Africa, among the Soosoos, Bulloms, etc.*, 1845

    The Church of England Mission in Sierra Leone; including an introductory account of that colony, and a comprehensive sketch of the Niger expedition in 1841, 1847

Wallace, James, A General and Descriptive History of the Ancient and Present State of the town of Liverpool... Together with a circumstantial account of the true causes of its extensive African trade, etc

Ward, Leonard G, *Stepney Meeting House: a history: 1644-1978*, 1978 [typescript, TH]

Warner, Rebecca, *Original Letters from Richard Baxter, Matthew Prior [and others, including John Newton]*, 1817

Warren, Robert Hall, *The Hall Family*, 1910

Watson, Isobel, *From West Heath to Stepney Green: Building Development in Mile End Old Town 1660-1820*, London Topographical Society Record, vol 27, 1995

Watts, Isaac, *A Discourse on the Way of Instruction by Catechisms, and of the Best Manner of Composing them*, 1736, 3rd edtn

    A Short View of the Whole of Scripture History, 1732

    Catechisms: or, Instructions in the Principles of the Christian religion, and the history of Scripture, Composed for Children and Youth, to which is prefix'd A discourse on the way of instruction by catechisms [&c.], 1730

    Divine Songs Attempted in Easy Language for the use of Children, 1715; facsimile edtn OUP, 1971

    Horae Lyricae, Poems Chiefly of the Lyric Kind, 1706

    Hymns and Spiritual Songs, 1707

    Memoirs of the Life and Writings of Isaac Watts. With extracts from his Correspondence, 1806

    Psalms, Hymns and Spiritual Songs 1812 a new edtn, corrected and revised by the Rev G Burder, 1812

    Sermons on various subjects, 1721

    The first sett of catechisms and prayers: or, The religion of little children under 7 or 8 years of age, 1734, 5th edtn

    The second sett of catechisms and prayers: or Some helps to the religion of children and their knowledge of the Scripture, from 7 to 12 years of age, 1733, 4th edtn

    Two setts of catechisms and prayers; or The religion of little children under 12 years of age, 1774

Useful and Important Questions Concerning Jesus, the Son of God, freely proposed [etc.]. To which is added, A charitable essay on the true importance of any human schemes to explain the sacred doctrine of the Trinity, 1746

Welch, Edwin, *Two Calvinistic Methodist Chapels 1743 - 1811, The London Tabernacle and Spa Fields Chapel,* 1975

Wesley, John, *The Almost Christian,* 1741

The Journal of John Wesley, Standard Edition, edited by Nehemiah Curnock, 8 vols, 1909

The Letters of the Rev John Wesley, 8 vols, edited by John Telford, 1931

Wheatley, Henry Benjamin, and Cunningham, Peter, *London Past and Present: its history, associations and traditions, based upon the handbook of London by P. Cunningham,* 1891

Whitefield, George, *A Letter to the Rev Dr Durell ... occasioned by a late expulsion of six students from Edmund Hall,* 1768

A select collection of Letters, With an account of the Orphan House in Georgia, 1772

Select Sermons of George Whitefield, With an account of his life by JC Ryle and a summary of his doctrine by R Elliot, 1958

Sermons in London Chapels, 1738

The Almost Christian [on Acts 26:28] [preached at Wapping, St John's], 1738

Whitefield's Journals. To which is prefixed his 'Short Account' and 'Further Account' with appreciations by H Aitken, Cowper and J Foster, ed by W Wale, 1960

Whitley, William Thomas, *A Baptist Bibliography,* 2 vols, 1916, 1922

Wilberforce, Robert Isaac and Samuel, *The Correspondence of William Wilberforce,* 2 vols, 1840

The Life of William Wilberforce, 5 vols, 1838

Wilberforce, William, *A Practical View of the Prevailing Religious System of Professed Christians in the Higher and Middle Classes in this Country Contrasted with Real Christianity,* 1797, reprinted 1989, 1996 as *A Practical View*

[Wilcox, Thomas], *A choice drop of honey, from the Rock Christ; or, A short word of advice to saints and sinners,* 1690? [42nd edtn 1757]

Williams, Gomer, *History of the Liverpool Privateers and Letters of Marque with an account of the Slave Trade etc,* 1897

Williams, Robert, *Memoirs of the life and correspondence of Mrs Hannah More,* 4 vols, 1834, 2nd edtn

Williamson, David, *Lectures on Civil and Religious Liberty; with reflections on the Constitutions of France and England and on the violent writers who have disgraced themselves in the controversy about their comparative goodness; and particularly on Mr Burke and Mr Paine. To which are added two sermons, on the "Influence of religion on the death of good men",* 1792

Williamson, Matthew, *The Universal Advertiser,* 1756

Willison, John, *The balm of Gilead, for healing a diseased land; with the glory of the ministration of the Spirit ... The seventh edition. To which is added, five sermons preached upon sacramental occasions, by the same author,* 1765

Wilson, Walter, *The History and Antiquities of Dissenting Churches and Meeting Houses in London, Westminster and Southwark, including the lives of their Ministers from the Rise of Nonconformity to the Present Time,* 4 vols, 1808-14

Wing, Vincent, *Reminiscences of the Rev Thomas Ford , LLD, Formerly Vicar of Melton-Mowbray,* [1864]

Winter, Richard, *A Sermon [on 2 Peter 1:4] occasioned by the death of Thomas Bradbury,* 1759

Wood, Arthur Skevington, *Thomas Haweis,* 1957

Woodd, Basil, *A Memoir of Bowyer Smith, A Pious Child who died January 30th 1811 Aged 7 years and 2 months,* 1811

Woodward, Josiah, *The Seaman's Monitor: wherein particular advice is given to sea*